FOREWORD

Your Gloria Diehl Book Club selections are chosen by an independent review board with members all across the United States. Board members are carefully chosen to represent all backgrounds, views, and reading interests. Any romance novel which bears the imprint *Gloria Diehl Book Club Selection* has been reviewed and recommended by the committee for its originality, reading interest, plot, and character development.

MASKED LOVER

His hands cupped her face and with a thumb across her lips he silenced her. His arms came around her waist and Averil was pulled full against him, feeling the hard length of his body, his wide chest and the firmly muscled thighs, pressed to her. He held her head against his chest and the dull erratic thudding of his heart was loud in her ear. The sound was somehow strangely thrilling to Averil. Her own heart beat more rapidly and the nerve endings of her body quivered with a sense of expectancy.

Unable to change the direction of her thoughts, she wondered what it would feel like to be kissed by the Tottman. She lifted her head to peer at the mask, suddenly fearful of what lay behind it. Trembling within his embrace, she whispered, "Can I not see your face?"

KATRINA HAMILTON

MOONLIGHT MASQUERADE

*For my husband, Ron, and my agent,
Joyce A. Flaherty, with warm appreciation.*

Book Margins, Inc.

A BMI Edition

Published by special arrangement with Dorchester Publishing Co., Inc.

Printed in the United States of America.

CHAPTER
ONE

From out of the dawn's dusky grey light they appeared on the road—seventy men, soldiers. Mud sucked at their boots, clotted on the hooves of the officers' horses, bogged the wheels of the carts that trailed them. The road they traveled led through sloping fields crisscrossed by ancient stone hedges. A timeless, drowsy landscape. Far ahead, gathering shape in the veiled morning light, was a broad stone dwelling known as Maslin Manor.

Built in 1320, the manor had seen the sunrises of more than three centuries and had witnessed 132 births and 74 deaths within its walls. From its square central tower extended two newer grey stone wings twined with ivy. Newly blooming white cyclamen, hollyhocks, wild pear trees, and fragrant sweetbriar framed the walls. From all sides it exuded a magnificence, an endurable grace and solidity only time could bestow. Diamond-paned windows imbedded deep in its walls glowed pink in the sunrise; from the surrounding fields the lilting songs of meadowlarks invaded the stillness.

As Averil listened drowsily from her bed within the manor, the song of the morning birds abruptly ceased. Caught between waking and sleeping, she was not at first aware of the change and gave a long, untroubled sigh as she stretched and rolled over. She was just curling deeper under the goose-feather tick when the first crack of musketfire shattered the morning hush.

Groaning in protest, she buried her head deeper under the bedclothes, sure that her father was beginning earlier than usual this morning in his relentless drilling of the servants and men from the estate. But when an agonized scream penetrated to her ears, she snapped awake with alertness so acute it bordered on pain.

The inner walls of the manor echoed with the screams of servants; rapid footfalls resounded through the halls and down the stairs. The sounds mingled with the shouts and gunfire and drumming of horses' hooves outside, creating a horrifying cacophony in her ears. Without pausing for a dressing robe, Averil ran from her bedchamber into the small adjoining room.

"Lottie! Lottie!" she cried, but the serving woman was not there. Her bed had not been slept in. Because of the war, many of their servants had secretly fled. Had Lottie now left, too? Distraught, Averil ran on and emerged into the wide upper hall. She was enveloped by a stream of those servants who remained in the manor—pages, the little blond kitchen boy, the serving girls. When she reached the head of the stairs, she heard Mrs. Fairchild shouting instructions to the servants below.

"Emma, where's the silver? Didn't I send you to fetch it? Quick spot, girl! We've got to get it all hid!"

Mrs. Fairchild supervised the serving girls and was under the direction of Francis Bowers, Averil's father's steward. She had dragged a high stool to one wall and was balanced on it as she tried to pull down a tapestry of a rosy-hued pastoral scene. She was fiftyish, a tall woman, and her white day cap was askew above a taut, grim face.

Averil's small bare feet flew as she raced down the crowded staircase. Through two deep windows at the end of the room she saw a haze of black smoke, horsemen flashing past, heard the clang of steel on steel. Over the chaos of shrieking and gunfire, Averil screamed out, "What is this!" Her teeth chattered and she shook violently.

"God o' mercy, it's the Roundheads!" Mrs. Fairchild exclaimed, all her attention on the heavy fabric she was futilely attempting to bring down. But an instant later, noting the ashy color of Averil's delicate face, the green eyes rounded in fearful anxiety, and the tangled fair hair that framed her young body in disordered waves, the woman let go of the tapestry and struggled down from the chair.

"My *lady*—! You shouldn't be down here!" She gripped Averil's arm, and with concern that sounded close to anger, said, "Hie yourself back to your room! Mrs. Shapwell," she cried, looking around, "go with her! See that she's kept safe."

"Where's my father? I want my father!" Averil's father was all the family left to her; four years earlier her mother, after numerous pregnancies and still-births, had died attempting to give birth to the last doomed infant.

A stray musket ball shattered one of the bright, glazed windows nearby, and both women ducked as splinters of glass showered over them. A servant entering from the dining hall dropped the tray of silver she was carrying and threw her hands to her ears, shrieking, as she fled up the stairs. The silver utensils clanged against the dropped tray, and bowls rolled away on the polished wood floor.

Mrs. Fairchild exclaimed impatiently, "Go! Now!" She spun around, crying, "Mary, pick up that silver! Emma, help me get this tapestry down! D'ye want the Roundheads t' take it all?"

Averil scrambled toward the stairs. Bits of glass cut into her feet. Hardly aware of the pain, she fled alone to her chamber and cowered on the bed, ears covered tightly. Blood from her feet soaked into the immaculate white linen sheet.

Looking at the crimson smears, Averil began suddenly to cry. In one of the coffers she found cloths to tie around her feet, and then she huddled on her bed, more helplessly terrified than she had ever been in her life.

It was Thursday, March 30, 1643, two days after Averil's sixteenth birthday, and England was engaged in a civil war that had begun as a power struggle between the King, Charles Stuart, and Parliament—the forces of which were called Roundheads because of the cut of hair many had adopted.

Averil's father, William Maslin, Earl of Armondale, supported the King. Though many of his peers had ridden off proudly to join the war, William Maslin had remained at home. "His Majesty has nought but officers all ordering each other about!" he had grumbled of those who joined the King's army. "To win this war 'tis money he needs and honest soldiers." To that end the Earl had given great sums and sent off to the army every available man from his estate. Until this day it had seemed a remote struggle to Averil, and though she heard the battle reports and listened to her father and his friends debate the issues by the hour, it never actually occurred to her that they might be in danger.

Her father had worried about it, however. Of the men who remained on the estate, most were old or lame, but Averil's father coached them patiently in the use of muskets and devised plans for the defense of the manor. He waited eagerly for reports of the battles and often rode out to stop passing coaches or pack trains on the road to enquire for news.

But there had been no reports of Parliament troops in the area, nothing to suggest an attack was imminent.

When the echo of the last shots died away, Averil eased herself from the bed and tiptoed across the bare floor to the door. Hesitantly, she leaned her ear to the panels to listen.

She heard nothing—no voices, no footsteps.

As she reached for the bolt to throw back the lock on her door, one of numerous shiny brass locks her father had recently installed in all the rooms, she heard a distant crash as wood splintered and gave way somewhere near the rear of the manner. Her hand stayed, her heart leaped into her throat; forced entry could mean only one thing—the Round-heads were the victors.

An instant later she heard Mrs. Fairchild cry out with ragged screams that seemed to echo and grow as the sound tunneled through the corridors. So heartstopping was the sound that Averil felt the room tilt sickeningly around her.

When she heard deep shouts and thuds of heavy boots in the hallway below, she spun about, horror riding her till she could not breathe. She had to hide! But where? Her eyes stabbed about wildly. Her room held a massive four-poster bed enclosed by blue velvet drapes, two wardrobes, a heavy trunk at the foot of her bed, several smaller coffers, a heavy-legged table—nothing that would safely conceal her for long. Below stairs in the main hall, a heavy piece of furniture crashed down, fabric ripped, and hard-soled boots, many of them, pounded up the stairs.

The windows? she wondered frantically. It was a two-story drop to the garden, and even if she did not slip from the ivy and fall, she would still be visible to any soldiers lurking below.

But she had to do something! Anything!

From somewhere in the manor, coarse laughter erupted. Screams of women echoed through the halls, such screams as Averil had never heard before—of terror and pain and anguish. As in a nightmare, the cries seemed to come from all directions around her. She clenched her fingers into tight fists, holding them against her ears, against the nightmare, as if she could make it disappear by not hearing. But the agonized screams penetrated to her very core, and she retched in fear.

Harsh voices nearby caught her attention. From the shouted words Averil realized the soldiers had seen the trail of bloody footprints and were following it to her door. The voices grew louder as the soldiers approached through the adjoining rooms. And though she tried to make herself move, though her brain demanded it feverishly, Averil was paralyzed by her own terror.

It was not until the handle of her door creaked as someone tested it and a rumbling voice just inches away from her on the other side called out to a companion for assistance that she erupted into motion. As she spun about to flee, her foot, encased in the soft cloths, slid out from beneath her and she sprawled full length on the floor. When she lifted her head, she looked directly into the yawning mouth of the huge old hearth. Though not as massive as the fireplace in the main hall below, which a man could stand upright in, the one in Averil's chamber was nonetheless built on the same design, with the ancient and inefficient straight chimney flue.

With a sob catching in her throat, Averil ducked into the fireplace, treading on the cold ashes as she felt the size of the flue. Behind her a heavy object struck her door and she heard splintering as the panels weakened. Quickly she lifted first one knee and then the other, bracing her weight with outward pressure as she tried to inch her way up the black interior. Rough projecting stones served as footholds but were slick with soot and bruised her legs. The soot she dislodged swirled up around her and she held her arm across her nose and mouth, fearful of inhaling any and revealing herself with a cough of sneeze. At the last moment she realized that the hem of her dressing gown trailed down within view of the room and she clutched at it frantically. The final shower of soot had settled into the ashes below when the panels of her door finally gave way and the soldiers burst through.

Averil had no idea how long she braced herself within the flue; it seemed hours as she listened to the sounds of men moving about her bedroom, dragging furniture from against the walls, ripping down the bed draperies. They had followed the crimson footprints to this room and found blood in the middle of the bed but not a soul in evidence.

As one of them approached the fireplace, Averil held her lips tightly against a cry of hysteria. But the soldier who knelt before the ashes was thumping experimentally at the hearth plate in the black wall, and she realized that he was looking for a priest hole. In previous generations, Jesuits had escaped persecution by hiding in specially designed compartments behind chimneys. But there was no priest hole here, and the soldier abandoned his quest at the back of the hearth without discovering Averil's hiding place.

The voices died away as the intruders departed her room. Averil waited. Her nose and lungs were burning with the stench of the flue, but she dared not move. She heard the soldiers comb the floor above her own, then the next. When they returned to the main floor, she heard the whimpering of servants. The noise of the intruders grew indistinct, and she realized they had left the manor and were outside again. Still she waited. After what seemed an interminable time, they rode away on horseback and the last sounds faded into a solid and alien silence.

Averil slid slowly into the cinders. As she crawled from the fireplace, her eyes widened. Her room was in shambles— wardrobes knocked away from the walls, her garments strewn about in vibrant, multi-colored disarray, the bedclothes snatched from the bed, the feather mattress ripped open. Light pierced the gloom in an odd slanting ray from a shutter snatched open and hanging askew. Dust motes swirled densely in the air.

Swaying with shock, Averil climbed to her feet and reached for the door. The bolt had been broken from the wood casing and what remained of the door swung loosely from its hinges. She crept through the ransacked adjoining rooms. From over the carved newel post at the head of the stairs, she looked into the ruins of the main hall below. Tapestries had been yanked from the walls, some slashed beyond recognition; books, papers, candlesticks, and knickknacks were strewn about, furniture upended. From the interior of the spinet case on a table against the far wall, broken wires curled like spider legs.

When she lifted her hand from the newel post, Averil found

blood on her palm. She stared at it uncomprehendingly as she descended the stairs. Filled with dread, she sidestepped twisted chairs and crossed the hall into the broad, high-ceilinged dining room. The doors of the cupboards containing their plate and silver hung wide, the interiors empty. The family's finest linen tablecloth was unfurled on the floor, a gaping rip at one end showing where a soldier must have speared it on his sword before flinging it across the room. The paintings were gored; some had slid down and their frames had cracked on the floor, others hung askew on the wall. Averil tiptoed through the room in horrified fascination and ran ahead to the long narrow hall at the rear.

She almost stepped on Mrs. Fairchild.

The woman lay in a crumpled heap on the floor, eyes staring, blood and vomit sticky around her mouth. The handle of a kitchen knife protruded from her chest and her long fingers were clenched around it as if she had tried to remove the blade in those last moments of life.

Beyond her, the rear door opening into the garden was smashed, splinters of lighter, raw wood jutting out. Dazed, Averil groped her way toward it and pulled the door open. A weak ray of morning sunlight fell across her. She stood in the doorway, and her nostrils flared at the rank perfume of crushed roses and the acrid sting of gunpowder smoke.

"Father?" she whimpered.

Blinking rapidly, Averil looked across the garden. Splayed across the neat rows of herbs and yellow blooming marigolds were the bodies of three men she knew—two were gardeners, the third a footman. The gardeners had been slaughtered while at their work; each held only small garden tools.

Averil ran down graveled walkways as she searched about the garden and found Thomas Kateley, her betrothed, face down amongst the rose trees. He wore only breeches, a shirt thrown on in such haste that the tails were left out, and a pair of boots he had thrust his bare feet into. His shirt had tangled in the rose thorns as he had fallen and the hem was held up tentlike over his back, suspended by a thorn and flapping carelessly in the wind. Negotiations for a marriage between Averil and Thomas Kateley had been proceeding and the young man had been their guest for the past week. His home was some thirty miles south, near Reading. Though an agreement had been reached, the papers had not yet been signed.

Averil gave a small whine of fear and dropped to kneel beside him. His smooth white back felt cold beneath her palm. Unhooking the fabric from the thorn, she tried to turn him over to see his face, but he was too heavy for her. Genuinely fond of the shy man, Averil pressed shaking hands to her mouth and turned away.

Lifeless, as if in a dream, she passed through the gate set in the tall juniper hedge that bordered the garden. Her feet slid in the mud of the outer yard. Here she saw more dead, some she knew, others not. The bodies lay in oddly disjointed heaps, arms flung wide, legs buckled under them. The metallic smell of blood lay heavily on the air.

"Father!" she screamed.

She searched in the stables. The coach was gone, as were all the horses. She ran on to the small forge, the mill-house, the sheds where the hams and strips of beef had hung for smoking, the cooking house where rope baskets that had once held meats and cheeses swung emptily, but nowhere could she find her father or any other living being.

Exhaustion broke over her and she paused near the center of a grassy meadow some distance from the manor. Her hands and arms were smeared with soot, her gown equally black-stained and spotted with mud. She wiped at her cheeks, discovering as she did so that she had been crying. The lingering haze of gunpowder smoke diffused the sunlight into a red, sourceless glow; she could not tell how much time had passed. As she turned slowly to survey the land, the wind lifted her hair into gentle streamers and tugged the hem of her gown. She could see nothing moving but the rippling grass and the gentle swaying of the tops of the distant trees surrounding the manor, hear nothing but the rush of wind in her ears.

It was then that she realized she was alone.

Her father was gone; there were no servants, no friends, no other living person around her. Never in her young life had she been so alone. The realization chilled her and she swung around, suddenly fearful of seeing something or someone watching her. She saw no one. But still the goose-bumps stood out on her skin and she trembled as though an icy wind touched her.

Suddenly, with fluid, rapid steps, feet leaping through the high grass, Averil ran for the safety of her home. She ran wildly, recklessly. Every fear she had ever known, every tale she had heard whispered by believers reared up in her mind—tales of witches flying out of hell, of evil spells and omens, of fairies and demons and spirits that wandered the roads by night.

With lungs burning, she burst into the manor and recoiled in horror as she realized there was no way to bolt the shattered door. She paused there for only a moment before running on through the great hall and sprinting up the stairs. Passing her own room, Averil ran on to her father's bedroom, and after throwing the bolt on his door, climbed into the bed her father had left only a few hours before. She pulled the coverlet high and buried her face in the pillow that still carried his scent.

Anguish coiled through her; her body shook, wrenched by sobs. The room was dim with the shutters closed, the air dense and still. She remained huddled in her father's bed as the day wore on. Like the protected child she had always been, she expected someone to come for her. Someone who would know what to do. So she waited. Evening drew on and still the manor remained silent.

Averil jerked awake. Her body was wet with perspiration and her gown stuck to her skin. Her eyes burned; the lids felt thick and swollen from her tears. The manor had never been so intensely silent, and though she could not be certain she had not dreamed or imagined it, she thought she had been

awakened by a distant voice. The chamber was dark now.
She could barely make out the shape of a tall wardrobe against
a lighter wall opposite the end of the bed.

When the noise of a voice was repeated, she reared up
in fright. Someone was downstairs! She panted with fear.
Then she had a new thought. Could it be her father? Since
she had not found his body, she was convinced he still lived.
Eagerly she lit the candle on the bedside table, left the
chamber, and swept down the corridor till she could see into
the hall below. Here she lifted the candle and leaned over
the rail, her hair falling around her face as she peered down
into the semi-gloom.

The two men below paused in their search and looked up.
She stared back at them in stupefied wonder. They were filthy
and unkempt. One had long black hair shiny with grease and
wore an odd assortment of fine clothes rich blue satin
doublet and matching loose breeches, limp yellow ribbons
tied about his waist and one knee, and fine leather boots caked
with dried mud. The other sported a dusty beaver hat, wide-
brimmed and sprouting feathers in the Cavalier style, a long
black coat, and a sword belt. He wore black velvet breeches
and wool knit stockings folded down over his boot tops. Their
clothing was ripped, the material heavily stained with sweat
and dirt and food.

The first man held a long sack and paused in the act of
stuffing a small mantel clock into it. When he saw her, he
grinned, and Averil looked into a mouth with black gums
and broken teeth.

She remembered then the stories she had heard of the
scavengers who trailed the army and lived off the blood and
defeat of others. The clothing these men wore had been
stripped from corpses, their sacks bulged with articles from
her home they could either use themselves or sell.

Averil straightened with a jerk, and the two men dropped
their sacks and started toward the foot of the stairs. With
a shriek of panic, she ran back to her father's room and
slammed the door. She threw home the bolt and backed away

as she heard the sound of their boots clattering up the stairs at a run. Wildly, her eyes scanned the room, seeking some weapon. She put the candle on a low table and jerked open the wardrobe doors. Frantically, she groped about through the jumbled heap of clothing left in the wake of the Parliament soldiers' search that morning. She tossed out breeches and shirts and knocked over one shiny boot. Her father's sword, where was it? The soldiers had torn apart the room to such a degree that Averil felt disoriented now, as though she hunted through a different room entirely. She whirled about in confusion. There had to be something!

A memory came to her of a morning some months previously when the first major battle, at Edgehill, had been fought. Concerned for her safety, her father had brought her to this room and showed her a case containing two slender, foreign pistols. As Averil had watched, he showed her how to load and fire them. Then he had returned the case to its hiding place.

Eagerly now Averil clawed her way across the room to the tall wardrobe, and kneeling down, groped behind it, low, near the floor. She found the narrow ledge and then her fingers bumped against something else. She pulled the case out and sank back on her heels as her fingers fumbled with the catch. The lid fell back, revealing two long-barreled pistols on a bed of black velvet. To the side was a flask of powder and a drawstring pouch of balls. Could she remember how to load them?

The rattle of the door caught her attention and her head snapped up. "All's well, sweetheart," a slurred, uneven voice called out. "Y' can open this door now."

Averil remained silent. Her fingers shook as she spilled dark powder into the barrel of one of the pistols. It felt cold and heavy and alien in her palm. She rammed a ball home quickly and twisted the small wheelock at the side of the weapon. When the first booted foot rammed the wood panels of the door near the lock, she jumped with fright. The small lock bent under the onslaught of the men's shoulders and boots, but Averil worked on feverishly, sprinkling more of the black powder into the flash pan. She would have time to prepare only one pistol.

When the lock broke and the door swung open, she was standing rigidly in the center of the room, a pistol in each hand. Though only one was loaded, Averil prayed the men would think they were both ready and be frightened off. The intruders froze in their tracks. The man with the long black hair eyed her warily and lifted one grimy hand to stop her.

"Begone!" she screeched.

The other man seemed unconcerned by the weapons she waved warningly. By the way her hands shook he could tell she was not confident with the power she held, and he was likewise sure she had no notion of how to prepare or use the pistols. What woman did? As his eyes swept her from head to just-visible toes, his grin widened. Her thick flaxen hair hung in tangled waves to her waist, and her green eyes were glazed, blinking quickly. Even with the grimy black smears and tear stains, he could tell she had an exquisite face. Though the stained, ivory gown was voluminous with yards of flowing material that concealed her figure, the outline of firm young breasts was clearly visible beneath the lace bodice.

"Surely, sweetheart," he murmured to her soothingly, as one calming a frightened, cornered animal. "Aye, and it's sure we will." He walked toward her without any abrupt movements.

"Stay away!" Her steps faltered back. "Leave me be!"

He crooned, "Here now, lass—here, sweetheart. I'll not harm ye." He thrust out skinny arms and reached for her pistols.

Averil screamed. One of the pistols barked and spit flame and a puff of black smoke. The ball caught the man square in the chest. He shrieked as his body was thrown back from the impact, and he slammed against the floor. The other man paused only to gape at the second, leveled pistol before dropping his candle and disappearing into the hallway. The candle flame hissed as it was extinguished in a river of blood running out from under the fallen thief. Averil heard the man run down the stairs and clatter through the dark toward the rear door.

She stared at the still form of the thief where he lay half in the room, half out. In the sputtering light cast by her candle on the nearby table, the blood puddling under him looked black. Was he really dead? Or would he, if she moved to him, spring up suddenly?

Averil's hands shook. With legs as limp as bread dough, she tiptoed closer to the figure on the floor. The oddly sweet stench of his blood choked her. After poking him several times and getting no response, she grew braver, put the pistols down, and grabbed him by one arm. As she dragged him into the hall, the stink of his body almost made her retch. His skull bumped on the bare floor.

When he was clear of the threshold, Averil dropped his arm and jumped back into the room, slamming the door behind her. She loaded both pistols and sat on the side of the bed to wait out the night, like a pale sentinel, keeping watch. During the long hours she had time to think. What if the other one returned—what would she do? There might be others even now gathering around the manor under cover of night. She whispered a childish prayer aloud: "Please, God, please send the Tottman."

Averil had heard of the Tottman from many sources. He was an elusive figure whose exploits in aiding Royalist sympathizers and their families escape London was a much-discussed topic from the meanest street urchins to the highest government leaders. Parliament and its supporters denounced him as a traitor and a murderer and laid the blame on him for every grisly calamity. A reward of 500 pounds was offered for his arrest. Averil's father and many others, however, believed him a hero of uncommon valor. Tales of his deeds, whether praised or condemned, traveled with amazing speed, and he was rapidly becoming a legend throughout the whole of England.

With the threat of scavengers closing in on her, Averil knew she could not stay another night at the manor, but she did not know where to go. The nearest neighboring house lay almost three leagues to the west, but what if it had been attacked as well? Or soon would be? Her only relative, her mother's sister and her family, lived in London. But not only did the city lie a full three days' journey to the east, it was also the Parliament stronghold since the King and his family had fled the city many months previously. Perhaps she could find help in Abingdon; it was less than a day's journey away, and her father had friends there.

She toyed with that idea momentarily, then discarded it with a feeling of desperate hopelessness. How was she to reach Abingdon? How could a woman travel the highways alone? No escort, no protection, not even a coach or horse was available to her. The soldiers had taken everything they could move. And there was always, war or no war, a danger to any traveler; highwaymen and thieves swarmed the roads and some innkeepers were secretly in their pay. Rising, she paced about the room, shuffling her feet through the jumbled clothing on the floor and nudging her father's boots with her toe. If she were a man it might be different. Even a boy stood a better chance than she did!

The idea that next occurred to her was so stunning, so frightening, that she climbed back onto the bed. But the thought persisted. Could she pass herself off as a lad? The idea was unthinkable. But it was unthinkable to stay here.

By the following noon, Averil was on the road to Abingdon.

In the living quarters of the stable boy Jeremy Halmes, she had found clothing to fit her—a pair of brown, linsey-woolsey breeches; a cotton shirt and soft wool doublet laced across the front; a stained sugar-loaf hat; an old pair of boots; and a well-mended cloak. Using strips of sheet from the bed, she had bound her hair atop her head, knowing she needed only to conceal it until she reached Abingdon. As an afterthought, she had bound her breasts as well.

On a rough-hewn table in the grooms' quarters, she had found stale food and surmised that the attack had caught someone in the midst of a meal. Too hungry to pass it up, Averil finished off the rest of the meat pie and downed a tankard of ale. Clouds were blowing over from the west when she finally departed the manor.

At first Averil trudged quickly, engulfed by her fear and unhappiness, but gradually her thoughts shifted. The rough fabric of the breeches felt alien, rubbing as it did on her inner thighs, and she began to consider her appearance. She experimented. She tried a devil-may-care swagger as she had seen some boys do, then a bouncing lope the way Jeremy Halmes himself walked. Pitching her voice low and husky, she tried out impromptu, one-sided conversations and matched the comments with wide-flung gestures and exaggerated facial expressions.

Late in the afternoon she found a shaded glen some yards from the road and sighed with relief as she kicked away the boots and stretched out on her back on the tall, cool grass. A soft wind rippled through the grass and caressed her face, carrying with it the rich smells of fertile soil, mosses, wild flowers. Somewhere a bird broke into song. She felt as if she floated on the surface of a great body of water, rising and falling softly, and was thinking of never moving again when she heard the clatter of hoofbeats approaching on the road. Fearing it was the Roundheads, she scooted behind the nearest tree. But when the riders, four of His Majesty's Cavaliers, rode into view, she released her held breath with relief.

The men were obviously officers, resplendent in doublets and breeches in rich shades of blue and scarlet velvet, white shirts with lace-trimmed collars and cuffs. They wore black satin capes that soared out behind them and wide-brimmed hats with feathers furling from the crowns as they galloped past. They were heading toward Abingdon.

Sure that they would be willing to help find her father, Averil leaped up. She jammed her feet into the boots and shouted out to the Cavaliers as she hurried back to the road. But they were far ahead and turned a bend in the road without hearing her. Dust hung thick in the air in their wake, and she coughed, biting grit between her teeth.

Overhead, the clouds had bunched up and darkened ominously. Evening was coming on. She hoped to reach town before the rain began and tried to run the last few miles to Abingdon, but in such oversized boots she achieved nothing more than a clopping gait. The rain fell lightly at first, but shortly turned into a downpour. It cast an eerie pale shroud around her and created a dismal rushing sound as it pelted the leaves and road. Averil's hat drooped. Water cascaded over the brim and soaked her to the skin. She was miserably wet and shaking with cold when she reached Abingdon.

Wagons slogged past in the early gloom, their drivers cursing and pulling on the lead animals' harnesses. Foot travelers hunched into their cloaks while rainwater ran from the brims of their hats in steady rivulets; stray dogs stared menacingly from the corners of dry doorways. In the center of the town, the houses were nestled so closely together that their eaves touched, and the streets grew increasingly dark and narrow. Shutterless lower windows had iron bars across them for safety.

Averil hurried her steps until she stood before a broad, four-storied home past the other end of town, where the road widened again and there was space for trees and tall hedges to grow. It was the home of her father's closest friend, Sir John Walford. The servant who answered her knock was a woman Averil had never seen before. She shook her head briskly when Averil asked for Sir John.

" 'E be gone now, lad. Take yer beggin' elsewhere."

"I'm not a beggar!" Averil exclaimed in surprise. "You see, I'm not really a boy, I'm Lady Averil Maslin, his Lordship William Maslin's only daughter. Wait! I can show you!'' Averil whipped off the hat, preparing to unwrap the linen cloths from her hair. But the woman misunderstood Averil's intent and slammed the door.

"Please!" Averil cried, rapping on the door with a wet fist. "You don't understand! Sir John knows me. He would want me to wait for him, I know it!''

"Not likely 'e'll return for some weeks. And I don't believe yer story none! No lady like ye say ye are 'ud be out like that—it 'ud be *indecent*!''

Averil dropped her hand. Weeks! It no longer mattered to her to prove herself to the servant; she could not wait that long to present her case to her father's friend. She clattered down the rain-slicked steps and hurried farther on to the home of another acquaintance. But here there was no answer to her knock, though she waited and pounded repeatedly and with increasing vigor.

At last she turned away and stood dismally in the rain. She wanted to sit down in the mud and cry. Oh, I should never have left home! she wailed silently to herself. What will I do now?

Darkness was fully upon her when Averil slogged back into town. Ahead, visible in the weak glow of a lantern, a sign swung sluggishly from a wrought-iron arm over a doorway. It was the Three Bells Inn. Hoping the Cavaliers had taken refuge there and that they might be able to help her, Averil approached the front window. A quick glance at the few seated patrons proved the Cavaliers were not there. Were they taking supper in a private room upstairs? Or had they stopped elsewhere?

She trudged behind the building toward the stable to see if she could find their horses. Through an archway in the back wall, she entered a broad, enclosed courtyard. The stable door was ajar and the glow from a lantern inside slanted out onto the wet cobbles of the inn yard. Averil entered the structure hesitantly. The interior was warm and humid and bore the strong odors of hay and fresh manure. The four horses she saw within the stable were unusually healthy specimens.

Beside the lantern hanging from a nail on the right wall, a hunched man with thin greying hair worked quickly, wiping dry the gleaming dark flanks of a horse. When he caught sight of Averil, the man straightened and squinted at her. His cheeks were ruddy, eyebrows and eyelashes pale, his chin was grizzled with a few day's growth of beard.

"No free meals." He spoke in a growl. "Git away wit' ye."

Averil stepped closer to the light, feeling the warmth penetrate her wet garments. Steam rose from her cloak.

"Did four Cavaliers arrive here tonight?"

"Them gentlemen are nothing to do wi' the likes o' you." The man hawked and spit into the straw. "Begone now or I'll lay the 'eavy portion of a stick to yer 'ind end!"

"Please," Averil begged. "I must—!"

The man flung down his rag to come after her, but a new voice stopped him.

"Wait, Samuel."

A young woman, still beautiful although hard work and worry had prematurely added deep lines across her forehead and at the corners of her eyes, had stepped into the stables. She held a pale grey scarf around her shoulders and tiny drops of moisture on it gleamed in the lamplight. She had a generous mouth, but her round blue eyes were fathomless as she surveyed Averil's garments. "What is your name, my sodden friend?" she inquired.

Averil hesitated, her heartbeat quickening, and decided against going into the story of her identity and the strange clothing. "Jeremy Halmes, ma'am," she muttered. It was the only answer she could summon at the moment. "It's about the Cavaliers, I must talk to them. It's urgent."

"Aye, I can see it's important to you, Jeremy, and I'm thinking you need a hot supper as well. My name is Mrs. Brimby. I own this inn."

The man protested, "Ye're not goin' to let these young pups get away wi'—"

"Samuel," Mrs. Brimby said, and in that one word conveyed affection, regret, and a determination to have her way.

The kitchen Mrs. Brimby took her to was warm and fragrant. Huge joints of beef, veal, and pork hung suspended from the beams across the ceiling, and handfuls of drying rosemary, twigs of bay leaves, and other aromatic herbs hung upside down in bunches from hooks beside the fireplace. Several fat, roasted chickens newly pulled from the spit lay on a table, and Averil felt faint with hunger when she smelled the aroma of the cooked meat.

The fire crackled pleasantly, and as the heat invaded her clothing, Averil drooped with exhaustion. By the time Mrs. Brimby had her seated on a three-legged stool beside the fire with her plate of supper, she was almost too weary to enjoy it. Around her bustled the cook and Mrs. Brimby. Trays of steaming food were carried from the kitchen, and a huge pot of water was swung onto a hook above the fire. Averil's eyelids felt weighted. It was not long before she put aside her plate and, much like a drowsy cat, curled herself on the warm stones beside the hearth and fell asleep.

She was awakened by a nudge as a booted foot prodded her ribs. "Ho there, we need more wine upstairs." The voice was deep, slurred.

Though her mind was clogged with sleep and she felt as though she were seeing through a heavy piece of lace, Averil recognized the rich red velvet doublet and wide bucket-topped boots of a Cavalier. Excitement surged through her. The man stood with feet braced wide, one dark green bottle tipping in his relaxed grip. His face was broad, the skin heavily pitted. Through half-closed eyes he regarded her. "We need wine," he repeated. "And hurry up with it."

Averil looked around, the kitchen was empty. Since the officer was obviously more interested in wine at the moment, she decided to oblige him that before asking any favors. With a lantern from the wall in one hand, she crossed to a trap door, pulled it up, and cautiously descended the wooden steps into the cellar. The interior was cool and smelled musty. She emerged with an armful of dusty green bottles which the officer took.

"Sir, please, I would have a word with you," Averil begged when the man had turned to leave. At her words he looked back in surprise and surveyed her dubiously.

"Please, sir, have you knowledge of a Roundhead attack on a manor near here just yesterday morning?" She spoke in a rush before he could leave, and the man's puzzlement turned to interest. He bent down to her.

"A Roundhead attack, you say?" His breath reeked of sour wine. "Where was this?"

"The Maslin Manor, sir. About two leagues to the north."

The eyes narrowed, the face retreated from hers. "Come along," he said. "Rupert will want to hear of this."

Could he mean the King's nephew, Prince Rupert? Averil's eagerness mushroomed as she followed him. The room they entered was lit by a tallow dip on one table. Two men were seated at the table, leisurely picking the last bits of meat from a platter piled with gnawed bones and cold vegetables coated with congealed grease. A third man stood smoking a long clay pipe near an open window. The three were comfortably attired, their cloaks tossed over a chair in one corner, their shirts and doublets open at the throat, hats canted back on their heads.

One of the men at the table had shoulder-length black hair curling around a face that was tragic, handsome, aristocratic. His eyes were expressively dark, his nose straight and slightly tipped down at the end. Averil knew at once that this must be Prince Rupert; his black ringlets were a legend. At her entrance he tossed his bone to a small white poodle at his feet, picked up a napkin, and wiped his fingers and mouth with it. As he surveyed her, his eyes took on a glint of humor.

''What's this, Mumbry, your entertainment for the evening? But why bring him here? You know we don't share your tastes.''

The other men laughed heartily, and Mumbry, the officer who had escorted her to the room, scowled as if this joke represented a long-standing aggravation. Averil waited nervously, not understanding their jest.

With a clinking of glass against glass, Mumbry deposited the wine bottles on the table, and as the other men reached for their share, Rupert gestured to Averil and asked impatiently, ''Why is he here?''

Mumbry prodded her closer to the table. ''He told me he had news of a Roundhead attack on Maslin Manor.''

''Maslin Manor?'' Rupert fixed his dark gaze on Averil. ''When?''

Though she had been eager for this opportunity, once confronted by Rupert, Averil's stomach leaped fearfully. ''Yesterday morning—'' She tried to keep her voice husky, but realized to her consternation that she was breathless—''at about daybreak, m'lord.''

''Have him sit.'' Rupert gestured to Mumbry and the man pushed another chair up to the table. Averil sidestepped a few scattered napkins and bones that littered the floor and sat in the chair just opposite Rupert. She looked across the flickering yellow tallow dip at him. His dark eyes were steady, searching.

''Your name?''

Her mouth felt dry. ''Jeremy Halmes, m'lord.''

''You saw them? You're sure they were Roundheads?''

''Nay, m'lord, I didn't see them, but the Earl is a firm Royalist, so it could only have been Roundheads. I mean . . .'' She peered around to the other men who watched her curiously, and then finished in a weaker voice, ''. . . It does seem that way.''

''Were you there at the time, or did you chance upon the manor later in the morning?''

She looked back to Rupert. "There, m'lord."

"Where?"

"In the manor." She added in a strange uneasiness, "It's where I work. But I have a question—"

"Were you hiding in the manor?"

"Hiding?" Averil repeated after a hesitation.

"You felt no urge to take up arms and protect his lordship?" The deep eyes fixed on her were keen and probing. "Or were you protecting something else? The lady perhaps?"

Averil dropped her gaze, confused and nervous. "The lady?"

"The Earl of Armondale's daughter," Prince Rupert said impatiently. "She's missing and I want to find her."

Averil studied him. Something in Rupert's voice and the questions he asked made her wary; she was not sure she should reveal herself just yet. "The Earl is missing also," she ventured.

Mumbry sniggered. Rupert looked at him sharply, and the man shrugged and lifted his wine bottle to his lips.

Prince Rupert sat back in his chair. At last he said, "The Earl is a traitor. Official dispatches, ammunition, supplies—all are disappearing into the Earl's household. And one of my messengers was murdered on that property not a week ago."

Averil's heart beat painfully as she tried to make sense of what she had just heard. Rupert pushed himself to his feet and walked around the table to stand beside her. When he leaned down, his black curling hair swung forward.

"Look at me!"

Averil looked up.

"Do you know anything about this?"

Averil shrank from him. "Nay, nay—the Earl is a firm Royalist—"

"Don't bleat to me of the Earl's loyalty to our King!" Intensity gripped Rupert and made his eyes darken dangerously. "*Someone* in that household is a traitor and I *will* find out who it is. Now look, you, tell me what you know of the Earl's daughter. Where was she yesterday morning?"

The full meaning behind his question exploded in her mind, and Averil's eyes snapped wide as she stared at Rupert. "You!" she croaked in stunned amazement. "It was *you* who attacked the manor!"

Prince Rupert straightened and veered away from the table so abruptly that the tallow flame danced wildly in the draft. The other men remained silent. From under the table, the dog whined.

Looking at him as he paced the room, Averil could feel the consuming energy scarcely within him; there was a barely checked violence in his movements. Averil grew cold with fear. When Rupert stopped in front of her, she cringed.

"We have the Earl. But his daughter escaped us. She should have been there! Where were you hiding? Was she with you?"

Averil cowered in her chair, fear clotted her mind.

"Answer me!"

"There was no one else with me," she choked out.

"Where is she then? You know, don't you?"

Averil shook her head dumbly.

"By God's wounds! What a sniveling disgrace to manhood you are!" He leaned down, his hair falling before her face. "*Coward*, you hid in the manor instead of taking up arms like a man. I can get what information I need from the Earl, so go. Get from my sight! You *disgust* me."

He yanked her chair from the table so violently, she was almost spilled to the floor. When Rupert turned his back on her, Averil ran.

She clattered down the stairs and thrust open the main door so forcefully it rebounded against the outer wall with a crash. Down the narrow mud-clogged street she ran blindly.

CHAPTER
TWO

The night was thick and noisy around her; insects chirrupped, night birds screeched, somewhere a frog flopped into water. With no moon, the darkness was so dense as to seem palpable. At some point Averil had wandered off the road and was now surrounded by a forest that seemed to throb and hum with a life all its own. She slumped to her knees at the base of a tree. The matted leaves and mosses on the ground around it were dry, having been protected from the rain by the tree's branches.

At some time in the night she bolted awake, heart pounding. Something had awakened her, some sound alien to the gentle rustlings of the forest. The rain clouds had dispersed and full moonlight bathed the woods. Fearfully, she looked around and realized she was in a clearing. In the moonlight, the trunks of the surrounding trees looked made of pewter, and the leaves had a silver cast. A cold wind caressed her. Turning her head, she strained her ears to catch any sound.

Then she heard it. A horse. Some distance to her right, its hooves churned damp leaves in the undergrowth. The noise increased as the animal sped nearer and Averil wondered frantically if it was Rupert or one of his men coming after her. Had they realized she was no boy? Perhaps guessed her true identity? Would they try to kill her?

The sounds grew louder as the horse approached and crashed through the underbrush. Averil's heart hammered as she wondered wildly which way to run. For a split second the noise stilled and then she saw it—the horse and its rider became airborne as the animal leaped a fallen tree. Gracefully the horse landed on its front hooves and continued its head-long rush toward her. The beast had a massive chest and head and its muscles bunched and stretched like waving satin in the blue moonlight. The breath streaming from its nostrils formed white banners in the night air.

Astride the animal, with cloak rippling behind him, was a man in a black mask. It was the kind of fashionable mask Averil had seen occasionally in London on lords and ladies bound for a masqued ball, but here in the night and with the silver light full upon it, it took on a strangely humanless cast, like a death mask.

Terrified that one of the night spirits said to haunt the highways had found her, Averil choked on a scream as she tried to scuttle from the specter's path. Her hands and feet slid through the leaves, crunching them in her panic-spurred haste.

"Hold there!" The voice split the night like a crack of thunder, and the great beast pawed the air as the rider jerked back abruptly on the reins.

Averil fled. She plunged into the trees to her left, then stumbled wildly as she encountered the edge of a stream bed. The strange specter was coming after her. In panic, she flung herself over the edge of the embankment and scrambled into a low clump of brush to hide herself. The brush grew beside a tree that was dead and leaning sharply over the embank-

ment, and she pushed herself as far under the trunk as she
could manage. Several feet below her, a shallow stream
trickled past, the surface flecked with tiny splinters of
moonlight.

She heard twigs snapping behind her, and the irate snorting
of the beast's breath. The apparition appeared in her range
of vision and stopped barely three feet from her hiding place.
The animal was mammoth to her and blue-black in color.
Above him the man rose tall and menacing. His masked face
was lost in blackness beneath his hatbrim, but the exposed
white front of his shirt glowed like snow in the moonlight.
The horse's head snapped up and down in restless protest,
but the man held the reins taut as he waited, watched, listened.
The horse and rider were so near she could feel the heat
radiating from them.

Averil held her breath against the loud and frantic pounding
of her heart. Surely he could hear it! Abruptly the man
clucked his tongue, and with a gentle prod from spurless
boots, he urged the horse across the small stream. Tiny, icy
drops of water were flung up at Averil and stung her face.
After a slow tour of the other bank, the man returned past
Averil's hiding place, shook out the reins, and the horse
lunged across the clearing. An instant later the man and beast
disappeared into the trees.

Averil released her breath slowly. Fully awake now, she
knew the man had been no apparition. Frightened and forlorn,
she wanted desperately to be with her aunt and uncle, regardless of where they lived or how far away.

Though the roads were unmarked, Averil thought she could
find the way from previous visits to London. She had not
been there since her mother died, but when she could not
remember a particular turning, she asked directions of passing
travelers. At any time there were those who wandered home-
less and begging, but with the war many had been burned
out of their homes, forced to flee destruction, and the
wanderers were plenty in number.

She was never to remember much about that journey. She begged for her food and passed one night in a cottager's shed, two more in copses of trees she found alongside the road. A fever from exposure and exhaustion built in her, and she slept deeply for two hours on a cartload of firewood when she was offered a ride one morning.

As she neared London, the villages and cottages crowded closer to each other until they all but lined the thin path of a road. Traffic increased. A woman with geese and chickens hanging by the feet from a long pole slung over her shoulder brushed past. The fowl she carried squawked and flapped their wings in protest, and Averil ducked clumsily out of the way of their snapping beaks. Three young girls with empty milk pails sauntered home through the long shadows cast at day's end. They laughed together and swung their brightly colored skirts in hopes of catching the eye of one of the thin farm boys sitting atop carts that rattled past them.

For the defense of London, the Lord Mayor, Isaac Pennington, had ordered that a string of forts be built around the city and joined by earthwork trenches. To raise revenue for the army and to keep a closer watch on the comings and goings, a pass was required to enter or leave the city. Averil remembered all this as she neared the queue of people halted before a crude gate. A guard, his halberd braced in the dirt beside him, was admitting people one at a time. The fort at this site was only half built, but a cannon squatted beside it aimed threateningly at the road. Behind this and stretching out to the distant horizons were the encroaching, dark, crowded buildings of London. Spires of the more than one hundred churches thrust upward into the hazy smoke that clung to the city.

Averil hung back in momentary panic; she had no pass. She could not have come all this far only to be turned away! Shaking with fever, clutching the cloak even tighter around her, Averil worked her way into the small crowd converging at the gate. When the man in front of her showed his pass, she pretended to be with him and as the guard waved the man on, she followed close on his heels. But the halberd slid deftly between them and barred Averil's path.

"Pass," the guard said. "Show yer pass."

Alarmed, Averil mustered her flagging courage and replied in what she hoped was a street urchin's whine, "I've come to see me aunt and uncle. Me uncle's sick, ye know, an the poor old dear can't cope wi' the chores and seein' to a sick'un and all, an' she needs me t'help or she'll be awastin' away a'for—"

"Two shillings," the guard interrupted. "No pass, ye pay two shillin's."

Averil tried to suppress another deep shudder that went through her. She scoffed, "Me? Two shillin's! Now there's a good 'un. Lud, if I had two shillings I'd be a fair rich man."

"Git on wi' ye," the soldier growled ill-humoredly and waved her through.

As she wandered dim streets made even darker by the overhanging smoke from limestone furnaces and soapboilers, Averil cringed from the noise and confusion. Harnesses jingled, coaches creaked and bumped, hooves and wheels clattered on cobblestones or slopped through mud; shouts and distant cries and sporadic laughter echoed in the dust around her. Beggars clutched at her as she passed. A linkman paused in front of her to fire his torch, and the smoking light illuminated a dusty hackney coach as it rattled past.

When at last she reached Aldersgate Street, the darkness was almost complete, but she counted the houses until she found the one she sought. It was a narrow, four-storied house built of lathe and plaster with decorative cross-timbering.

Averil's knock was answered almost at once, and the last thing she remembered from that night was the sight of her aunt's fleshy pink face illuminated by the candle in her hand.

Averil vacillated in and out of consciousness for two days. Her Uncle Jacob hired a man to come with his smoke pots, and the chamber where she lay was filled with the smoke

of burning pitch and frankincense to drive away the illness.
The windows were locked to keep out the night air thought
to be deadly to a sick person, and through it all her Aunt
Mary Geneva stayed at her bedside, cooling Averil's feverish
brow with cloths dipped in vinegar.

Mary Geneva Kirkland was a confirmed and dedicated
housewife. But with her son away fighting with Colonel
Cromwell's troops and her daughter indifferent to her, she
was feeling somewhat useless and unneeded at that time.
Averil's arrival excited her dormant maternal instincts. With
all the gusto of a general laying siege to an enemy castle,
Mary Geneva fought Averil's fever and illness. She was an
optimistic woman, still handsome at the age of six-and-thirty,
though overly round and with one front tooth freshly missing.
She had an abundance of energy and bustled in and out of
Averil's chamber. She brought soup to spoonfeed her niece,
applied poultices to her raw, infected feet, and personally
changed the bed linens whenever Averil's fevered body
soaked them through. When, on the third morning, Averil's
eyelids fluttered open and she looked at her aunt with full
recognition, Mary Geneva experienced the searing pride of
victory.

Two evenings later, as she sat on a stool at Averil's bedside,
Mary Geneva was joined by her husband and her daughter,
Lynna. It was the same bedroom Averil and her mother had
shared during their many visits. Situated on the second floor,
it was a small chamber dominated by the wide tester bed
and decorated with a few pieces of heavy, carved furniture—a
single chair, a wardrobe, and two stools covered in turquoise
satin.

Feeling stronger now, Averil related the events that had
forced her flight to London. Only Jacob made any sound
during her recital, and that was an occasional exclamation
of anger or a soft whistle of disbelief. He sat in a straight-
backed chair drawn up before the red-glowing hearth and
drank wine from a pewter mug. Averil remained dry-eyed

through the account, feeling strangely removed, as though the events had happened to someone else.

When she finished, Jacob scowled and slapped his palm on his knee. "It shouldn't surprise me *what* those shaddle-pated Royalists attempt, but accusing the Earl of being a traitor—! Hey day!"

Mary Geneva was aghast. "Poor sweet Mrs. Fairchild." Imploringly, she turned round, shocked eyes on her husband.

"Unfortunately, it's happening all over, madam. His Majesty can't raise the revenue to pay his soldiers their wages, so they loot the damned countryside! Swine! You remember what happened after Prince Rupert attacked Brentford last autumn—sacked the damned town, burned it, raped all the wo—"

"Jacob!" Mary Geneva exclaimed and nodded her head to Lynna and Averil, warning him not to talk of such things in front of them.

Jacob clicked his tongue against his teeth in impatience but said nothing. He was a short man with a plump belly and thin legs. His hair was straw-colored and combed straight back from his face to hang in wispy curls on his shoulders. He had a long nose below squinting brown eyes, and his mouth was a narrow groove of displeasure. Though an economic depression had been building for the last twenty years, Jacob had worked diligently and prospered. A wine merchant by profession and a supporter of Parliament in the war, he had been at the height of his career two years before. Now he had been forced to dismiss nearly a third of his employees and was working desperately to keep his business from being wiped out altogether. Heavy taxation to support the war affected the entire country, but London in particular, and trade fell off steadily. As a result, many businesses had been forced to close, and unemployment and poverty were rampant.

Now he had not only his business to worry about, but also a niece who had suddenly thrust herself upon him. To make matters worse, she was the daughter of a prominent Royalist and was being sought by Prince Rupert. A damned sticky business, this! he thought impatiently.

"It's very clear to me that we can't let your identity be known," he said at last. "Instead of Averil Maslin, you'll have to be Averil Kirkland, and we'll say you're my brother's daughter sent here from Reading because of the fighting."

"But Jacob, what about those who might remember her from past visits?" Mary Geneva pointed out.

"That was almost four years ago. She looked different, don't you think?"

"Not unrecognizably so."

"We'll just have to be discreet then, madam! Can you think of any better way? We can't lock her up!"

Averil sank back against the pillows. "How much longer will this war go on? Perhaps, if it is over soon, they'll let my father go free."

Jacob shifted uneasily in his chair. "Charles is stubborn and won't relinquish any of his power to Parliament. Right now he's claiming most of the battles, and if he emerges victorious over Parliament, it'll be very bad for any accused of treason against him."

"What are you saying, uncle?" Averil looked out at him from the flickering shadows cast into the head of the bed by the candle on the nearby table. Jacob drank the last of his wine and stared sadly into the crimson glow of the sea coal in the grate.

"Your father's as good as dead," he said at last.

"Nay, nay! There must be something we can do! My father has many friends in the King's army!" She pleaded with desperate eagerness. "Why, there are Lords Somersfield and Ames, and Sir Peterton, and so many more. We could send word to them and they'd vouch for my father. They'd have him released!"

Her beseeching words increased Jacob's chagrin. He rose to place his mug on the mantel and stood with his back to the hearth, hands clasped behind him. He felt duty-bound to give shelter to and provide for his wife's sister's child, but not to endangering his family and reputation by sending messages to the King's officers. Every man was in a precarious position, and it might be disastrous for his business and his family if he were considered a Royalist sympathizer. Letters were seldom sealed and anyone who so wished could read the contents. He tried to explain this to her, but Averil was too distraught to accept his reasoning.

"But, Uncle Jacob, there must be some means!"Averil protested. "If you won't help, then let me go back to Abingdon. He must be near there somewhere!" She was too passionately concerned for her father's safety to curb her tongue or even to recognize that Jacob considered the matter closed and was frankly astonished that she dared argue with him.

Lynna looked at her cousin with candid surprise. She had tangled with her father often enough in recent years to recognize his limits, but her cousin was too trusting. Since it was not she herself pushing him over the edge, Lynna kept her silence and watched the two with increasing amusement. She was sixteen months older than Averil and had hair so pale blonde it seemed white in sunlight. Her eyes were a delicate blue which at the moment were bright with an almost impatient excitement but which could quickly grow heavy-lidded with boredom. She might have been considered a pretty girl but for the trace of petulance in the way her thin lips curled down at the ends and the arrogant carelessness in her manners. As she listened to the conversation, there was a curbed wildness in her movements, and she alternately paced the chamber or sat on the end of the bed.

Mary Geneva saw the tightening skin around her husband's mouth and knew his patience was fraying. "It's just the fever talking," she explained.

Jacob considered himself a beneficent man and was a good Christian as long as he did not have to exert himself. So he accepted the excuse of fever. He smiled to show Averil he could be understanding. "I applaud your high intentions, my dear Averil, but you must be practical. Your father could be almost anywhere in England at this moment. Besides," he added in the tone of voice an adult might use in humoring an impetuous child, "how would you get by in the country with a war going on?"

"You would have me do nothing?"

Jacob's loose jawline quivered. "You certainly cannot run about the countryside with that—" he brushed the air with his hand in a gesture of dismissal —"that boy's costume on that you arrived in! Though it stretches my sensibilities, under the circumstances I can understand why you were forced to lower yourself to this charade in the first place, but to voluntarily go off like that is out of the question!"

With tears burning behind her eyes, Averil looked down at the soft feather mattress tucked over her and picked at a loose thread. While under his roof and thus under his protection, she had a duty to her uncle. But she had an even greater duty to her father.

"What can I do?" she begged. "Is there no one else who would help?"

"Who, for instance?" Jacob responded sharply.

Lynna spoke out with tart sarcasm. "How about the Tottman?"

Jacob turned on her in fury. "Don't you *ever* mention that name in my house!"

At the pleading look his wife gave him, he shrugged and continued more gently to Averil, "Your father is a known Royalist and therefore enemy to Parliament. On the other hand, the Royalists claim he is a traitor. The Earl is now an enemy to both sides, Averil. Who is in a position to risk everything they have to argue his case? I'm sorry, my dear— terribly sorry."

"Uncle Jacob, my father is not a traitor. You know that, and I know—"

Jacob's voice exploded across the room and he advanced rapidly to stand at the foot of her bed. "Nay, young woman, I do *not* know!" He glared at her; thick purple veins on his forehead throbbed, and his face filled with blood. "How do any of us know for a certain *what* he was doing? He could be guilty as a whore with a full belly for all I know! I'm not saying he is or isn't, I'm just telling you I'm not risking *my* neck to find out!"

His hand flashed out and one plump, quivering finger pointed to her. "And I don't want to hear another whimper out of you about it, or I'll exercise my rights as head of this household and give you a cuffing you'll not soon forget!"

Averil stared hard at him, then abruptly turned away and threw herself down onto her pillow. She had never in her life been spoken to in such a manner and the experience mortified her. She trembled with helpless rage.

She heard him storm out of the room, slamming the door behind him with such force that the window panes rattled. Though Mary Geneva tried to comfort her with excuses for Jacob's words, Averil refused to speak or even look at her. Eventually Mary Geneva tiptoed out, firmly pulling Lynna with her.

She did not see Jacob again for two days. He never returned to her room and Mary Geneva insisted that Averil was still too weak to be up and about, so she did not go downstairs. More than ever before she was aware of a great chasm that separated her from them and of how insubstantial her position was in their household. Until that moment facing Jacob, she had viewed these people in much the same way she had as a child—with simple trust and the expectation of love. But now she saw the relationship with the eyes of an adult. She was the daughter of an earl who supported His Majesty, Charles Stuart; they were a merchant family on the side of Parliament. The only thread binding them to her now was Mary Geneva's continued loyalty to her dead sister. There was nothing else to bind Jacob to any sense of responsibility and she became inordinately fearful that he would turn her over to the soldiers or turn her out of his home altogether.

When she began joining the family downstairs, she was nervous and on edge. But Jacob was friendly in a detached sort of way, politely concerned about her activities and welfare. The message was subtle; he would treat her fairly and provide for her if she would put no demands on him or endanger his political reputation in any way.

Soon after Averil's arrival, Mary Geneva called in a seamstress, and the two designed and stitched gowns, chemises, and petticoats for Averil. As Averil's strength returned, so did an unhappy restlessness, and she took to joining her aunt and the seamstress to learn the intricate details of dressmaking.

Once she asked Mary Geneva what had been done with the boy's clothing she had worn to reach London, and when she discovered they had been put away in a chest with other articles to be distributed to the parish poor, she retrieved them, including the hat and boots, and hid them away in her room. Though she had no plan in mind for their use, the disguise had served her well and she had not given up hope that someday she might be allowed to return to Abingdon to search for her father. The thought plagued her that he may have already returned to Maslin Manor and was mourning her, believing her to be dead. A multitude of wildly impossible means of finding him filled her head every waking moment.

At night she had dreams of soldiers and black smoke, and she was running up a staircase that had no end. The staircase became a hill of mud and below her, emerging from a cloud of smoke, a man in a black mask swooped upward on a winged horse. Though she tried to scream, no sound came from her, and the demonic figure flew ever nearer, closing over her. The wings of his horse beat the air with a deafening noise like the cracking of thunder.

The first of May dawned clear and hot. As if in prelude

to the summer months to come, the day was airless and still. The stench of rotting garbage and human waste rose, and flies swarmed over the city. Averil threw open the windows of her room to catch whatever slight breeze might pass, and dust and insects filtered in. The massive oak tree just outside her window was grey with dirt. She and Mary Geneva went out in the coach that afternoon to purchase more buttons and a length of silver taffeta for an underskirt.

It was May Day and in previous years would have been a day of intense frivolity and celebration, with dancing and music and feasts to remember for weeks afterward. But due to the spreading Puritan influence, the practice was shunned, and in some places the maypoles had been chopped down as ungodly.

Rather than return to the closed and stifling house, Averil and Mary Geneva decided to seek out what coolness they could find along the open river. They rattled past Charing Cross and down the narrow King Street, viewing the broad, sprawling buildings of the palace at Whitehall, and then on through the village of Westminster. When they reached the fields beyond, Mary Geneva leaned forward and rapped on the front wall of the coach.

"Stop here, Morton!"

After the two matching horses were reined in, the driver, who was also gardener and all-purpose assistant in the household, climbed down to open the door. Short, wiry, grey-headed, Morton had been dutiful in his employ to Jacob for some fifteen years. After seeing the two women from the coach, he led the team farther down the road to where three other drivers waited with their horses and coaches. The coachmen stood in the shade cast by the conveyances and talked among themselves, exchanging news and bits of gossip concerning their respective employers.

Arm in arm, Averil and Mary Geneva strolled toward the riverbank where small groups of people clustered about in the broad swath of shade cast by a line of towering oaks.

Children ran shrieking between tree trunks and sometimes stopped to throw rocks into the river. If one of them approached too close to the water's edge, an adult would call out scoldingly. A girl selling fresh cherries from a basket on her arm sauntered past, calling out her wares in a high clear voice.

In the field a band of young men forming a volunteer militia marched about half-heartedly. Usually these bands were composed of apprentices who trained zealously, but the heat had eroded their fervor. They now complained loudly among themselves and exchanged insults with several men who stood close by, observing them. On the river, small boats moved past as the watermen ferried their passengers up and down the Thames. All along the bank the air felt weighted—with heat and sluggish insects and the decaying smell from the river.

Mary Geneva spread her skirts and sat in the tall grass beneath a tree, patting the space beside her in invitation for her niece. "I've made plans for us to visit my dear friend Eleanor Devenish and her son, Edmond, tomorrow." Mary Geneva cast a sidelong glance at Averil's profile. "Do you remember Edmond?"

Averil squinted her eyes against the sunlight flashing off the water as she recalled the boy who had been a childhood friend. "Of course I remember him! How is he?"

"La, child, he's near twenty now. A most attractive man. He's unmarried still."

"But aunt, if Uncle Jacob has been so careful to have me be known as his brother's child, as a Kirkland, is this wise to seek out people who remember me?"

"Oh, pish, child. Your uncle is frightened of his own shadow! Eleanor and her son are dear, dear friends and wouldn't dream of saying or doing anything that might be harmful to us. Why, I'll have a little talk with Eleanor and explain the whole situation to her. Would that make you feel better?"

Averil shot her a wry smile. "I feel fine. It's what Uncle Jacob will say that worries me."

"But he's going along with us! So there's nothing to be concerned about at all."

Avoiding Mary Geneva's eyes, Averil shaded her face and looked to the open field where the volunteer soldiers were abandoning their practice and heading toward the nearest tavern. A moment later she gave a cry of surprise and picked up her skirts as she started at a run across the sun-drenched field.

"Sir John!" she called eagerly and waved as a man leading a horse onto the road turned toward her. "Sir John!"

He hurried forward to greet her. He was tall, his brown hair richly accented with grey. His black velvet doublet and breeches were well tailored, and he wore an old-fashioned, starched ruff and high-tongued shoes with shiny silver buckles. Despite his forty-eight years and the severity of his clothing, he exuded a boyish vitality. The lines at the corners of his eyes deepened in laughter as he swept Averil up in an embrace.

"Averil! Be gad, sweetheart, what a surprise!"

When he released her, Averil stood back, laughing, but kept his hand in hers. She had known Sir John Walford since before her mother died, and the knight had been a frequent visitor to the manor during the last few years. He and her father had spent many a day together, hunting and riding, sharing wine and arguing politics. Once a year they traveled to the horse-fair together and Averil had always accompanied them.

"By gad!" he repeated. "What are you doing in London?"

"I'm staying with my aunt and uncle. Do you remember them?"

"The Kirklands, am I right? Is your father here, too? It's been months since I've seen . . . What is it?" As the laughter died from her lips, and her eyes grew stark, Walford asked gravely, "What's happened? Is it the Earl?" He put his arms around her as Averil's lips quivered. "Come, tell me."

Haltingly, Averil described the recent events to him. His mouth drew tight as he listened. "And you?" he questioned when she had finished. "Nothing happened to you?"

Averil shook her head. "I hid."

"You hid? But where?"

When she told him how she had squeezed herself into the old chimney flue, Walford laughed. "In the chimney!" he repeated in amused delight. "Well done. By gad, well done!"

"But my father," Averil pleaded. "You'll find him, won't you?"

Walford looked over the top of her head as his hand tightened reassuringly on her shoulder. "Of course. Had you doubted I would? But is this your aunt approaching?"

Mary Geneva had discreetly kept her distance while the two greeted each other, but now she joined them, smiling. "Sir John Walford, is it not?"

Walford slipped his arm from around Averil and greeted Mary Geneva with the customary kiss. He held one arm for Averil, the other for Mary Geneva. As the three strolled past wandering clusters of people, Mary Geneva invited Walford to join them for supper that evening.

"Thank you, madam, but I must decline. I'm departing London today on business. I've delayed too long as it is, but having just found Averil here and learned of this sad business concerning the Earl, I'm loathe to take leave of her just yet."

Mary Geneva waved the fan gently in front of her face. "Another time perhaps. But now, if you will excuse me, I see an acquaintance of mine."

When Mary Geneva had moved beyond earshot, Averil looked urgently to Walford. "You must leave so soon? When will you return?"

"It's only for a few days, Averil. A week at most." He tethered his horse to the tree under which Averil and her aunt had been sitting. Averil spread her skirts and sat in the warm grass while Walford took a seat with his back to the tree.

"Who brought you to London?" he asked.

Now that sufficient time had passed and no harm had been done, Averil felt almost absurdly proud of her accomplishment, and she replied, "No one. I traveled to London as a lad."

"As a lad? Why that's the most ludicrous thing I've ever heard! Where were the servants?"

"There were none I could find."

Walford considered her for a moment, then shrugged. "At least you're safe," he said and added, "Perhaps the servants were captured and pressed into the King's army."

"The King cannot be so desperate for soldiers."

Walford smiled in faint amusement. "Sweet innocent, he needs all the soldiers he can muster, and there are ways to convince almost anyone to join."

Averil pinched a flower petal as she brooded on this. "I tried to find you in Abingdon."

"Did you? I'm sorry I wasn't there."

"Are you living in London?"

"I've had a home near Southwark for years. Didn't you know?"

Averil shook her head. "Is it not dangerous for you to be in London now?"

"Ah, well. . . . There are Royalist sympathizers aplenty in London, we just must not be overly zealous or risk damage to our property or person."

Averil bit at her lower lip as it began to tremble. "Oh, Sir John! I don't know where my father is now or even if he lives still! And Uncle Jacob refuses to discuss it or to help in any way or even to allow me to return to Abingdon to seek news."

Walford snorted in disbelief at her. "I can hardly blame him! Someone must protect you from your foolishness, and that's exactly what it would be if you tried to return now."

At her look of anguished protest, Walford shook his head. "You could hardly make a convincing boy, sweetheart, and even so, the way is full of soldiers now. The King is trying to block all the roads to London in hopes of starving the city into submission."

Frustrated at the critical note in his voice, Averil stubbornly refused to meet Walford's gaze. He continued in a quiet tone. "Be patient, Averil. I shall be returning by the end of the week, and I'll see you then."

As Walford rose to gather the reins of his horse, Averil jumped to her feet to halt him. "But it's been over a month since my father was taken! Every delay counts against him!"

Walford ignored her outburst.

"Then what about the Tottman?" she cried out on impulse.

"The Tottman?" he repeated in surprise. "What do you mean?"

"Could *he* help my father?" Suddenly, at his look of astonishment, Averil buried her face in her hands. "Oh, I don't know!" she wailed. "There has to be some way!" She looked up at him and her eyes brimmed with tears. "I just cannot wait in this forced idleness! I'm willing to try anything!"

Walford's brow furrowed. Absently he stroked the leather bridle as he murmured half to himself, "It might work."

"But how do we find the Tottman?"

Walford exhaled loudly and took both her hands in his own. "Not long ago, a knife grinder, an old half-blind man named Darby Kipp, was arrested. The leaders of Parliament have spies everywhere and they were certain this peddler was in some way connected with the Tottman. I don't know the particulars, but this Kipp fellow was questioned and released after a few days in Newgate. It may be that Darby Kipp *is* but a simple peddler, or it may be that he is very clever." Walford shrugged. "Wait until I return and then we shall see."

Averil nodded as she slipped her hands from his grasp.

She watched as he mounted his horse. After waving to her, he urged the animal onto the road and headed north toward Westminster. Though her eyes were on the puffs of dust flung up from the horse's hooves, Averil's thoughts were far away.

If Sir John was correct and this Darby Kipp was in some way a link to the Tottman, she had no intention of waiting through another torturous week to find out. She was too passionately concerned for her father's safety to wait a moment longer than was necessary. Tomorrow, she promised herself. Tomorrow . . .

CHAPTER
THREE

"You do feel somewhat feverish, Averil. Are you sure you wouldn't rather I stay with you?" Mary Geneva pressed her moist palm to Averil's forehead. Worry creased both women's brows.

Eager to be about her quest for Darby Kipp, Averil had remained in bed that morning with the excuse of feeling poorly. With Mary Geneva, Jacob, and Lynna planning to visit Eleanor Devenish, and the serving woman, Honor, given permission to use the hours to see her family in Deptford, Averil knew she would have most of the day to herself. But Mary Geneva was being too solicitous about her niece's welfare. Averil was alarmed.

"Please, don't worry about me," she pleaded earnestly. "Just a little rest and I'll be fine."

"Are you sure, dear? We'll be away till late with all the things Eleanor has planned." As Mary Geneva fretted with indecision, the color rose higher in her doughy cheeks. "Nay,

nay, I can't leave you ill abed and unattended. I'll speak with Honor.''

"Oh, nay!" Frantically Averil reached for her aunt's arm to detain the woman. If Honor remained with her, she would be unable to seek out Darby Kipp. "She was so eager to spend time with her family, it would be cruel to make her stay now.''

A shout from the street intruded into the room. Jacob was waiting with the coach. Mary Geneva hurried to the window, threw open the casement, and leaned out. "Be right down, Jacob,'' she called with a wave.

Jacob's voice sounded a gruff warning from below. "Quickly, madam, or you will be running along behind us!''

With a little sound of disgust, Mary Geneva pulled the window closed. She took up a thin black cloak she had dropped on the end of Averil's bed and adjusted it about her shoulders. This morning's weather was considerably cooler than the previous day's, and a misty fog rising from the Thames had penetrated the streets.

"I suppose I should take this up with Jacob, but I expect you'll be doing for yourself today, dear. I'm sorry,'' Mary Geneva said with a vague frown as she waved good-bye.

Averil waited, listening to Mary Geneva's heels clack on the stairs as she descended. Then she threw back the bedclothes and dashed to the window to peer out. Morton, dressed in his best livery of midnight blue satin, was seated on the driver's bench of the coach. Lynna was already settled inside, and Jacob paced the short distance from the coach to the front door as he waited for his wife. A moment later Mary Geneva and Honor emerged from the house. After a brief exchange during which Averil knew they were discussing her, Jacob threw up his hands. But in the end, with an angry expression on his face, he handed Mary Geneva into the coach and doled out some coins to Honor for her boat trip to Deptford.

When the fog had hidden their respective departures, Averil

turned from the window. If she had to venture alone through London, it would be far safer, she knew, to wear the boy's clothes she had hidden away. With a silent apology to Mary Geneva and a promise to replace it, she ripped a long linen towel into strips to bind up her breasts and hair. After donning the rest of her costume, she wiped her face and hands with ashes for good measure. The sugarloaf hat rested low on her head, the brim meeting her eyebrows.

She left the house through the rear and circled back to the street through a side alley. She had no idea where to find this Darby Kipp; he could be anywhere in the city or any one of hundreds of peddlers. But she had to make the effort.

She encountered numerous peddlers, some with cloth goods, some with pots and pans clanking from their sacks. But it was not until she reached the square in front of the massive St. Paul's Cathedral that she saw the first knife grinder. In times past, the main aisle in the cathedral had been a gathering place for businessmen, shoppers, and vendors, but now it was used as a stable, and Parliament soldiers and their horses occupied the space. Outside the church people had set up stalls and were crying their wares—jewelry, spices, fresh baked tarts and pastries. Averil maneuvered through small queues of shoppers, keeping her eyes on a man pushing a whetstone. He could not be Darby Kipp; he was not old, nor was he partially blind as far as Averil could determine.

When she questioned him about Darby Kipp, the man spat once and replied, "Fleet Street, 'ats where 'e goes."

Eagerly, Averil hurried across the square and into Fleet Street, a main thoroughfare choked with inns and taverns and shops. A coach, pausing to let its passengers look over the wares of a fruit seller, snarled the traffic and the air filled with loud curses and shouts from the drivers behind. Nearing the Fleet Street bridge, Averil smelled oysters and gingerbread for sale. Though her stomach rumbled emptily, she hurried past; she had neither the coin nor the time to spend here. She passed shops where apprentices lounged in doorways, calling out to passersby, urging people in. Porters sweated under heavy bundles on their backs and cursed the slow-moving fishwives who shouted out their offers for the day as they went from house to house.

It was nearing the noon hour and the fog had thinned considerably, but the air was still damp, and Averil felt clammy and uncomfortable. At last she stopped and leaned in angry weariness against a high brick wall dividing the road from the garden of some more privileged resident. She had reached the Strand and was surrounded by stately homes.

How had she missed him? Perhaps the knife grinder had not come out today, or perhaps he had been arrested again. Bitterness threatened to overwhelm her. But with lips compressed in determination, Averil once again searched the surrounding faces and forms for that of an old, half-blind knife grinder. She *would* find him!

On her return journey through Fleet Street, as she crossed the bridge over the Fleet Ditch once more, she spotted a man who gave her pause. He was small, stooped, and at the moment was applying the edge of a shining knife to his whetstone. He pumped the wheel with his foot and sparks flew from the blade. The man had white puffs of hair curling under a broad-brimmed hat. His clothing was faded by age and weather and was the color of dirty water. He wore a long coat that fit his thin frame like an oversized sack, breeches that were loose and fraying where they ended at mid-calf, and stiff, coarse wool socks. His shoes had the look of quality—probably a gift from a customer at one time—but the leather was cracked and lusterless, the buckle of the left shoe only half attached and flapping loosely. He bobbed his head as he handed the knife back to a young apprentice and held out a gnarled hand for the coins due him.

He was so unseemly a character to have any traffic with one such as the Tottman that Averil fleetingly wondered if he was not, after all, a mere peddler with no more information about the Tottman than she herself possessed.

His transaction completed, the little man picked up the handles on the frame of his whetstone and pushed it down the street. Averil sprinted after him, dodging the people in the road until she had caught up with the stooped form. Mentally giving herself a shove, she fell into step beside him and questioned, "Mr. Kipp?"

The man set down his wheel and cocked his head at her. One eye was coated by a milky blue film, but the other was clear and sharp, glittering at her through a hundred tiny wrinkles.

"Eh? Who be calling Darby Kipp? Ye 'ave knives to sharpen?" The clear eye ranged her form.

"I have a matter to discuss," Averil said breathlessly, her heart hammering. "About the Tottman." She dropped her voice and cast a furtive look around. "I have to find him. It's urgent."

"Eh? Who'd ye ask for?" His grizzled chin hung down as he gazed at her blankly; he had only one upper tooth and that was blackened.

"The Tottman! Please, do you know where I might find him?"

The grey head jerked back and forth in agitation. "Nay! Nay! I told 'em I don't know!" In a wide-eyed panic, he bent to pick up the handles of the whetstone. Averil threw herself in front of him.

"Please wait! You don't understand! I mean you no harm. I just want to talk. I've heard of your recent arrest, but I—"

The old man began to whine. "Ol' Darby, 'e knows nothing. Leave this poor ol' Darby 'lone."

"But my father's life is at stake! He's been arrested and they'll kill him, I know!"

But his head was swinging from side to side, his small dry face just opposite hers. Averil's heart plummeted. Stinging tears blinded her, but she grasped his arm to hold him back. He tried to shake her off, to reach again for his whetstone, but she clung to the bony arm. Several passersby turned to stare at them.

"Go 'way!" he begged. "Leave Darby in peace. I know nothing!" His lips were shaking, the thin, parched cheeks growing whiter.

"But you must! You must help me. You're my only hope."

"Nay!" he wailed, plucking her fingers from his arm. "I done ye no 'arm."

As though awakening from a dream, Averil released his arm and stepped away. She had not realized they had attracted so many people, and she stood rooted to the dusty street in mute humiliation. Though her eyes were blurred with tears, she saw the curious glances, the ugly, grinning faces. For one sharp, bitter moment, she hated them all. She watched as Darby Kipp shuffled away from her, and then, one by one, the people who had stopped to watch began to drift away. Averil stood alone in the street as she looked at the receding figure of Darby Kipp.

She had handled her approach all wrong, she chided herself. She had given him no reason to trust her, and—but of course!—he would not have answered her while a crowd gathered around! How foolish she had been! In her eagerness she could have caused them both to be arrested. No wonder he had shunned her!

With newly recovered hope, she followed him and waited some yards behind while he sharpened a butcher's heavy cleaver. When Darby Kipp caught sight of her, his good eye widened. After that, he quickened his shuffling pace as he moved from shop to shop, pausing for briefer and briefer times. From where she watched, Averil could see his hands begin to shake, and once he cut himself on a tavern maid's paring knife. As he sucked at the injured finger, he shot Averil a furious glare that gave her momentary pause. But when he moved on again, she followed. After several more blocks, the knife grinder turned down an alley between a cookshop and a blacksmith's forge. Averil hesitated. Was he merely going to a back entrance to ply his trade or was he trying to lose her? She cast a furtive glance around. There was no one paying her the slightest heed, so she dodged into the alley's narrow opening.

It was much dimmer here, the walls of the buildings on either side rising up to block out all but a thin strip of the sky. She could not see Darby Kipp and wondered if he had ducked behind one of these buildings or passed on out to the street at the far end. A small crowd of flies on a head of rotting cabbage buzzed up angrily as she passed but quickly settled again in her wake. She approached the end of the cookshop wall.

Just as she reached the corner of the buildings, a hand shot out and grabbed the front of her shirt. She saw the deadly blue gleam of a knifeblade as she was yanked into the narrow space just behind the blacksmith forge and brought face to face with the one-eyed man. Averil started to scream in terror, but with surprising swiftness, the old man whipped his arm around her head and clamped a hand over her mouth. The blade of his knife quivered within inches of her nose.

"No sound! Not a squeak," he hissed. "Ye came near t' costing me m' freedom earlier, ye know that?" He jerked her vehemently. Averil winced at the strength in his thin arm, but she kept her eyes on the dangerously close blade that seemed ready at any moment to slice into the flesh of her upper face. As she watched, the blade split into two blue flashes wavering in her vision, and Averil wondered if she would faint. She remembered the claims she had heard that the Tottman was a murderer. What nest of criminals had she disturbed now? Why had she not waited for Sir John to return before seeking out the knife grinder!

"Ye wanted t' talk, eh? Remember this—if any o' them soldiers comes lookin' fer me again, I'll know who t' blame." The knife twisted in a slow, graceful arc before her eyes. "Not only do I know 'ow to sharpen 'em, but I know 'ow to use 'em as well. D'ye ken?"

Cautiously Averil shifted her eyes from the blade to Kipp. His clear eye bored through her. She managed a small nod, though he still held her rigid, the brim of her hat mashed down around her ears and neck. He loosened his hold on her and replaced the knife in some inner pocket hidden under his large coat. Gingerly, Averil touched her sore jaw and licked her bruised lips, tasting salt and sweat. She had an impulse to flee but held herself back.

The old man said grimly, "So ye wants me t' tell ye where the Tottman might be. I can 'elp ye there, so 'appens 'e's 'ere in the city. Now, I wouldn't be tellin' this to just any Jack-a-nod, but I could see ye was in dire straits, miss."

At her look of frightened astonishment, Darby Kipp exclaimed, "Aye, I knew ye were no lad! Ye gave yerself away any number o' times, y'did. First it was yer voice, all cultured and polite, and then ye took me arm—'at's a woman's way if ever I knowed one. Had ye been the true lad ye're dressed like, ye would've cursed me soundly in yer anger 'stead o' crying. And only a sweet young miss could be as soft to the touch. Don't let anyone put a 'and on ye again or yer game's up."

Averil felt a hot blush sweep into her face. With it came a scorching humiliation. She had been sure of her pose as a lad—how many others had guessed?

"But the warning still 'olds true, be ye boy or woman." He fingered the knife through the fabric of his coat, and his good eye was a slit of hatred.

"Aye, I understand," Averil murmured, aghast. "I'd never reveal you to a living soul. I just have to find my father."

The peddler snorted in exasperation. "Yer father! Aye! Aye! Everyone needs something! But fer a woman such as yerself—quality, I'd say—to stoop to this, ye must be in great need. 'Tis courage ye 'ave, miss, and I'll not be the one t' stay ye from presentin' yer case t' the Tottman. But if 'e turns ye away, ye cannot come begging back t' me."

Averil's heart surged with wild excitement. So she would find the Tottman after all! It was unthinkable that he might turn her away, she was so sure of herself and her cause. Tears of gratitude threatened to fill her eyes, but on seeing them, Darby jerked a warning finger at her.

"Ye're the lad fer as long as ye wear them clothes! Now, 'ere," he said, drawing something from his pocket which he put into her hand, "take this coin and use it t' buy yerself an ale at the Nag's Head Inn in Cheapside. D'ye know where it is?"

Averil looked at the coin in surprise. "But aren't you going to take me to the Tottman?"

"Take ye t' the Tottman!" the one-eyed man exploded contemptuously. "All's I know is, 'e's in London now. If ye want t' find 'im, ye use this coin 'ere to buy yer ale. It's a sign, d'ye ken?" Darby Kipp turned to retrieve his whetstone and nodded to her as he angled it back down the alley toward the street. "Luck t'ye, miss."

Alone in the alley, Averil studied the coin. Aside from several scratches and something sticky on one side, it was an ordinary shilling as far as she could determine—rather an expensive cup of ale. But there had to be something in the scratches, some meaning not evident to the ordinary observer. For a moment she had the unnerving thought that the coin was a simple joke played by Darby Kipp to rid himself of her presence. There was only one way to find out; she tucked the coin into a pocket and returned to the street.

Cheapside and the Nag's Head Inn lay halfway across the city to the east. Averil turned eager steps in that direction, her tiredness and hunger all but forgotten now. Possessed as she was at that moment by youthful exuberance and single-mindedness, Averil paid no heed to her surroundings. She failed to notice the growing crowds in the street. In her imagination she considered various means of disclosing her predicament to the Tottman. Should she reveal her identity before telling her story? Or should she use it as a last, crowning point? She would be convincing, she was sure. The Tottman couldn't help but be moved by her predicament.

How long would it take him to find and free her father? Surely not more than a few days. Oh! And then they could return home! She thought of her father in his study, the precisely clipped beard on his smiling face, the warm brown eyes glancing up with affection whenever she interrupted him, as if he had been waiting to see her.

Her protecting bubble of preoccupation was shattered when an apprentice, brandishing the heavy stick every shopkeeper kept behind the counter to help guard his property, dashed from the doorway beside her. Almost knocking Averil down in his haste, the young man ran out into the street, shouting, "The Cross! God help us all, they're tearing down the Cross!"

Baffled and alarmed, Averil watched the agitated people pushing past her toward Cheapside. She recognized the rage and dismay in their faces. What was happening? Averil moved forward with the crowd, tentatively keeping to the farthest edges so as not to be caught up in the growing crush. As they headed toward the square, the masses of people rushing up from behind squeezed the mob into a seething crush of bodies, and Averil found herself surrounded, trying to keep her footing. She was borne along, unable to escape until the river of humanity emptied into the square surrounding the oversized, ornate Cheapside Cross.

Parliament soldiers, some on horseback and others on foot with long, menacing pikes in their hands, attempted to hold back the crowd. Ladders were being raised against the old Cross. Other soldiers stood by with great lengths of rope.

Several weeks earlier, a mob of zealous Puritan citizens had descended on St. Margaret's Church in Westminster, destroying religious relics and shattering each of the magnificent stained glass windows. The Puritan leaders in Parliament had seized eagerly on this activity and, in an attempt to be encouraging, had similarly doomed the Cheapside Cross. But the Cross was a beloved ornament. Decorated with ancient religious sculptures, it was adorned

with garlands on holidays according to the old custom.
Parliament had seriously miscalculated the sentiments of the
people. Now the soldiers were forced to raise their weapons
as rioting erupted in the square.

"Damn Puritans!" screamed a voice beside her, and she
curses and shouts increased.

"Not the Cross!"

"Hang John Pym! Hang the Puritan devil for taking our
Cross!"

Rocks, bricks, and pieces of cobblestone hurtled through
the air at the soldiers, but they fell without hitting their marks
and smashed on the cobbled square.

Thoroughly frightened, Averil held onto her hat and
squeezed and shoved her way toward the outskirts of the
crowd until she emerged in front of a shop. She huddled in
the doorway in panic. Straining her eyes, she searched the
square until she spotted a picture of a horse's head on a sign
swinging from a wought-iron arm. The Nag's Head Inn.

With her boots crunching broken glass beneath her feet,
Averil inched her way along the shopfronts, pausing in the
sheltering lee of each doorway, her eyes riveted on the one
door she sought. As ropes were lashed around the Cross,
the mob surged and fell back like a pacing, enraged beast.

When she reached the Nag's Head Inn, Averil slipped
quickly inside. The common room was dark. She waited as
her eyes adjusted to the gloom. Five men were seated at
scattered tables and almost all were heavily into their cups.
It was a long room with a fireplace at the far end; over the
low, glowing fire hung a row of chickens roasting on a spit.
In a chair beside the fire sat a rotund, half-bald man who
alternately sucked at a bottle of wine and swung the handle
on the spit. Averil sank onto a bench at a table against the
wall and huddled there gloomily as she looked around. Who
would be the person to recognize the coin?

"Peter Oxton!" shouted one of the men as he rolled blood-
shot eyes toward the figure seated at the fire. "It's dry,"

he complained, swinging a tin mug from his forefinger for the other to see. The man called Peter Oxton pushed himself up to a standing position and threaded a broad, slow path through the tables. After picking up the empty mug, he crossed to Averil's table.

"Ale," Averil answered his bored look. Self-consciously, she pushed the coin from her pocket across the rough, splintered table and watched his face closely. He picked it up without a flicker of emotion or recognition and turned away to fetch the requested drinks.

When Peter Oxton silently set a brimming mug and her change down on the table and returned to his seat beside the fire without so much as a nod or a sign of any kind, Averil's disappointment was so keen she almost cried out. So the coin meant nothing to him! Either it was a cruel joke on the part of Darby Kipp or Peter Oxton was not the person who would recognize it and help further her efforts to contact the Tottman. Averil bit at her quivering lower lip and tried to still the impulse to weep.

Outside, the tumult continued. The other patrons seemed not to notice; they were sunk in their own private desperations, saying little to one another. Knowing she had to continue her charade, Averil downed a portion of the ale, wiping her mouth on her sleeve for good measure. She was still shaken by how easily Darby Kipp had seen through her disguise.

When she set the mug down again, Peter Oxton caught her attention. He had put aside his bottle of wine and retrieved her coin from his pocket. She held her breath as he studied it, held it in front of the firelight, rubbed it with his thumb. After experimentally testing it with his fingers, he frowned, then rose and came toward her table. Averil's pulse hammered frantically. Peter Oxton wrenched the shirt fabric at the back of her neck and Averil squeaked in surprise.

"You little whelp!" he roared. "Givin' me false coin fer me good ale! I'll thrash ye good fer this, I will!"

The man was perspiring heavily as he yanked her from the bench and dragged her through the room toward a door to the left of the hearth. Surprised out of their lethargy by this unexpected entertainment, the other patrons snickered gleefully and banged their fists on the planked tables as they shouted encouragement to Peter Oxton.

"Thrash the runt good!"

"Ungrateful pup!"

With one swing of his foot, Peter Oxton booted the door open and shoved Averil into the room beyond. She fell against a long low trestle table in what appeared to be a kitchen area. He followed her and kicked the door closed behind him.

"Yell," he told her. Averil was too stunned to respond. "Damn you, lad! Yell like yer bein' beat!" he ordered harshly.

When she remained dumb, watching him with eyes bright with fear, he grasped one arm and shook her roughly until Averil let out a yelp of surprise and pain. From the other room filtered the sounds of hooted laughter.

"Again." He shook her arm, more gently now, and Averil, at last realizing his ploy, emitted a screeching yell that surprised both of them with its intensity.

"That'll do," he said. He released her and flicked a drop of sweat from his chin with a short, pudgy finger. "So ye've met the knife grinder?"

At Averil's nod, he ordered, "Wait here. I'll fetch me wife down to tend the fire."

He had just pulled open the door to return to the common room when a piece of flying brick crashed through the narrow, multipaned front window. Angry voices rushed in to fill the room. One of the sotted patrons wove a path to the shattered window and eyed the turmoil.

"Lud!" he exclaimed as he staggered around to look at his companions. "They're tearin' down the Cross!" He raised his fist to the mob in the street. "Damn Puritans! Damn Isaac Pennington! I piss on ye, Pennington! The Lord Mayor is a Puritan whore!''

From somewhere in the room, a voice rose in song. It was a scornful ditty about London's Lord Mayor, and as other voices took up the melody, Peter Oxton rushed about the room trying to quiet them. Undaunted by their host's curses and urgent pleas, the drunken voices rose higher in volume.

> "Farewell little Isaac, with hey, with hey,
> Farewell little Isaac, with hoe,
> You have made us all like asses,
> Part with our plate, and drink in glasses
> While you grow rich with two-shilling passes,
> With hey, trolly, lolly hoe!''

When the song was entering its third round, the door to the inn swung back forcefully on its hinges and a stream of Puritan soldiers wearing lobster-tailed helmets and waving swords before them burst into the inn.

Peter Oxton lunged toward Averil and dragged her back into the kitchen, swinging the door closed again behind him. Sweat drops were flying from his round red face.

"Quickly now, do ye know the Red Gate Tavern?'' Amidst shouting and scuffling sounds, a table in the common room fell with a splintering crack. Averil jumped, shaking her head anxiously in the negative. Peter Oxton's fleshy face had gone white.

"Threadneedle Street by Cornhill. Go there now and get the Tottman. Upper floor, last door. Run!'' He let go of her, but Averil could not move. Oxton shoved her toward the rear door. She saw naked fear in his eyes.

"Run!''

The kitchen door burst open and Oxton spun around as three Puritan soldiers pushed their way in. Two of the men grabbed the owner of the inn as a third lunged at Averil and grasped her roughly by the collar. Before he could utter a sound, Peter Oxton's mid-section was split open with a long heavy blade.

Averil screamed. It was a ragged, piercing sound that seemed to shatter the very air in the room into a thousand tiny pieces. Recoiling from the horror, she flung herself backward. The soldier who held her had been braced to keep the lad from running away and was not prepared for a backward assault. The momentum threw him off balance. As he felt himself falling, he released his grip on her. Averil swung her arm frantically against the soldier and leaped past him as he fell. In an instant she had wrenched open the heavy rear door. Behind her the other two soldiers were scrambling over the massive, inert form of Peter Oxton, but she was into the alley and running before either had cleared the door.

Averil dodged barrels and leaped debris. She was young and agile, unencumbered by a helmet or heavy leather buffcoat or weapon, as were her pursuers. The thick boots were her only impediment, but in spite of this she managed to keep several yards between herself and the soldiers. The narrow, twisting alley led her out into the crowded square once again, and she ran full tilt into a screaming crush of people. Mindlessly, she pushed into the sea of bodies. Her progress was sluggish. She screeched aloud in desperate frustration at the people in her way.

Sobbing with terror, she tore clear of the mob and ran on down the street without looking back. A pain bloomed in her side. She passed street after street, her breathing growing more labored as the air burned a path in and out of her lungs. Finally, unable to manage another step, she collapsed against a wall and dropped to her knees in the dirt.

In the door of the lodging house against which Averil slumped stood an old woman in a soiled smock. She was barefooted, twin long grey whiskers hung from her chin, and she stared at Averil with an immobile and childlike expression.

Averil moaned softly, trembling as she mopped at her damp face with the sleeve of her doublet. Her pursuers were nowhere in sight. Though her muscles protested and her legs were shaky, she pushed herself to her feet. She looked around, then at the woman in the doorway.

"Do you know Threadneedle Street?" Averil ventured.

At this attention the old woman assumed an air of vast pleasure. She pointed to the nearby cross street.

"And the Red Gate Tavern?"

"In a fair wind I can spit and hit it," the woman crowed. With a slow wave of her finger, she indicated a northerly direction.

She was so close! Briefly Averil struggled with herself, undecided whether to risk anything further that day. But she was so *close*!"

The woman was right about the distance. Averil had only rounded the corner when she spotted a sign announcing the tavern in question. An arrow indicated entrance through an alley, and within that shadowed area was a structure surrounded by a wrought-iron fence joined by a red gate. Entering by the main door, Averil stepped into a crowded room that smelled of pipe smoke laced with the pungent fragrance of rosemary. The space was thick with patrons, some seated and engrossed in conversation, some clustered around a game of darts, still others casting dice on a table. None gave Averil more than a passing glance as she picked her way through the room and climbed the squeaking, narrow stairs to the upper floors. When she reached the third floor, the voices could still be heard, though the sound sifting through the floorboards was filtered into a muted clamor.

Candles set in wall sconces, one at either end of the hall, lit the corridor. There were three doors—one to the right, one to the left, and one directly at the end of the hall. Remembering Peter Oxton's directions, Averil approached this last door and stood before it. Her stomach fluttered nervously. So it was here that she would find the Tottman, she thought as her gaze touched the fresh wood planks of the door—here that she would either find help for her father or be turned away.

Her fingers were clenched together to still their shaking,

her eyes squeezed tightly shut, when the door opened suddenly and a man leaving the room almost collided with her. Averil stifled a gasp of surprise and her fingers flew to her throat. The man eyed her strangely. He was of medium height with short blond ringlets and wore a clean, well-cut black doublet and breeches.

"Who are you? What are you doing here?" the man asked brusquely.

Averil stammered. "Jeremy Halmes." She added in a whisper, "Peter Oxton sent me."

The blond man frowned. Could this be the Tottman? Averil wondered, feeling at once both relieved and disappointed. The door behind him was still open. From within the hard blackness of the room beyond, a rasping voice questioned, "And where is Peter Oxton?"

Averil started at the sound and peered unsuccessfully toward the source. The candle in the hall cast a faint, wavering rectangle of light across the threshold and illuminated only a dusty strip of floor and the edge of a rush mat.

"He's . . ." she bit at her lower lip to still its sudden trembling. "He's dead."

"Dead?" queried the blond man.

Averil nodded as she peered anxiously between him and the yawning blackness of the room. She was sure now that whoever waited within the darkness there was the Tottman. Her heart jumped painfully in renewed panic.

"In Cheapside," she began, trying to calm herself. "The Puritan soldiers were pulling down the Cross and after that some came into the Nag's Head Inn. One of them stuck"— she paused—"stuck a knife into him. I think he's dead, I didn't wait. He told me to come here and I did."

"Had you known him long?" questioned the strangely grating voice from the room. "Why did he send you here?"

Averil shook her head. "I only met him today. I was told to seek him out. A knife grinder, Darby Kipp, sent me to him." At the silence that greeted this news, Averil added defensively, "He gave me a coin to buy ale—"

"Come in," said the heavy voice within the room.

Averil looked at the blond man, but he stepped aside and motioned her ahead of him. She saw him nod slightly in response to some muted signal from the occupant of the room. Cautiously Averil stepped over the threshold. Though this meeting with the Tottman was what she had desired, a sense of foreboding overtook her now. Behind her, the man in the hall reached in and pulled the chamber door closed. Just as total darkness descended, a lantern was unshuttered and light flooded the room. As it revealed the lone occupant, Averil gasped involuntarily.

At a small table on one side of the room sat a man wearing a shiny black satin mask. It fit his face loosely and gave no hint of a man beneath it but appeared malevolent, cold, a mask of evil and death. The lantern on the table shot a brilliant fire-yellow streak across the vizard but missed the eyes behind the eye-slits entirely, leaving the two openings black, unfathomable, inhuman. Fear shot Averil's blood upward and outward through her body.

She recognized him at once as the spectre-like being she had encountered in the woods the night she ran from Prince Rupert. The nightmares she'd had—of a masked vengeance swooping toward her on a winged horse—returned to her mind in terrifying magnificence. Sweat seeped from her pores; her breath escaped in tiny, constricted pantings.

The mask obscured his features from hairline to neck to ears. It was secured by black ribbons extending past his ears, another parting the crown of his head. Around the mask, black curling hair fell with healthy thickness to his collar. Over powerful shoulders, he wore a crisply fresh white shirt with voluminous sleeves gathered in at strong wrists. His plain brown wool breeches were dusty over hard thighs, his boots tall and equally dusty.

As he shoved aside a sheaf of papers on the table and shifted himself to face her, Averil trembled under a wave of overwhelming raw, primitive fear. Though he appeared relaxed, there was blatant strength and agility in his form, in each small movement.

In the same hoarse rasp she had heard from the hall, he said, "Tell me now, why are you here?"

"Oh . . . I . . ." Every instinct warned Averil to flee. "It's about my . . ." Gone were the easy speeches she had rehearsed earlier. But her charade as the boy lent her a certain comfort, and she blurted, "Be ye the Tottman, then?"

The masked head dipped in answer.

"Well . . . It's about m'father." She licked dry lips and plunged ahead. "Y'see, he was taken prisoner by the Royalists, by Prince Rupert, and . . . and I need you to help me."

"Why was he taken? Was it a battle? Was your father fighting for Parliament?"

"Oh, nay!" Averil protested breathlessly and twirled a fraying patch of threads on the cuff of her sleeve. "He always supported the King. Prince Rupert thought he was a spy and so attacked our home. The soldiers took my father away."

"Why would Rupert suspect your father of being a spy?" Was there a hint of sarcasm in that hoarse voice?

"He said m'father was taking his guns and letters and such like as that."

"Where was this?" The words were steel-hard in the air.

Averil faltered. "Near Abingdon."

He stroked the side of the mask absently, as if it were his own flesh he touched.

Averil flinched at the gesture and tore her eyes from him. She looked around the room to keep from meeting those empty, inhuman eye-slits. They were in the sitting room of a suite. On the right wall the only two windows were heavily shuttered, and the fireplace, now cold and dark, was in the wall on the left. Two large, gold-brocade covered chairs rested before the empty fireplace, and on the spindly-legged table where the Tottman sat stood the lantern, a tray bearing the remains of a meal, two green wine bottles, and several papers. The wall sconces were dark. Across the way the door to the bedchamber stood open. When she looked back to the Tottman, the black eye-holes were fixed on her, and Averil squirmed.

"How did you find Darby Kipp?" he asked.

Averil muttered anxiously, almost apologetically. "A friend, Sir John Walford, told me about him."

"Did he also tell you how he came to know about Kipp?"

"He said only that he had heard about the knife grinder's arrest and that he might be a connection to you somehow."

The Tottman uttered an unintelligible sound of exasperation. "My lad," he said in a suddenly tired voice, "the Royalists will most likely press your father into service on their side. Sooner or later, during the confusion of some battle, he'll escape and return home. It's not an uncommon occurrence."

As his meaning registered, Averil crumpled in dismay. "You refuse to help me, then?"

"My help is unnecessary. As I said, sooner or later your father will—" He stopped and regarded her. "Are you alone or do you have other family to provide for you?"

"I'm living with me aunt and uncle, if that's what ye mean." Averil lifted her chin in a brief show of defiance. "But it's not the same."

"You're better off than most."

"You don't understand!" Averil protested desperately. "Rupert thinks my father is a spy! He'll kill him!"

"But I do understand. I know who the Royalists seek as spy, and I can assure you it is not your father." He added more gently, "I am sorry about your father."

In desperation, Averil took a small step toward him, clenching her fingers to keep her hands from shaking. She knew she must do something to convince him! With courage she didn't know she possessed, Averil announced, "My father is William Maslin, Earl of Armondale, and my home is Maslin Manor. Prince Rupert himself informed me he had my father prisoner.''

''Maslin!'' the Tottman muttered to himself. The sound whispered eerily through the thin mouthstrip of the mask and set off a ripple of goosebumps along Averil's arms.

Abruptly he rose out of his chair and his height was such that the mask towered over her. With a cry of alarm, Averil skittered from his path, brushing against a heavy cloak on a peg as she tried to the find the door. The faint scents of horses and night air enveloped her from its folds, and she was engulfed again by the terrors of that night in the forest.

He was evil! He was a murderer!

''Stand still!''

Averil spun around, every muscle trembling as he loomed before her. In one lightning movement, he yanked the hat from her head. She gasped in utter shock and tried to duck away, but the Tottman grasped her upper arm and held her still. ''What in the name of the saints is this?'' He plucked at the bindings around her head.

''Nay!'' she cried, but already he was unwrapping the head linens with his free hand. Averil struggled against him and wrenched at the fingers that held her. It would have been easier to pry apart iron bars. When the linens were stripped free, he pulled her around into the lantern light and the bright silvery gold waves of hair swirled around her shoulders and waist in soft curls that caught and flung back the light.

Abruptly his head tipped back and he began to laugh. To Averil, his laughter had a surprisingly pleasant sound, not harsh, but rich with exuberance.

''So you're Lady Averil Maslin, eh?''

Scorching humiliation flooded her. She glared at him as she gave one last futile tug of her arm. ''Let me go,'' she demanded.

''One thing more before I do,'' he said, and his voice was softer, like dry leaves brushing together.

He held the back of her head in one hand as he wiped the

streaks of dirt and dust from her face. Averil squeezed her
eyes closed in dark frustration at this, only to fling them open
again in surprise when he lifted her face by the chin and
turned her head from side to side to study her features in
the light.

As if reflecting the light of her thick flax-colored hair, her
face glowed like rich ivory, with a crimson flush staining
her cheeks. Her eyes were wide and glittered angrily at him
like matching emeralds between veilings of feather-soft
lashes. She had a slender nose, and her small, full lips were
parted slightly with her breathing. Between them, the tips
of white square teeth gleamed in the light. Her chin was
tapered, pert.

"Aye," he said softly, confirming something to himself.

When he released her, Averil backed quickly away and
rubbed her arm where the feel of his warm fingers still
lingered. "How dare you treat me this way!" she said,
fighting back tears of outrage and fear and exhaustion.

"Were you behaving as a lady should?" The mask dipped
as he stepped back to survey her doublet, breeches, and boots.
Shaking his head slightly, he tossed her hat and the linens
on the table.

"I didn't know anything about you! I had to protect
myself!"

He agreed. "Your point is a good one. Better than you
know, probably." He rolled up the papers from the table
and plucked up a thin ribbon to tie them with. "There is
a small meat pie and some wine remaining—are you
hungry?"

Averil shook her head and asked defiantly, "How did you
know who I am?"

He did not answer at first but crossed the room and tossed
the roll of papers onto the bed in the next chamber. His every
movement displayed the grace of a natural predator.
Returning, he explained, "Prince Rupert has instigated a quiet
search for you, for the only child of William Maslin."

The news disturbed Averil to a greater degree than she revealed. "Do you know him?"

"Rupert? Nay." The Tottman hunkered down before the cold hearth and took a handful of sticks and a large chunk of wood from a battered bucket on one side. After placing these on the grate, he rose and retrieved a long box from the mantel. He looked at her over his shoulder.

"Here, sit down." He indicated one of the gold-brocade chairs in front of the hearth. "I don't bite, nor am I a ghost, though I've been accused of both."

Averil approached the chair and sat stiffly. She was still on her guard. "You're not going to turn me in to Rupert, are you? He's wrong, you know. My father is not a spy."

"Nay, I have no intention of turning you over to him." He struck a spark to a partially burned taper and hunkered down again to light the fire. As he worked, the folds of his shirt stretched taut across his back, and Averil found herself uncomfortably aware of the sleek, hard muscles bunching across his large frame.

"Then you'll help me find my father?" she asked, hardly daring to breathe until he answered.

He stood up, his long frame stretching straight and tall before her. "Aye," he said absently, staring into the infant flames.

Averil knew a relief so overpowering she almost wept.

When the Tottman had taken a seat in the chair opposite her, he said, "Now tell me all that's happened. You mentioned you had seen Rupert."

Encouraged, she related her story to him, slowly at first, but with growing intensity as she relived those moments. She frowned as she tried to recall precise details. When she described her interview with Prince Rupert, the Tottman grunted. "He thought you were not man enough! You're clever with that disguise."

"Perhaps not," she admitted. "Darby Kipp saw through it."

"Did he? I might have expected it—he's shrewd, that one. That must have been why he sent you here."

Averil clenched her fingers together as she added, "I saw you in the woods that same night. You saw me too, but I hid."

"That was you? Were you traveling *alone* to London?" When Averil answered in the affirmative, he unexpectedly laughed in enjoyment. Again, she noticed how pleasant the sound of his laughter was, how different from the rasping voice.

Her voice firmer, she told him of her meeting with the knife grinder and Peter Oxton. At mention of the latter, the Tottman turned to stare into the flames, and Averil caught a glimpse of a dark glitter behind the eye-slits.

"No one else knew what you were about today?" he questioned.

"Nay. I couldn't tell my aunt and uncle, or they would surely have prevented me from seeking you."

"And this man Walford?"

"Nay, he didn't know either. He left London yesterday and asked me to wait until his return before embarking on the search for you." She asked cautiously, "Do you suspect something?"

The masked head turned full upon her again. The firelight played over the surface contours of the mask in flickering orange and blue-black streaks. "Oxton's cold-blooded murder doesn't seem odd to you?"

"But the fighting, the riot outside—"

"A convenience merely. It gave them an excuse for their actions."

"Murder," she repeated. In spite of herself, she shuddered, and the movement sent a ripple through the soft, loose hair that spilled around her shoulders.

The Tottman pressed, "Are you absolutely certain no one followed you to the Nag's Head Inn? That no one could have known what you were about?"

Just as she was shaking her head, the image of the curious

spectators who had stopped to watch the odd scene between her and Darby Kipp flashed to mind. What had she said to the knife grinder in those moments? Had she mentioned the Tottman then? Given anyone reason to follow her? Had *she* caused Peter Oxton's death?

With a groan, Averil related these things to the Tottman and continued with an account of the soldiers who had pursued her from the Nag's Head Inn. "The woman!" Averil added with a gasp. "I met a woman living nearby, and she knows I came here. Oh, oh!" She shuddered with misery and self-rebuke. "If anyone should question her—oh, I've been so stupid!" she cried. "I never realized how these things could be linked together! How easily someone could trace me! And what about Peter Oxton? What if I'm responsible?"

The agony she felt was evident in her voice, and this time the emotions she had held in check through the day burst forth, uncontrollable. Heavy tears slid from her eyes, and she leaned forward letting her hair fall around her like a veil to hide her shame and misery.

For several long minutes the silence in the room was broken only by the sporadic snaps from the fire and her own choked gasps.

The Tottman spoke finally and his whispering rasp was gentle. "Peter was aware of the dangers. He made his choice, as we all did."

"But it was so unnecessary!" she cried, flinging her hair back and looking at the Tottman with tear-drenched, pleading eyes. "It should never have happened to him!"

"Fight the guilt, Averil!"

Momentarily taken aback by his intensity, she pressed her hands to her temples. "I don't understand you," she mumbled.

He rose and stood with his back to the fire, hands clasped behind him. He seemed unaccountably to steel himself, as though he braced against something. "Ah, guilt," he said with a sigh. "Sometimes, Averil, exposure to death, to war, can create very destructive reactions. One is guilt, and it will destroy you if you let it. But the worst reaction is boredom. Watching men die can become very boring. I know it sounds heartless, but it's a fact of our miserable, depraved, undeserving existence.''

As Averil listened, his voice grew harsher beneath the oppressive rasp and seemed to echo centuries of human despair and anguish. Behind him the fire leaped up, and she had visions of demons and fairies, the spirits of the night said to fly out of hell in search of luckless human prey. She shook her head in denial.

Watching her, the Tottman continued. ''You don't believe me? Tell me then, have you never considered the reason for the wide variety in the manner of executions? Or the incredibly diverse forms of torture used in the Tower, even at this moment?''

Averil began to shiver in the grip of some dread fear, as if a wintry midnight wind touched her heart.

As if he knew her emotions, he spoke in a lighter tone, almost apologetic. ''I have the information I need, so we'd best see about returning you to your home now.''

Averil felt small and lost inside as she pushed herself to her feet slowly. ''Have I put you in danger? If anyone should have followed me here—'' She could not voice her sudden fears.

''It's highly unlikely there is any immediate danger. Tell me where you're staying in London.''

When she had given him the information, she asked, ''Should I need to speak with you again, would it be wise for me to return here? Considering what happened?''

The Tottman reached past her for the hat and linen cloth on the table. ''I never tarry long in any one place, Averil. I'll contact you.'' He handed her the items. ''There's a looking glass in the other room, you'd best prepare yourself now. I'll return shortly.''

Averil watched until the door had latched behind him, then

took up the lantern and carried it to the bedroom. The chamber was spacious and adequately furnished, but contained nothing to suggest occupancy, save for the roll of papers flung on the quilted bed covering. She set to work binding up her hair.

Just as she tucked the ends of the cloth strip under at the nape of her neck and donned the hat, the Tottman returned. He entered the bedroom and stood just inside the door. "Your face is too soft," he commented.

He crossed to the cold hearth opposite the bed and knelt as he wiped his hand across the blackened inner walls. Returning, he lifted her chin with one hand and deftly applied the camouflaging soot. Averil's head was tilted far back and she looked up at the mask as she waited stiffly. The light from the lantern was behind him and his masked face was swamped in shadows. He was too near for comfort, and his size and easy strength and the contact of his hands on her face reminded her of the moment when he had stripped her hair of its bindings. She experienced the same frightening sense of vulnerability and grew breathless with the tension.

At last, just as he finished, the Tottman said, "I must have your word that you will tell no one about me, or about this day. Do you give it?"

She nodded her head slightly.

"Let me hear it."

"I give you my word I will tell no one," she answered.

She followed him into the sitting room and found the blond man waiting there. He cast her a long, curious glance, and Averil wondered if the Tottman had told him who she was.

No words were spoken as the Tottman's companion escorted her from the tavern. Outside, the sun was beginning to set and Averil was surprised to see daylight still. The Tottman's rooms had been as dark as midnight.

As she walked beside the blond man, she wondered what it was like for the Tottman—to surround oneself with darkness, to live with the ever constant threat of exposure, of arrest, of death. Was he even now leaving the Red Gate Tavern for some other place of safety in the city? Why, she wondered, did he live as he did?

When they reached her home, Averil was relieved to see that the windows were still dark and no one had returned yet. She turned to offer her thanks to the man, but he was no longer there. In the deepening twilight shadows across the street she could just barely detect his receding form.

CHAPTER
FOUR

After the brief display of clemency two days previously, winter had reasserted itself. On this morning a grey pallor hung over the city, and chill winds swept through its streets, rattling windows and whistling down chimneys. Along the Thames a light mist was falling.

Jacob Kirkland sat in his office, situated in an upper corner of the warehouse he rented at Paul's Wharf. He was concentrating on a column of dismally small figures and ignored the occasional gust of wind that rattled the panes in the single window above his head. His profits were declining. It was not due so much to the lack of demand, though that had indeed dropped off and taken its toll, but rather to the lack of supply. The barrels of wine remaining in his stock filled barely a fifth of the space he rented. The ship he had purchased and outfitted just prior to the outbreak of the war had been seized and plundered on its second voyage back from France. On the edge of his desk was a stack of papers, all orders for the cargo his ship would have returned with and which he knew he could not fill now. In the wake of that setback he had raised his prices as high as he dared and left off syphoning the wine into bottles—a service he had previously offered his customers, but which he could no longer afford to provide.

It was not only wine that was growing scarce in the city. Ever since Royalist frigates and privateers began attacking merchant vessels, the number of ships venturing for London had dwindled, though the rewards for reaching port were great. The prices the shipowners could command for their cargoes had climbed to unprecedented heights.

Jacob retotaled his figures, hoping he had made an error, but he had not. Disgusted, he threw down his quill pen and fingered his earlobe.

As on every morning for the past few weeks, he had made a stop at the wharf office on his way to the warehouse. Usually he was disappointed, but this morning good news had awaited him. A ship had arrived in port with a full cargo of wine and would be coming in to dock shortly. Eagerly, Jacob had climbed the stairs to his office and lit a candle against the day's gloom. He intended to corner as much of the cargo as he could, but first he had to be sure of his capital. Not only would there be other wine merchants like himself vying for the cargo, but taverners, innkeepers, and gentlemen replenishing their private stocks had begun traveling to the docks in hopes of bargaining directly with the ship captains for the wine they needed.

Rising, Jacob peered through the fine mist sprinkling his window and looked toward the ship that waited in the middle currents of the Thames. As he watched, the anchor was lifted into a small boat and carried dockward, and the ship began to kedge itself across the currents. It used to be that ships finagled for docking space as soon as possible after they arrived, and a merchant could pick and choose among the cargoes. Now some waited, as this one had, letting the news of their arrival spread in hopes of attracting the highest bidders and increasing the competition among the merchants.

Quickly Jacob donned his still damp cloak and hat and blew out the candle on his desk. He closed the office door behind him and hurried down the stairs. The wind pushed at him as he left the warehouse. Despite the inclement weather, the wharf was clotted with people and wagons. Three other ships were already docked and cargoes of all kinds were being unloaded. There were spices and woolen goods, tobacco and sea coal, even white stone from the quarries on the Isle of Wight.

As Jacob maneuvered himself toward the forefront where the new ship would dock, he scrutinized the other wine merchants he knew. Some had most likely paid visits to their goldsmiths this morning, he speculated, and had sacks of coin ready in hopes of swaying the odds of a substantial purchase in their favor. Jacob mouthed a silent curse that he had learned of the ship too late to seek out his own goldsmith. He and Mary Geneva had stayed late visiting their friend, Eleanor Devenish, the previous day and he had tarried overlong in bed this morning. It was a known fact that some merchants had of late been unable to meet their bills of exchange, but Jacob hoped he could persuade this captain that his credit was good.

The small boat dropped the anchor at the dock and those on shore heard the creaking as the capstan in the 'tween decks of the ship was turned, hauling at the anchor rope. At last the ship scraped against the dock and was moored fast. A gangplank was run out. Jacob and nine other men filed onto the main deck and awaited the man who strode toward them from the quarterdeck.

He looked to be in his early thirties and wore a short black cloak against the mist. As he walked, it blew about him in the wind, revealing a handsomely tailored burgundy doublet and breeches trimmed in silver braid. The sleeves of the doublet were decoratively slit from wrist to shoulder and beneath it he wore a white shirt with wide lace-edged collar and cuffs. He was tall and braced himself with a broad stance as he addressed the gathered men.

"Welcome aboard." His resonant voice carried easily across the deck of the ship. "I am Camden Warrender, owner and captain of this ship, the *Indomitable*. You're welcome to look over the cargo of wine I carry. My men have tapped two barrels and will be happy to draw you a sample should you so desire it. I'll be in the great cabin and look forward to meeting with each of you." He smiled as he bowed slightly, his dark hair blowing about under the broad black brim of his hat. Then he turned and disappeared down a hall under the quarterdeck. Three merchants followed immediately after him.

As Jacob descended into the hold with the others, he found himself looking forward to meeting this captain. He had an intelligent and shrewd look, and Jacob felt his pulse quicken at the prospect of bargaining with the man.

The hold was lit by lanterns for them and rich with the smells of damp wood and tar and trapped salt air. According to Jacob's quick estimate, there were near five hundred barrels and puncheons, stacked five high and filling the cargo area except for the space directly below the ladder, which was used for the ship's own provisions. In the weak light he could see the sign of a lion burned into the side of each container, and he sucked in his cheeks in surprise. It was the sign used by M. Lebecque, a French winemaker distinguished in the business for his excellent claret. This Warrender fellow must be very shrewd indeed to have come away with such a cargo from M. Lebecque.

Who was this Camden Warrender? Jacob wondered. He had never heard of this ship or its captain. The other merchants were thinking the same thoughts, for they began murmuring together and questioning each other.

"Ho, there!" called one man to the sailor who was occupied with drawing a glass of wine for them. "This ship and captain are unknown to me—have you been to London before?"

"Aye, sir," came the reply as the sailor looked up. "But this is the first wine cargo she's carried. 'Tis been cloth and coal and tobacco and suchlike." He brought them the glass and they each accepted a taste.

"Whence does your captain hail? Is he a Londoner?" Jacob inquired of the sailor.

"Nay. From Jamaica, but more recently from the colony in the New World."

Jacob was first up the ladder. The three men who had followed the captain into his cabin previously were now departing the ship. Seizing the opportunity to speak next with the captain, Jacob burried aft to the hall beneath the quarter-deck. At his knock he was granted entrance.

He stepped into a great cabin that was richly appointed with leather-cushioned chairs and colorful hangings. It was what he expected, for the captains of such ships spared themselves no luxury. At a table in the center of the cabin sat Camden Warrender, with papers, ink pot and quill set before him. Behind him fine porcelain gleamed in the upper shelves of a cupboard, and below that were leather-bound books numbering two dozen or more.

As Jacob introduced himself, the captain rose. He stood tall and erect, his feet braced wide from long experience on a rolling deck. His eyes were a brilliant grey in a face tanned by wind and sun.

"Have a seat, Mr. Kirkland. I take it you've had an opportunity to look over the cargo."

"I have, and I must say how impressed I am. M. Lebecque is a well-known name in this business. How came you to acquire such a cargo, especially for your first venture in wine trading? I must assume you know M. Lebecque well."

"Only recently," replied the other man easily as he took his seat opposite Jacob at the table. "It seems he was in danger of losing his market in England when Mssrs. Tobias and Matthews grew skittish of pitting their ships against the Royalist navy in the Channel. I'm willing to venture it, but only with a cargo whose price will be worth the risks." With a small half-smile that held no humor, he added, "You can appreciate that, I'm sure."

"Of course, Captain Warrender," Jacob nodded as he replied. He suddenly wished heartily that he had a pocket full of coin to help sway the bargaining to his side.

"I have one hundred and eighty-six puncheons of claret and three hundred and seventy-five barrels of burgundy. How many of each would you like?" The long tan fingers stabbed the quill into the inkpot and waited over the paper.

"I'd like your entire shipment," Jacob answered evenly.

The quill hesitated, the flinty eyes of the captain looked up. "What are you prepared to offer?"

"Four thousand, three hundred pounds."

"I can't sell at that price." The quill scratched hasty figures across the paper. "What you are offering is approximately thirteen pounds a puncheon and five per barrel. In order to meet my expenses—and paying a crew to risk their lives is a damnably high expense—and still see a profit, I cannot consider any offer under eighteen pound a puncheon and eight for the barrel. The quality of the wine itself is worth far more."

"You do have a fine cargo, Captain Warrender," Jacob began slowly. He sat back in his chair and crossed his legs at the knee. "But perhaps it is too fine for any of us at this moment. London's economy is severely depressed, if you haven't already made yourself aware of that. Demanding the price you mentioned of any of the merchants in these parts would see you with no takers and a cargo you couldn't unload. Even selling piecemeal to every individual who came along would take weeks, even months, and that would be time and money lost for you. Perhaps you should reconsider."

"I'm sorry, Mr. Kirkland. I'll not change my mind on that. What you've offered is an impossibly low amount for my entire cargo."

Jacob pulled at his lower lip thoughtfully. "I could take one hundred and forty puncheons then and twice that many barrels off your hands for fourteen pound six a puncheon and five pound ten a barrel.''

The captain rose and crossed the cabin to a cupboard. From inside he extracted a long-stemmed clay pipe and leather pouch of tobacco. ''Do you have the money available?'' he inquired as he returned to his chair and filled the pipe.

''It is with my goldsmith.''

The other man regarded his visitor steadily, then commented, ''I've grown distrustful of bills of exchange, Mr. Kirkland. I'm well aware of London's economic problems, and 'tis not London's own, but a situation that permeates the whole of England.''

An impatient rapping at the door interrupted him.

''A moment more,'' he called out. Turning his attention again to Jacob, Captain Warrender shrugged apologetically. ''I have others to meet with this morning. If I have cargo left, perhaps we can discuss this again, but it doesn't appear that we can do business at this time.''

''I'm not offering you any bills of exchange, sir,'' Jacob pointed out. ''If you would but delay your business here an hour or two, I can return with payment.''

''Perhaps you should do that, but I can make no guarantees on price or quantity. Your offer is still low to my reckoning.''

''Do you guarantee this, though,'' Jacob questioned as he jabbed a plump finger on the center plank of the table, ''that there are still a full one hundred and forty puncheons and two hundred and eighty barrels unsold?'' He was thinking of the three men who had spoken initially with the captain and departed.

''Aye, that much I can vouch for,'' Captain Warrender replied through a pale circle of smoke.

''My name is not unknown in this business, sir—''

''Aye, I know that,'' the captain interrupted. ''I made inquiries this morning at the wharf office.''

''—and I've been engaged in this occupation long enough to say with certainty that, though your cargo is of a higher quality than usually seen here, you'll not get more for it than what I have offered.''

"I appreciate your opinion, but we shall see."

Jacob pushed his chair back and rose. "I'll pay a visit now to my goldsmith and return within an hour."

With a little smile playing about the corners of his lips, the captain replied, "I look forward to your return."

Jacob departed, pushing his way past the few men clustered in the narrow hall outside the cabin, and emerged on deck. Though the wind buffeted him and set up an eerie whine through the rigging high above, his spirits were keen and he felt refreshed and full of energy.

Averil slept late that morning. She was stretching her sore limbs gingerly beneath the covers when the door to her bed-chamber flew open and Lynna swept into the room. She crossed to Averil's bed and peered at her cousin.

"Are you awake?"

"Aye," Averil murmured drowsily, rolling over and pulling the covers to her chin. She kept her eyes closed, irritated with Lynna. "What's brought you here so early?"

"Father wants to know if you feel well enough to join us for dinner. He's brought a guest." Lynna laughed briefly, but her excitement was evident.

Averil hurled back the bedclothes in surprise. "What o'clock is it?"

"Near one."

"I had no idea I'd slept so late!" She left the bed hastily and, dipping a towel corner in the basin of water, scrubbed the sleep from her face. "Who is his guest?"

"A ship's captain he met this morning." Lynna smiled slyly. "He's mightily handsome."

As Averil drew a gown and a fresh chemise from the wardrobe, Lynna strolled to the door. "I'll send Honor up to you."

"Thank you. And please tell them I'll be down shortly."

"I saw him first, remember that."

Averil acknowledged Lynna's parting comment with a shrug. As she dressed, her thoughts and energy were taken up by her concern for her father. She thought of the Tottman's promise to help and quivered with raw excitement. Her father would be safe again very, very soon!

With Honor's assistance, she was quickly attired in one of her recently completed gowns, a deep green silk gown that was drawn up slightly in front to reveal a taffeta underskirt embroidered with pink rosebuds amidst green leaves. The sleeves were cut full and long, but with space to allow the lace cuff of her chemise to fall over her wrists. The neckline was a deep oval, adorned with a small white bow at her bosom. Knowing the others awaited her, Averil separated and twisted into shape the small curls framing her forehead as Honor wound and secured the long back tresses into a soft knot.

As she approached along the downstairs hall, Averil caught a glimpse of Jacob's guest seated near the door of the dining room. It was immediately apparent to her why Lynna had already put a claim on him; he was striking. She saw his profile—a smooth brow, straight nose, a prominent and strong jawline. His face was dark from the sun, his faintly waving hair a dark walnut shade with stray bronze highlights. He was relaxed in his seat, his knees spread wide, his long tanned fingers resting on his thighs as he listened to Jacob.

At her entrance into the dining room, the newcomer pushed back his stool and rose to face her. He was tall, with a broad-shouldered frame that filled out his expensive and well-tailored burgundy doublet. Crossing his chest was a leather shoulderbelt that held a sleek silver scabbard at his left hip. The hilt of his sword was intricate and glittered brightly in the candlelight from the table.

As she stopped just within the doorway, his brilliant grey eyes searched her face and gown in a swift but thorough assessment. When his gaze met her shocked one once more, there was a strangely intense appreciation in the crystal depths of his eyes. And Averil was immediately aware of the potent and compelling handsomeness of his features. She responded to him without understanding that the face she looked on was a mature face that bore the imprint of a brutal life and the long-enduring patience of a man who has accepted the loss of dreams and illusions.

She was startled by him, startled by his appraisal, startled by the sudden rise of goosebumps on her skin. There was no experience in her past to prepare her for this moment, and though she did not realize it, inwardly she was retreating from a masculinity that was overwhelming to her and not a little threatening.

Jacob introduced them. "My dear, this is Captain Camden Warrender; Captain Warrender, my niece, Averil Kirkland."

"Your servant, Mrs. Averil," the captain intoned politely, sweeping a bow. His voice was a rich and resonant baritone that pleased her even as it augmented her uneasiness. He had used the more mature form of address reserved for adult women, and Averil felt oddly complimented.

It was customary to acknowledge introductions with a kiss, but when Averil realized the captain had begun to step toward her, she turned away swiftly. The thought of being touched by him, however innocently, caused her a terrible anxiety. As she took her seat on the opposite side of the table, she missed the slight frown that crossed his face and her uncle's swift, apologetic glance to the captain.

They helped themselves from dishes of sausages and capons, herring pie, pickled radishes, and glazed fruits. The thin, grey light from the windows was dispelled by the glow of a dozen candles set both on the table and around the room. Jacob had insisted on this show, despite the depletions caused by the war.

"Captain Warrender," Lynna began sweetly. "How fared you in the crossing? We've heard so many tales of piracy and plunder, isn't it terribly dangerous?"

"We were chased on this crossing," he admitted, "but managed to cripple our pursuers and get through. Fortunately, I possess a letter of marque and reprisal, so I carry guns— ten twenty-four pounders. Not sufficient to engage a ship of the navy successfully, but they provide some protection, and are quite useful at any time.''

Averil's uneasiness grew as she watched the captain and listened to him, but not being able to define her feeling and deal with it made her impatient with herself. Anger formed a temporary refuge. She aimed it now at the source of her discomfort as she inquired with a frown, ''Do you speak from experience, Captain? Have you attacked and taken other ships?''

He answered with brisk surprise. ''Of course. Wars are not mere exercises in maneuvers.''

''I am aware of that, Captain,'' she answered, remembering with anguish the attack on her home and the death of Peter Oxton.

Jacob raised his wine glass. ''A toast to your continued success, Captain Warrender. And may I add, to our continued relationship.''

''I look forward to a long and profitable one.'' The captain lifted his own glass and smiled. His teeth were straight and white. ''Fair warning though, Mr. Kirkland, I'll never again let you cheat me as you did this day.''

''Cheat?'' Jacob laughed jovially and drank the toast. ''Why, I'm the one cheated. From any other ship my money would have purchased twice the cargo.''

''Even were it peacetime, that would be an exaggeration. But when a cargo has been brought through the threat of death, it is far more valuable. As you well know.''

''Is it really that dangerous?'' Lynna asked, awed.

''Most assuredly so,'' he said.

Unable to control herself, Averil broke in, ''Then why do you risk it?''

With long, lean fingers the captain lifted his glass and held it near the candle. The wine glowed in the light. ''Like liquid rubies,'' he said softly, reverently. His gaze flickered over the top of the glass and met hers. ''For the money, Mrs. Averil,'' he said. ''What else would there be?''

Mary Geneva and Lynna lifted their own glasses against

the light. Frowning, Averil demanded bluntly, "You would risk the lives of your men for mere profit?"

"*Mere* profit?" He chuckled, though it was not a pleasant sound. "I risk my own life as well! Besides, I pay my men well for their services. I assume from the comforts you're familiar with here that you've been sheltered from war's ravages. But without men like me to bring goods into port for you, you'd soon feel the deprivations." The crystal eyes dipped and his glance covered her breasts. "So you see," his eyebrows lifted slightly and his gaze returned to hers, "we do serve a worthy cause."

Jacob applauded. "Well said!"

Under his look, Averil had felt again the skittering of goosebumps on her flesh and a flush of something faintly intoxicating in her veins. At that moment she wanted to flee.

The grey eyes probed hers. "I see I have offended you, Mrs. Averil. I extend my apologies if I have insulted your delicate nature."

Averil blushed profusely at the amused unconcern in his voice, and to what she was sure was a subtle reference to his indecent stare. "You mistake principles for delicateness, Captain," she insisted, matching his gaze. "But then I suspect you have lost sight of whatever principles you may once have possessed."

Mary Geneva pinkened with embarrassment, and Lynna shot her looks like rapiers. Jacob was aghast. "Child! Captain Warrender is an invited guest in this house and deserves—"

But he was interrupted as Captain Warrender put up a hand and said, "Nay, 'tis not taken as insult." He looked back to Averil and the expression in his face was bland. "I know what is coursing through your mind—that I should turn my ship and crew toward the efforts of Parliament in this war and take to battle in the cause of right. But there is precious little money available to support the effort. London's economy is slowly strangling and cannot sustain itself, much less an army and navy. I bring support in the form of goods to be traded and purchase London's goods to sell to other ports, thus stimulating the economy. In so doing, I assist the war's 'holy' efforts.'' He grinned at her. ''It's a very simple concept.''

Unhappily aware that she had embarrassed her aunt and uncle by her thoughtless comment, and dismally upset by her own lack of control, Averil retreated. She merely nodded to him and looked away without making any reply.

Mary Geneva beamed. ''Well phrased, Captain. And we do so need your help.''

''The ship I financed was recently taken and plundered,'' Jacob commented. ''I'm greatly hoping to be able to outfit another as soon as I can afford to do so. Have you many backers here in London, Captain?''

Captain Warrender drew his gaze away from Averil's averted eyes. ''I was approached this morning by three men looking to hire my ship, but as long as I can afford it, I prefer to act indepentently. Actually, unusual as it may sound, I like the freedom to choose and buy according to my own preferences and instincts. It does at times prove difficult to find markets, but there again is the challenge.''

Throughout the remainder of the meal, Averil could feel the man's attention on her. She tried to focus her thoughts elsewhere, but even so she was keenly aware of him, of every movement he made, every inflection of his voice. He had the easy, thoughtless manner of one accustomed to wealth or power and sure of his own position in the world. In spite of her best intentions, Averil's attention remained riveted on the captain, and she was listening to his smooth, pleasant voice.

''—But unfortunately we took a chance ball that splintered the main mast, and with the shrouds as tangled as they were, we were unable to veer away as I would have liked. We did manage to strike a good blow to their running gear, but even so, they luffed and kept abreast of us.'' He smiled often as he spoke, enjoying himself. ''It proved their undoing, however, as we got off several balls at rapid pace into their hull before they could reload. We lost her then. By first light of morning we jury-rigged the sails and managed to limp into port at Portsmouth.''

Mary Geneva was wide-eyed. ''I hope you didn't lose many men, Captain.''

''Surprisingly, nay. My men are well trained and highly disciplined. I can't afford to take on a coward or laggard— my cargoes are too valuable for that. And in this particular incident we were able to bring the entire cargo into port, though we only barely achieved that.'' Though he addressed Mary Geneva, his eyes glittered at Averil. ''Brought a very handsome profit, so it was well worth the risk.''

Averil wondered if he put a value on anything else besides his profit, but she dared not voice another comment in front of Jacob.

Lynna asked eagerly, ''Why don't you add more guns to your ship, Captain? Wouldn't that be safer?''

''Hardly. I carry about as many as my ship can maneuver with,'' he explained patiently. ''She's not designed for fighting as the frigates are. She'd grow top heavy and sluggish with the imbalance were I to add any more. Besides, the King's ship, *Prince Royal*, alone carries near fifty-six guns.''

''Tell me, Captain,'' Lynna continued, attempting to keep his attention to herself. Dinner was at an end and Honor was clearing the table. ''How long do you expect to be in port?''

He inclined his head toward her as he considered this. ''Two to three weeks, depending upon how long it takes me to refit my ship. At present, with so few vessels working the London market, it's relatively easy to obtain worthy cargoes.''

''I suppose you work quite diligently preparing for these voyages of yours?''

As if recognizing Lynna's hidden meaning, he responded with a grin of amusement. ''Though my work does keep me busy, Mrs. Lynna, I do not forego a social life and other entertainments.''

* * *

Lynna reminded her mother of this comment two days later when Mary Geneva expressed a desire to hold a supper party. Her visit with Eleanor Devenish had whetted her need for more active social entertainment, another aspect of life the grip of war and the Puritan influence had severely curtailed.

"You heard him, Mother," Lynna insisted. "He said he had time for entertainments. Please invite him."

Mary Geneva and Honor were kneading bread dough in the kitchen and Lynna sat watching from atop a nearby stool. Averil had received no word yet from the Tottman; she chafed with worry at the delay. To keep her mind from its persistent churning, she had donned a simple gown and an old apron and was vigorously working her own mound of bread dough. It was a new experience for her. Jacob was home that morning. He stood beside Lynna and sucked a small chunk of sugar as they discussed details of the supper party planned for that Monday evening, three days away.

"After Averil's rudeness to the man," he pointed out, sending a stern look of reproof at his niece, "I think it would behoove us to invite him. He's of great value to me in my business and I would like to remain on good terms with him. I can try to get a message to him this afternoon at the wharf."

Averil sighed inwardly. With the back of her flour-dusted hand she pushed a stray tendril of hair from her face.

Shortly after Jacob had departed for his office, a visitor arrived, and Lynna and Mary Geneva went to the door together. Lynna returned to the kitchen house where Averil still fussed over an unruly mass of dough and announced, "It's your friend, Sir John Walford, and he asked to see you. Mother is inviting him to the party."

When Averil entered the front room, her hands cleaned of tell-tale flour, she found her aunt and Sir John discussing her. Her aunt was explaining, "And it is for her own safety, of course, but we introduce her as Jacob's niece, Averil Kirkland, from Reading."

Averil crossed the room eagerly and leaned up on tiptoe

to kiss the man's cheek. "Sir John, I'm so glad to see you again! I understand my aunt has invited you to the party Monday evening. You *will* be able to come, won't you?"

He smiled at her obvious pleasure. "I'm frankly delighted by the invitation and expect there should be nothing barring my presence." Nodding to Mary Geneva, he added, "Thank you, madam, I'll remember what you've said. Now, as much as I find your company charming, I'd like a word alone with Averil, if I may."

"Oh, my! Forgive me. But of course, Sir John." She held up her floured hands and waggled her fingers at them. "I must see to the bread now. Excuse me."

When the door closed behind her, Walford came right to the point, inquiring earnestly, "Is your mind still set on seeking the Tottman's help? For if it is, we should be about the business of finding this knife grinder as soon as is convenient."

Averil looked at him in helpless confusion, not knowing what to say. Though she desperately wanted to talk with him about all that had occurred, she remembered her promise to the Tottman to tell no one of their meeting. Her first loyalty was to her father and to helping him, and to do that she had to trust the Tottman. She shook her head slowly.

"You've changed your mind then?" Walford questioned, studying her guarded features. "Why, sweetheart? What happened? Is there something you're not telling me?"

"It just wouldn't do any good," she said with a half-hearted shrug.

"Averil, in this last week I've had time to consider this course, and I really believe that an attempt to get the Tottman's help is our only chance of saving William. With or without you, I intend to pursue the matter. I'll let you know how I fare in locating that knife grinder."

"Nay!" Averil exclaimed. "There *is* something I haven't told you." If the Tottman were approached by Sir John, he might think Averil had broken her vow. She could not risk alienating the Tottman, for if he considered her untrustworthy he might refuse to help. Until she could get the Tottman's permission to include Sir John, she had to persuade him against this course of action. "I suppose I was just ashamed to tell you about it," she faltered. "You see, I acted impatiently and have already sought out Darby Kipp, the knife grinder, on my own."

Walford's eyebrows shot up in surprise. "But how? When?"

"The day after I met you in Tothill Fields. I wore the same costume I escaped to London in—you know, the boy's clothes. I told you about it."

"Aye, I remember." Sir John frowned uncertainly at her. "What happened, did he tell you where to find the Tottman?"

Averil shook her head, relieved that at least this part was no lie. But it pained her not to be able to explain it all. "He didn't know any more than you or I about where the Tottman was."

In the face of Sir John's stunned disbelief, Averil turned away. After a moment he emitted a long sigh. "I was so sure," he muttered, half to himself. "Blast!"

He seemed so greatly disappointed, Averil was tempted to rush to him and tell him everything. Her heart was full of gratitude for his concern, and she struggled bitterly with herself to keep the words in check.

Interpreting her silence as grief, Walford approached and laid his hands on her shoulders. "Averil, sweetheart, I'm sorry this idea turned out so poorly. Have patience. Somehow we'll find your father. I'll do what I can—you know that." After giving her a brief squeeze, Sir John took up his hat and cloak and let himself out.

In the kitchen of the Three Bells Inn in Abingdon, the owner, Mrs. Brimby, sat hunched over a ledger at a table in one corner. With painstaking care she scratched figures into the ledger. The ponderous form of the cook appeared beside her.

" 'Scuse me, madam, but there's a man what wants t' see

ye. 'E's in the common room.''

''At this hour? Why it must be near one in the morning! All right. You can go ahead to bed now. I'll see that everything is secured for the night.''

When the cook had gone out, Mrs. Brimby remained sitting. She was alarmed. The taxes were overdue and she did not have the money yet. Was the man here because of that? But at this late hour? She closed the ledger, rose, and went through the door into the main room. By the light of the dying fire, she detected the shape of someone seated at a table in the center of the room.

''Bring a candle please, madam,'' the stranger said. His voice was firmly official and bore a trace of a scratching rasp.

Mrs. Brimby did so and set the light on the table. The stranger wore a plain black doublet of broadcloth and a white round collar. He had a low-crowned black hat on his long, dirty blond hair, and his face was an unhealthy shade of white. Behind a pair of spectacles his eyes were pale and squinting.

''Sit down, if you please,'' he said, and she complied, stilling the trembling in her hands.

''And you are Mrs. Brimby, am I correct?''

When she nodded, the man drew a paper from inside his doublet. He spread this on the table and turned it for her to see.

''Whatever your current political beliefs, Mrs. Brimby, I must request that you cooperate with me and answer the questions I shall put to you with complete truthfulness so far as you know it.'' He pointed a long white finger at the document and said, ''This will explain that I am acting as agent for our Parliament.''

Mrs. Brimby saw only the official mark of Parliament; her skills at reading were minimal and she glanced only briefly at the closely scripted words without understanding them. She did, however, see the name of John Pym, leading power in Parliament, penned at the bottom. Her alarm intensified into fear.

He asked her about Prince Rupert and his stay at the inn

some weeks previous. How many men had he had with him? Were other soldiers quartered in the town? Where? Had there been any others in his party? Any prisoners? How long had he stayed? Had anything unusual happened during that day? When she mentioned the boy who had been there, he questioned her more closely.

The stranger never gave her his name, and she never requested it. She was eager to comply so that the frighteningly official stranger would leave quickly.

At last he seemed satisfied and rose, tucking the paper back into his doublet. A pouch heavy with coin thudded onto the table in front of her. "An expression of gratitude. Good night to you, madam."

CHAPTER
FIVE

After a four-year separation, Edmond Devenish and Averil were both genuinely pleased to see each other again the night of Mary Geneva and Jacob's party. They laughed together as they recalled some of the happier experiences they had shared as children—the puppy they had adopted one summer and tried to keep a secret from the adults; the masquerade of pirate and queen they had amused themselves with on many a hot afternoon in Jacob's garden; how Edmond had shared his lessons with Averil, tutoring her in languages, mathematics, geography, philosophy—subjects not generally available to women.

As they talked, Averil studied the well-remembered features that had been slimmed and planed by the years into a decidedly rugged, masculine cast. His eyes were tawny brown, matching almost exactly the shade of his hair, his nose hooked slightly, and he sported a thin moustache above soft lips and squared chin. He was slightly taller than she, and dressed in black satin.

A silence fell between them when they had exhausted their supply of memories, and Averil murmured, "I'm sorry I was unable to join my aunt and uncle when they visited you last week."

"That's quite all right," he assured her with a ready smile, "though I did miss you. I had, in fact, planned to travel to Maslin Manor. Damned nuisance, this war. But it brought you to London, so I shouldn't complain overmuch."

Averil's eyes brightened. "You're going to the manor? When? Oh, please say it's soon, Edmond—my father may be there and he doesn't know where I've gone. You could—"

"Whyever would I go there now?" Edmond broke in with a smile of astonishment. "It was you I wished to see, and since you're here in London I have no intention of leaving."

Her surprise was evident.

"Come now," he said. "You haven't forgotten our last parting?" Briefly, annoyance crossed his features. With uncharacteristic soberness he dropped his voice, saying, "We pledged ourselves to each other, Averil—and sealed that pledge with a kiss! How could you have forgotten?"

Averil laughed at the memory. "I haven't. We were but children, though." She began to falter under his scrutiny. "You weren't thinking it was serious!" Impulsively she put her hand on his forearm. "Oh, Edmond—"

They were standing just inside the door of the large parlor, and Averil was interrupted as the figure of a late arrival filled the doorway beside them. She looked up and met the disturbingly perceptive grey eyes of Captain Warrender.

"It's a pleasure to see you again, Mrs. Averil," he said, his voice deep with the hint of a smile. His attention shifted pointedly to Edmond's arm where Averil's hand rested in a seemingly loving gesture. Feeling almost guilty, Averil withdrew her hand as she introduced the two men.

Edmond was instantly congenial as he began in a conversational tone, "Delighted to make your acquaintance, Captain. And are you in the service of our Parliament?"

"Nay," the captain replied bluntly, dismissing Edmond,

his attention returning once more to Averil. His glance took in the length of her long-sleeved, red satin gown, the skirt of which was parted in the center and drawn high at the sides to reveal a petticoat embroidered with silver thread. Above the lace-trimmed neckline the upper curves of her breasts were fashionably and partially exposed. Her silvery gold hair was drawn up in the back to a loose knot draped with strings of pearls, and small, short curls framed her face. She wore a simple pearl necklace and teardrop earrings.

As the captain cast a swift glance over her, Averil's heartbeat quickened anxiously, and when his eyes returned to hers, there was something sweetly grave in his look that tore at her.

At that moment, Lynna swept up to the group, a vivid turquoise velvet gown swirling around her. Her eyes were vibrant with excitement, her lips parted and smiling as she greeted the captain. Without her usual expression of bored sulkiness, she looked exceptionally pretty. After a token apology to Edmond and Averil, Lynna steered the captain away to introduce him to the other guests.

Edmond watched them, his expression mild. "So who the devil is he?" he inquired, leaning toward Averil. "How do you know him?"

Averil's eyes were still on the captain. "He is captain of a merchantman. My uncle is doing business with him."

"Not for long, I hope." Edmond finished his wine and turned again to look at Averil. "Watch out for that one," he said earnestly. Then, as if shaking off a disagreeable mood, he laughed and exclaimed, "Shall we resurrect our old games? I'll protect her ladyship from the wicked, wicked captain."

Averil felt her earlier good spirits returning and she smiled at his teasing remark. She had forgotten how very dear Edmond was to her.

Around them, the large parlor was lit brilliantly with candles placed in every conceivable location. In the kitchen

Honor tended to the cooking. As she moved in and out of the house to the dining room, the aromas of roasting chicken and spiced ham wafted through the room and mingled with the heavy perfumes.

The guests had all arrived now and the room was colorfully crowded with people talking animatedly and laughing. Percival Osgood's rust-hued doublet flared open over a bulging belly that protruded even farther when he laughed. His daughter, Cecelia, was especially dainty in a rose-pink dress, the skirt of which was split and drawn high over a spangled pink underskirt. Percival, his wife Esther, and Cecelia were talking with Mary Geneva, who forgot her lost tooth as she grinned broadly.

Edmond's mother, Eleanor—slender, regally composed—was in conversation with Sir John Walford. Averil looked fondly at Sir John. She was delighted to have him present and had earlier talked at length with him. By his association with her father, his presence was a source of comfort to her. This evening he had forsaken his usual starched ruff for a more modern wide flat collar. The change enhanced his youthful looks.

Also present were several men from Jacob's warehouse. One was Gilbert Woodby, the foreman, with his young wife, Maureen. They were listening to Jacob, who argued some point with finger-jabbing insistence. Three other men from the warehouse were crowding the wine bottles on the trestle table and sampling the refreshment liberally.

Most of the guests had brought musical instruments of some type—lutes, guitars, flageolets—and the promise of singing and dancing later was implicit.

Though Averil tried to ignore him, her eyes were drawn repeatedly to Captain Warrender. Lynna was keeping one hand possessively on the captain's arm as she introduced him to the other guests. From a distance, and without his attention on her, Averril was able to study him freely. His clothes were expensive. Beneath a deep blue satin doublet trimmed with gold thread, he wore a lace-edged linen shirt. The snowy whiteness of his collar and cuffs made a striking contrast to his sun-darkened face and hands. He wore the same leather swordbelt with the band extending over his shoulder, and the scabbard at his hip swung with each step. As was the fashion, his doublet was buttoned only halfway down his chest and parted to show the lace of his shirt over a taut stomach. His breeches were tied below the knee, and white hose hugged thickly muscled legs above black shoes. She was forced to admit that his was a singularly striking figure in this group.

Watching him kiss Cecelia Osgood when he was introduced to her, Averil experienced a soft flush of yearning that confused her. Cecelia's eyes were shyly bright when the captain straightened. She appeared to stammer as she spoke to him. The captain's eyes were friendly and he was smiling at her as he carried the conversation. To Averil's surprise, Cecelia's distress evaporated and she was soon talking with animation. The captain at first ignored Lynna's attempts to draw him away from Cecelia, but at last he allowed her to lead him on to be introduced to the remaining guests.

He was confident, smiling and at ease as he moved through the gathering, and Averil wondered at the charm he used. Defensively, she decided it was like a poison. He had melted Cecelia quickly enough! In fact, each of the guests seemed to greatly enjoy his conversation. She and Edmond were apparently the only ones with sense enough to see through him!

When the captain's gaze unexpectedly slanted across the room and met her frowning regard, Averil quickly looked away. There had been some expression in his face—amused speculation?—that pricked her. With a falsely bright laugh, she spoke again to Edmond.

A short time later, the guests were called to the table, and as she entered the dining room, Averil found Captain Warrender behind her.

"I understand there is to be music later," he said, leaning down to speak into her ear. "Will you share a dance with me?"

Averil turned in swift surprise at the sound of his voice and looked up into his smiling grey eyes, startling and vivid in the dark face. She had never before noticed his inky lashes, or the tiny lines at the corners of his eyes that gave evidence of years spent searching a distant horizon. He was far too close to her, and Averil felt herself stammering and blushing nervously, much as Cecelia had done earlier. The sensation infuriated her.

"Thank you, Captain Warrender, but I'm afraid I—"

She was on the verge of refusing when Jacob materialized beside them and she saw the reproof in his eyes. He had earlier extracted her promise to be cordial to the captain, but did it also include dancing with him? Apparently Jacob thought so. Oh, these two men! she thought irritably.

"Thank you, Captain Warrender," she began again, not meeting his eyes but staring at the line of a gold thread on the front of his doublet. She was aware of his smile and faintly heard his breathing. "I look forward to sharing a dance with you later."

When all the guests had taken their seats, the captain was at one end flanked by Lynna and Esther Osgood, and Averil sat at the other end between Edmond and Sir John. Supper was served and Percival Osgood, a clerk for the House of Commons, began the table conversation with one of his favorite topics, the Tottman.

"Parliament was abuzz like a nest of angry hornets today," he announced with a frown of incredulity. "Seems the Tottman managed to break three Jesuits out of Newgate early this morning."

The ensuing comments of surprise and disbelief aroused Averil's attention. Beside her, Sir John shot her a reassuring glance.

Prodded by the others, Percival continued, "From what

I understand, he got himself arrested for assaulting a member of the Watch last night. Of course, no one knew it was the Tottman at that point—haggard, crying drunkenly, begging as if his life depended on it not to be taken to Newgate. Who would have guessed? But then this morning the truth was discovered. Two guards and a handful of inmates had been assaulted. By that time he was gone, and the three priests with him.''

''Are you sure the guards weren't bribed?'' Jacob inquired with a short laugh.

''Certainly a possibility,'' Percival agreed, ''but I doubt they'd admit to such a thing. Anyway, as it stands now the Tottman is proclaimed the responsible party.'' Percival spread his hands and looked to the right and left along the line of listeners. ''Who else would attempt such a thing, eh?''

Each of the guests present knew that Newgate, like the other London prisons, was guarded only on the outside—internal order was maintained principally by the prisoners themselves, and murder, thievery, and every form of debauchery was practiced there.

Along with the other dinner guests, Averil had hung on every word of Percival's tale, but while the surrounding dinner guests broke into exclamations of indignation, she felt a flush of hideous excitement.

From the other end of the table, Captain Warrender was watching her and noted the strange light in her eyes. It gave him cause for wonder. It was in his nature to be observant, to search for the hidden meaning, the touchstone of weakness that each man guarded carefully. He watched her with interest. Though very young, she had nevertheless a fully matured form and was undoubtedly a beauty by any standards. She also possessed an unusual quality of allurement, a suggestion of luxurious fulfillment, that he had been instantly and very pleasantly aware of when they were first introduced.

Averil felt Sir John squeeze her hand beneath the table

as he questioned Percival with unrestrained excitement, "What did the Tottman look like? Someone surely gave a description!"

Percival sighed. "Not as good as we'd have liked, I'm afraid. For one thing the light was poor, but still the Watch did say he was a big ruffian—blond hair, reddish beard, not full, rather thin—and that he had a scar like a knife wound from temple to chin."

As Sir John looked again to Averil almost triumphantly, she tried to hide her confusion. The Tottman had black hair, coal black. And the beard and scar . . . ? With a mask hiding the Tottman's face, she would never have seen those.

The conversation turned to the subject of the war, something never far from the minds of everyone gathered. Voices grew bold and loud; sentiments were vehemently announced. The exercise of expressing themselves thoroughly was a gratifying experience for many of those present. By the time the meal was finished, the mood at the table was one of pleasurable satisfaction. They were now ready to enjoy the music with the same wholehearted enthusiasm.

Jacob called for the wine bottles to be refilled, and Gilbert and Percival moved the furniture from the middle of the large parlor to prepare for the dancing. The captain opened the doors leading out to the small flagstone terrace that overlooked Jacob's large and highly prized garden. Torches had been placed at intervals along the main path, and in their flaring light he surveyed the garden. Averil watched Lynna follow him into the fragrant evening air.

When the music began, Jacob and Mary Geneva were encouraged to lead the first dance. After that they called for an allemande, and Edmond appeared at Averil's side. She accepted his offered arm, eager to join in the dance, for she had heard no music for some time.

The participants formed two lines, men on one side, women on the other. As she swept through the required steps, Averil felt her mood lightening. She felt exhilarated and laughed along with Edmond when he made light, bantering conversation. Hearing her laughter above the conversation and the music, the captain glanced to his left and watched Averil as he absently led Lynna through the steps.

Several guests took turns playing the music so that all had an opportunity to dance, but Edmond stayed possessively at Averil's side. He offered no further mention of the pledge they had made as children, and Averil did not remind him of it. They danced jigs and lively country dances, sang rounds of songs, and enjoyed the quieter moments of improvisational music. Soon Averil had entirely forgotten her promise to dance with Captain Warrender.

But when Edmond left the room, the captain excused himself from a conversation with Eleanor and started toward her. Suddenly realizing his intent, Averil retreated to the trestle table where Sir John was tasting a glassful of the newly replenished supply of claret. When she begged his arm for a dance, Sir John laughed his particularly boyish, infectious laugh and she felt herself smiling in response. "Sweetheart, with one so lovely as yourself, it would indeed be a pleasure."

After that, she danced in turn with Jacob and two of the young men from his warehouse, then again with Edmond and Sir John, until her legs ached, and she was wearying of avoiding the ever watchful Captain Warrender.

At last she slipped away. She would have liked to retire to her room for the night, but Jacob expected them all to behave as proper hostesses and stay till the last guest departed. He had made himself especially clear to Averil. She went out past the dining room and left the house.

The door into the kitchen was open, and Honor was visible in the amber-tinged firelight, scouring the last platter. She was fifteen years old, small, with an enchanting liveliness.

"Are ye not enjoyin' yerself, ma'am?" Honor called out as Averil passed the door. "I've been tappin' me foot to the tunes the whole time. A mighty fine party, I vow and swear. Can I fetch ye anything?"

"I was just going to step out for a bit of air, Honor, thank you."

To the left in the light of the torches she could see Percival Osgood and Sir John in conversation on the small terrace and hear the laughter and music straying from the open doors behind them. Keeping to the shadows in the border of cypress hedges, she slipped quietly through the kitchen garden and on into the night, not pausing till she reached the farthest corner. Thick fragrant rose bushes and flowering orange trees hid her from view of the house. Almost no sound of the party penetrated to this end of the garden and she relaxed, breathing deeply of the heavy perfume from the orange blossoms. Nearby, a tree frog grated its call to the night in steady rhythm.

Averil relished the peace of the moment, willfully draining her mind of all thought, stilling the tension that buzzed in her head.

"Mrs. Averil."

The voice shattered her fragile inner calm. With an involuntary jerk of surprise, she looked up to the black-etched shadow of a man who stood only a few feet from her. A faint shaft of light from the last torch penetrated through a break in the foliage and touched a bronze streak in his dark hair. She recognized those bronze highlights; it was Captain Warrender.

She had heard no sound, no scrape of pebble against pebble on the path, no whisper of brushing leaves to warn her of someone's approach. A strange sensation of fear and excitement invaded her.

"You've been avoiding me," he said. She could not see his face, only hear the voice that grew slightly sharp as he continued, "But how could I forget—you think me disgracefully lacking in principles, am I right? You label a person unprincipled merely because his differ from your own."

Furious at herself now for being discovered and especially by the one she had worked so hard to avoid, Averil exclaimed, "Whatever principles you possess are about as weighty as the coin that will buy them!"

The captain's voice was tinged with genuine surprise. "Are you always so rude?" When she made no reply, he reminded her, "You owe me a dance."

"I'm sorry, Captain, but I'm not feeling well and plan to retire now. If you will excuse me." She made as if to step by him but was halted as he caught her arm just above the elbow.

"You also owe me a kiss," he said. When Averil uttered an involuntary sound of surprise, he added, "I didn't even get so much as a curtsy from you when we were introduced. I expected better manners."

She was just starting to pull away in indignation when he reached one arm around her waist, caught the back of her head in his other hand, and bent his lips to hers. Though the kiss was light, his mouth was warm, expressive, and he held her hard against him. Averil was stunned by the un-expectedness of his actions, by the contact of his mouth on hers, the powerful muscles of his thighs against hers. Her hands were trapped against his chest, and after the first paralyzing moment of incredulity, she pushed herself away.

She was shaking, overwhelmed by the physical contact with him and alarmed by the resulting warmth that seeped through her breasts and legs. Her breath hissed sharply into her tightened lungs.

"How dare you?" she cried. She struck one small fist against his chest.

"We had yet to acknowledge our introduction," he pointed out mildly, catching her fist. She tugged it away.

"But you go beyond propriety!"

"I make no apologies for it." He sighed slightly and said in a softer tone, "You've never been kissed, have you?"

As a stray night breeze moving through the foliage tossed sparks of light over his face, Averil caught the unmistakable tenderness in his eyes. Surprise robbed her voice of its anger as she answered defensively, "I'm not accustomed to such insulting behavior."

He lifted his eyebrows in faint wonder. "A kiss such as I gave you is not an insult but a compliment, Mrs. Averil. Now, about that dance?"

Unsure of herself, Averil replied, "I'm afraid you've sorely misjudged yourself—and me. Let me pass, Captain."

"Jacob may be unhappy with your decision."

In spite of her desperate urge to escape, Averil was caught by some veiled meaning. "What are you referring to?" she asked guardedly.

"I'm aware of the undercurrents between you and your uncle. I also detect pressure for you to be—kinder?—to me." He lifted his shoulders slightly in a shrug. "If our business arrangements disintegrate, for any reason whatsoever, who will he blame?"

"You would toy with people in this way?"

"I would certainly take it amiss if you deny me the simple pleasure of one promised dance."

Averil grit her teeth. "Captain Warrender, don't try to blackmail me."

Through the foliage the sparks of torchlight danced over them both as the breeze stirred the leaves. The shrewdly contemplative grey eyes held hers. His teeth gleamed in a smile.

"I never blackmail," he said. "My business with Jacob does not concern you in the least. I was merely warning you of what your uncle might construe from the situation, and I don't think he's the sort of man to react kindly to any setback. He'll find a scapegoat. But you owe me one dance. Shall we bargain then, Mrs. Averil? I give you my word that once that debt has been paid, I'll not trouble you again tonight."

"I don't know if I trust your word."

"You'll have to risk it."

Averil realized she would be far safer if she could return to the house and the protection of the other guests. "I have no choice, I see," she answered. "So be it."

He moved to the side to let her by and held out his arm for her. She placed her hand on his sleeve. Beside his long strides, her high-heeled shoes rapped smartly on the flagstones of the main path. The torches sent out flickering shades of light over her stiff features and his impassive expression.

When they entered the large parlor, Lynna and Edmond were both watching them with sharp, unhappy stares. Averil waited as the captain spoke briefly to the three young men from Jacob's warehouse who were presently playing the music. Almost immediately they nodded and began the music for another dance, a slow and stately pavane.

The captain extended his hand to Averil, palm down, and she placed her fingers atop his. She held her head up as they began. Though she remained poised, her face was flushed, eyes clear and brilliant with angry frustration. She glided with practiced grace through the movements of the dance—curtsies, advances and retreats, moments of held poses. The captain's execution of the steps was faultless, though he never moved his attention from his partner.

Averil's eyes met his during one face-to-face movement, and she was held fast by the beckoning in the silvery grey light of his eyes, by the powerful magnetism of his broad-shouldered frame. There was a secret in his masculinity that drew her even as she fled from it.

When the dance at last concluded, Averil dipped into a weak curtsy, grateful that the music had ended. The captain straightened from his formal bow.

"I'm true to my word," he murmured. A warm reluctance touched his eyes. "Good night, Mrs. Averil." He stepped back, turning as he sought out his host and hostess.

When he had departed, Lynna glided to Averil's side. Her blue eyes were slitted, the thin lips tight against her teeth as she demanded, "What happened out there in the garden? You were alone with him, weren't you?"

Feeling weary and drained, Averil had no patience left for Lynna's vicious insinuations. She pulled a face at her cousin, then whirled away, ignoring Lynna's sharp "*Oh!*" of indignation.

CHAPTER
SIX

All the following morning rain thundered against the rooftops and windows of the city. The Thames boiled and heaved in fury. As if brought to their knees by a violent, frenzied god, trees bent their leaves to the ground, and anxious humanity hid itself away behind doors and walls. The city waited.

Averil wandered the house with a morose restlessness, stopping often to stare out the windows. Across the road the outlines of houses and distant rooftops were grey lavender, veiled and wavering. It had been a week since she had seen the Tottman. Why had he not sent her a message of some kind? Anything!

She leaned her forehead against the dining room window. The cold pane stung her skin and a small cloud of steam from her breath formed on the glass. Her pensive mood was further deepened by thoughts of her encounter with Captain Warrender the previous evening. She stroked her lips absently with the tip of one finger as she thought of him. Why had he thought she had never been kissed? She had spent frequent moments alone with Thomas Kateley, her late betrothed.

Poor Thomas, she thought, and hugged herself with her arms, pressing hard against the blooming lump of sorrow in her chest. Thomas's kisses had been sweet, almost as one might kiss a pampered pet. But the captain had evoked within her a blatant awareness of him as a man, of herself as a woman, of a contrast between them that awakened secret, formless needs deep in her. She was no longer a child content unto herself.

Afternoon brought a clearing of the skies and a brisk wind to sweep away the rain. Still restless, Averil asked Mary Geneva if she could go riding in the coach now the storm had passed, and her aunt seemed equally excited at the prospect of an outing.

Lynna was still furious with Averil. She was certain in her mind that her cousin had been purposely attempting to gain the captain's affections, knowing full well that Lynna had laid claim to him first. When her mother invited Lynna to accompany them in the coach, she pointedly refused.

Cloaked against the wind and moisture in the air, Averil and Mary Geneva set out. As they rolled through the streets, the rear wheels of the coach spat up twin streams of muddy rainwater. Morton expertly guided the coach around the worst mires. Mary Geneva requested that they stop first at Jacob's warehouse. He had been busily at work ever since purchasing the captain's wine cargo and missed dinner entirely that day, so she had packed a light meal for him. When the coach dragged to a halt at the busy wharf, Mary Geneva alighted with her fragrantly warm, cloth-wrapped bundle.

"I'll be but a moment, Averil. Would you prefer to come in or wait here?" Averil chose to wait, and Mary Geneva hurried into the warehouse.

There was a general hubbub of activity at all times on the wharf, and Averil watched the goings-on with only a half-minded interest. Morton climbed down from his perch to talk with a fellow he knew. Wind whipping through the windows finally forced Averil to don the black hood she had brought and tie it securely under her chin. There was no glass in the coach windows, and rather than draw the heavy leather shades, she and Mary Geneva had left them open to enjoy the sights.

When the warehouse door swung open, Averil turned, expecting to see Mary Geneva returning, but it was Captain Warrender who had stepped out of the building. Holding the brim of his hat against the wind, he strode toward the coach, his jet black cloak swirling.

Averil's eyes were riveted on the tall man in sudden acute alertness, and she felt alarmed and breathlessly pleased—and not a little shaken—by the very sight of him. Then she snapped her head around, hoping desperately that he might pass without stopping. But that hope was not to be realized.

"Mrs. Averil—this is a pleasant surprise." He leaned his elbow on the window frame and shoved his hat back on his head.

"Aye, it is a surprise," Averil answered, avoiding his gaze. She kept her eyes leveled on one of the distant ships dotting the river and hoped he might take the hint and leave. The captain followed her gaze.

"She's a beautiful ship, isn't she?" he said.

"What?" Averil shot an instinctive, perplexed look at him and caught the warm vibrancy of his eyes. She was aware of the broad line of his shoulders more than filling the window. As the moments in the garden flashed with unnerving vividness to her mind, Averil's eyes dropped to his smiling lips. She remembered the texture of that mouth on her own and blushed furiously.

He answered. "You were staring at my ship, the *Indomitable*."

"Oh." Ruffled by his stare and furious with the direction of her own gaze and thoughts, Averil tugged the edges of her cloak closer about her and commented sharply, "I might have expected you to apply such a pretentious name to your ship."

"It is not pretentious if it expresses the truth, Mrs. Averil." She heard the amusement in his voice.

"You've had a spell of luck."

He paused before replying more seriously, "I don't believe in luck. It's the crutch and excuse of weak men who can't shoulder the responsibility for their own actions—or lack of them."

Averil turned to stare at him. "Then you believe you have complete control of every situation—is that what you're saying, Captain?"

He smiled oddly, only one side of his mouth stretching back. "I can't control the actions of others. No matter how much I might wish it."

"You're very sure of yourself."

"I try to be." With one finger he softly stroked her wind-flushed cheek. Instantly she pushed his hand away. "Do you so detest me?" he inquired, wholly serious.

"Aye! I do!" she cried. "There is nothing in the least honorable about you!"

"I'm true to my word," he reminded her. "Didn't I convince you of that last evening? Will your doubting mind not grant that I do possess some integrity?"

"You dare call that integrity? When you manipulated me as you did? I wish to have nothing more to do with you. You claim to possess integrity—prove it by honoring my request!"

"I do not possess a fool's integrity, Mrs. Averil." He made a small noise of disgust, then his voice sharpened as he explained, "I said I do not believe in luck—nor destiny, fate, fortune, or whatever else other men may rely on to gain what they desire. I desire you, Mrs. Averil. Thus I decline to accept your rejection of my attentions."

Before Averil could find words to express her utter outrage, he stepped away from the coach. With a smile, he added, "And that's no insult, Mrs. Averil." He settled his hat down on his brow and said formally, "Your servant."

When he departed, Averil saw the plump form of her aunt returning to the coach. The woman climbed in and dropped onto the seat opposite Averil. "Such a delightful man," she murmured, watching the captain's receding figure through the window.

Averil bit hard on her lower lip, afraid she might scream aloud in frustration or burst into tears. At Mary Geneva's return, Morton climbed back to his perch and the coach rolled in a wide circle as it turned to leave the wharf, the wheels rumbling on the wooden planks.

Mary Geneva smiled broadly and her eyes were round and bright as she leaned toward Averil. "This is a secret—just between the two of us," she said excitedly, "but Jacob and I have been discussing a possible match between Lynna and Captain Warrender!"

Averil's eyes widened in sharp dismay. "But aunt," she protested. "Have you given no thought to his character?"

"What do you mean?"

"Why, he could already have a wife somewhere for all we know!" The words sprang from her without thought, but once they were uttered, she experienced a drop in her spirits. What if he really *did* have a wife? The possibility unaccountably depressed her.

"Pish-pish. Jacob has already asked him about that, and he is neither married nor betrothed. And as for his character—why, Averil, he's so utterly like a gentleman and so handsome into the bargain. Lynna is well into the proper age, and I truly believe marriage is what she needs to settle that wild spirit of hers. And it would be a profitable arrangement for Jacob as well!"

"But this is . . . terrible!"

"Don't be so naive, Averil," Mary Geneva scolded sharply. "Lynna is infatuated with the man, and why should Jacob not continue to do business with him? Prosperity is desirable, is it not? To quote Reverend Pritchard's last sermon, it is a sign of God's favor. I don't know why you so disapprove of Captain Warrender, but you might for our sake at least pretend to be pleased!''

"Has Jacob suggested this to him yet?"

"Nay, we've only just begun to consider it ourselves, and nothing has been mentioned to Lynna. But I think we can all guess her response." Mary Geneva smiled as she envisioned her daughter's pleasure with the news.

"He's an immoral—" Averil began darkly. "For Lynna's sake, I hope he refuses."

"And he might! Especially if you can't govern your tongue around him!"

"I'm sorry, aunt, really I am," she murmured distractedly. "I just don't know what's wrong with me."

The outing was cut short; the cheerful anticipation of both women had been dampened considerably. As the coach rolled toward the house, they passed a hunched knife grinder plying his trade along their street.

Averil gasped audibly with shock as she recognized Darby Kipp. Was this a mere coincidence, or was he here to contact her with a message from the Tottman?

"God's grace, Averil!" Mary Geneva exclaimed in irritation. "Whatever is the matter with you today?"

Averil colored and stammered lamely. "I just saw a knife grinder— It's my sewing shears. Impossibly dull." She fidgeted as Morton climbed down from his seat, and he seemed to take an eternity to lower the step and unhook the door for them. When he did, Averil alighted first and with her skirts held high she dashed ahead into the house. On her way back out carrying her shears, she passed Mary Geneva just entering. Her aunt observed her flight with stiff distaste.

Darby Kipp was waiting in the street. Averil slowed her pace to a sedate walk as she approached. His one good eye gleamed at her as she presented the shears.

"Have you news for me?" she inquired in a whispered voice that barely concealed a tremor of excitement.

A chuckle rattled from Darby Kipp's throat as he set his

stone wheel spinning. "Ye've certainly changed from the last time I seen ye, miss. Almost didn't know if it be ye or not." He applied one blade to the stone. "The Tottman wishes to see ye tonight."

"He does? When? Where!"

"About ten o' the clock, Nicodemus—he's a big man with black 'air and beard—will come by 'ere. 'E'll take ye to the Tottman. Come as the lad, like ye did before."

Averil's excitement was so intense she felt as if she stood high above the cobbles. But a minute later she came crashing down as Darby finished with her shears and handed them back. She accepted them in sudden acute embarrassment. "I have not brought a coin with which to pay you."

"It's of no consequence, miss. The Tottman pays me for m' services. But thank ye all the same."

As Averil returned to the house she was plagued by a fresh concern. Darby Kipp had said the Tottman paid him, but who paid the Tottman? It was a subject that had not been discussed during their meeting. How much did he expect for his services? And how was she to pay him? She had nothing but the few coins Jacob allotted her as he did to all the household for their small, incidental expenses. It was nothing to what the Tottman must charge for his work, but once he found her father they could settle with him in some way. In the meantime, he had contacted her, so that must mean he had news! Her heart skipped a beat in tumultuous excitement as she picked up her skirts and ran the rest of the way back into the house.

At supper she found herself able to eat little. Her stomach was tight and fluttered with apprehension. The hours spent with the family around the hearth after the meal seemed interminable, but when at last the time neared half-past nine, she excused herself gratefully and retired to her room. There she donned her disguise with eager, fumbling fingers.

After extinguishing the single candle in her room, she pushed open the casement windows and peered out. The broad-limbed oak tree that grew beside the structure reared blackly in the night's gloom. Several of its many branches spread within a few feet of the window and Averil climbed up to perch on the narrow sill. The ground below seemed so far away; the nearest oak branches receded. Dizziness rolled around her head, but she took two deep breaths to orient herself, vowing that nothing would prevent her from meeting the Tottman this night.

She kept her eyes on the oak tree, and with one hand clutching the window frame securely, she leaned out to grasp the nearest branch. The bark was scaly and damp to the touch. With her heart in her throat she jumped, and on impact wrapped her legs securely around the broad, swaying branch. From there she half slid, half climbed to the ground and crept around the front corner of the house. Aside from a small coach that rattled past at that moment, the street was deserted. Averil knelt in the shadow of the house and waited.

Would this night see her reunited with her father? The thought made her almost weep with the waiting and wondering. Or would the Tottman have other news, terrible news, to impart? Nay, she wouldn't think of that possibility. Hope brought tiny butterfly flutterings in her stomach.

She scanned the street again and this time a movement far down on the opposite side caught her attention. Eagerly she watched as the form of a man took shape. When he was closer Averil could discern the heavy black curling hair on his head and full long beard. It was the man Darby Kipp had told her about, she was sure. She waited a moment longer and when she saw the man's walk slow as he neared the house, Averil stepped from the shadow and hesitantly crossed the street toward him.

In the bleak moonlight his eyes were narrow black slits shadowed by thick, overhanging brows. She approached him cautiously.

"Nicodemus?"

"Aye." His face split open in a broad grin as he surveyed her. Was her appearance a joke to him? "So come along." His voice was a glutinous rattle, deep, seeming to come from far inside him.

Averil fell into step beside him. He moved with an amazing quickness for so heavy and bear-like a body. Averil took two steps to his one as she hurried to keep up with him.

"Where are we going?" she questioned when they had emerged into Fleet Street and headed east.

"Ye'll find out soon enough."

Nicodemus seemed unwilling to offer any further comments and Averil was too breathless from trying to keep up with his brisk pace to ask more questions. It crossed her mind that she was completely vulnerable, going alone into the night to an unknown destination with an unknown man, and no one but Darby Kipp knowing where she had gone. But she trusted Darby Kipp now.

Nicodemus turned into a side street and at the next street turned again. A goat bleated loudly somewhere nearby; a dog whined. Something scuttled softly in a blackened doorway. Instinctively, Averil moved closer to her companion as she swept a wary eye around. Nicodemus led her through a maze of crooked, unlit streets and alleys until Averil realized she was lost and could not have found her way back again had she the need. It seemed he walked for a long time. Her legs began to tire, and an ache in her side sharpened.

They came out at last into a main road bordered by taverns and cook shops and lodging houses rising some four and five floors high. Several structures were built across the roadway, leaving dark tunnels beneath for coaches and traffic to pass through. They passed a small alley between two buildings, and for the first time Averil became aware of a steady rushing sound of water. With a start, she realized they were on London Bridge.

Fog seeped along the road and swirled in thick tendrils in the glowing light that spilled out from several open tavern doors. Just as they passed one establishment, the door swung back, resounding sharply as it slapped the outer wall. Averil froze as the figure of a soldier stumbled out through the boisterous sound of merrymaking and a thin cloud of tobacco smoke.

Nicodemus looked away as the soldier eyed them. Averil felt her companion grasp her arm to lead her away, but she stood transfixed by fear. Though the soldier was a stranger, the sight of his buff coat and helmet brought back to her forcefully the terror of that day the soldiers had attempted to catch her in Cheapside.

"Get away with you!" the soldier barked, and the heavy stench of ale wafted towards Averil. She was jerked away abruptly, but looked back as the soldier marched unevenly across the road, his sword swaying at his hip, and entered another building.

Nicodemus had an iron grip on her arm and Averil said contritely as she hurried along with him. "I'm sorry, I don't know what came over me."

" 'E was so drunk 'e might have spitted ye fer merely standing in 'is way," he growled, angry and harsh.

Nicodemus led her across the street and into the building adjacent to the one into which the soldier had just disappeared. It was a lodging house. She followed Nicodemus up the narrow stairs, passing a door at each landing. When they gained the top floor he ushered her into a meagerly furnished room.

The Tottman stood at the window and turned at their entrance. The malevolent, inhuman power of his mask turned her legs watery. Would she ever be able to look upon him without this fear?

"I'm thankful you came," he said in the grating, rasping voice she remembered. "I have need of your assistance this night."

"Have you any word of my father?" Averil could not conceal the sudden tightening fear that he had some horrible information.

"I'm afraid this search may prove more difficult than I'd earlier expected. Here, take a seat." He indicated chairs and a couch and the three moved to sit, Averil and Nicodemus

on the padded couch, the Tottman in a rush-bottomed chair
facing them. He was attired in black, a wide leather swordbelt
around his lean waist. A single candle burned in a wall sconce
just behind the Tottman, and his masked face was lost in
shadow.

"I talked with Mrs. Brimby, the woman who owns the
Three Bells Inn in Abingdon, and learned that your father
was at the inn with Prince Rupert."

"He was there that night?" Averil drew in her breath with
sharp dismay. "So close! Oh, that I had known!"

"You could have done nothing for him, Averil. He was
heavily guarded."

"How was he, do you know?" Averil questioned softly,
her eyes large with concern. "Did he look well? Had they
mistreated him?"

The Tottman was slow in answering. The description he
had been given revealed that Averil's father had been half-
carried into the inn, but he hesitated to have her know this.
At last he said, "He was well, Averil. The next day Rupert
and his party departed Abingdon and headed north. On the
third of April, Rupert attacked Birmingham. No one
remembers seeing your father there, so I suspect he may be
in Oxford now, though I cannot say for sure." The Tottman
looked to Nicodemus. "How much time do you need?"

Nicodemus shrugged briefly. "Twenty minutes, no more."

The Tottman nodded and the mask swung again to Averil.
"I have something to ask of you tonight, Averil. There is
a young couple of my acquaintance who are in grave danger
unless they can leave the city soon. I will not go into the
details of their plight, but suffice it to say they are under
guard and accused of publishing treasonable statements in
a circular they print and distribute. At this moment they are
in a room of the inn next door here. Soldiers have been set
to guard them for the night, but tomorrow they will be moved
to a prison ship. I was able to get in to see them earlier and
there is no way to get them out but through a window overlooking the river. Nicodemus will be waiting below in a boat

ready to row them ashore and away from the immediate danger if I can find a way to get them out that window.''

The Tottman watched her as he spoke and noted with some satisfaction that Averil listened carefully. She was obviously intelligent as well as compassionate, and he would have need of both those qualities in the course of the night. Before he could continue, she frowned.

''How did you get in to see them?''

With a sharp sound, the Tottman warned, ''Never question me about what I do, Averil.'' She seemed to shrink back into the couch at the sound of his voice. ''It is for your own protection that I tell you only what you need to know. The problem I have is that there is no way to anchor a rope on the roof. There is but one chimney and that is decaying and crumbling dangerously. It would never hold my weight to allow me to lower myself to their room or lower either of them to the river. But if I stayed on the roof myself to hold the rope, I could lower someone else to their window.'' He paused. ''That is what I need you for, Averil. Would you allow yourself to be lowered by rope to their window and relay the plan to them in my stead?''

A jolt of apprehension shot through Averil. She looked from the Tottman to Nicodemus. They were both watching her closely, awaiting her reply. Her first reaction was one of denial—she had been frightened of climbing down a tree earlier, how could she manage to go down a rope along the side of a building, and over the river? It was mad! He was mad to even suggest such a thing to her!

''If I refuse,'' she began hesitantly, ''How would you get those people away from the inn?''

The Tottman replied simply, ''I don't think I could. At least, not tonight.''

Averil was silent as the full weight of the Tottman's words registered in her brain. The entire success of his plan rested on her alone. ''But isn't there someone else?'' she protested. ''Why me?''

''Believe me, if I could use someone else, I would, and

thus spare you this, Averil. I can well understand if you're frightened, but will you help these people?''

Even as her mind cried out in its agony of indecision, she thought of her father and wondered if she would be able to do such a thing if he were waiting this night. Though it was not her father, the people held there were kin to someone, somewhere. She raised round, shimmering eyes to the Tottman and said tremulously, ''Aye, I'll do it if I can.''

Though she could not see it, behind the mask the Tottman smiled his approval before turning to Nicodemus. At the Tottman's nod, the large man rose and let himself out of the room.

When they were alone, the Tottman said, ''We have time, Averil. Would you like some wine to settle yourself?''

Averil shook her head jerkily. The very thought of ingesting anything made her feel sick to her stomach.

For several long minutes they remained silent. Averil clenched her fingers together, tugged at her sleeve, dried her palms on her breeches. The Tottman remained motionless, a statue carved in ebony.

At last Averil ventured, ''Who is Nicodemus?''

''A friend,'' he said, and seemed disinclined to add more.

''I have an old friend, Sir John Walford,'' she said, remembering her desire to include him. ''He was the one who told me about Darby Kipp. He's a dear friend of my father's, and I know he could be of help if I could tell him about you.''

The Tottman stretched his long, straight legs out before him and crossed them at the ankles. ''I've made inquiries about this Sir John. Born in Dorset County in 1595, youngest son of the family, a black sheep from what I've learned.''

Averil couldn't resist a smile. ''Aye, my father's told me he had quite a wild streak in his youth. But he's much different now—very settled and wise.''

''Married once, and a professed supporter of the Crown,'' the Tottman continued, but Averil interrupted.

''He never married!''

"Aye, he did, many years ago, but his wife died in their first year of marriage."

Averil whispered softly, "I never knew that. Poor Sir John."

"He lost a goodly amount of money in a speculative venture in the New World. From what I can determine, he's virtually penniless at the moment."

"But may I tell him about you?" Averil pressed.

"Nay."

Though disappointed, Averil dared not argue with him. She hesitated before bringing up another question that had been on her mind. "How did you come by the name 'Tottman'?"

After a lengthy pause, he answered, "The first person I aided, quite by chance actually, was an old friend of my own father's. He called me that. It means 'watcher' or 'lookout,' if you will." The Tottman rose and crossed the room to peer out the window. "Come, let me show you what we'll be about tonight."

Averil followed him to the window on shaking legs.

"It's an easy climb from here to the roof," he explained.

Standing so close to him, she could not control the sudden shivering apprehension that gripped her. She looked up at him, at his masked features looming over her. Her gaze traveled upwards to the eyeslits in the black mask and strained to see into their depths, to find some image of those eyes that were locked with hers.

"The window, Averil. I want to show you."

Averil jumped as if struck, and with color staining her cheeks, she looked obediently to where his finger pointed. They were just below the roofline; Averil thought she could almost touch the low, sloping eaves. Just visible over the side was a short length of rope.

"I have attached that rope to the chimney of this building. It's newer than the one on the next building and with luck will hold my weight. I'll go first, and when I call, I want you to stand upright here on the ledge and take hold of that rope. I'll help you up from there. Can you manage that much?''

Averil bobbed her head in response, not trusting her voice, for her throat had suddenly constricted and she felt a tight pressure in her chest.

''Good. The rest should be easier.'' He looked down out the window and raised his hand. ''Nicodemus is ready.''

The Tottman returned to the couch and from beneath it extracted a coil of heavy rope and a cloth pouch that clanked with a heavy metallic sound when he moved it. The latter he attached to his belt and, with the rope in hand, returned to her. He tied one end securely around her, under her arms, adjusting and testing the knot till he was satisfied. After unwinding a generous length, he thrust his arms through the coil of remaining rope and settled it on his shoulder.

With quick, sure movements he climbed out of the window. His lithe, black-garbed form swung away into the darkness, and Averil leaned out to watch as he pulled himself easily over the eaves and disappeared from her sight.

It was then that Averil looked down.

Visible through idly shifting currents of fog, the broad expanse of wall fell in a sheer drop to the river far below, where black water foamed and crashed thunderously between the stone arches. Averil's pulse beat frantically. Fear squeezed the breath from her lungs. How stupid she had been! Why, oh *why* had she agreed to this? She gripped the casement ledge so tightly the muscles in her arms ached.

From somewhere above her his voice whispered urgently, ''Averil! Are you ready? You can start now, I'm holding the rope.''

She released her hold on the ledge and flexed some feeling back into her fingers.

''Don't look down,'' the whispered voice commanded. Averil nodded, though the Tottman could not see her response, and carefully, holding tightly to the side of the window, eased herself up to a kneeling, then a standing position. She forced herself to look upward, never down.

"The rope around you is secured up here. You can't fall. Grab the rope hanging over the edge."

Obediently she stretched out her hand and closed it tightly on the end of the waiting rope. For one long moment she held her breath, her eyes blinded by the force of blood pounding into her head, then released her other hand from its grip on the casement and reached desperately for a hold as her body swung free of the window. Immediately she was lifted, a strong hand grasped her arm and swung her over the eaves to the roof.

She lay flat on the rough, sloping tiles, panting sharply in fear and relief. The Tottman relooped the rope and settled it again on his shoulder. With his help she drew herself up to a crouching position. A chill wind flapped the brim of her hat as she looked around. To the east, tall masts of ships riding at anchor near Tower Wharf pierced the fog, and over their skeletal forms the Tower of London squatted with silent menace, the four turrets atop the White Tower appearing clearly through the fog like specters in formation.

Because the eaves almost touched each other, Averil and the Tottman crossed to the next building easily, and there he made her wait. He scaled the steep rise of the roof and knelt behind the chimney, part of which had collapsed. While Averil watched, shivering in the wind, he withdrew several items—two large nails and a small mallet—from the pouch at his waist and hammered the nails into the roof just behind the chimney. Then he slid back down the roof to her.

"I've just put in some spikes to brace myself with. The bricks below the roofline are not as weathered as those above, and will hold me." He adjusted the rope around her, testing the knot as he spoke. "Wait until I'm in place—I'll tell you when—and then I want you to ease yourself over the edge of the roof there." He pointed to a spot just to the left of a blunt cornice piece. "Hang onto the rope as I let it out slowly. Go down to the second window from the top, and explain to the people what we're doing. Then I want you to go down to the boat first. Jerk twice on the rope when you're ready to descend from their room. Tell them of the code—one jerk is for me to raise the rope again to them, two for me to lower it.''

''But what will you do?'' Averil questioned through the pressure in her throat. ''How will you get down?''

''I'll go back the way we came and meet you later. Nicodemus knows. Guards are occupying the chamber's outer sitting room, so be as quiet as you can when you reach their room.''

She nodded mutely and the Tottman cupped her chin in one hand. ''You are an incredible woman, Lady Averil Maslin,'' the hoarse voice whispered. His thumb brushed across the flesh of her lips in a soft caress. ''Were I without this mask—'' Abruptly he dropped his hand and turned to climb upwards to the roof's peak.

Averil released her breath slowly, too aware of the sudden glow that pervaded her body and the way her lips had seemed to burn under his touch. Confused not only by his actions, but by her response as well, Averil watched as he settled himself behind the chimney, feet planted against the spikes, the end of the rope wrapped around his back and shoulders.

When he was ready, he called down to her and Averil began to crawl toward the spot he had indicated on the edge of the roof. She peered tentatively over the side and her stomach leaped up sickeningly. The river slid away in a sheer, dizzying drop and the crash of foaming water around the bridge supports seemed to come from a great distance away.

She rocked back and forth on her knees, her body trembling violently. Tears splashed down her cheeks. How could she do this? It was impossible!

The rope around her tightened firmly. ''You're safe, Averil,'' the Tottman called to her softly. ''Don't look down.''

She nodded and swept her tears aside with her fingertips. The strength in the rope around her was reassuring, but she held tightly to the corner of the roof as she lowered herself hesitantly over the edge. Unable to test the ability of the

Tottman to hold the rope with her weight on it, Averil hung onto the eaves by her fingers. Her legs swayed loosely in empty space and she squeezed her eyes closed as a small sob escaped her pinched and trembling lips. Ever so gingerly, she released her hold on the roof, transferring her grip to the rope.

She hung poised over the water, her body descending slowly and smoothly along the outer wall. The rope bit into the skin over her shoulder blades and bruised the underside of her arms.

On either side of her, the fog was banked against the buildings and glowed here and there with a thin, cottony light from various rooms of the inns up and down the bridge. She kept her gaze fixed on the appropriate window below and to her right. It was partially open, and a very faint light emanated from within. As she neared it, the sound of muted voices drifted out. Though she could not make out the words, Averil detected the obviously tense tones of a woman.

When she drew near, Averil swung out with one foot but was not close enough to hook the toe of her boot on the window frame. On the second try she was more successful and was able to pull herself close enough to grab the edge of the window with one hand. It was with a feeling of intense relief that she felt the firm ledge of the window beneath her feet, and then she was climbing through the narrow opening.

She heard a gasp from somewhere in the shadows, and almost immediately a young woman took shape before her, eagerly helping Averil the rest of the way in.

"He's here!" the woman exclaimed softly, and then, "But you're not the Tottman! Who are you? Where's the Tottman?"

One shuttered candle lit the room and its light was turned full upon Averil. From what she could see, it was a shabby room; the floor was bare and there was grit beneath her boots. The woman was several inches taller than Averil, dressed in a black gown, her shadowed face etched with deep lines, her thin lips pinched in disappointment. Averil tried to reassure her.

"It's all right, I'm here to help," she said, still gripping the rope as if she derived strength from it. "There is a boat waiting below and you'll be lowered to it one at a time. Where is your husband?"

The woman turned her head and Averil followed her gaze, squinting her eyes to peer into the deep shadows behind the shuttered candle, but she was unable to discern anything. The woman spoke sharply.

"But I thought the Tottman would be coming! Where is he?"

"He's on the roof, holding the rope. But please, we must hurry!"

In the next instant the room burst into life with an uproar. Several figures sprang out of the shadows. The woman grasped Averil by the back of the neck, and someone laughed in eager triumph. Averil could do no more than gasp in the utter shock of the moment. Across the room a man pulled the door open, and as he did so a broad shaft of light from the outer room fell upon him.

Recognition hit Averil like a stinging whip. Then the full impact of the situation burst upon her as the man at the door cried, "He's on the roof! Catch him!" and a commotion of men bearing swords and muskets bolted from the outer room to race upwards, their footsteps pounding on wooden stairs.

It was a trap! A trap for the Tottman, and she had been caught as well! In horror, Averil kicked out at the woman and heard a harsh grunt as her boot struck a shin. The woman cursed loudly and struck Averil across the face, bringing a rush of tears to her eyes and knocking her hat to the floor. A brawny man sprang up in the light, and in a frenzy Averil struck out at the two of them with fisted hands and kicking feet. The woman stumbled backwards as a flailing fist found her nose, but the man caught Averil by the front of her shirt. His fingers tangled through the laces of the doublet and grasped a handful of shirt. As she twisted to free herself, Averil's shirt fabric, thinned from wear, was wrenched apart in a gaping tear. The bindings beneath had loosened and shifted in the struggle and now the unmistakable roundness of one heaving ivory breast was bared.

The shock of discovering that he had a woman and not the boy he had expected momentarily halted her assailant. Averil leaped onto the ledge of the open window, hoping to escape the room by the same means as she had entered, but before her horrified eyes, the Tottman's end of the rope twisted past and dropped away into the darkness below.

When she spun on the ledge, the man was lunging for her, and she was knocked backwards. A thin, high scream of terror tore from her. Fingers splayed, arms out, she clawed for a hold. The man tried to reach for her but caught only the bindings on her head. The linen strips came free in his hand and from them erupted a cloud of brightly shining hair that filled the window for an instant as she fell.

CHAPTER
SEVEN

Averil hurtled through the darkness. She felt herself somer-saulting, heard her own agonized scream as she plummeted downward. The black water rose up and she hit the foaming surface with an impact that sent a shock of pain through her. Her mouth filled with water, then her lungs, and she was choking as she sank. Her arms and legs thrashed frantically, the weight of her water-filled garments dragging her deeper into the blackness. Her body convulsed in its effort to get air.

For an instant something large and hard and tangible brushed against her, but it was gone again when she grabbed at it. The currents of the river sucked her down and carried her along, rolling her body over and over.

Gradually the agony gave way to a peculiar bliss; the water became a warm and comforting haven. She ceased her struggles. Her arms and legs were free and seemingly un-connected to her as she swirled through the smooth, sleek corridor of black water. But a hardness entered the soft world around her and pulled her back to the agony. She fought against it weakly.

The Tottman broke the surface, dragging a small, limp form. When the boat drew alongside, he gasped, "Dear God in heaven, I almost couldn't find her!"

Around them musket balls struck the water with angry, stinging sounds, and voices cursed and shouted from the bridge upstream. With Nicodemus' help he dragged himself and Averil into the boat. As Nicodemus returned to the oars and pulled with long, powerful strokes to carry them out of range of the muskets, the Tottman turned Averil face down in the small boat and planted his hands on her back, pressing down again and again.

The water was forced out through her nose and mouth and replaced by clean air. Averil returned to hazy, painful awareness as she choked and coughed. When she began to retch, firm hands lifted her and held her head over the side of the boat. Her stomach heaved as she rid herself of the river water she had swallowed. When the spasms subsided, strong arms encircled her and she was held close against a warm, wet chest.

She awoke feeling hot, smothered. Warm bricks were packed around her feet and layers of heavy blankets surrounded her. She pushed away at the blankets that seemed to press her deep into a thin, sagging mattress. Had Aunt Mary Geneva placed these many blankets over her? But why? As her fingers plucked ineffectually at the rough materials, memory flooded back and she cried out. She struggled to rise, but firm hands pressed her back into the mattress and a familiar voice said, "Nay, rest."

Averil managed to peel open her eyes, though the lids felt heavy and weighted down. The Tottman, mask in place, was seated beside her on the mattress. His clothes were damp and wrinkled, and a broad smear of mud marked the wide chest.

"How do you feel?" the rasping voice questioned.

"You . . ." Averil began, then frowned slightly as she

tried to untangle the web of her thoughts. "They didn't catch you. . . . You pulled me from the water?"

The masked head nodded, then the Tottman rose and reached across to a table. They were in a small room, barely more than a hovel. In addition to the straw-filled mattress she lay on, there was a rough-hewn table with one chair and, on the wall above it, several sagging shelves bearing chipped crockery and some wooden trenchers. A small glowing hearth sent up a thin, foul-smelling haze of smoke into the room. The Tottman returned with a steaming mug.

"Where are we?" she muttered weakly.

"This is where Nicodemus lives."

"Where is he?"

"Away. Here, drink this."

Her stomach felt weak and she turned her head away. "I don't think I should."

"Do as I say, Averil." The rasping voice was quiet but the authority in it made Averil eye him uneasily. The black emptiness behind the eyeslits was complete. She shivered with the knowledge that she was being watched from those dark depths. He explained, "This will help you regain some of your strength."

Obediently Averil lifted her head to sip from the cup in his hand. It was wine, thickly sweetened. With the Tottman's hand behind her head to hold her up, she was able to drink several swallows, and the mixture warmed her throat and middle. She lay back, moving her legs beneath the blankets, and choked on a cry as she realized she wore no clothing.

Clutching the blanket close under her chin, she eyed him warily, too distressed to speak aloud the question that burned in her mind.

As though able to read her thoughts, the Tottman said, "Your clothes are over there, drying by the fire." With a gesture of one hand, he indicated the meager hearth. Draped on stools set in front of the glowing coals were her breeches and shirt.

Averil reddened in mortification as she looked back at him. "Did you—? Was it you—?"

"You were shivering and your lips were blue by the time we reached here. Propriety was the last thing that mattered. But nay, Nicodemus was not present."

He crossed to the stools, felt the garments and, satisfied they were dry enough, carried them back and dropped them onto the bed beside her. "For the sake of your modesty, I'll wait outside if you feel well enough to dress now."

Averil, her face darkening to crimson, fingered the stiff material of the breeches as she nodded, unable to look at him.

When the latch clicked behind him, Averil rose unsteadily. The floor beneath her feet was littered with stale rushes. She pulled on the garments he had given her, then looked around curiously. There were no boots in evidence, nor her doublet, and she realized with a start that they must lie somewhere at the bottom of the river. The thought that it could just as easily have been herself lying in those murky depths brought a chill of horror to the surface of her skin, and she shivered.

The Tottman's knock sounded on the door after a few minutes and she called for him to enter. When he stepped into the room, she was sitting on the edge of the mattress holding the torn edges of her shirt together.

Hesitantly, she stammered, "I owe you my life and I am truly grateful. Thank you."

He sat on a stool opposite her and watched her with an intensity Averil could almost feel—as if his very being was a palpable force that emanated from the central core of him and enveloped her with a dense and smothering power. "Don't be grateful," he said curtly. "I put you in that danger."

Confused and hurt by his tone, she wrapped her arms around her middle and rocked on the mattress as she looked up at him. "Why do you do this?" she begged. "Why do you involve yourself in these activities?"

He wiped his hand over the mask absently and dropped his hand to his leg before speaking, emotionless. "Sometimes, Averil, seeing others' suffering, participating in it, can become meaningless. It's like a sickness. And when you've got that sickness, the only way out of it is to make a conscious and deliberate decision.'' He paused, watching her. ''What I do now is the result of just such a decision on my part.''

Averil shut her eyes, unable to look upon the deadness in his mask. She knew a ghastly fear and grief.

The Tottman leaned forward, resting his elbows on his thighs, and studied her. ''Tell me what happened when you reached the room at the inn tonight.''

Startled back to the moment, Averil uttered a sudden exclamation. ''The man! That man in the room—I knew him! It was Francis Bowers! He was my father's steward.''

''Holy sweet Jesus,'' the Tottman muttered. ''Did he recognize you?''

''Nay, I don't see how. I was there only a short time, but—'' she looked down at the front of her shirt, shivering slightly as she remembered the struggle with the hulking man in the room and the moment when he had ripped it open. ''He could not have doubted I was a woman,'' she murmured softly. ''Still, I have no reason to believe he would have known that woman was me.'' She sucked at her lower lip thoughtfully. ''What worries me is that if Francis did this to you, he may be the one who is responsible for all those actions that Prince Rupert believes my father guilty of. He is the traitor! Oh!'' She pounded her fists into the mattress on either side of her. ''Oh, how could he do this? And my father had been so patient with him! He'll pay for—''

She broke off as the Tottman leaned over and grasped her arms. He half lifted her from the mattress and she cringed at the feel of the steel fingers biting into her flesh.

''Promise me,'' he said warningly, ''you will say nothing— *do nothing*—and you will steer well clear of the man! Promise me!''

There was such intensity in his words that Averil could offer no response. She nodded. The Tottman released her. She sagged back on the mattress, her arms limp. "We must hurry," he said. "It's very late and I have work to do."

"Are you going to find Francis Bowers?" she asked hopefully, rubbing her upper arms.

"Not this night," he answered. "There is another cause more dear, namely that of the people who should have been in that room tonight! I suspect they've already been taken to the prison ship. Tell me all you saw and heard."

Averil complied, including descriptions of the woman and the heavy-set man in her account. "But what will you do?" she asked when she had at last satisfied him as to the details of the evening's events. "Where will the prison ship take them?"

"Nowhere. The Tower and prisons are overly crowded now, and some of the frigates at Tower Wharf are being used to house the overflow of prisoners."

He rose to his feet, stepping back as he surveyed the tangled mass of her unbound hair and the small bare feet. After searching about the room he came up with a battered hat which he presented to her. "This belongs to Nicodemus, but you have the greater need of it at the moment. But there is nothing that will serve you for shoes. I have to see you home now. We'll take my horse, so get yourself arranged as best you can."

The hat was much larger than the one she had been wearing, and without the linen strips to hold up her hair, the loose strands kept sliding out from under the wide brim. As she worked to tuck up the tresses, the torn front of her shirt parted and closed slightly with her movements. The Tottman waited, glancing away and then back again to the shadowed soft inner curves of her breasts revealed intermittently as she worried with the hat. At last he muttered, "I'll get my horse. 'Twill be a few minutes—the stable is some streets away."

Averil waited for him at the door. He returned, materializing out of the dark night and leading a horse by the reins.

She recognized the massive black beast she had seen him on in the forest the night she met Rupert.

The Tottman lifted her onto the saddle, then swung up behind her. He settled her across his lap and coaxed the animal into a steady pace as they picked their way up the shoulder. Though the sensations were pleasant, she shifted

Averil was acutely aware of the feel of his hard thigh pressed to her own, and his warm broad chest against her shoulder. Though the sensenations were pleasant, she shifted position uneasily and sat up straighter.

"What is it?" the Tottman asked. "Aren't you comfortable?"

"Aye," Averil murmured. "But this is so . . . well, *improper.*"

A burst of amused laughter answered her. "After all that's happened, you're concerned now about sharing my horse? What is damned improper is you in those rags—I wish to God you'd burn the wretched things." His voice grated more softly in seriousness as he said, "In fact, Averil, you should do just that, for I'll never again endanger you as I did this night."

At his last words, Averil felt a smudge of tenderness and peace in her heart. She said nothing, not knowing how to respond to him. But she relaxed at last and let his chest cushion her.

The ring of the horse's hooves on the cobbles was the only sound. The streets were empty at that late hour of the night; not even a linkboy or a late reveler passed them as they traveled along Fleet Street. The city was intensely silent. Averil wondered how the Tottman could see the way—there were no torches to light the street, nothing but a silver glow of moonlight in the fog.

They continued their journey in silence and the steady pace of the horse lulled Averil, and she felt a lethargy steal over her. His arms held her on either side and in drowsy contentment she sighed against his chest.

When the horse slowed to a standstill, she jerked upright.

"Where are we?" she whispered in alarm. "What happened?" She peered cautiously into the night around them. Faintly she discerned the shapes of broad, tall houses looming upwards against the misted sky.

"That's your uncle's home just across the way. We'll get down here. How do you want to go in?"

"Around the side there," Averil whispered. "I can climb up the tree to my window."

Because of her bare feet, the Tottman dismounted first and lowered her into his arms. He carried her across the cobbled street and when they were beneath the limbs of the oak tree outside her window, he set her down. Before she could move away, he pulled the hat from her head and buried his fingers in her hair. For a moment Averil stood silently, then she whispered, "I must go in, my aunt may be—"

His hands cupped her face and with a thumb across her lips he silenced her. His arms came around her waist and Averil was pulled against him, feeling the hard length of his body, his wide chest and the firmly muscled thighs, pressed to her. He held her head against his chest and the dull erratic thudding of his heart was loud in her ear. The sound was somehow strangely thrilling to Averil. Her own heart beat more rapidly and the nerve endings of her body quivered with a sense of expectancy.

Unable to change the direction of her thoughts, she wondered what it would feel like to be kissed by the Tottman. She lifted her head to peer at the mask, suddenly fearful of what lay behind it. Trembling within his embrace, she whispered, "Can I not see your face?" She was afraid of seeing, yet more afraid of not seeing.

He shook his head.

"Never?" She looked up at him imploringly.

His fingers traced the line of her chin, drifted down the slender column of her neck, and lingered, drawing slow circles over the soft, pulsing hollow above her collarbone. "That's hard to say."

She emitted a ragged sigh and pressed her cheek to the

warm front of his doublet. He stroked her back and his arms
dropped lower as he pressed her hips to his. Averil felt a
rigidly solid force against her abdomen and she pulled away
slightly in confusion and alarm.

"Nay, Averil, stay," he whispered against her ear. She
shivered as his warm breath touched her cheek.

"I must go in," she protested breathlessly.

"Soon," he promised, and then abruptly, regretfully, he
set her away from him. "You're right, you should go in now.
Go in before I'm tempted to take you away from here."

He prodded her gently and Averil turned and climbed into
the tree. Once in her room, she leaned back out but could
see nothing within the deeper shadows beneath the tree. Then
her ears caught the sharp ring of horse's hooves on the
cobbled street.

She disrobed slowly and stood in the darkness of her room.
With a sense of wonder, she stroked the skin of her breasts
and stomach, still flushed with the warm longing which the
Tottman had aroused in her. She found herself wishing he
was there within her room.

Immediately ashamed of her thoughts, Averil hurriedly
donned her nightdress. She pulled open the linen side curtains
of her bed, then recoiled in shock. A pale human form lay
upon the mattress.

"Where have you been?" demanded a shrill, feminine
voice.

"Lynna!" Averil pressed the palm of her hand against her
breast to still the sharp beating of her heart and exclaimed
breathlessly, "You gave me such a start! What are you doing
here?"

"Waiting for you." Lynna lit a candle beside the bed and
Averil could see her cousin, attired in a vivid yellow nightdress, sitting back on her heels in the bed.

"You've frightened years off my life. You might have
made your presence known a little sooner."

"What? And interrupt whatever sweet little moments were
happening out there? Who was it? Edmond?"

"Nay," Averil replied sharply, feeling a thin thread of apprehension twine about her chest. She threw back the thick coverlet and climbed onto the high bed.

"Well, who was it, then? And where have you been? You smell like the river."

"Lynna, does anyone else know I've been gone?"

"Nay, and I didn't tell. Not yet, anyway. Whoever it was, he kissed you, didn't he? I couldn't really see anything, but I could *hear*."

"What did you hear?"

"Oh . . ." Lynna idly trailed a finger across the crisp edge of the bedsheets, "I heard him say he wanted to take you away. . . ."

Angrily, Averil exclaimed, "I don't know why you're here, Lynna, but if all you want to do is—"

"I came to tell you Captain Warrender was here tonight, but when I found your room empty I just had to wait for you. And oh, how sweet this is! You've taken a lover and have secret rendezvous."

"That's not true! Who gives you leave to say things like that!"

Lynna watched her stonily for a long moment. Sweeping aside the hem of her thin gown, she stepped down from the bed. There was a hint of a sneer in her voice as she said, "Whoever he may be, you're welcome to him. As long as I have the man I want I care nought for your sordid little escapades. Captain Warrender has asked us to be his guests for an outing Saturday afternoon. *If* you attend at all, see that you keep to yourself!"

The oily black surface of the river was cleaved by a pair of splashing oars as a small boat carrying three soldiers and a large plump man approached the frigate anchored off Tower Wharf. Their lantern picked out the high, steeply angled stern and the elegantly carved figurehead. The gun-deck ports were closed. It was near three in the morning and the guard on middle watch on the quarterdeck was dozing lightly, but he snorted awake when the boat drew alongside. After calling to a companion on the forecastle, he rushed to the rail, musket in readiness, and peered down. The small lantern in the boat illuminated its four occupants and the guard called out, "Identify yourself!"

The overweight man addressed the guard. He had light, greying hair and was attired in a somber black suit and hat. "I am George Hassenby, here at the request of the Committee of Safety. I must speak with your commanding officer, Captain Moorcross."

The other guard had joined the first and the two conferred for a moment before the newly arrived guard disappeared to rouse his commander.

A short time later the officer in charge stepped to the railing. He was attired in a nightshirt stuffed hastily into a pair of breeches. When the man in the small boat had identified himself again, the officer had a ladder dropped to them and the man climbed onto the ship's deck, leaving the three soldiers to wait in the boat.

"I presume you are Captain Moorcross?" the man inquired.

"Correct, Mr. Hassenby. What is the nature of your business?"

"Shall we go to your cabin first, sir?"

Captain Moorcross inclined his head. Accompanied by one of the soldiers, they proceeded to a cabin below the quarter-deck. The soldier took a stance inside the room by the door as the two men seated themselves.

It was a cramped, though elegant cabin, and the newcomer looked around curiously. On the narrow bunk was a rumpled red satin quilt; framed stitchery pieces, probably made by the officer's wife, adorned the walls. The table they sat at also served as his desk—papers and silver inkpot were pushed to one side.

"Whatever your business, Mr. Hassenby, could it not have held till morning?" demanded the officer. A single brass sconce lit the room, and in the light the officer's face looked haggard from disturbed sleep. He appeared to be in his forties and had a thick stubble of beard on his cheeks and chin. His nose twitched at the unpleasantly pungent odor of onions that emanated from his guest.

"I was called from my bed as well, Captain Moorcross, so I can well understand your feelings. But the Committee considers this matter of utmost importance, so who am I to argue?"

George Hassenby had a heavy, square frame with a pronounced bulge in his mid-section. His cheeks sagged, his hair was grey, his eyes weak with a tendency to water excessively. At frequent intervals he dabbed at his wet nose with a delicate linen handkerchief.

"Though your name is familiar, I'm afraid I don't recognize you, Mr. Hassenby. Would you be so kind as to enlighten me regarding your position with the Committee of Safety?"

Mr. Hassenby eyed him coldly. "I am aide to Mr. Holles and the Earl of Essex."

"Oh, aye! Please forgive me, sir. I meant no insult."

"No insult taken. We've not had the pleasure of being formally introduced, and I recognize the caution you must exercise, especially with an unusually timed visit such as this." Mr. Hassenby wiped his nose with the lace edge of his handkerchief. "I'm here concerning the matter of two prisoners who were brought on board today—Mr. and Mrs. Lambreth."

Captain Moorcross's eyebrows shot up. "Aye! They were removed here as part of a plan—"

"I know, I know." The other man waved his handkerchief in the air and blinked rapidly. "Unfortunately, the ruse failed and the Tottman escaped the trap laid for him. I've been sent now to escort the prisoners to the Tower."

The officer clasped his hands together and looked uncomfortable. "Considering the nature of this request—and I regret the necessity to question you—but do you have papers, Mr. Hassenby? I must see written authorization. You understand.''

"Of course." Mr. Hassenby pressed the handkerchief to his moist nose and passed a folded paper from his doublet to the other man.

Captain Moorcross opened it and scanned the close writing. The terse instructions were signed by Denzil Holles, one of the members of the Committee of Safety. He folded the paper and handed it back. Then he addressed the guard who waited just by the door.

"Have the new prisoners, Mr. and Mrs. Lambreth, brought on deck."

The guard let himself out and Captain Moorcross looked again to his visitor.

"Are you at liberty to divulge just why those prisoners should be transferred?"

"The Tower would be a safer place to keep them, don't you agree?" Mr. Hassenby shifted his bulk in the straight-backed chair and rubbed his eyes with his fingertips. "Dear God, but I'll be glad when this business is completed and I can return to my bed."

"But why tonight?" the captain pressed. "Wouldn't morning have been soon enough?"

"My dear sir," Mr. Hassenby addressed him with exaggerated patience, "the Tottman is a particularly clever fellow. Having been frustrated in his attempt to secure those people at the inn, he may try something desperate. It is for your security as well that we are removing them to the Tower tonight."

"May I offer the services of several of my men, then? Those three soldiers waiting in your boat, no matter how worthy, are a poorly insufficient escort should the Tottman be lying in wait."

The watery eyes of the other grew chilly. "You question the aptitude of our committee members, sir. There are others waiting at the wharf, and Traitor's Gate is open even now.''

"Aye—well, that's good.'' The captain nodded, shifting uneasily in his seat.

"Captain Moorcross," the other man began, steepling his fingers and examining the nails on each hand. "You've not been paid your due wages for two months now, am I right?''

"Aye, sir, though I'm not complaining. I know the Committee is doing what it can to raise revenue.''

"That is correct.'' He smiled, lifting one eyebrow appreciatively. "Your attitude is commendable. But I've been authorized to give you this.'' He pulled a sack from his doublet. Coins clinked as he deposited it in front of the officer. "Two months' wages. Count it if you like.''

The captain's mouth widened in a broad, surprised smile. "Thank you, sir.'' He took up the pouch and weighed it in one hand.

"A word of caution—mention this to no one. The Committee is expecting to be able to secure each soldier's wages soon, but until then there might be bad feelings were it to become known you'd received your due earlier. We don't need the kind of divisiveness that might result. You understand.''

"Most assuredly.'' The officer nodded as he rose and hid the pouch beneath a mound of clothing in a wall cupboard. The guard returned then to inform his captain that the prisoners were waiting on deck. When the door closed again behind him, the officer turned to the visitor.

"Is there any other way I can assist you tonight?''

"Thank you, nay. I'll be departing now.'' Mr. Hassenby tucked the handkerchief into his sleeve as he rose. "Perhaps with luck I can be abed again before the sun rises.''

On deck, the two prisoners waited together, the husband holding an arm about his wife's shoulders both protectively and for warmth. She was shivering in the brisk night wind. Her hair was loose and tangled as it fell about her shoulders, and the ship's large bronze and glass lantern behind her cast a kind of golden halo around her. Neither looked mistreated.

"Quickly now, into the boat," Mr. Hassenby directed. He bowed slightly to the officer as the prisoners were assisted down the ladder by the soldiers waiting below in the boat. Then he himself descended, his copious mid-section slowing his movements and causing him to pant slightly with the exertion.

He took his seat facing the prisoners in the center of the boat as two of the soldiers laid hands to the oars. Captain Moorcross waited on deck, watching until the boat disappeared into the fog-laden darkness.

In the boat, Mr. Lambreth murmured consolingly to his wife. As they neared the wharf he lifted his rigid, proud features to the man sitting just opposite them.

"Where are you taking us now?" he demanded.

"Where would you like to go?" was the quiet response. "And I would keep my voice down if I were you—sound travels too far over water. You're free now, the both of you. Where would you like to be taken?"

Mr. Lambreth's eyes narrowed. "What trick is this, sir?"

"No trick, I assure you. We'll be at the wharf soon and we cannot stand about arguing in front of the Tower."

The young man looked perplexed, then ill-at-ease. At last he said, "Who are you?"

"The Tottman, Mr. Lambreth."

The young woman gasped as she lifted her face to the stranger. "But you can't be—"

"Hush!" her husband warned. "This may be a trap."

In the faint, shuttered glow from the lantern, the two peered at the shadowy man with dubious eyes. The man known as Mr. Hassenby calmly removed several sets of women's cosmetic plumpers from each side of his mouth. Wetting his fine handkerchief in the water, he wiped one side of his grey head and revealed a broad streak of dark hair.

"You haven't told me yet where you would like to be taken," he pointed out, the inflection of his voice warmer, deeper.

The young wife began to cry quietly. "Can we get to Cambridge?" she asked with a small catch in her voice.

"I'll have you there in two days," the Tottman promised. He started to wipe his face with the handkerchief, then stopped abruptly, muttering "Damn!" as he hurled the wet cloth far out into the water. He chuckled slightly as he looked to the startled couple.

"I had too much onion juice in it," he explained. "I only wanted to cover my features with the disfigurements of a slight illness, but it damn near overwhelmed me a few times back there!"

CHAPTER
EIGHT

Through the lead-patterned window, a square of milky moonlight fell across the edge of the faded blue counterpane and spilled onto the floor. It was not quite eleven o'clock and Averil sat brushing her hair in preparation for retiring. Beside her on the dressing table, the candle flame flickered in the draft from the movement of her arm. Its light was not strong enough to dispell the moonlight, but illuminated her scowling face in the looking glass tilted before her.

If she went on the outing planned by the captain? Now what did Lynna mean by that comment? Did her cousin expect her to be frightened into staying at home because of Lynna's knowledge that she had been out that evening? By the mercy of God, at least the bed curtains had been drawn and Lynna had not seen her in the boy's clothes! Wouldn't that have caused some questions! She snapped the brush through her hair with angry vehemence.

Her irritation had been growing in the two days since the disastrous events of that night on London Bridge. On the first morning after, she had awakened feeling bruised and exhausted. After a few hours of limping painfully around the house—her entire body felt as if she had been rolled under coach wheels—she had returned to her bed and slept through the day. But that night she had lain awake, restless, tossing uncomfortably as she listened to the bellman call out each passing hour. Her thoughts had been in a turmoil. The irritation she felt with her cousin had spread like a fever until she was frustrated and upset with everyone.

Not only had Lynna's snide, accusing glares and outbursts pushed Averil's patience to the limits, but she had become the brunt of Mary Geneva's ill-humor as well. Ever since Averil had expressed her dismay at her aunt and uncle's intent to match Lynna with the captain, her aunt had grown decidedly cool toward her. Though this development alarmed Averil, for she knew her security lay in this household and she owed her aunt and uncle a debt of gratitude she could not hope to repay, she also felt dispirited.

It was all the captain's fault! Damn him! Her profanity shocked her, but scarcely surprised her—after all, the man was a devil, and certainly no gentleman!

The candle flame danced wildly as her arm yanked the brush with renewed irate energy through her hair. Even the Tottman had toyed with her! Who was he, anyway? She thought again of what he had told her about himself and felt the strange fearful dread. She lowered the brush, her hand falling idle in her lap. Oh, what had she been thinking to trust him as she had? To nestle in his embrace? Shame and fright flooded her at the memory. Oh, I'll not let that happen again! Never! I'll not be used by any of them!

After snuffing the candle flame, she climbed into her bed and sat with her arms around her drawn-up knees as she fumed. I *will* go on that outing Saturday with the captain, she decided. I don't care if Lynna tells—I'll deal with that somehow—but I'll not be intimidated by any of·them!

The following day, Lynna returned from a morning ride

in the coach and burst into the house like a wayward tempest. Cheeks flushed, eyes fiercely bright, she scrambled up the stairs to her mother's room where Averil, Mary Geneva, and Honor were sewing two new shirts for Jacob. She was too breathless to find voice immediately.

"It's Mr. *Markham*!" she cried at last. "Quickly now, *quickly*!"

Mary Geneva thrust aside her sewing and stood up, but Lynna was already out the door. Exchanging swift, anxious glances, the others hurried in her wake.

Farther down the street, a crowd gathered at the gates of one of the finer homes. Still some distance away, Averil could hear murmurs of discontent, shouts of zealous anger, sporadic cheers. Her heart was racing as rapidly as her feet as she caught up to Lynna near the outskirts of the mob.

"What is it?" She tugged at her cousin's arm. "Tell me, Lynna, please!"

Lynna shook her away. "It's Mr. Markham. He's been a Royalist all this time and now they're arresting him!" She bounced on her toes to see over the rows of spectators. "Come on, we can see better over there."

Fright sliced through her, but Averil followed her cousin automatically, not really wanting to see better, but not wanting to be left alone. Over the heads of those in front of her she saw furniture—a small table, several stools, a mirror—being hurled from an upstairs window. The articles smashed in front of the main entrance. Four men slipped through the barrier of soldiers holding back the crowd and broke into the house through a downstairs window. When they emerged and dashed off with small vases, candlesticks, a musket, and an ornamental rapier, the crowd could no longer be contained. With wild screams of victory, others ran into the house and the looting and destruction began in earnest.

Mary Geneva and Honor caught up to them. The four women waited along the outer fence, peering between iron railings at the commotion within. Honor held the hem of her apron to her face, only peeping out every few minutes to make sure she had not been deserted by the others.

Mary Geneva was indignant. "This is a mistake! A terrible mistake! Mr. Markham is no more a Royalist than you or—" She shot Averil a sudden look, blank with surprise.

"Oh look! There he is!" Lynna exclaimed.

Amid cheering, a frail, grey-haired man in a well-tailored suit of clothes was being led from the house. He paused for a moment, eyes wide and staring at the melee taking place around him, then climbed awkwardly into a cart that had been drawn up before the door. He stood in the back of the cart, a soldier at each elbow. As the crowd parted to release the cart into the street, eggs and rock were hurled, pelting the prisoner. Mr. Markham seemed oblivious, stunned, but the two guards shouted angrily as they were hit. Using their musket barrels like clubs, they struck indiscriminately into the crowd, leaving a bloody wake behind them.

Watching, Averil felt a deep thrill of fear run through her.

Saturday morning the sun was hot, heavy, brilliant as a diamond against a blue velvet sky. The crowds of people in the streets were unusually noisy with laughter and greetings and a general air of congeniality.

When Captain Warrender arrived in a hired coach to escort his guests on the outing he had planned, he found Edmond Devenish in the parlor talking with Averil.

She was wearing a gown of apple-green lawn trimmed with small black bows, one at the deepest curve of the neckline, the others sprinkled over the skirt. Beneath the bodice of her gown a lacy chemise peeked between the braid-trimmed slits of the voluminous sleeves. But her face was unnaturally pale, and the captain noted the confused and alarmed look in her eyes as she rose from her conversation with Edmond. He wondered what the young man had been saying to her to cause such consternation. As Edmond came to his feet at the captain's entrance, the two men's eyes—one with an angry, tawny hue, the other's with flinty directness—met and challenged each other.

After admitting Captain Warrender to the house, Mary Geneva had gone off to fetch her daughter. Now Lynna burst into the parlor with a high-pitched laugh.

"Why, Captain, you're here already! I should have known you'd be so prompt."

She sidled next to him possessively, the bright painted color of her cheeks heightened by the reflection of the pink gown she wore. "Could you not invite dear Edmond to go along today?" she begged. "Father's working and sends his regrets, so that leaves room for one more." It was in her mind that Edmond would keep Averil occupied and leave the captain free for her.

He grinned as he turned his attention from Lynna to Edmond.

"An excellent suggestion. Mr. Devenish, would you care to join us? We're off for a picnic, but if you have other business in London—"

"Thank you, sir. I'd be most pleased to join the outing." Edmond pointedly put his hand to the small of Averil's back in a possessive gesture designed solely for the other man's benefit; noting it, the captain's look became slightly derisive.

Averil, at the moment, could have cared less about the picnic, or the captain, or even Edmond's joining them. As they all climbed into the waiting coach and settled themselves amidst a profusion of gaily colored skirts and cloaks—Mary Geneva and Averil on one side with Edmond between, and Lynna and the captain on the other—her emotions were in chaos, with fear taking the upper hand.

Edmond had arrived just a few minutes before the captain and had drawn her to the parlor window, asking, "See those two men yonder across the street? Do you know who they are?"

She had gazed at the figures he referred to, not recognizing either. Both men were of average height, wearing dark, nondescript clothing. One had medium brown hair and a thin moustache, the other black straight hair and moustache and T-beard in the style worn by the king. For a moment the two men had conversed together, throwing furtive, curious glances toward the house. After what appeared to be a small argument, they walked away.

In confusion she had answered Edmond, "Nay, I've never seen either of them. But why? Should I know them?"

Edmond frowned slightly. "I waited for a moment and watched them before I came up to the door. They exhibited an unusual interest in this house. I wondered if they were business acquaintances of your uncle's, or perhaps suitors to you or Mrs. Lynna?"

"Nay! They are none of those things." Why was she growing so sharp? "At least, I really don't know for certain. They *could* be waiting for Jacob." She turned away from the curiously probing gaze he fastened on her.

She tried to dismiss the matter of the two men, but her thoughts burned in her mind. Were they sent by the Tottman? Or did their presence have something to do with her participation in the Tottman's attempt to rescue the people at the inn? Had Francis Bowers indeed recognized her and was she now under surveillance by Parliament? Or were they Prince Rupert's men? The Tottman had said Rupert was conducting a quiet search for her—had she been traced here?

Now as the coach jostled them and she felt Edmond's thigh brush against hers and remain there, she grew annoyed, then angry. Why had he even pointed those men out to her? They were most likely innocent passersby, and he had let that wild imagination of his take hold and alarm her.

Captain Warrender sat across from her, and in the cramped interior of the coach his knees almost touched the opposite bench. He had been watching the play of shadows across Averil's face as she sat lost in thought, her eyes focused on some faraway spot out the window. He looked from her to Edmond, who was studying a spot on the window frame, and considered the young man. The thought suddenly occurred to him that Edmond was much closer to Averil's age, and the captain felt himself age greatly in that moment.

He returned his attention to her speculatively. When he saw Edmond's thigh press against hers, he stretched his legs, and under the guise of shifting his position, maneuvered his knee against Edmond's and pushed it aside. Though Edmond shot him a glare, he pretended not to notice but kept his booted feet planted on either side of Averil's small black satin shoes and his knees spread wide to ward off any future such intimacies toward her from Edmond.

Unaware of the undercurrents, Mary Geneva addressed the young man beside her. "Edmond, how is your dear mother?"

"She's doing well," he responded stiffly, then relented, adding, "I brought her and her woman, Sarah, into London today so she could take care of some shopping and visiting."

"Oh, I'll be sorry to miss her."

"As she will you, but I'll carry your greetings to her. I know she wanted to ask you about your cherry trees and how you achieved such a sweet harvest."

Mary Geneva launched into a brisk analysis of the care of cherry trees, and across the coach Lynna maneuvered herself as closely as she could to the captain without drawing her mother's disapproving looks. She pretended a great absorption in the conversation between Edmond and Mary Geneva. When the coach rocked, she made full use of the moment and moved against the captain so that her breast pressed his arm. When he turned to peer at her, Lynna lowered her lashes in feigned embarrassment. Never had she met a man who so attracted her, and it was all she could do to sit placidly beside him. She had not yet been able to keep his attention away from her cousin, and the fact fired a vengeful hatred in her toward Averil.

On a grassy meadow in Southwark, overlooking London and the sluggishly glittering Thames, the five of them partook of the picnic dinner the captain had brought—chicken, pickled radishes, anchovies and artichokes, glazed fruit tortes, a basket of fresh Kent cherries, and wine. The hot sun blazed down around them, but where they sat beneath a leafy tree, they were sprinkled with dancing sparks of light in the shade.

The panorama of the city spread before her was breath-taking to Averil and she drank in the sights with pleasure— all but the grim row of grisly, pickled heads set atop spikes that crowned the Great Stone Gate at the south end of London Bridge. The heads of criminals, and now some Royalists, were cured at Newgate and set proudly aloft in the wind above the bridge.

Averil sat on one corner of the blanket the captain had provided, Edmond beside her. At the opposite corner the captain sat beside Lynna, who chatted gaily and with obvious affection. Lynna ate little as she talked, plucking at pieces of roasted meat with her fingers and scattering the bones into the meadow grass.

"Tell me all about yourself, Captain," she begged in invitation. "Where are you from?"

"Originally? England, of course." He shifted away from her slightly and leaned his back against the tree trunk, one leg up, his forearm resting on his knee. He wore black broad-cloth breeches and over-the-knee boots of soft brown leather. Because of the heat he had earlier removed his doublet and the white linen shirt clung damply to his skin.

"I know *that*," Lynna pouted prettily as she held out a basket of ripe cherries to him. "Where *exactly*?"

"Near here, but I left when I was eighteen. Went to Jamaica." He seemed bored and refused the cherries, so Lynna passed them to the others.

Averil accepted a handful. They were warm and sticky. As she sucked the moist skin of one, she shot another glance over the city, wondering idly where the Tottman was at that moment. Unconsciously, she sighed. Beside her, Edmond was unnaturally quiet, his attention on the captain.

"I took to the sea from Jamaica," the captain continued. "I found that I loved it—some aspects of it, not everything.

After I acquired my own ship, I worked a trade circuit covering Jamaica, the Levant, and England. I did that for close on eleven years. Then I switched to plying the markets between England and the New World.''

Averil was awed by his so casual mention of places that to her were only vague marks on an equally vague map. Studying him, she could begin to read some of that vast experience in his face, and she felt her own world broadening just at that contact with him. It was an extraordinary sensation to her. She tossed aside a cherry pit and took up her wine cup.

''Acquired your own ship?'' Edmond repeated with an engaging smile. ''That would take some doing. Tell us how you managed that, Captain.''

The captain scrutinized the younger man. ''It helps to know certain people,'' he answered bluntly.

''Oh, Captain, I can't tell you how utterly distressing this is,'' Lynna interrupted. ''I can't help but wonder how much longer you'll be here before you set out across that ocean again. You'll probably be away for months and months.''

Averil caught the flash of annoyance in his features. But he answered calmly, ''Not for some time. I'm exploring the European markets now.''

Edmond asked, ''Is it a search for markets only that has brought you back to England, then?''

''I have several other matters to settle as well.''

Gradually, as they each had their fill of dinner, the conversation grew more sporadic. The day's heat pressed heavily on Averil's skin and she sipped her wine in drowsy contentment. Edmond lay on his back, eyes closed, seemingly asleep.

The captain chewed the end of a strand of grass in thoughtful silence. Though Averil was not looking directly at him, she was conscious of him. And whether it was the wine, the heat of the day, or the fact that she could feel his attention on her, she grew flushed with a heavy languor.

Lynna and Mary Geneva were making casual conversation. Their voices became droningly monotonous in Averil's ears. They were discussing the Bartholomew Fair held in this meadow every September. Though Averil tried to revive herself with comments and questions concerning the fair which she herself had never attended, her attention slipped repeatedly and her languor increased. The warm, rich tones of the captain's voice as he added a remark or responded to a question from Lynna wove around her pleasantly, increasing her sensation of utter well-being.

From where Camden sat, with the sound of Lynna's idle chatter like the irritating buzz of an insect in his ears, he watched Averil. As always, she intrigued him. She displayed a curious blend of innocence and full-bodied allurement, so that her every move, by its very artlessness, was expressively tempting. And he was aware of the beguiling suggestion of pleasure that emanated from her.

He chewed on the grass absently. As Averil shifted position, he caught a glimpse of slender ankles before she again tucked her skirts around herself, and he envisioned proportionately slender, tapering legs. The image was disturbingly pleasant. He shifted the piece of grass to the other side of his mouth. As she leaned her weight on one hand to sip her wine, his attention turned to the indentation of her waist. When she reached to put the cup down, the lace edging of her bodice dipped and he contemplated the curves of her breasts. His teeth clamped hard onto the stalk of grass.

His interest mounted higher when he noted a soft pink flush steal across her breast and saw the heavy-lidded, drowsy contentment in her eyes. The thought hit him with sharp pleasure that she looked as if she had been making love. His own eyelids dropped slightly as a thick rush of desire thudded through him.

When Lynna had repeated a question to the captain and he still had made no reply, Averil glanced to him curiously. His full attention was focused acutely on her, and his eyes were narrow over a glittering, hot stare.

In response, the flush of languor rose higher in her and spread over her shoulders and into her face. The heat of it was a rich and heady pleasure to her, and her gaze clung to his in strange fascination.

Abruptly, the captain plucked the grass from his mouth and flung it aside as he pushed himself to his feet. Without a word to any of them, he strode away. He stood looking down the sloping meadow and out over the river. Watching him, Averil felt an odd ache that was almost tender.

At three of the clock, Edmond rose to take his leave. He had to rejoin his mother to see her home, and he thanked the captain politely as he untied his horse from behind the coach.

After Edmond's departure, Averil rose, shaking crumbs from her gown. She felt still a lingering sweet languidness and decided that a short walk might clear her mind of its haze and break loose the lethargy from her muscles. Swinging her feet through the tall grass, she strolled across the meadow to the spot where the captain had stood earlier. She shaded her eyes and looked along the Thames, wondering if she could recognize his ship from here.

"Can you see it?"

She swung around at the sound of his voice so near. The captain stood beside her, searching the river, and he pointed for her. "There's the *Indomitable*."

"Why would I be looking for your ship?" she exclaimed in confused surprise.

"Weren't you?"

She stared at him, unable to find a suitable answer. He was watching her face, studying it. Alarmed suddenly, she dropped her gaze.

He chuckled as he said, "You must know how revealing your eyes are!" After a short pause he asked, "What did Edmond Devenish say to you this morning in the parlor before I arrived?"

Averil looked at him sharply, all of her defenses springing up. "What do you mean?"

"I saw it in your face when I entered the parlor. You were quivering like a hunted rabbit. Was there some trouble? Believe me, Averil, I can help—I want to help."

The familiar use of her given name without the formal address sparked anew her anger and fear of him. He seemed entirely too perceptive and she feared inadvertently revealing something to him. Without so much as a word or glance, she turned away and retraced her steps across the sun-baked meadow.

Jacob returned from the warehouse at a quarter to four. The women were not home yet and he shut himself into his study. His hands shook as much from fear as from anger as he smoothed out the paper on his desk and reread the message that had been delivered to him a short time ago at his office.

When it arrived, he had been busy composing a letter to a fellow wine merchant with an invitation to meet with him. It was in Jacob's mind to inquire if the merchant would put up a sum of money with him to outfit a ship for the purpose of importing not only wine but perhaps ammunition and guns as well. Running the Royalist blockade could be especially profitable.

Then Gilbert Woodby had interrupted him to bring in the message some young ragamuffin of the streets had delivered, and with that piece of paper, Jacob's high hopes, like shooting stars, had turned and fizzled in downward flight.

The young delivery boy had scampered away, and there was no way to run him down to learn who had hired him to bring the paper to the warehouse. Throwing away the letter he had been writing, Jacob had left the warehouse to return straight home.

Alone in his study, as he waited for the women to return, he reread the message. The words burned into his mind.

"Let it be known, Mr. Kirkland, we are aware that your niece is in league with the Tottman to return London to the King. Her activities, as well as your own for housing and protecting this traitor, will not go unpunished. *Traitors all*! In the name of God, we will destroy your wickedness!"

By all the saints, by all that was holy—what did this mean? Averil? In league with the Tottman? It was a lie!

But lies held a weight no man could dismiss. Jacob knew the reality of this and it made him shudder with fear. Neighbor harbors a grudge against neighbor and with a few words whispered in the right ear, the wrongly accused man forfeits his property, his wealth, his freedom. Tempers were high, vindictiveness flaring—not even a hundred honest men vouching for him could save the man once the lies began to spread. Jacob had seen it happen all over London!

Heavy-hearted and shaking, he heaved himself from his chair and gazed out the window at the late-afternoon May sky, at the sleepy, quiet day.

Why him? Why him? Whom had he angered? Whom did he know who was capable of harboring such hate and bitterness? And why the blatant accusation that Averil was involved with the Tottman? By all the powers! If there was anything so sure of tainting a man by mere inference, it was that!

The ring of horses' hooves on the cobbles brought his attention around and he peered out the window to see a plain hired coach draw up before the door. Captain Warrender's tall frame emerged from the interior, and then he reached back in to help Mary Geneva alight.

Jacob hurried from his study and down the hall to the main door, pulling it open as the three women of his family, escorted by the captain, approached the entrance.

"Jacob! Did you miss us? I didn't realize you'd be back so soon." Mary Geneva greeted him with a kiss on the cheek, then stood back. "Has something upset you? I'm sorry we're so late." Jacob's dark eyes were almost black, and Mary Geneva faltered. "Would you like to invite Captain Warrender to sup with us?"

"Thank you, madam, but in any event, I must decline." The captain made a small, polite bow.

When he had departed, the others entered the main hall, Mary Geneva chatting to her husband with almost frantic enthusiasm. But Jacob did not hear.

"Averil," he called, as he saw his niece begin to ascend the stairs to her room. "If I might have a word with you."

Averil turned, her eyes round with surprise. The stiff expression in his face frightened her. "Aye, uncle, of course."

"Shall we go into my study?"

Averil's steps were wooden as she crossed the hall. He had never before wished to speak alone with her; she had never even set foot in his study.

Mary Geneva and Lynna watched them enter Jacob's room and close the door. With a last glance at her daughter and a shrug, Mary Geneva continued down the hall toward the kitchen to see if the preparations for the evening meal had begun. But Lynna, once her mother was out of sight, moved to the closed door and tilted her head in an effort to hear what was being said behind the thick panels.

Averil took a seat on a low, bare wood stool while Jacob lit the two candles in their wall sconces. As the light forced the shadows into the far corners, Jacob walked to his desk and stood behind it. It was a solid, ornately carved piece of furniture that dominated the room and was cluttered with papers and ledgers, several broken quill pens, and an empty wine bottle. Behind it were framed maps of England and France, three high shelves that contained only a few books— for Jacob had no time and no interest in reading—and a small gilt clock that ticked away the minutes.

At last Jacob cleared his throat and said, "Really, there is no graceful way to begin. I'd just like to show this to you. It was delivered this afternoon to my warehouse. I know you have had more than your share of troubles, and I don't mean to add to them, but perhaps together we can find a solution to this threat."

He waggled a paper as he spoke, and Averil, growing more apprehensive by the moment, could not contain herself. "Please, uncle. If it is something I should see . . ."

She held out her hand and Jacob came around the desk to give her the paper. He watched as she read the message, saw the small, oval face clench with pain and fear. Her hand dropped into her lap and Jacob bent to slip the paper from her slack fingers.

"I'm sorry, Uncle Jacob," she murmured in a thin voice. "I don't know what to say."

"I know, I know. It is a vile act by vile people. Averil, do you know of anyone, anyone at all, who could have written this?"

Averil looked down at her lap where her hands were clasped together so tightly her fingers were turning red. Who knew she had met the Tottman? Francis Bowers must have recognized her after all. How could she tell Jacob? Even admitting one small fact would mean having to relate the whole story. The Tottman had sworn her to secrecy; she could not betray him. But neither could she lie boldly to her uncle and claim complete ignorance about either the writer of the letter or the contents. Lifting her head, she caught the pain in Jacob's eyes and realized she had delayed too long in answering. He would have expected her to deny it all with immediate protestations.

"You *do* know something about this letter." His voice cracked. "Dear God, Averil—what have you done!"

"I have done nothing treasonable, uncle, believe me! The letter is false—I have never plotted to return London to the King's power!" She started to rise, but with two fast strides, Jacob was in front of her. The incredulous fury in his eyes held her rooted.

"What is the cause for this letter? *Have* you seen the Tottman?"

The room began to tip around her. How could she reply to him? But he was involved now, she told herself remorsefully, and thus had a right to know. She nodded slowly.

"Aye," she murmured. "I have seen the Tottman." She owed him that much.

"My God!" Jacob looked stunned. He ran short fingers through the stringy, straw-colored hair above his forehead. "All right, my girl, let's have all of it." His face hardened. "How did you meet him? When? And why, tell me *why*?"

"I sought out the Tottman with the intention of securing his help to find my father. He was my only hope! You can surely see that? I have done nothing wrong, uncle!"

"How do you know *what* this Tottman is involved in, eh? How do you know what his purpose is? What if he is, in fact, attempting to restore London to Charles?" He clapped his hands together in impotent fury. "How, in heaven's name, did you even track him down? Where did you meet him?"

All of her nerves jumping, Averil answered softly, "At an inn."

"A public inn!" Jacob's voice exploded at her and she winced. "And were you escorted there? Who else in this household has met the Tottman!"

Averil's mouth was dry. The words had to be forced out. "No one. I went masquerading as the boy. We met in a private room, and I'm sure no one could have recognized me."

"You did *what*? Met him in a private room! Masquerading? It's a wonder the soldiers aren't tearing down our door this minute! You've put all of us in danger!" Jacob paced a short line in front of Averil, muttering. His face was contorted and ugly as he looked at her. "What in *hell* were you thinking of! My God, we could all be arrested!"

With sudden, unexpected fury, he struck her across the face and the force threw her to the floor. He stood over her, shaking his fist in unrestrained rage. Averil sat up, touching her burning, bleeding lip. She was shaking with shame and horror, and her eyes blurred from tears of pain. The new pearl-tipped bodkins in her hair had come loose and several tangled strands of hair slid down her cheek. One side of her face throbbed. It felt hot and swollen.

Slowly she pulled herself to her feet and faced her uncle. She wanted to scream at him, hurt him; she wanted to run from the room and hide forever. She did neither. An expressionless mask sifted over her features and her eyes were glassy as she said in a hard voice, "Have you given no thought to the real danger to my father? Is his life not worth a risk?"

Jacob rubbed his chin as he warned her, "Don't put me in this position, Averil! I worry a great deal about you and your father, but my first responsibility is to the safety of my family. That is how it must be and that is how it is! I must ask you to henceforth have no contact with the Tottman. For as long as you are residing within this household, you will conduct yourself in an exemplary manner! You will not see this Tottman again! Do you promise me that?"

"Aye, I promise you that." Her voice was so soft as to be almost inaudible, and it hid the agony that ground her heart into a tight, painful knot. The Tottman was her one hope, and it seemed to her that her father died in that moment.

"And another thing, young woman," Jacob continued. "I want that wretched costume delivered to my hands. I personally intend to see to its removal from this house!"

Averil made no response past a brief acquiescent dipping of her head. She was feeling a curious detachment, as if Jacob stood at the end of a long shadowy tunnel.

He fixed her with a keen look, pulled gently at his lower lip, then clasped his hands behind his back. "Y'know, girl," he began, rocking on his heels. "There's still the matter of the threat in this letter. Now if we could turn over the Tottman—"

The meaning of his words struck her like a blow. She broke in sharply. "Nay, I cannot help you."

Jacob's sparse, straw-colored eyebrows shot up. "You cannot help me?" he repeated. "You cannot help *me*? I'm talking of *your* predicament as well! If we turn the Tottman over to the authorities, 'twill completely negate the accusations against you! And we'll be five hundred pounds the richer!''

But though her uncle threatened to strike her again, Averil would tell him nothing further. In those moments her loyalty to the Tottman grew strong and surpassed her sense of duty to Jacob.

When at last, in disgust, he dismissed her, Averil crept up the stairs to her room. She locked the door to her chamber and crossed through shafts of flickering shadows cast into her room from the flames leaping in the hearth. She stood as near as she dared to the fire, but no warmth touched her. She found no comfort in her thoughts, and though she wanted to cry, she could shed no tears. The barren space within her breast was dry and arid and aching.

CHAPTER
NINE

Though the other members of the household were curious about Averil's split lip when they saw her the following day, neither Averil nor Jacob would say anything about it, or about their discussion. It was not uncommon for Honor to sport a swollen lip or a bruise here and there from Jacob, but he had touched none of the family members until now. Jacob had the rightful authority to so discipline any in his household, but he was always ashamed and embarrassed by the visible signs of his disciplinary measures. What man liked it to be known he was having trouble keeping his family and servants in line?

Jacob turned away Mary Geneva's questions about the reason for the scene with Averil, having no desire to alarm his wife with the knowledge of the letter and its contents. Only Lynna knew what had been said within the room, and she was not about to let anyone know she had been eavesdropping.

On Tuesday morning, three days after the encounter

between Averil and Jacob, Lynna was feeling restless and in need of a bit more excitement than the tense and gloomy atmosphere her home provided. Jacob had already taken their coach for the day, so Lynna begged some coins to hire a vehicle for a few hours, promising to see to some necessary errands. They needed another loaf of sugar, some herring for supper, and another half a yard of black broadcloth from the draper so Mary Geneva could finish Morton's new suit of clothes.

Her mother gave in and Lynna was in high spirits as she and Honor rolled through the streets. She called to the driver to stop here and there as she spied something of interest. Though the day was warm, she wore a cloak and muff, for no woman of quality ever went out without them even on the most scorching summer days.

Alighting at the head of a street of small shops, Lynna told the driver to bring the coach around at the end of the street and wait there for them.

She swung her skirts jauntily as she and Honor sauntered past a meatseller's shop and a book stall, but paused at an appealing array of hair ribbons and adornments at a stall farther down. Idly, Lynna picked through the ribbons, pulling out one and then another to hold up to her hair, viewing the effect in a hand mirror held up by an eager shopgirl.

''Oh, la! That yellow one, ma'am,'' the shopgirl piped encouragingly, ''Just the color of sunshine in yer hair. 'Twould look lovely on ye! And that be the truth, I vow and swear!''

Lynna ignored both the comment and the yellow ribbon. She plowed through the array, seeking something darker. Midnight blue, perhaps? Ever since overhearing her father and Averil, Lynna had been sure that the strange man she had heard with Averil under the window late that night had been the Tottman.

She had never been as afraid of him as that timid goose Cecelia Osgood, but rather had thrilled to the tales of his exploits. Now that Averil had actually seen him, been with

him, touched him, he seemed no longer an illusive shadow
to Lynna, but a real man of muscle and bone and flesh. And
his voice! The whispered voice she had heard excited her.
The merest thought of him now sent a thick, heady pleasure
throbbing in her veins. It made Lynna almost suffocate with
the stifling confines of her daily life. To know the Tottman!
To experience the dangers and excitements and wildness of
that kind of life! How had Averil managed to meet him? By
what manner of conniving had she accomplished that? Not
only was she snaring the captain, but now the Tottman as
well!

Just to think of it was almost more than Lynna could bear
and in a high frustration she hurled down the handful of
ribbons she had been searching through. "A paltry display!"
she exclaimed angrily.

The surprised shopgirl, so sure of a purchase from a well-
dressed, pretty young woman, watched in disappointment
as the two hastened away.

The day had lost a good measure of its brightness for
Lynna, and she grew vexed with the mildness of the shopping
expedition. So it was with a feeling of intense speculation
and interest that, upon hearing her name called by a slow,
male voice, she turned to find Francis Bowers lounging in
a shop doorway.

He was thinner than she remembered and wore a stark black
suit of clothes that emphasized the pallor of his skin. His
hair was brown and wavy, and he had a narrow face that
was high in the forehead and shadowed beneath prominent
cheekbones. His mouth was small, lips fleshy and soft, and
his nose was straight between wide-set, light brown eyes.
Though not as appealing as the captain, Francis Bowers was
still very attractive to her. His position as steward to the Earl
of Armondale made him a distinguished man with a certain
enviable power. Lynna had always thought him a very fine
man and had been in awe of him whenever she had stayed
at Maslin Manor. His presence now created the diversion
she craved.

"Why, Mr. Bowers," she called, smiling coyly. "What are you doing in London?"

He picked his way across the narrow, muddy street to where she stood and made her a small, gallant bow as he said, "What am I doing in London? Before joining the Earl's household I resided in London. Now I've been forced to return here. Maslin Manor has been confiscated—did you know?"

"Aye." She dismissed the comment. "But it is such a pleasure to see you again. Honor and I were just browsing in the shops, taking care of some errands and such like. Tedious business. I do hope you don't have to run off soon?"

"Not a bit." He laughed and there was an eagerness in his look that stirred Lynna. "In fact, I was to have met someone here over an hour ago, but he never arrived. I'm frankly glad now that he didn't. May I offer you good women my services? Escort you on your errands? Or perhaps offer you some refreshment? There's an excellent establishment just down the way."

"What a delightful suggestion!"

Lynna took his arm and as the three strolled along the street, her thoughts were winging madly. She had been in such a temper earlier about her placid existence that this chance encounter with Francis Bowers threw a shock of excitement into her. The surprise of it made her bold and she determined to enjoy herself fully. But then there was Honor, drab little Honor, whose very presence beside her suddenly reminded Lynna of a prison guard. She had to find a way to rid herself of Honor for a while.

When they reached the door to the inn, Lynna turned swiftly to Honor as if a thought had just occurred to her. "We have so little time this morning and there are so many errands!" She faltered and looked prettily confused for a moment, then her face brightened. "You have the list of things we need, don't you? I'd like you to continue with the shopping, Honor. You can take the coach."

"But, ma'am," Honor protested, dropping her voice to

prevent Francis from hearing. "It isn't fittin' for ye to be alone—"

In a moment of pique, Lynna pinched the girl smartly on the arm, then drew her several steps away from Francis, who waited in puzzlement, one hand on the door.

"Do as I say!" she hissed. "And don't you dare breathe a word of this to anyone, d'ye hear! If you do, I'll make your life so unhappy—" She pinched the unfortunate girl again viciously to underscore her meaning.

Honor nodded briskly, wincing.

"And bring the coach back here for me in two hours!"

As Honor hurried away to where the coach was waiting at the end of the street, Lynna walked back to Francis, smiling apologetically for the delay. His eyes held unmistakable elation; he grinned, but said nothing as he held the door for her.

Before entering, she drew on her hood and pulled the edges close about her face. Once inside the crowded, boisterously noisy common room, Lynna leaned toward Francis and murmured, "I really should not be seen alone here with you. If any acquaintance should recognize me and inform my father. . . ." She let her voice trail off with the unspoken implication. Though Jacob had long ago learned to turn a blind eye and a deaf ear to his only daughter and her personal activities, she knew that should she publicly embarrass him he would most likely descend on her with swift fury.

Francis touched her arm. "A private room would be better. Wait for me in the upstairs hall."

When she had ascended the stairs beside the door, he went off in search of the owner to order a room and refreshments. The suite he showed her to some moments later comprised two bright and spacious rooms. The sitting room was furnished with large and comfortable-looking cushioned chairs, several small tables, and a small hearth; from its two windows overlooking the street, a steady stream of noise from coaches, vendors' cries, and music from some distant flute trickled in. The other, connected room held a high canopied bed draped with folds of thick burgundy velvet.

They were expensive rooms and Lynna beamed her delight. From the doorway to the bedroom she looked back at Francis who was breaking the seal off one of the bottles of wine he had brought upstairs with him on a tray. In addition to the wine, the tray held a dish of glazed orange segments and a plate of tiny steaming pastries.

Would he want to kiss her? Should she let him? As she watched him furtively, she toyed with the idea. Perhaps just once . . . and then she would protest in embarrassment that she didn't know what had come over her. It wouldn't do to let him think her kisses were too easily won; she had a reputation to consider. But it was delicious to be contemplating such a thing. Thank goodness a reputation wasn't based on one's thoughts!

She crossed the room and removed her cloak, hood, and muff and carelessly dropped them onto a table. Francis handed her a glass of wine and they sat in opposite chairs as they chatted of inconsequential affairs—the high price of food, the lack of good materials for the making of new gowns, his coach throwing a wheel—and tasted the delicacies he had ordered. The tiny pastries were stuffed with a mixture of artichoke hearts and onions, a delectable combination, and Lynna relaxed as they ate and talked, and began to enjoy herself immensely.

But when every crumb had been consumed, a silence fell between them. Lynna drank her wine self-consciously. Francis took up the wine bottle and drew his chair around to sit beside her.

"Tell me," he said when he had settled himself, "what has become of your cousin and her father? Have you had any word?"

"You don't know? Weren't you there?"

"Nay, the Earl had sent me to London on business and when I returned some two weeks later, the manor bore the

seal of the Crown and there was no one about. When I sought
news in Abingdon, I learned it had been attacked. No one
I questioned seemed to know what had become of his lordship
or Lady Averil.''

Lynna swallowed the last sip of her wine and held out her
glass for more. ''Then allow me to tell you. I know the whole
sad tale.'' She sampled the freshly refilled wine in her glass
and darted another glance at Francis' smooth face. He
watched her from beneath slightly lowered eyelids. ''First
of all, the Earl was taken captive—''

At Francis' quick intake of breath, Lynna nodded eagerly.
''Aye! The Royalists have accused him of some form of
treason—conspiracy against the King and such.''

Francis grunted his disbelief. ''The Earl? Now where did
you hear such a fanciful story as that?''

''Fanciful! You said you'd seen the mark of the Crown
on their door. And it was Averil herself who told me all about
it!''

''Lady Averil? Where is she?''

Under his scrutiny, Lynna lowered her eyes. ''Averil
escaped and made her way here to London.''

''She's living with you?''

Lynna nodded. Absently Francis reached out and fingered
a shining blond curl at the nape of her neck. Lynna shivered,
wondering if it was the wine or his attention that made her
feel so deliciously reckless.

He murmured, ''Has she told you much about that day?
Or anything else?''

''Nay. At least, not much. Why?'' She studied him
cautiously, defensive anger welling up in her. ''*You're* not
in love with her, are you?'' When she heard what she had
said, Lynna could have bitten off her tongue.

Francis squeezed his eyes closed and laughed. ''Oh, my
dear Mrs. Lynna! Nothing could be further from the truth.''
He tipped the wine bottle and drank deeply. A drop of liquid
trickled onto his chin and he wiped it away with his sleeve

before returning his attention to her. Gently he wound the ringlet of her hair around one finger. "She's neither as lively, nor as exciting as you. I was merely"—he shrugged elaborately—"curious, I suppose. I've always been more interested in you."

Lynna's pulse fluttered wildly and she dropped her gaze. I *will* let him kiss me, she thought. She tried then to think of something to say to debase her cousin. How richly rewarding it would be to see him smirk at Averil! They would laugh quietly together, shaking their heads over Averil's faults and failings.

"You know," she said leaning close and looking at him coyly out of the corner of her eyes. "My cousin, highborn though she is, actually dressed herself as a common cottage boy to reach London. You can't believe how grimy and smelly and dirty she was when she arrived! I could hardly bring myself to be in the same room with her."

"Disgusting."

"My mother and father were greatly disappointed with her behavior. Father was especially appalled." Lynna drained her second glass of wine, and the room rocked slightly. She smiled conspiratorily at Francis and he poured her another portion. "And do you know what else she's done?"

"Tell me."

"She's been meeting the Tottman."

"Come now, Lynna! Where did you get such a notion?"

"It's no fabrication!" she insisted and smiled at him over the rim of her glass. She told him of the scene she had overheard one night from the window, and also the details of the conversation between Averil and Jacob in the study. Francis seemed properly stunned and impressed by the tale.

"Have you ever seen the Tottman?" he asked.

"What do you take me for? I'm no traitor like she is."

"Of course not," Francis answered soothingly. "You'd turn him in if you could and be properly praised as a heroine."

"Aye. Aye! That's what I'd do."

Francis' eyes were glowing with a strange light in their brown depths. "I knew you were brave as well as beautiful. Has Averil told you anything about the Tottman? Who he is? What he does? How she met him?"

For a moment, the earlier frustration emerged in Lynna. She thought of the intrigue surrounding the Tottman. How bold and recklessly daring he must be! Her own interlude here with Francis paled. Francis himself seemed now as dull as Newcastle coal compared to the Tottman. Desperate to recapture her initial feelings of excitement with Francis, she set aside her glass and leaned close to him, putting a hand brazenly to the front of his shirt. She looked up at him with imploring eyes. She wanted him to kiss her immediately, to do something shockingly exciting and make her forget the Tottman.

Francis circled her shoulders with his arm and leaned near to kiss the curls over one ear. "Do you know why I'm here in London and not fighting in the war?" he whispered.

"Nay, I don't," she said impatiently. She did not add that she didn't care.

"I'm working for Parliament in a secret capacity."

"Secret?" Now what was this? Her interest perked up and, emboldened by the wine, she leaned her head back against his arm. "Can you tell me about it?"

"I shouldn't." He lowered his head, and as she had hoped, kissed her. It was a light, chaste kiss. Lynna squirmed closer to him when he lifted his head.

"Why can't you tell? You're not worried I'd give you away, are you?"

He laughed in what seemed like relief. "Nay, you're right. I shouldn't have been worried. You wouldn't do anything like that. And I'd like to tell you—you might even be able to help me."

This possibility added a keen edge to Lynna's curiosity. She slid her hand into the hair at the nape of his neck and widened her eyes in feigned surprise. "How could you possibly need *my* help?"

"What tameness do you pretend now, Lynna?" He tightened both arms around her with a sudden passion that rekindled Lynna's exhilaration. "Where is the spirited, bold girl I've dreamed about all these years?" When he kissed her again it was with a feverish insistence and Lynna clung to him as her head grew dizzy. Francis pulled away slightly to look at her, and his features were set. "As an agent for Parliament, it's my mission to find the Tottman."

"Find the Tottman!" Lynna struggled to sit up straight again as the words bolted through her wine-sluggish brain.

"Aye. It's by far the most challenging job yet entrusted to me. Do you know how keen his wits are? But I will succeed, Lynna. I can feel it."

Lynna's eyes flashed her fervor. "How can I help you? What did you mean by that?"

"Can you keep a close eye on your cousin? Follow her and report to me where she goes and who she sees?"

"Is that all?" Lynna almost pushed him away with her impatience.

"But it's vitally important. She could lead you to the Tottman. Haven't you ever been even a little curious about him?"

He had her there. Lynna frowned with concentration as she pictured the scene. An alley somewhere perhaps, dim and shadowed, she wearing a long, sweeping cloak and a vizard and trailing a scurrying Averil. A form would step from the shadows. A tall, exquisitely made man of incredible power and control. He would look over Averil's head and see her, Lynna, and their eyes would meet. He would push Averil aside and stride toward her to learn the identity of this woman who could so challenge him.

Beyond this point she could not decide. Should she be triumphant and laugh as soldiers waiting in the shadows suddenly surrounded him? Or should she surrender and join him, riding away in the night with the Tottman, and leaving a bitterly disappointed Averil behind? She looked again to Francis and caught an unexpected calculating coldness in his gaze. But so suddenly did his expression shift to one of concern that she could almost believe she had been mistaken.

"What is it, Lynna? You're thinking it's too tame for your tastes?"

"Tame or not, it won't work. Have you forgotten I told you my father has forbidden Averil to contact the Tottman?"

"But he cannot forbid the Tottman to contact Averil. And I'll wager that if you are successful at keeping watch over her, you'll find him."

For a moment Lynna was transfixed by the possibilities. He was right, of course. Who could stop the Tottman if he chose to contact Averil? Oh, and she could do as Francis asked! She would be perfect—stealthy, discreet, watchful.

Aloud she said, "Aye, I'll do it! I'll find him!"

There was harsh triumph in his eyes and Lynna looked at him in surprise. He said, "I knew I could count on you."

A note in his voice touched the very core of her being and thrilled her more deeply than anything she had yet experienced. He kissed her again, and within his arms she tensed momentarily, then grasped his shoulders tightly with a strength that surprised him, returning his kiss with a frenzied eagerness.

When Honor returned with the coach at the appointed time, Lynna stood waiting and ready at the window. Francis escorted her to the coach and after handing her in, returned to the room.

He opened the last bottle of wine and dropped wearily into a chair. What a performance! he thought, and toasted himself with the wine bottle. After drinking deeply, he rubbed the back of his neck to ease the tension.

Actually, the plan had been easier to execute than he had anticipated. And he had not expected she would let him bed her, but she had. All in all, a most encouraging morning!

Only one thing plagued him. Who had written that threatening letter to Jacob Kirkland?

CHAPTER
TEN

Averil dug her fingers into the moist spring earth, hooked them around a particularly stubborn weed, and yanked. The stalk came free with its root system intact, and she sat back on her heels to drop it into the basket beside her.

Under the blanket of hot sun she was beginning to perspire. A sheen covered her nose and cheeks and the skin below her collarbones. Her hair, loosely and untidily secured that morning, was bursting from its bodkins and several strands were free and looped over her shoulder.

In the three days since her explosive meeting with Jacob, she had remained closed up in her room. Feeling devoid of any emotion or life, she had moved listlessly through the days. Time had been meaningless. Each moment was disconnected, hanging suspended, isolated, then slipping away to be replaced by the next. Mechanically she went through the rituals of dressing, of combing her hair, of carrying on polite conversation with Honor when she came to light the hearth fire and tidy the chamber. But her heart was locked away tightly. She felt nothing. Jacob had swiftly and devastatingly killed all her hopes of ever resuming her life again at Maslin Manor. Now she had no goals, no hopes, no dreams. . . . Nothing.

Then, that morning after Jacob had departed and Lynna had gone off in a hired coach to do the errands, Mary Geneva had forced herself into Averil's world.

"Come now," she had announced as she marched into the airless, dim room. "You're going to go downstairs and do something useful. So what if Jacob struck you? That's not the end of the world. You act as if nothing like it has ever happened to anyone!"

While Mary Geneva went about tidying the chamber, Averil drifted out to the garden. Her slippered toe had encountered a basket and she knelt beside it and began to fill its emptiness with the weeds. Time was marked by weeds—two weeds, five—until she lost count.

Mary Geneva had braved the direct, brilliant white sun to talk to Averil. She had been disgusted.

"What kind of a lady are you? On your knees in the dirt like that—and wearing one of the gowns I spent so much time and money on. Just look at you!" she had muttered. "On your knees, and getting browner by the second in the sun. You'll look as if you came from some hovel! Your nose will peel—will that make you happy?"

Mary Geneva had waited, but Averil gave no response, no apology. She had not looked at her aunt, but kept her eyes down and picked dirt from beneath a fingernail.

"What has come over you, Averil? Have you no pride?"

At last, Mary Geneva had departed, storming back into the house with her own hands tucked beneath her apron to preserve their whiteness.

Captain Warrender came calling. Mary Geneva thought his presence might shake Averil out of her doldrums, so she pointed out to him the splotch of peacock blue holland barely visible through the bushes in the garden. He walked slowly out into the sunlight and along the pathway.

"Good morrow," he said when he stood just beside the small bent form.

Averil looked up. Nothing mattered to her now, so the sight of the captain and his faintly frowning expression did not stir her. She returned to her work.

He sat on his heels beside her and put his fingers under her chin, turning her face to him. "Lord Almighty," he said in a hushed voice. "What happened to you?"

" 'Tis no concern of yours," she said dully.

With gentle fingers he felt the swollen, bruised edge of her lip. "Who did this?"

There was something about him, about his gentle touch, that made Averil begin to hurt inside, to ache with an untouchable longing and need. She looked down again to the dirt and to the slender green weed she had just ripped up. The ache became scalding, and she shook her head as much to deny this fresh pain as to answer him.

He raised her to her feet and cupped her face, tilting her head up till she looked into his eyes. The probing keenness in his gaze alarmed her. She felt as if he could see straight into her soul, and she held secrets and pain there she could not relinquish and lay bare to him.

"Who did this?" He tried to control his anger. "Was it Jacob?" She flinched slightly and he had his answer. "Why did he hit you?" But she lowered her head and he stepped back, dropping his hands.

"Just look at you," he muttered, grimacing. A bit of weed with dirt clinging to its roots swung from her fingers. He plucked it from her grasp and flung it away, then began to speak in a low, insistent tone. "Do you know, when I first met you I was struck by a rare spirit in you, Averil. You had vitality, loyalty, a strength of purpose. But now I see before me only a faint shadow of the woman I know you to be."

She stared at his wide-spread leather boots, felt his hands grasp her upper arms. "What happened? I told you I could help. Trust me.'' He stroked her arms as he said, "I *care*, Averil. Can you believe that?''

Suddenly, unable to bear the sweetness of his words or the gentle touch of his hands, Averil snatched up her skirts and ran. He was after her immediately.

She felt the sobs of grief welling up into her throat. Her carefully guarded illusions were gone, wraithlike; the reality that was too painfully shocking to face reared itself at her. The people she loved were lost to her forever. Her home was an empty shell she would never walk through again. The life she had known was over. Finished. She had never allowed herself to look beyond the immediate future. Every day of the past two months had been looked at through the frame of her hopes and dreams, in which this time was only temporary, a brief interlude before she and her father returned to the manor and resumed their lives. She had looked to that day with all the passion she possessed, believing she could make it come true if she just wished for it hard enough. Childish dreaming!

She was no longer Lady Averil Maslin, but Averil Kirkland. Her identity as well as her past had been eradicated. She was not allowed to talk of her father. Both were gone. Buried. Dead. Face it. *Face it!* her mind screamed at her.

She had gone no more than a few steps before Camden caught her into his arms. Averil gripped the soft fabric of his doublet as she wept with abandon. Her agony was too great to be stifled any longer. Once the tiniest bit had been released, the mass of it flooded her and she felt as if she were drowning and would never—not this time—return to the surface of that black, roiling river.

Her tears eventually slowed, though the hurt was still as strong. For the moment, she had exhausted herself and she leaned against Camden, limp and drained.

The arms around her were warm and held her securely; the chest beneath her cheek was solid and comforting. As he stroked her hair, the last loose bodkins scattered to the ground. He shifted one arm slightly and put a handkerchief into her hand. She dried her nose and leaned her cheek against his chest again.

His head bent and his lips touched her hair, her brow, her tear-drenched cheek. He cupped her face and turned it up to him, like a blossom to the sun. Her eyes were closed, the black lashes resting on her cheeks were spiky with tears. His mouth moved over the drawn, pale side of her face then shifted to her lips. He was gentle, careful of the tender bruise Jacob had inflicted. She felt his mouth brush hers, kiss the upper lip, then her lower lip, which quivered slightly under the butterfly stroking of his lips.

Her need for tenderness, for someone to care, was too keen to be blunted by her previous anger with him and the fear she had known. He had held her while she wept and had shown neither embarrassment nor impatience. There was a new sensation blooming within her heart; it ached, yet was not a hurt. It was the sweetly painful ache of feeling loved.

His head lifted and he gazed at her gravely, his strong, warm hands stroking her face and slender neck, and he kissed her again with infinite care. How kind he is, she thought. In wonder she reached up hesitantly, between his arms, and touched his face.

When he raised his head to look at her, her fingertips slid along his hard jaw. His face was shadowed by the wide black brim of his hat, but the grey eyes glimmered in surprise. As her fingers moved over his mouth, his gaze softened.

His arms curved around her and drew her into an urgent embrace. Against the sun-warmed hair beside her face, he muttered, ''Ah, that I could love you as I want!''

Trembling, Averil stood on tiptoe within his arms. Taking his face between her hands, she pulled him down to her. He kissed her with a hunger, tightening his arms around her till she grew breathless.

Though at first her bruised lip stung, that soon fled before the yearning pleasure that filled her and warmed her. She moaned softly under the force of that pleasure. Mistaking t for an exclamation of pain, he broke off his kiss, though his mouth lingered lightly on hers. His breath was warm in her mouth.

"Why, Captain Warrender!" The shrill voice was like a knife cleaving the air between them.

Averil jerked away in horror. Her eyes were wild, her face crumpled. Picking up her skirts, she ran for the house.

Lynna stood on the path. She had seen the two locked in an intimate embrace and had witnessed the captain's kiss. The sight had ignited a rage in her so forceful she had very nearly run shrieking to claw them apart. As Averil rushed past, Lynna glared furiously at her. Then she carefully composed her features before facing the captain once more. It was all she could do to keep her manner calm. She tried a sweet smile, pretending she had seen nothing.

"What a surprise to find you'd come calling. I do hope you'll stay and take dinner with us. We haven't thanked you properly yet for the delightful picnic." If she could just get him to spend a little time with *her*, she was sure she could wipe any thought of Averil from his mind. The brazen little slut! Kissing him right there in the garden!

Camden looked at her with frank annoyance. "Thank you, nay," he said, casting a glance to the door through which Averil had disappeared. "I have other appointments to keep."

Lynna trailed him to the street, hoping to convince him to change his mind, but he was preoccupied and ignored her. When he departed, she returned to the house in disappointment.

The setting sun was shedding a rosy glow over the streets and shops and church spires of London when Camden bid his third and final good-bye to the Osgoods.

Percival had remained in the dining room to finish the last of the spiced fruit pie that topped the extravagant supper, while Esther and Cecelia saw Camden to the door. Amid their good-byes and requests for him to join them again, he kissed each woman's hand. Esther had been absurdly obvious

in her intention to bring her daughter to his eye, and Cecelia
had been blushing and acquiescent throughout his visit.
Though pretty enough, Cecelia Osgood was not to his taste,
and he experienced a good measure of relief when he had
at last extricated himself from their company and turned his
steps toward the wharf.

As he walked, he settled his cloak over his shoulders and
shoved his hat far back on his head. His stride was long and
purposeful as he made his way through the dusky rose
twilight.

At the street corner, another man caught up to him and
fell into step. They walked together in silence for a minute.

"You know," said the newcomer, "I have yet to determine
your purpose here in London."

The captain looked at his companion. "I thought I'd already
made it clear to you, Francis."

Francis Bowers answered angrily, "I don't want your
help! I told you before, I don't need any help finding the
Tottman."

"Suit yourself." The captain shrugged.

A linkboy on the next corner tried to stop them. "Would
you two good men be needin' a light?" he piped, waving
his torch for them. "Tuppence an 'our."

The captain shook his head and tossed the small boy a coin.
They were in front of a well-lit tavern, the Rose and Holly
and he turned to Francis. "A pot of huffcap?" he suggested
lightly.

Francis nodded his head, the wavy brown hair swinging.
"You're buying, of course. You can afford it."

"Of course."

They entered the noisy room and the captain steered them
away from the common table to a smaller one near the low-
burning hearth. As Camden took a seat, Francis sought out
the tavern maid, a young, black-eyed girl who was bringing
in a tray of mugs from the kitchen.

"Well now, Kat, my sweetheart, how 'bout some ale for
me and my friend there. And bring a couple of pipes as well."

He tried to pat her rounded backside, but she sidestepped adroitly.

"Kat's the daughter of the owner," Francis explained as he rejoined Camden. They watched her swing between the tables and deftly avoid any number of similarly attempted contacts from other patrons. "Half the customers here come just to see her. She's the only thing now that keeps this place in business."

When Kat placed the ale and two long-stemmed pipes on the table, she smiled secretively to Camden and murmured, "Been a long time. Didn't think you'd ever come back. Thought mayhap the King's men had sunk your ship, or the press gangs had caught you." She touched his arm with a plump, pink hand. "You've the muscle they're looking for."

He winked at her and patted the hand on his arm. "They'll never catch me, Kat. Don't you know that?"

"Aye," she murmured, her black eyes softening.

"How's your father?"

Her eyes dulled slightly. "He takes longer t' get out of the bed in the mornings, his cough's so bad. Those herbs you brought him seemed t' help a mite, though."

"I'll get some more for him next time."

Kat smiled again, then leaned down and kissed his firm mouth. When she straightened, they were both laughing.

As she turned to see to her duties, Francis Bowers leaned back and laughed until his eyes watered. At last he pulled out a handkerchief, dabbed his eyes, and shook his head wonderingly.

"I should have known you'd have charmed her as well. As God's my life, you're a rogue! You would know just how to get in sweet with good little Kat—herbs for her ailing father. And she's generous with her gratitude, I'll wager!"

Camden grinned as he pulled out his pouch of tobacco and began filling one of the pipes. "Did you learn anything, Francis?" he remarked lightly.

Francis drank a good portion of his ale and held out one hand in an unspoken request for Camden to share his tobacco.

The pouch was tossed to him and he filled the other pipe for himself. As the blue, trailing smoke mingled over their heads, he said, "So aside from dallying with dear Kat, you're also back in London to see to the same business I'm pursuing. Want to catch yourself a five hundred pound reward, eh?"

"It's a pretty figure, isn't it?" The captain showed his teeth in a brief smile, then was serious. "But there are other reasons as well."

"Aye, so I hear, Captain," he answered, stressing the title oddly. "Trading is bringing a good profit for you, isn't it?"

"War has definite advantages, I must admit. Incidentally I paid a call today on Goodman Osgood and his family," he said conversationally. "He's a clerk for Parliament and has never heard of you. If you're not working for one of the Committees, who *are* you dealing with?"

"Who said I was working with anyone at all?"

"I know you well enough, Francis, and you've never been inventive enough to operate alone."

Though Francis Bowers' knuckles showed white as he gripped the bowl of his pipe, he gave no other indication that he was affected by the slur. When he spoke, his words were measured and delivered with careful precision. "I've been following you since last week after we encountered each other again. You seem to be insinuating yourself into the Kirkland household. Business deals with Mr. Kirkland that have not been particularly profitable for you, a supper party, a picnic for the women. I find it unusually interesting." He raised his mug to his lips and watched his companion over the rim as he drank.

The captain shrugged. "Why should that concern you?" In an elaborate gesture, he snapped his fingers as if he had just recalled something. "Lady Averil Maslin, the daughter of your former employer. Surely you're not jealous, Francis? Come now, you'd never stand a chance of winning the lady's affections."

This second jibe struck a sensitive chord in Francis, but

he covered his discomposure with a tight smile. "Are my chances any worse than your own?"

"Most definitely. I happen to know something of your record of employ at Maslin Manor, and it seems the Earl was about to dismiss you. Something about fraudulant accounts."

The other man's face paled visibly in the firelight, his cheeks sucked in, and he demanded rigidly, "Where did you hear that lie?"

"From your mother," Camden replied easily. "Dear Mum loves her buttered ale, and I took her a packet of spices for her brew."

"Lord, but you're a devious son-of-a-bitch," Francis remarked softly.

Camden grew solemn. "She's getting on in years, Francis. You shouldn't leave her alone as often as you do."

"She's no concern of yours! Stay away from her!" Francis swilled the last of his ale and banged the tankard on the surface of the table. "Kat!" he called to the serving girl chatting with a customer at the main table. When she sauntered near with eyebrows raised questioningly, he gave her a weak grin.

"How 'bout another tankard, sweetheart? And be quick with it, eh?" He gave her a fond pat. She ignored him and turned her bright black eyes to Camden inquiringly, but he shook his head.

When she set a brimming mug before him, Francis took a hearty swallow. Fortified, he replaced the stem of the pipe in his mouth and worked it with his small, fleshy lips as he studied the captain. Camden was staring out at the twilight through the window above a nearby table. He seemed lost in thought. Francis leaned over the table and said softly in amazement, "*You* wrote that letter to Jacob Kirkland, didn't you?"

Surprised, Camden looked to his companion. He had been puzzling over Averil's strange behavior and the reason for

Jacob's apparent anger with her, but at the mention of a letter, his curiosity was aroused. Was there a connection? "So what does it have to do with you?"

Francis snorted. "It was a stupid move! You've slit your own nose."

"How is that, do you figure?"

Francis' lips tightened in another smirk. "You thought to get to the Tottman through the lady, didn't you? And now, as a result of your rashness, Jacob Kirkland has forbidden Averil to have anything further to do with the blackguard."

At the quicksilver flash of anger in Camden's narrowed eyes, Francis shook his head. "Why did you do it? Was it spite? Jealousy? You've never learned to control your temper, have you?"

Camden put down his pipe and rubbed his jaw. "How did you learn about the letter?"

"I have my means," Francis answered vaguely, "and a good sight more patience."

"Let me see. . . . Three people in the household, not counting Lady Averil. Ah, but I'm forgetting the maid. That's more your style, isn't it?"

Francis broke in sharply. "Why discount the lady? She's troubled, unhappy, lonely. A bit of sympathy goes a long way with her."

The captain shook his head, grinning and relaxed. But Francis pressed on, nettled by a long history of always being a step behind his companion. "Why do you consider it impossible for Averil to trust me? After all, I'm someone from her past, someone who was a member of her household, close to her and to her father. She's so lonely now, she loves to reminisce. Or haven't you been able to sneak that close to her yet?"

Camden grunted in disbelief. "You mean she's willing to discount your ignominious conduct regarding her father's accounts? From what I know of her, I don't think she'd forgive you so easily."

But even as he spoke the denial, Camden was pricked by

doubts. He had seen for himself that Averil's defenses were gone. She was vulnerable and entirely too susceptible right now. Had Francis discovered that fact and made use of it? He felt a quick lick of fear.

"She never knew about that. Not an inkling!" Francis crowed with his triumph as he saw the surprise in Camden's eyes. "So there you have it, my friend. You'll not have a leg to stand on when I'm finished with the Kirklands—and our dear Lady Averil." He leaned back and a smile pulled at his face. "You were always a man for a wager—care to wager now? A hundred pounds to the one who manages to catch and hand over the Tottman?"

Camden smiled unpleasantly. "I hope you can afford it."

CHAPTER
ELEVEN

"**B**y all the saints!" Jacob exploded. He stared around in awestruck disbelief. His cheeks were mottled with red and white splashes, the red stretching until the blood filled his face. He raised his clenched fist high. "Damn and blast!"

Beside him Gilbert Woodby looked ashen. "I still can't believe it myself."

"Who was supposed to be on watch through the night?" Jacob demanded, fury choking his voice.

"Old Tim, sir."

"Where is he? I want to talk to him!"

Jacob followed his foreman from the doorway through the splintered, reeking wreckage of the main floor of the warehouse. They splashed ankle deep in wine—burgundy, claret, canary—all run together and raising an overpowering sour stink. The horror of it was just beginning to seep into Jacob's stunned brain. Someone had come in the night and hacked apart the barrels, spilling his wine, his profits, the very blood of his business on the dusty warehouse floor. Not a single barrel or puncheon had been spared. Whoever had done this had been methodical, as well as thorough. This was no simple act of anger or vandalism, but a coldly thought-out maneuver to ruin him.

Who had done it? Why?

His mind faltered as he recalled the anonymous, threatening letter he had received a few days previously. The last line seared across his mind: "We will destroy your wickedness!" He stood still in shocked incredulity. Ahead, Gilbert Woodby paused and glanced back at his employer uncertainly.

Jacob looked around at the floating, maimed barrels; the splinters of wood and debris; the slowly rippling lake of dark wine that filled the warehouse and lapped softly at the base of the walls; at his morbidly excited employees milling in doorways and on the stairs. So this was it—the move to destroy his "wickedness" for housing Averil.

Something bumped his ankle and he looked down to see a large, drowned, grey-black rat floating around his feet. With a roar of fright and anger, he kicked it out of his way and followed his foreman.

Old Tim was sitting on the stairs leading to Jacob's office. Three men were bunched around him, one bandaging a split and bleeding lump on the rounded back portion of Tim's skull. His shirt collar was soaked with blood, and he looked white and tired as he watched Jacob ascend the bottom steps toward him.

Jacob knew the man for as honest a laborer as he had, and he questioned sorrowfully, "What happened, Old Tim? Can you tell me anything?"

Old Tim looked back from eyes filled with mortification. "Don't know," he said at last, wincing as the friend bandaging his head finished and tied off the ends of the cloth. Already fresh blood was staining the bandage. "I was just finishing me second round of the warehouse, checking the doors and windows, just like ye want it done . . . it were 'bout three in the morning then . . . everything tight, it were. Then two o' the windows—there 'n' there," he said, pointing a shaking finger to two shattered windows in the north wall, "were broke in. Rocks, I think. Afore I could jump, they was in and comin' at me. Had axes and sticks, they did."

"Who was it?"

"Wish I could tell ye, Mr. Kirkland. But I 'ad just me one rushlight. Only saw a couple o' them—mean sorts. One o' them must o' snuck up behind and fetched me a good 'un on the head. I never seen 'im coming and 'at's God's truth. Next I knows I'm locked in yer office upstairs an' all's quiet down 'ere."

"All right. Thanks, Tim. You couldn't have done anything more. Now I want you to take yourself on home and rest. There's no need to come back here for a few days at least." Jacob straightened. "The rest of you"—he turned and looked at the main floor of the warehouse, and a shadow of anger darkened his face—"start bailing the place out."

As the milling employees set to work with leather buckets, Jacob went past Old Tim and on into his office. He lit a fresh candle and looked around. His desk was generally littered wildly with papers and notes, but he always knew where everything was and could readily find his place again in the confused jumble whenever something interrupted him at work. So he could tell at a glance that nothing had been disturbed.

He stood in the center of his office, momentarily at a loss as to how to proceed. Like a stupefied bull, he shook his head to clear it of the nauseating odor that clogged his brain. He looked at his desk and wondered if he should set himself to work. But, oh dear God, what was the point? He had all of eternity now to count his losses.

Who could possibly hate him so much to do this kind of premeditated evil? If he could just find out and put a stop to it! Nothing he did to rebuild his business would be safe until that first step was accomplished.

Rebuild? His eyes jerked about blindly as he envisioned what lay before him. To start all over again. He had some money with his goldsmith and some notes due him from customers who were paying on credit. But when would the next ship with wine in its hold reach London? It could be months, for all he knew. In the meantime, with no money coming in and overhead to pay, how much of a wine cargo could he afford to purchase? It was a mean, competitive business these days. He would be reduced to bidding on the leftovers, the sourest of the lot, after the other, more prosperous merchants took their shares. And they would take his customers too. Why had he not put his money into land!

Dismally, he dropped into his chair. His toes were numb when he wiggled them inside his wine-soaked shoes. Suddenly, he wanted to be away from there, far away from the smell of disaster and defeat. Somewhere warm and dry and smelling of love.

He still wore his cloak and hat, and he rose quickly to yank open the office door. Below on the main floor, the men had formed lines and were passing buckets of wine out to be dumped into the river. The debris was settling. There were mangled barrels, chunks of stained wood, splinters big and small, tiny glittering shards of window glass, bits of paper, spiders, insects, several dead rats, some empty bottles, all floating on the dark liquid.

Outside, wispy cirrus clouds high overhead laced a blue, sun-washed sky. It was a buoyantly cheerful day that seemed to mock him in his defeat. The coach was waiting beside the warehouse, and Jacob looked around for what establishment Morton might be found in. He had taken no more than three steps toward one of the nearby taverns when he was hailed and he turned to see Captain Warrender approaching, boots barking on the wooden wharf. A look of consternation filled the captain's face.

"What the devil has happened here?" He gestured to the line of men passing buckets out of the warehouse.

"It's too detailed a story to go into now, Captain Warrender." Jacob waved him away, distraught and beginning to feel sick in the pit of his stomach. He was eager to return home where he could think more clearly in his study. "Vandals, vandals," he muttered. "Good day to you, Captain."

The captain caught his arm. "I was just on my way to see you because of a note I've received. Perhaps you and I should have a talk."

Jacob was on the verge of lashing out verbally when his sluggish, preoccupied brain caught the severe urgency in the other man's face and tone of voice.

"It must be quick, Captain. I've many things to see to this day." Jacob paused. "Better yet, come along with me. We can discuss whatever it is in my study at home. Would that be satisfactory?"

"Very. Lead on."

With the captain at his heels, Jacob found Morton in the second establishment he searched through, and they were promptly ensconced in the coach and on their way. Aside from an occasional comment, both men were silent. Sunlight through the open windows splashed on their laps.

The house was silent when they arrived, and the two men saw none of the family members as they went directly into Jacob's study. Jacob took a seat behind his wide, littered desk while the captain pulled up a straight-backed chair.

Without formality, Camden came directly to the point. He extracted a slip of torn paper from inside his doublet and flattened it on the desktop. Amazement was plain in his voice and features as he said, "I've received a warning letter, and it mentions you, Mr. Kirkland."

Jacob's sudden stare was filled with horror. He snatched the paper and held it gingerly as he read. The message made no mention of Averil or the Tottman, but warned Captain Warrender that Jacob was a traitor to Parliament and advised him to have no further dealings with the merchant. It was unsigned.

He tossed the paper back on the desk. "This is preposterous! It's a lie, Captain Warrender. Someone is trying to ruin me.'' He leaned forward. ''They vandalized my property during the night. Split open every last barrel of wine I had in there! Do you know what that will do to me?'' With the end of his right forefinger, he flicked the edge of the paper Captain Warrender had just shown him. ''Now this. No doubt other shipowners and captains have received similar messages, all designed to rob me of an opportunity to restock my warehouse!'' His voice grew reluctantly pleading. ''Captain Warrender, I hope you don't believe the charge of traitor made against me.''

''Who would have reason to injure you? For what purpose?''

''If I only knew! Whoever they are, they're cowards! Digging up filth—''

Camden interrupted. ''Did you receive such a letter yourself?''

''Aye.'' Jacob sighed and stroked his forehead with a shaking hand. ''Several days ago it was delivered to my office.''

''Do you still have it? I'd like to see it.''

Though his weakened spirit struggled, Jacob at last decided to oblige the other man. He would have need of all the help he could muster. He unlocked the desk drawer that contained the letter and quickly passed it across to the captain.

Camden scanned the message, laid it alongside the letter he had brought, and studied them both. ''The handwriting is the same,'' he commented. Looking up, he asked, ''Your niece knows about this letter?''

''Aye,'' Jacob said uneasily.

''Your wife? Your daughter?''

''Nay, they know nothing. Only Averil. I had to confront her with the letter, you understand. If she had been putting my family in jeopardy by any foolishness, I wanted to know.''

''Have you, yourself, told anyone else about this letter?''

''Only you,'' Jacob said, and added with harsh bitterness,

"It's not something I take pride in."

The frown that creased Camden's forehead caused Jacob a good measure of alarm. But Camden was remembering a recent conversation with Francis Bowers. The fact that no one else in the family knew of the letter proved Francis' insinuation that Averil had been the one to tell him of it. His frown deepened.

"And what did your niece say when you showed it to her?"

Jacob cleared his throat. "She has not been involved in any treasonous activities, I assure you."

"Is there any truth in these accusations?" Camden's features grew hard, his eyes speculative. "*Is* your niece involved with the Tottman in any capacity?"

Jacob could feel the condemnation and worried that the captain would turn on him now. He felt his chest grow hot and wet with perspiration. He shook his head, saying adamantly, "Nay, none. It's all lies. All of it, just as I told you."

Camden's nostrils quivered with the stale, sweating stink of Jacob's unmasked fear. He knew Jacob was lying—and he understood the implications. Averil had to have admitted to knowing the Tottman; for what other reason would Jacob so have lost his temper with her? And Averil had shared this knowledge with Francis Bowers.

Camden chuckled absently and without humor. Rising, he strolled to the window. He stood washed in sunlight; sunlight drenched the cobbled street and gleamed off the helmets of two soldiers trotting past on horseback.

He spoke thoughtfully, without turning around. "I take it you have no idea who sent the letter?"

"None!" Jacob exclaimed. "Not even the whiff of a clue!"

Camden walked back to his chair and sat. He needed time to think. "Do you have a pipe, by chance?"

Jacob rummaged through another drawer and pulled one out to offer his guest. "I'm frankly at a loss now, Captain. I don't know what more I can do to put a stop to this! I'm near ruined now."

Camden accepted the pipe and filled it from a leather pouch he drew from his doublet. Using Jacob's tinder box, he struck a spark to a blackened straw he found on the desk and lit the tobacco.

"There is something more you can do," he said, cradling the pipe bowl gently between his thumb and first finger. Smoke sifted between his lips and rose, veiling his features. He was frowning in thought. "Whoever is behind all this is harboring a grudge against your niece. The accusations in the letter are very specifically pointing to her. As long as she resides in your house, you, as head of the household, are held responsible for what she does—or is accused of doing."

"Blast it, man, are you suggesting I turn her out? There is nowhere else for the child to—"

"Send her back to her home in Reading. Surely your brother would understand, considering the circumstances."

"That's impossible!"

"Why?"

Jacob's face grew mottled and he stuttered ineffectually for a moment. "Because my brother and his wife have left Reading and I don't know precisely where they are now. That's why."

"Then perhaps you should see her married off, and without delay. You have to remove her from your household or face total ruin."

Jacob realized Captain Warrender had hit the hard truth with his statement, and there was more truth in it than he suspected the captain would ever know. Prince Rupert had already captured William Maslin and proclaimed Averil a traitor as well. Should the King's army prove victorious, Jacob and his family could be imprisoned as conspirators against the Crown for harboring Averil. On the other hand, Averil's name had been linked with the Tottman as a conspirator against Parliament. Should the forces of Parliament succeed in this war, he and his family would suffer the same fate. She was considered a traitor to each side and

Jacob would be damned either way this war turned out. He shoved his fingers into his hair and propped his elbow on the table, leaning his head wearily into his palm.

Camden said, "I didn't realize this suggestion would cause you so much difficulty. I was merely offering a reasonable solution to your dilemma."

Jacob looked up and smiled wanly. "Unfortunately, it's an impossible suggestion. The girl has no dowry and I'm in no position now to offer any."

"But if she did have a dowry, you'd consider it a plausible solution?"

"Aye," Jacob answered. The entire idea was merely hypothetical, but there had to be *some* means of removing Averil from his household. Saving his family and his business demanded that he do so. He drummed his fingers on the desk, taking no notice of the captain's leisurely watchful attention. By God, he'd *have* to marry her off—there was no alternative!

"Aye!" he cried again, and this time with vehemence. "I'd marry her to the first decent soul who'd take her." He spread his hands in mute appeal. "But tell me, where am I to find a dowry?"

"I think we can work it out," the captain answered flatly. "And I'll marry her."

Jacob was taken aback and stared in disbelief at his visitor. "You're entirely serious, aren't you? What of the dowry?"

Camden removed the pipe from his mouth and leaned over to knock the ash from the bowl into a waste basket beside the desk. As he straightened he said, "It's been in my mind, Mr. Kirkland, that though blockade running now is lucrative, when the war ends, I'll be competing with every half-baked shipowner and merchantman on both sides of the ocean. Frankly, I can't see that it'll be that profitable for me. Unless, of course, I could strike a bargain with someone such as yourself and be assured of a ready market."

Jacob's brows knit. "I'm not sure I understand you correctly, Captain. Are you looking for financial backing for your voyages?"

"Nay, not in those terms, nor am I seeking a partner. But I need a contact in London for the disposal of whatever cargoes I bring in. You possess a goodly knowledge of the London market not only for wine, but for other commodities as well, am I right?"

"It's true that at one time I dabbled in the cloth trade, and I do have some connections still in the cloth market at Blackwell Hall."

"Spices? Cloves, raisins and such? How about tobacco?"

"It's possible. But now what exactly are you suggesting?"

Camden chose to ignore the question. "The war has created a greedy market for guns, powder, shot, swords and the like. It's a fast profit for anyone dealing in such commodities. Have you ever considered munitions dealing?"

Jacob's recent plans in that direction returned afresh to his mind and he narrowed his eyes as he answered, "Not only a fast profit as you say, but a guaranteed one if Parliament can afford it. Are you seriously contemplating this course?"

"Aye. I've a number of contacts who might be persuaded to supply us with munitions for a fair price. If you put up whatever capital you can manage for the first shipment, I'll supply the remainder of the necessary funds. Profit would be split along the same percentage lines. I estimate two or three such shipments would help restore your financial status. Beyond that it's clear profit, and you'll have your business restored as well."

"I don't doubt it. It's a generous offer you make. Tell me, how does this relate to my niece and her dowry?"

"It's this: I take over the responsibility for her and you in turn agree to purchase and market whatever cargo the *Indomitable* brings in after this war for a specified period of time—two years, three—we can discuss the time element. I would guarantee in writing a fair price for the cargoes based on whatever standards we can agree upon in the contract. The munitions dealings now would put you in a position financially to accomplish this."

Jacob tugged thoughtfully at his lower lip. "Whatever cargo you bring in?" he repeated as a frown gathered his brows together. "This might prove touchy. Who knows what trading monopolies may be granted in future?"

"I would be careful of the cargoes I shipped."

Though Jacob's eyes had taken on a glimmer of excitement, he was as yet unconvinced. "This is an incredible stroke of good fortune for me, Captain. Provided, of course, we can agree on the exact terms of the contract." He shook his head. "I hope you know what you're doing in agreeing to marry my niece."

Camden laughed briefly. "Whoever is responsible for the damage to your stock may well turn on me after the marriage."

"And I may suffer retribution still for my business arrangement with you."

"Do you judge your present situation as better?"

"Nay, nay—of course not."

"Shall we call it a bargain then, Mr. Kirkland?"

For a long time, Jacob stared ahead, silent, lost in his thoughts. The more he listened to the captain, the more plausible the entire scheme sounded. The man did not know of Averil's father's arrest—how could he? So he did not realize the full ramifications of this decision to marry Averil. Jacob was not about to enlighten him now and possibly see this whole plan collapse. The captain would eventually learn her true identity—after the marriage—but by then the deed would be done and he could not undo it.

And as for Averil, she was without even a penny's worth of dowry. This was her only chance as far as Jacob could tell. Otherwise, God forbid, she would be dependent on him for the rest of her life. And with the brand of traitor on her from every side, the sooner he removed her from his household, the better.

Jacob's mouth turned down at the corners as he observed, "She'll have to give her consent to the marriage, for I'm not her legal guardian and cannot force it. This may prove troublesome—she's not exactly enamored of you, Captain.''

''Aye,'' the captain nodded somberly. ''I've thought of that, but I think I could persuade—''

''Nay!'' Jacob held up a hand. ''I'll talk to her, Captain. I can handle this to our satisfaction.''

''Do you intend to beat her into submission?'' The captain's voice was hard with sarcasm and Jacob was momentarily taken aback. ''I saw her face, and it bears the results of a recent encounter between the two of you, doesn't it? I don't care to take a bruised and disfigured bride to the altar, Mr. Kirkland. She'll be my wife, and I don't want her spirit broken. If you think you'll not be able to restrain yourself, then let me talk to her. I've never struck a woman.''

Jacob's face flamed with embarrassment. ''You're quick with accusations when you don't even know the half of it, sir.''

''What don't I know?''

Blustering for a moment to cover his raw unease, Jacob's face grew even redder. He was not about to admit to Averil's connection with the Tottman now. ''Her character. Aye, her character! You don't know her as I do.''

''I'll have time to find out, won't I? Now when do you expect to discuss this with her?''

''As soon as I can, though it may take some time.''

''After Averil gives her consent, we can draw up the contract. My business in London is concluded for the present and I'll be sailing as soon as this matter has been arranged. I expect to be gone a month. That leaves ample time for the calling of the banns, and we can hold the marriage ceremony immediately after my return. And I, in the meantime, can secure the first shipment of guns. An acquaintance in Amsterdam is awaiting my decision—he already broached this same subject with me during my last voyage there. Time is therefore of the essence.''

Jacob nodded. ''In light of your plans, I'll have her answer by the morrow.''

"Good. I'll await your visit then. Shall we say, one of the clock? We can draw up the contract posthaste. By the beginning of next week I should be under sail, and we shall be in business, Mr. Kirkland.''

To Jacob's way of thinking, this called for a toast, and he poured them each a glassful of wine from a supply he kept in his office for his own use. He had already forgotten his damaged wine barrels and his earlier black mood. The two men congratulated each other.

Jacob drank his wine quickly and greedily. He knew he would need this fortification, for in the next few hours he would have to confront Averil and placate his wife.

CHAPTER
TWELVE

"It's for your own good," Jacob repeated, stoically. "You can surely see that." He perched on the edge of a stool he had drawn up before Averil in her chamber.

She was seated primly in a chair beside the window, with mid-afternoon's long streamers of light lying across her waist and arms. When he had announced that Captain Warrender had that morning asked for her hand in marriage, she had shaken her head in refusal. But he persisted, as he knew he must. There was too much at stake to give in to her stubborn pride and to what he was sure were girlish qualms.

Jacob continued nervously, "You're an intelligent girl. You can understand the situation. Without a dowry you'd spend the rest of your days here and what kind of a future is that for you?"

Averil shook her head in confusion. There was some missing element here in Jacob's argument. "You're saying I have no dowry, but then what is Captain Warrender receiving? Is he willing to accept me without it?"

Aware suddenly of a new path to her acquiescence, Jacob eyed her shrewdly. He insisted, "I'm not paying him a farthing for dowry! Does that satisfy you?"

"I find it hard to believe he would do something without making a profit by it."

"When was the last time you gazed upon your own reflection?" Jacob countered gruffly. "Can you not believe you're a lovely thing to look upon? Many a man would give his right arm to claim you, girl! Captain Warrender's a fine specimen of a man and I'll warrant you he's fully as susceptible as any man where love is concerned."

"Love?" she repeated.

Jacob pressed on, following this line of attack with fervor. "Aye! Why do you believe it impossible that he could love you? I realize 'tis sudden, Averil. But his offer of marriage is no less sincere. What do you answer him?"

"It's *too* sudden," Averil murmured. "Please don't press me."

"Don't be a fool, Averil!"

When she remained stubbornly silent, Jacob pursed his lips to stifle his anger. He would not leave this room until she agreed to the marriage, he vowed to himself. Damn if she wasn't an obstinate, prickly girl!

"Now look here!" Jacob began, propping his weight on hands spread over flaccid thighs. "There's been nothing but trouble for me since you arrived. You've drained my patience as well as my purse." He pointed his finger at her accusingly. "Because of your stupidity in meddling with the Tottman, my warehouse was destroyed last night. Every barrel ruined! *I've* been ruined!"

Averil's eyes flew wide, her mouth formed a small O of dismay. "Uncle Jacob, how dreadful—I had no idea! I'm so sorry!"

"*Sorry!*" Jacob shouted. "Sorry won't put my wine back in its barrels, or free me from fear of greater retribution to come!"

Averil thought of Francis Bowers sneaking into her uncle's warehouse and venting his hatred on the contents. Then the image of the two men who had been watching the house the morning of the captain's picnic sprang to her mind. Were they responsible? They had been waiting and watching. For what? For whom? In her mind she was surrounded by eyes, malevolent eyes, that knew who she was and condemned her for it.

She pressed her hands to her mouth as a sob broke free. "Oh, Uncle Jacob," she gasped. "I'm so frightened!"

"As well you should be! You're an omen as evil as the devil himself. I give you two choices, so listen well, Averil. Either you marry the captain quickly and respectfully, or you find another roof under which to shelter yourself. My home is henceforth closed to you!"

Averil paled. From the green depths of her eyes a murky, haunted shadow spread.

Rising from his seat, Jacob turned away with a scowl on his face. He had never intended to deliver such an ultimatum; the words had seem to spring from him of their own accord and he cursed his lack of control. Damn! But she had forced him to it by her obstinacy.

"I'll give you an hour," he said at last. "Then I'll return to hear your answer. Consider your choices well, Averil."

When he let himself out of the room, Averil rose and threw herself across her bed. Wearily she rolled to her back and flung one arm over her eyes to ward off the intense late sun that had crept across her bed.

One hour, she thought dully.

She slid off the side of the bed, pushed open the window, and leaned out through the casement. The street to her right teemed with activity—horses clopped past; a splintered grey wagon filled with firewood made its way past the house; a housewife in a black shawl and black, wide-brimmed hat led a young girl by the hand; a peddler with needles and threads for sale called his wares as he trod the cobbled street. The

mingled odor of animal sweat and hot cobblestones was thick
on the air.

A warm breath of wind stirred the curls over her forehead
and the thought came to her with a start that once out of
Jacob's house she was no longer bound by her promise to
him concerning the Tottman. She would be free again to
pursue the search for her father. In the warm afternoon air,
Averil's cheeks grew flushed with renewed fervor. All was
not lost—yet. There was still hope for her and her father.

What was she to do, though? Should she marry Captain
Warrender or go elsewhere? Where? Would Sir John be
willing to help her? But what if Sir John, in turn, received
a letter akin to the one sent to Jacob? Not only would he
learn that she had virtually lied to him concerning the
Tottman, but he might suffer retribution as Jacob had.

Through the confusion of her thoughts, the image of the
captain sprang to her mind. The crystal grey eyes gazed back
at her with tenderness, as they had in the garden when she
had grieved in his arms. She could almost feel again his warm
mouth touching hers, hard against hers. A sharp yearning
bloomed in her, fanned outward, and filled her with a tingling
eagerness. She squeezed her eyes closed as the sensations
and emotions shuddered through her body.

Did she love him? But she had warmed to the Tottman's
embrace as well. Was she truly so starved for some small
sign of affection? How was she to know?

Averil left the window and crossed to the wardrobe, where
she pulled out her cloak and hood. Downstairs, she found
Jacob in his study with his foreman, Gilbert Woodby. At
sight of her in the doorway, Jacob excused himself and
stepped into the hall, closing the door behind him. His face
was tight and frowning.

"Where are you going?" he demanded, indicating the
cloak. "What is the meaning of this?"

"I intend to seek out Sir John and determine if I would
be welcome in his home."

Jacob was aghast. "I gave you an hour to come to a decision. I cannot grant you more than that!"

"It is impossible for me to make my decision yet. But for the sake of preserving peace in your family, I promise you an answer by this evening."

"Nay, nay! I forbid you to go."

Averil pressed her lips together in exasperation. "I don't understand you, uncle. Believe me, I desire to be gone from your household as much as you want me gone."

Jacob's features went slack with surprise. "I'll not let you take the coach!"

"Why? Why should you be so against this when I am trying to accommodate your wish to have me gone?"

"Damn! You are impossible and impertinent, young woman. Can't you see I'm trying to do the best thing for you?"

"Then let me go."

"Nay!"

"Then I must hire a coach." Averil turned and walked to the front door.

Jacob was on her heels instantly. "You're going without an escort?"

"Aye."

Behind her, Jacob stopped. Averil pulled open the door and looked back before she stepped outside. His face was fixed and contorted. Briefly she felt pity for him and a small measure of regret. She made a silent apology to her mother and closed the door behind her.

The sun was arching in a slow descent; the winds had grown brisk. Averil drew her cloak around her and pulled on her hood to keep the gusts from tearing her hair from its anchoring pins. Her steps were firm; she felt an optimism that had been long alien to her.

Coaches for hire were to be found in the Strand and she headed in that direction. Though she was not sure where in Southwark Sir John resided, she was in such a mood to knock on each and every door until she found him.

When she reached the end of the street and looked around, she noted two men on foot approaching behind her. Though still many yards away, she recognized them immediately. Their clothing was dark, with nothing to distinguish them from other ordinary Londoners, but one man had a black moustache and T-beard, and their eyes were fixed on her, watching. They were the men Edmond Devenish had pointed out to her on the morning of the captain's picnic.

Panic whipped her thoughts. Who were they? What were they doing here again? Were they responsible for the letter and subsequent damage to Jacob's stock?

Their steps quickened when they saw she had noticed them.

In sudden fear, Averil hurried on. At the next cross street, she turned left and cast a swift glance behind to see if the men were in fact trying to follow her. She was dismayed to find them in pursuit and closing the distance with long strides. It was obvious they would catch up to her soon. What did they want?

Scanning the shops nearby, Averil chose one and entered. It was a small, sweetly fragrant shop offering wines, tobacco, soaps and pipes. At the counter near the door, a fresh-faced young proprietor was engaged in conversation with an elderly customer. The young man glanced to her as she entered, and Averil saw his eyes light with a smile. Deciding that he might prove chivalrous should she need help, she moved closer to him and let her eyes roam over the tins and jars of tobacco. The containers numbered only a dozen. She lingered over them, sniffing one, then another.

The door to the shop opened. Averil started in surprise and spun to face the newcomer. She felt weak with relief when she saw that it was not one of the men she was avoiding but Captain Warrender who had entered.

He was attired in black velvet doublet and breeches, his tall, straight-shouldered form filling the doorway. In her relief, Averil was unabashedly pleased to see him.

As he walked into the shop, he exclaimed, "Here you are,

my dearest heart! I didn't know where you had gone and it gave me a start when I couldn't find you.'' He put his arm around her solicitously as he spoke. He stroked her upper arm and Averil experienced a strange jolt of delight at his touch. She gazed up at him in surprise, but for the moment his eyes were fixed on the street through the window.

Camden led her to the door and under the guise of kissing her cheek, murmured, ''There are two men following you. Come with me. I have a coach.''

Grateful for his presence and assistance, Averil allowed him to lead her from the shop and to a waiting coach. Camden handed her in, inquiring, ''Did you have more shopping to do, or would you prefer to go back to your uncle's house?''

''To Southwark, please,'' she said.

He shot her a perplexed look, then quietly instructed the driver to turn toward Southwark. After a casual glance along the street discovered no immediate trace of the two men, he climbed into the coach. Camden ignored the empty forward seat and settled himself next to Averil as they started on their way.

''Did you know you were being followed?'' he asked.

''Aye, I saw them shortly after I left the house. The shop seemed a safe place in which to hide.''

''Do you know those men?'' he asked, surprised. ''Have you seen them before?''

''Nay. I mean, I don't know who they are, but I saw them once before. It was on the morning you arrived to take us on the picnic. They were standing across the street and seemed to be watching the house.''

She ventured a quick glance at him and met a slight frown of anger in the disturbingly handsome face. Her gaze trailed the brushed dark hair and the hard line of his jaw. In spite of herself, a slow, languid warmth invaded her and she grew shyly nervous. ''You were following me as well,'' she pointed out.

''Aye,'' Camden answered absently. ''But the two men—is that what had upset you that morning? When I saw you in the parlor talking with Edmond Devenish, you were visibly distraught.''

Averil nodded. "Edmond saw them and pointed them out to me. But why were you following me today?"

"I visited your uncle this morning on a particularly urgent matter." Camden glanced to her. "Has he by chance spoken with you yet?"

"Aye,"she said, hesitating briefly.

"And what have you answered him?"

"I've given no answer as yet," she said, turning away to stare out the window.

The coach rocked to a halt as traffic clotted the street. Shouts and angry threats filled the air in front and behind them. Their own driver added his curses as the jumble of traffic was slow to untangle itself.

"Why are you going now to Southwark? Does your uncle know?"

Averil nodded, not turning from the window.

Camden's voice took on a hard note as he said, "And he let you go unescorted—when anything could happen, and almost did?"

"But he didn't wish me to go," Averil said, rising to her uncle's defense. "If you insist on chastising someone, I should be the one."

"All right then, what you did was foolish. Going alone through London is an open invitation to any man who happens by."

"Such as yourself," Averil remarked, irritated.

"I'm different. I've offered you an honest proposal of marriage."

The coach was beginning to move again, inching forward. A slovenly beggar latched onto the side, swinging himself half into the window on Averil's side. She screamed in sudden panic and Camden snatched her away from the window. The beggar thrust an oozing, smelly stump of an arm at them. "Pity! 'Ave ye no pity fer a soldier maimed fer life? Spare some coins fer me poor starvin' wife and babes!"

Averil cowered within Camden's arms, shocked by the unexpected appearance of the beggar and sickened by the odor of his rotting flesh.

"Here," Camden flipped a coin to the man. "Now begone with you."

The beggar caught the silver and dropped agilely from the moving coach.

Though the beggar had departed, Averil stayed beside the captain. She found herself loathe to move away and drew a long, trembling breath as she struggled with herself. She was almost painfully aware of the powerful muscles of his chest and arms, of the strength and heat of him. Half of her shrank from him even as she felt an unequaled excitement course through her.

She lifted her head to peer at him. Her gaze touched the strong, corded neck, the firm mouth with its fuller lower lip. He stared long at her with eyes bright in intensity. The dark head dipped toward her.

Averil held her breath. His lips met hers, lightly at first. She felt his mouth turning over hers, and goosebumps chased crazily along her skin. It was a long kiss. When he lifted his head, Averil realized that she had clenched her fingers in the front of his doublet. She released them, shaken.

Before she could turn away, he had cupped her face with one hand and was kissing her again, this time with more urgency. When he parted her lips and his tongue touched deep in her mouth, she quivered within his embrace with a sharp, unfathomable pleasure. The secret longing she had known before flushed through her, a need, a warmth, seeping across her breast where she was held to his chest, into her back where his hand pressed her to him.

In those moments, all of her senses quickened. She grew aware of so many things about him she had not noticed before—each distinctly his and infinitely pleasurable to her. She could smell the leather of his swordbelt and the faint salty tang of sea air in his clothing, feel the soft velvet nap of the doublet beneath her fingers, see the glint of a silver strand in the dark hair at his temple as he lifted his head.

He seemed faintly surprised as he looked at her, his thumb stroking slowly along the line of her chin. Averil's hand rested on his chest and she could feel the dull thudding of his heart against her fingers. Her own heart pounded, her skin was almost unbearably sensitive and tingling where he touched her. She knew a strong desire for him to kiss her again and she slid her hand to the back of his head, unknowingly performing that ageless caress of invitation.

"Ah, Averil," he murmured. His fingers held her chin as he gazed softly down at her. "I don't think . . ."

He seemed on the verge of saying something more, but instead he bent his head and lightly brushed his lips over hers. With a soft, weak sigh, Averil reached her arm around his neck, and he held her to him in a hard embrace.

His tongue parted her lips and plunged between, filling her. Averil felt a sharp thrill stab through her. Shyly, eagerly, she met his tongue with her own and when he retreated, her tongue moved into his mouth. She felt a low groan vibrate in his chest.

When his hand moved up between them to stroke her breast, the incredible sensation of it shocked her and she uttered a small, muffled cry of surprise. Alarm mushroomed in her mind. She twisted her lips away from his and pushed at his chest. "Nay, nay! Wait!" she cried, feeling overwhelmed, frightened.

His eyes were faintly heavy-lidded as he looked down at her. "Marry me, Averil," he said. "Say yes to me."

"Nay!" she cried, twisting to escape the arms that closed around her. "I have to think! I'm not sure of anything!"

Camden's face closed up as he shut himself off from her. When he released her she retreated from him and crowded the window. Though she looked out at the street, she saw nothing. She was shaken by the clinging weakness she felt in her muscles, a weakness that was singularly pleasant but nevertheless alarming. A frown on her face, she stared out the window and tried to think of anything but the disturbing man beside her.

Camden lifted one foot, propping the sole of his boot on the edge of the seat opposite. Folding his arms over his chest, he tried not to think of her response in his arms, or of the lush promise in her young body. But his dreams of her haunted his mind. He turned his head to look at her but was presented with her rigid back. Even with the long draping folds of her cloak hiding her, he could just barely make out the curve of one hip and a sleek, soft thigh. The desire was acute in him to touch her and draw her back to him. He closed his eyes and rubbed his hands over his face.

"Let me see," he said slowly, recrossing his arms. "You're on your way to Southwark. If I remember rightly, your old friend, Sir John Walford, resides in Southwark. Were you by chance on your way to see him?" He shot a sideways glance at her, and Averil nodded. "Were you seeking out Sir John for his advice?"

Averil sat back against the seat, sighing, and shook her head. "My uncle has issued an ultimatum," she confessed in a small voice. "I must leave his household by one means or another. I thought to plead my case to Sir John and try to obtain his help."

"Bloody damn!" Camden exclaimed softly. "I had no idea he'd do anything like this. I asked him to let me speak with you, but he wouldn't hear of it. I was worried that he'd lose his temper and strike you again as he did over that confounded letter."

Averil glanced at him in swift surprise. "You know about the letter?"

"Aye."

Her voice grew sharp, rising on a high note. "Did you know as well that his wine was destroyed—because of me?"

He looked at her in silence, gauging her. "I know, aye," he said.

Averil searched the face that now seemed closed, unreadable, strangely sharp and formidable. "Uncle Jacob kept insisting I marry you," she murmured aloud to herself. There was something else in operation here, but she could not understand what. And then with complete and startling clarity she was reminded that the captain was very like her uncle—neither man did anything unless there was a profit to be made from it. And she had believed her uncle when he said there was no dowry involved. "Oh! I was so foolish!" she cried aloud in piercing disappointment.

Camden reached for her. "What is it, Averil? What did Jacob say?"

Angry and humiliated, she pushed away his hands. "He said you loved me—that there was no need for a dowry! But I know that can't be true!"

He gripped her hands to hold them still as he said, scowling, "Actually, your uncle in his demented fashion has told you the truth. I do love you. And I'll be gaining nothing from him for a dowry."

"How can I believe you!" she exclaimed.

A sudden sharp rap from the coachman's whip on the roof surprised them both. Averil jerked her hands from Camden's grasp. She had not realized they had stopped.

"This 'ere's Southwark, sir," the driver called from his perch. "Where might ye be wantin' ter go?"

Camden stepped out of the coach. The sun was dipping precariously close to the rooftops, spreading its hazy golden glow over the city. The cobblestones of the street gleamed like a mosaic of gold coins. Briefly Camden gave directions to the driver, then climbed back into the coach.

Averil looked at him in surprise. "You know where Sir John lives?"

"I asked him about it when I met him at the party your aunt and uncle gave."

When the coach drew to a halt, Camden helped her alight. She stood before a massive and stately stone house set well back from the road and surrounded by towering dark trees. No light shone from any of the empty windows. There were no other homes in evidence around it on any side. The only sound was the soft whispering of the twilight wind in the leaves high overhead.

Camden asked the coachman to wait and the man climbed down from his perch to light the matching torches on either side of the coach.

"I had no idea he lived so far away," Averil said as Camden placed his hand lightly on the small of her back and they started up the path to the front door.

"He's the last occupant this side of London, save for some cottagers, farmers and such."

"I doubt I would have made it here on my own. I'm glad you found me in the shop."

"I won't consider it fortunate if I have to turn you over to his care. I know less about him than about your uncle."

"Oh, but Sir John is like an uncle. I've known him since childhood, Captain."

"All that long, eh?" he remarked. When she shot him a swift, confused glance, he sighed. "Call me Camden."

"Camden," she said, then repeated the name, testing the shape of it with her lips and tongue.

They were close to the house now and Averil looked about uneasily. Weeds choked the walkway. The lintel over the door was chipped, and the door itself appeared badly in need of paint. Rotting leaves covered a good measure of the front garden.

"It doesn't look as if anyone is home," Averil whispered. "It doesn't look as if anyone has lived here for some time."

Camden shared her doubts, but said, "There should be servants or a caretaker. They could tell us where to locate Sir John if he is not here presently."

He rapped the door knocker sharply three times. After several long minutes, a faint glow of light appeared through a front window and grew brighter and wider as someone approached the door. It was pulled open and they were greeted by a simply garbed old man carrying a flickering taper dip. He looked at them with kindly curiosity.

"May I be of help to you good people?"

Camden spoke up. "We're looking for Sir John Walford. I understood this is his residence."

"Aye, aye indeed," the man replied, smiling eagerly. "But Sir John is out for the evening. I can't tell you exactly where—he doesn't share his business with me, you see."

They thanked the servant and walked back to the coach in silence. The coachman held the door for them and Camden gave him directions to Jacob's house.

When they were on their way again, Camden looked thoughtful. "Shall we try again tomorrow? I can come by for you with a coach and escort you."

"Nay," Averil replied. "I promised my uncle I'd give him my answer tonight. It would be unfair to further stretch his leniency. I fear I may have already overstepped the bounds when I left today. I refused to obey him, and even beyond that, I told him I was just as eager to leave his house as he was to see me leave."

Camden laughed loudly in the dark interior of the coach. "So you gave him back his own due! I wish I could have seen his face. Did you get any pleasure from it?"

"Nay, it saddened me. I felt sorry because of my mother and—" Averil broke off, realizing she had almost let it slip that she was related to them through her mother, instead of some shadowy cleric in Reading.

"Your mother?" Camden inquired. "What about your mother?"

"Oh, I just meant it would break my parents' hearts if I were disrespectful to Uncle Jacob."

"I see. What do you intend to do now—now that Sir John is no longer a possibility for you? Do you have someone else in mind to pay a visit to this evening? I'd be happy to take you anywhere you'd like. You seem determined not to accept my offer."

"It's not that," Averil protested. She did not explain that she felt lonely and unsure and wished that her father was there to advise her or to make arrangements she could trust—as in the case with Thomas Kateley. She apologized lamely, "Marriage is just such a momentous step."

"I agree with you."

Averil could not read his expression, though she tried. His face was shadowed. Only a faint bronze light slanted into the coach from the exterior lanterns.

"Where did you plan for me to live, if I married you? On board ship?" she asked lightly, though her heart pounded as she contemplated this course.

"I'd certainly welcome your presence there, but I wouldn't recommend it—ships are damp, cold, and crowded, and the food is incredibly bad. A home in London is not out of the question. Eventually, we might go to the colonies or settle here in England somewhere, whichever you prefer."

"And"—she paused in embarrassment, but chided herself because it had to be considered eventually—"children?"

He answered her seriously, "I hope we'll have many— I'll love them every one."

"What about your family?" she protested. "I don't know the first thing about your background."

The shadows deepened as he he pulled her to him and leaned his head to her. "We'll have time for all of that," he whispered.

Caught up in a web of hesitancy and apprehension, Averil tried to draw away, but he held her firmly and his mouth covered hers with gentle urgency. Perhaps she was acutely aware of him physically from earlier, but now his kiss, the pressure of his arms and body, were stunning. It was a distinct and unfamiliar pleasure that she felt like a streak burning all the way to her toes. She reached her arms around his neck, and when his head lifted, she pressed her mouth against the side of his neck, against a corded neck that was warm and hard. A pulse pounded under her lips.

He bent his head to her again, urged her mouth to his, and his lips crushed hers with an urgency that snatched the breath from her. As his arm curved hard around the back of her head, she felt her world spinning, reeling with a dizzying sense of imbalance. She was full against his chest, her breasts pressed to him, and she realized that she lay half across his lap. He shifted slightly and planted one boot on the edge of the forward seat, and Averil felt a solid, muscled thigh behind her back.

She looked up at him in confusion. From the exterior lamps, a shaft of bronzed light slanted across his face, creating hollows and planes in his features that surprised her. He seemed a different man, his face taut, his eyes unnaturally bright. Alarmed, she tried to pull herself back to her own seat, but the arm around her head tightened, and when he bent his head to kiss her again, his lips were coaxing, exploring, tempting her, drawing her with him. It was a breathless, shadowy, intoxicating experience. When his tongue slipped lightly over her lips, she caught her breath, slipping her arms around him, not wanting this moment to ever end. His tongue plunged between her lips, filling her senses as well as her mouth.

When he drew away, she clung to him, marveling at the distinct pleasure that made her feel so unnaturally weak. She tried to bring him back to her, murmuring, "Please . . ." She wanted more of this strange mystery of his mouth. His hands reached between them and Averil felt him untie her cloak and drag the garment open. She was transfixed by the glitter in his eyes. His fingers trailed lightly over her breasts, stroking through the gown, until the peaks of her breasts rose up hard against his fingertips. The sensation sent a lancing excitement through her, and she shuddered with the thick waves of pleasure that followed. With trembling hands, she pulled his head down to her again, holding him close. In that same instant, she felt the shudder that passed over him—a tremor in his muscles that quickened her excitement. She felt his breath against her cheek, and her own breathing was rapid. The arm behind her shifted and he was plucking the pins from her hair, twisting his fingers in the soft heavy mass.

Abruptly his head lifted. He gazed down at her and she saw the tightness in his features, the hot light of his eyes. "Averil—" he muttered. He was breathing heavily. She was still clasping his head and he reached up, dragging her arms away. "Averil," he said again. "You don't know what you're doing to me." His eyes stabbed about the dusty interior of the coach and he seemed almost pained. He grasped her arms and lifted her to place her back on the bench beside him. Muttering something incomprehensible, he dragged her cloak around her shoulders and tied it again.

Averil sat very still. She was at once both relieved and yet desperately disappointed. Her body felt alive and softly pliant, pulsing and throbbing with a new life all its own. She turned away from him slowly, feeling only half-awake, and began to repair her hair. The knot at the back of her head had been undone, and bodkins dangled from long trailing strands.

"What a sight I must look," she murmured distractedly, recovering as many of the pins as she could.

His voice was almost rough as he commented, "Actually, Averil, you look extraordinarily beautiful." She turned in look at him. His arms were crossed over his chest, knees spread, a rueful half-smile visible on his face as he regarded her.

He watched her as she fluffed the loose curls around her face and tried to gather the back tresses and wind them into a semblance of order. But her hands were shaking and the long strands slipped repeatedly.

"Here, I'll do it," he said, and pulled her around till her back was to him.

He deftly wound the strands for her and she handed him the bodkins meekly as he asked for them. It occurred to her then, devastatingly, that he had an ability that must have come from much practice. She had seen how Lynna and Cecelia Osgood had responded so warmly to him, yet she had never considered the fact that there might be other women in his life. Somehow she had thought she was as special to him as he was to her. The sense of humiliation was painfully strong.

When he finished, she self-consciously patted the back knot. He had done very well, and she commented more sharply than she would have liked, "No doubt you have to do this often."

With immediate rich amusement, he laughed. "Actually, the truth of the matter is that I have six younger sisters. The youngest two were wild little hoydens—rambunctious and always getting scolded for it. Many times I helped them repair their appearances before they confronted our mother." He chuckled softly to himself, remembering, delighted with the memories.

"Oh." Averil smiled in spite of herself. "I assumed you had—" She halted and blushed in embarrassment.

"Ah Averil, Averil." He was smiling at her, amused. He took her hand and held it lightly, his hand resting on his leg.

"Tell me more," she pressed. "Tell me about your family."

He squeezed her hand. "If you wish it." Tipping his head back against the wall of the coach, he closed his eyes. "I have nine younger brothers and sisters—I'm the eldest. My father died three years ago. When I was seventeen years of age, he moved the family to the New World. Don't ask me why. I chose to remain here. At least for a time."

"Then you went to Jamaica?"

"Aye."

He was silent and Averil pressed, "Go on."

"What else do you want to know?"

Averil blushed slightly. "You never married?"

"Aye, I did." Absently Camden stroked his thumb over her palm and continued in a heavier tone. "And we had two daughters, twins. Really they were no more than babes in arms when—We settled in the New World, in a small settlement between the James and York rivers. A beautiful, dangerous . . ."

Averil asked softly, "What happened?"

"Savages," he answered flatly, opening his eyes again. He looked tired suddenly. "I wasn't there at the time or—anyway, they were murdered."

"I'm so sorry," Averil whispered sadly.

He shrugged. "It was ten years ago."

"Is that your home still?"

"Nay."

"Where is your home?"

He stroked her cheek slowly with the back of one finger. "Wherever you want to live, Averil. In a few minutes you have to give Jacob your answer. What will you say to him?"

Averil pressed her hand to her breast, against the frantic, happy thudding of her heart. As if she had long ago made her decision, she answered immediately, "I'll tell him aye," she said. "Aye . . . Camden."

CHAPTER
THIRTEEN

Mary Geneva was furious when Jacob told her of the proposed marriage. "We had agreed to approach the captain on Lynna's behalf!" she exclaimed. Though he was loathe to worry her with the details of the vandalism and the reasons for it, Jacob knew she would give him no peace until she herself was convinced of the rightness of this course. When he had at last laid all of the details before her, she was profoundly shocked.

"I am amazed that Averil would act so carelessly—so irresponsibly! I had higher expectations of her," Mary Geneva said with tight-lipped resentment. "How dare she endanger us that way!"

Unfortunately, no one formally explained the situation to Lynna. Mary Geneva assumed Jacob would handle it, while Jacob considered his contract with the captain of supreme importance and conveniently forgot all else. It was not until early the following afternoon, when Lynna overheard a chance remark from Honor concerning a wedding, that she questioned the servant and learned the truth.

She flew to her mother's chamber, where Mary Geneva was engrossed in setting plans with the seamstress. Seeing her daughter's distress, and rightly guessing the reason for it, she dismissed the seamstress and opened her arms to comfort Lynna.

Lynna wrung her hands and tried to appeal to her mother. "How could father do this? Didn't he know how much I love the captain?"

Mary Geneva stroked her daughter's hair and cooed sympathetically. "Of course he knew. We had planned to approach the captain with a proposal for a marriage with you."

"What!" Lynna's tear-streaked face came up with a jerk. "Then what happened to change his mind!"

Mary Geneva fumbled helplessly for a way to phrase her reply, but at last said merely, "There were several— problems, Lynna. Your father was forced to make these arrangements."

"Oh! Oh!" Lynna's fury grew. She flung herself from her mother and stormed from the room in search of her cousin. Finding Averil alone in her room, lying across the bed and reading a copy of *Comus* by the popular poet John Milton, Lynna vented her fury.

"You weaseling little whore!" she screamed. "You *knew* the captain was mine, but you pursued him anyway!"

Averil's face pinched with anxiety and revulsion. "Lynna, please!" she begged. She slid off the bed quickly to face her cousin. "I had no hand in this—"

"Liar! *Whore!*"

Mary Geneva had followed her distraught daughter from the bedroom and now appeared in the doorway. "Lynna!" she cried in indignation. "I *forbid* you to speak thus!"

Lynna turned to her mother in supplication. "But she's ruined everything, Mother! She's ruined my *life*! Oh, I wish she'd never come here!" Abruptly Lynna swung back to Averil and for a brief moment, her eyes slitted with hatred. Then she rushed past her mother, and Mary Geneva and

Averil heard her loud sobs as she ran down the hall to her room. Seconds later, the chamber door slammed resoundingly.

Mary Geneva looked at Averil with ill-concealed impatience. It was clear to them both that the sooner the wedding took place and Averil was gone, the better it would be for everyone.

At four in the afternoon, Jacob returned from his meeting with the captain. The two men had deliberated the terms of their contract for several hours and had at last concluded the business. Gilbert Woodby and the captain's first mate, a man named Richard Cheyney, had been called as witnesses and had signed their names to the two copies of the documents. Jacob was well pleased.

He carried a leather-bound satchel and was smiling to himself when he entered his home. Lynna waited for him in the front hall. His smile vanished when he caught sight of the fury etched in his offspring's face. It was apparent to him that Lynna had heard of the intended marriage and had greeted the news with anything but grace. He knew Lynna had set her heart on the captain, but he was damned if he was going to let her disappointment put a damper on his high spirits.

Within the satchel under his arm rested his copy of the contract, duly signed by both the captain and himself and witnessed. Looking on the ugly twist of his daughter's mouth, Jacob was glad he had seen to the contract before facing her.

"Good afternoon, my dear," he said calmly. He walked past her and continued into his study, setting the satchel on his desk.

Lynna followed and called out from the doorway, "What manner of father are you? You see to the welfare of another before considering the fate of your own daughter! Is my happiness of so little importance to you?"

"Do not vex me, Lynna," Jacob cautioned. "I act always with my family's best interests at heart."

With a crash, Lynna threw the door closed behind her and

marched across the room to confront her father over the desktop. " 'Best interests?' Ha! I see nought but that the man I love has been betrothed to that—that scheming, unscrupulous *traitor*!''

"Now, daughter." Jacob wagged a finger at her as a tight, warning smile crept across her features. "Your ungoverned tongue will be your undoing." The smile disappeared and he stared her down, daring her to further test him.

He unbuckled the straps of the satchel and flipped it open. As he extracted the papers from the interior, he commented somberly, "Someday you will understand the why of this. I cannot now divulge the reasons. Bear this in mind though—I do what I must in order to protect you."

"You never do *anything* unless it is pleasing to you!" Lynna hurled her arm out as if she intended knocking the papers from his hand.

Jacob flicked the contract out of her reach and placed it in a drawer. Leaning his weight on fingers splayed on the desk, he fixed her with a hard, uncompromising stare. His voice thundered in the room. "Try my patience too far and you will find yourself wed to the first jingle-brains who'll have you!"

"How dare you say such a thing!" she screeched. "You're a coward to even pretend to do anything for my sake! You're a selfish, disgusting excuse for a father!''

"Get out of my office! Out!''

Lynna shook with rage. Her skirts whipped out behind her as she departed. Slamming the door again behind her, she fixed the panels with a vengeful stare.

She burst into the kitchen house, surprising Morton, who was seated at the big worktable and enjoying a mug of warm wine as he talked with Honor. The young serving girl was wiping out the interior of a large black kettle.

"You!" Lynna directed, pointing a finger to Morton. "Bring the coach out. Quickly!''

Morton put down his mug and, matching her finger-pointing gesture, said comfortably, "I've driven ye around

fer years without so much as a thank'ee on yer part, but I'll
not be budgin' from this seat till ye puts some Christian
kindness in yer voice this time.''

Lynna stamped her foot against the flagstones in impotent
fury. Gritting her teeth, she tried again. "Please, Morton.
I'd like to go out in the coach.'' Though her voice was
overlaid with forced politeness, her eyes snapped blue fire.

The coach and two horses were kept at a public stables
located at the end of the street, so when Morton finally guided
the conveyance up to the front door, Lynna was prepared
and waiting. Her cloak billowed in a sharp gust of wind as
she climbed in. Once settled, she directed him to take her
to Paul's Wharf.

Though it was only just past four in the afternoon, the sun
was banked behind a sheet of low clouds, and the day was
darkening prematurely. At the wharf, Morton remained in
his seat while Lynna shoved her way through the groups of
people thronging around a ship being loaded. Many cast her
an angry glance as she carelessly pushed them aside.

She entered the cramped wharf office and demanded of
a harried clerk, "Where is Captain Warrender's ship?''

"The *Indomitable*?'' the clerk queried. "There.'' He
pointed out the ship to her through a grime-smeared window.

When he returned his attention to a sheaf of tattered papers
on a table beside him, Lynna exclaimed in exasperation,
"Well, get me a boat to go out there in!''

The surprised clerk came to his feet. Lynna followed on
his heels as he stepped out of the building and motioned to
a greasy, unkempt sailor lounging against the outer wall. They
spoke together for a moment, the clerk gesturing earnestly,
while Lynna tapped her foot on the wood planking of the
dock. When the arrangements were made and Lynna had paid
him in advance, the sailor rowed her out to the *Indomitable*.

Her approach had been sighted on board the ship, and there
was a profusion of eager hands to help her up the thin,
slippery rope ladder. Gaining the deck, Lynna spotted the
figure of the captain rapidly descending the ratlines of the

foremast. Wind blew his hair around his face and rippled the loose folds of his plain, unstarched linen shirt. He was wiping his hands on a rag as he strode across the main deck. His brown breeches were stained with tar and bits of hemp. The sailors who had buzzed about her after her arrival returned to their various duties when their captain drew near. Lynna smiled coyly at the tall man.

"Mrs. Lynna, you amaze me," he remarked somewhat impatiently. Lynna's smile froze. "Don't you realize a young woman shouldn't visit a ship alone?"

She slid a surreptitious glance around. The sailors on deck were casting curious, amused looks their way, while on shore others strained to see the distant proceedings.

"Can't we go into the cabin?" she asked, flustered.

He looked at her in surprise. "That's an even better way to ruin your reputation."

"I don't care!" she cried. "I must talk to you. It's urgent!"

He nodded reluctantly and indicated a narrow hall beneath the quarterdeck. As Lynna hurried toward it, Camden requested of one of his crewmen nearby, "Ask him to wait." He gestured to the sailor in the small boat that had brought Lynna from the dock.

Camden followed his visitor and escorted her into the great cabin, leaving the door open behind him. The table was strewn with maps, and Lynna glanced idly over them. There were ocean charts filled with markings, a map of England also heavily marked, and several brief letters. Camden rolled all these up and laid them aside.

"What did you wish to see me about?"

Lynna removed her cloak as she stated, "I have heard of the marriage arranged for you and my cousin." She strolled around the table and dropped her cloak over the back of a particularly fine leather and brass-studded chair. All the hangings and furnishings of the cabin were luxurious and and well-tended. Its tidiness surprised her.

Camden prompted, "And?"

"I've come to warn you. You shouldn't go through with

this. Don't trust Averil.''

"Why shouldn't I trust her?''

Lynna moved to stand very close in front of him. "I'm here, risking my reputation, to help you save yours!'' she insisted.

"Oh?'' He grinned suddenly. "This is an unusual twist. Do I have a reputation that deserves protecting?''

Infuriated, Lynna cried, "Averil's a traitor! She's working with the Tottman, having secret night rendezvous with him! Is that not worth your knowing?'' When she saw the light of surprise in Camden's gaze, Lynna almost laughed aloud in her eagerness, but she suppressed the desire and looked at him with a solemnity befitting the moment.

"That's a serious accusation,'' he cautioned. "Do you have proof?''

Lynna lifted her chin a notch. "Averil herself informed me. She is quite proud of herself and cannot see that she is misguided and acting unwisely.''

"I assume you intend telling me all about it.''

However reluctant and wary his attention, Lynna sought to make good use of it. Once his illusions of a pure and innocent Averil were shattered, she would be there to comfort him and soothe away his disappointment with her caresses. She grew giddy with the thought of that magnificent body in her arms.

But it would never do to be caught as a complete liar or her cause would be irrevocably lost. So she was careful to seek out half-truths to twist into different meanings. She raked her memory for the details of the story Francis Bowers had given her, then she began speaking hesitantly, as if the truth was too painful to bear repeating.

"She told me of a night when she and the Tottman were trying to help some people escape London. These people were in an inn on the bridge, and Averil came down from the roof to their room by means of a rope.'' Lynna paused significantly and looked away in feigned embarrassment. "She was dressed as a common street boy! No good and decent woman would ever dream of doing such things. It pains me to have to say those things. But I couldn't bear the thought that you might have been duped into this marriage to protect her reputation.''

Lynna widened her eyes and said earnestly, ''For all I know she could even be with child by this Tottman.''

The starkness in his eyes momentarily halted her, but, recovering her thoughts, she decided she had scored a point and pressed on. ''Well, I know for a fact that there have been some . . . intimacies between them.''

''Averil herself told you these things?''

''Aye, everything! But there are some details I just couldn't repeat. Why, a decent woman wouldn't even consider such things!'' Lynna looked away. She pulled a handkerchief from the sleeve of her gown and twisted it nervously in a pose of intense embarrassment. She hoped that by this tactic the captain's own imagination would conjure up enough sordid images by itself.

From the tail of her eye she glanced swiftly at him. His face was closed and unreadable as he stared at her. Lynna paced in a show of agitation. When she returned to him, she looked pityingly into his eyes. ''To think how she's used you to protect herself.'' She placed her hand on his arm.

He gripped her wrist and held her away from him. ''Just what do you hope to gain?''

Taken aback, Lynna's mouth gaped wide. Then she snapped it shut again as a thought occurred to her. But, of course, she chided herself, his disappointment in Averil is making him irritable. He still wants to defend her.

''What do *I* hope to gain?'' she repeated, and met his scowl with a soft look. ''I love you. That is my reason. And whether you could ever return my love or not, I cannot stand by and see you caught within her trap.''

He released her. She watched his face closely for any signs of weakening, but there were none. He seemed more remote than ever as he walked a few steps across his cabin.

"Mrs. Lynna, perhaps you don't know this, but I really don't care a damn about this war. However, if Averil feels compelled by her principles to aid the cause of one side or another, that is her choice and I will not fault her for it."

"But she is consorting with another man—she'll make a cuckold of you!"

"Nay, I don't think so. At any rate, after we're married I'll make certain she doesn't."

Lynna spun around to hide an angry scowl. Oh, but he was being so stubborn! She had to try another tack.

"Captain Warrender," she tried again, "you said yourself that if Averil is drawn by her principles to help either side, you could not fault her for it—but she is *not* principled. She is devious. Averil is not merely helping the Tottman for a cause, Captain Warrender, she is helping set him up for arrest. She does it for the reward only!"

With a small, tearful sigh, Lynna let her shoulders droop. She continued slowly, as if with great effort. "My family has cast its lot with Parliament, my brother is a valiant soldier in the army, we are honorable in the means by which we seek to follow our beliefs. Averil is not. For all of her innocent demeanor, Captain, in her heart she is capable of great deceit. Believe what I say. I have known her far longer than have you."

Feeling hot and cross, she flung out her arms, saying almost impatiently, "She leads people on until they are no use to her! Why, even dear Edmond Devenish! She promised to marry *him* as well! So don't be tricked by appearances or any declarations of love from her. She's accomplished in deceit, and you'll find out just—"

"Get yourself away from me," he said quietly. His eyes had turned to ice. Lynna's voice deserted her. So powerful was the message physically radiating from him that when he tossed her the cloak, she fled the cabin, her footsteps echoing harshly down the short hall.

* * *

Two days later, on the day before he sailed, Camden paid another call to Jacob Kirkland's home. In sharp contrast to his first meal in their house, the dining room was only dimly lit from the meager grey light that managed to pierce the heavy fog outside the window, the hearth grate was empty and coldly reproving, and Mary Geneva offered Camden only the barest civility. To Averil she was indifferent. Lynna remained in her room throughout his visit. Jacob dominated the dinner conversation merely because no one else seemed eager to fill the long silences. Camden saw him exchange brief pleading looks with his wife.

Averil, he noted, ate little and offered nothing in the way of conversation. She seemed uneasy. Whenever she looked in his direction, Camden reassured her as best he could— with a partial smile, a softening in his gaze, a smoothing of the frown that grew on his brow.

But he watched and wondered about her. Would she truly reveal to her cousin such things as Lynna had claimed? Was she so sure of herself and her power? Or was it that her distress was so great? He chafed at the expanse of days that remained until they were safely wed and he hoped she would be able to withstand another month of the wintry antagonism in this household.

When Camden took his leave shortly after the conclusion of the meal, Averil walked him to the door. He paused beside the portal and said in a voice low enough to discourage any eavesdropping, "How have you fared, Averil? I detect animosity toward you here."

Averil met his gaze and smiled slightly, almost apologetically. "It shows, then? Uncle Jacob has spent nearly all of his waking hours at his warehouse or here in his study. After what happened to his wine, he's had to work long hours. I feel so sorry for him sometimes." She did not add that she was feeling weighted by guilt, for she knew she was responsible for his present predicament.

"As long as he leaves you alone," Camden said. "But your aunt is very cold in manner. That's not like her."

Averil dropped her eyes to a bright silver thread on his
doublet, undecided whether to explain the situation to him.

Camden pressed her answer by suggesting, "Does she
consider me unfit for you?"

"Oh nay," Averil's gaze lifted to his face. "In truth, she
had been hoping for a match between you and—and Lynna."

Camden gave a short chuckle, dismissing such an idea.
"And now, my heart," he said, drawing her to him and using
an endearment that made Averil's heart catch softly, "I have
to leave. We're still loading the ship and I have to return
to the wharf. Tomorrow I sail for Amsterdam, but I'll return
in time for the wedding."

"Is this so necessary?" she protested.

"Are you worried for me?" When she nodded, he smiled.
"I'll return to you, Averil."

Her eyes were large and unnaturally bright in the dusky
light of the hall. She seemed too tremulously fragile to him,
as though her defenses were crumbling again. It was an
alarming thought to him as he remembered the lost, susceptible woman he had found that day in the garden.

He thought of Francis Bowers and his claim that he had
gained Averil's trust. Apprehension niggled at him. Though
he wanted to question her about Francis, and about the things
Lynna had told him, he could find no way to begin.

At last, in frustration and urgency, he cupped her face
between his hands. "I know 'twill not be an easy few weeks
for you while I'm away, but be strong for me, Averil." He
leaned down and kissed her. When her arms rose swiftly
to catch around his neck, Camden dropped his hands to circle
her waist and draw her tightly into his embrace.

When he drew away, his eyes were anxious and intense.
He hated to leave her this way, vulnerable to whatever tricks
Francis Bowers might attempt. Silently he cursed the circumstances, cursed Francis Bowers, but most of all he cursed
the entire Kirkland family for their antagonism toward Averil.

As if sensing his mood and the frustration that left him
indecisive, Averil smiled. "Take this with you," she said

softly, happy in the moment, happy in the first pronounce-
ment, "I love you. And I will be strong for you."

He seemed to want to say more, and she saw the heaviness
in his features, but at last he shook his head. With a small
laugh he ran his finger lightly down the tip of her nose and
touched her lips. "You don't know how good that sounds."
He kissed her again, a solemn yet tender promise, then let
himself out the door.

CHAPTER
FOURTEEN

The night was clear, and blue moonlight etched the figure of a lone horseman speeding over the dusty, winding road that led west from London. At a discreet distance, two other riders followed. The single rider was unaware of their presence. Hidden in the skirt of his saddle was a missive given him by Sir John Walford to be delivered to Prince Rupert, temporarily in Oxford to meet with his uncle, the King.

It was nearing midnight, and he pushed his horse to a faster pace, knowing that an inn lay another half a league or less along the road. The two riders in the distance slowed their pace slightly.

Lynna and Francis Bowers exchanged glances as the barely discernable figure in front of them rounded a bend in the road and was lost to their view.

"Are you sure he intends to stop?" Lynna questioned irritably. "Why did you slow us down? What if he turns off on a side path and we don't see?"

"I'm quite sure of this," Francis insisted. "Are you growing weary, Lynna? You don't have to do this, you know."

"Don't call me by that name, not even when we're alone!" she exclaimed.

"All right, *Lady Averil*," he said with a sneer, "but I don't know why you feel you must muddy up this incident tonight by insisting on any kind of an identity. Total anonymity would be far safer."

"Please, Francis, this is of great importance to me!"

Francis shrugged his reluctant agreement. "I don't understand your hatred of Averil, but in truth I really don't care what happens between the two of you. Just remember everything I told you and keep your head tonight, do you understand?"

They traveled the snaking, moonlit road in silence. When they turned the bend in the road, an inn, nestled against a small sloping hillside, came into view. It was a two-story, rectangular building with several outbuildings dotting the hillside on either side of the main structure.

"Your friend was right!" Lynna exclaimed in astonished eagerness.

The entrance of the inn was lit on either side by large hanging lanterns, and in the flaring pool of coppery light, they could see the messenger dismounting and handing the horse's reins to a young ostler. When the man disappeared into the inn, Lynna and Francis increased their pace.

Hearing the sound of approaching horses, the ostler again came trotting out of the stables to meet the newcomers. Lynna reined in her horse and waited for Francis to dismount and assist her. She was attired in a full, flowing cloak of cherry-red satin, her eyes hidden behind a fashionable half-mask and her hair hidden by the hood covering her head. With Francis' help, she slid from her horse onto the hard-packed dirt of the innyard. Francis wore a threadbare servant's livery of black broadcloth with silver braid trim.

Lynna shook roadway dust from her cloak as she eyed the

young ostler with wilting distaste. She addressed Francis as she instructed imperiously, "You, see to my mount. Don't let this creature lay a finger on her."

With a deferential bow, Francis murmured, "Aye, my lady."

As Lynna approached the entrance to the inn, Francis and the ostler, a clean and cheerful boy, led the horses into the warmth of the stable some paces to the left of the inn. There was a single lantern lit within, and the interior was neat and recently swept. In five of the stalls, horses stood resting; aside from an occasional swish of a tail, the place was quiet.

The messenger's mount was as yet unsaddled.

"Ah, someone just arrived," Francis pretended surprise. "I saw no one on the road."

The ostler gave a single grunt as he unstrapped the saddle. "He wor in a hurry, than'un. I know nowt 'bout him, but he wants supper an' a new mount, then he's t' the road again." The saddle fell to the floor with a heavy thud.

"Here, my lad, let me give you a hand with this one." Francis rushed to his assistance and hefted the saddle. He fingered the skirt of the saddle as he lied, "This is ripped. Did that happen when it fell?"

The boy exclaimed in alarm, "I dunna know on't." He tried to look over the saddle to assess the damage, but Francis deftly shifted the leather around to prevent his seeing.

"I've a fair hand for mending," Francis said, smiling. "Why don't I fix it for you, and the owner will never know the difference."

"Thank ye," the lad stammered in relief. "An' I shall have yer mounts there set."

"Oh nay, lad. My mistress requested I see to our horses. Nothing against you, she's just very particular about her property."

"Who's yer mistress?" the lad inquired, curious.

After a moment's hesitation, Francis said, "Lady Averil Maslin. Now, do you have a good strong needle and thread?"

"Aye!" The boy took off into an adjoining room. In the lad's absence, Francis retrieved a small blade from his doublet and deftly slit several of the stitches in the saddle's skirt. From the interior he extracted a slip of paper which he pushed inside his shirt. He had just replaced the knife when the ostler reappeared and handed him an old metal box.

When Lynna entered the main room of the inn, she noted not only the man they had followed, who was seated at a table by himself and talking to the proprietor, but two other men at the long common table. They appeared to be local cottagers. One sported a generous belly protruding through an aged and colorless leather jerkin; the other had a shock of red hair that was greasy and tangled, a single piece of straw hanging in its matted length. To the side of the large open hearth across the room, a fat chunk of skewered meat was kept warm and the aroma filled the air. Four large lanterns hung from the walls, two on each side, and their wavering light scattered the shadows into the far corners.

Her arrival caused all heads to turn. She appeared to them as a lady of obvious quality and her presence here, unescorted and intending to sit in the common room, caused much confusion and speculation. It was what she had intended; she wanted them to remember her. Lynna took a seat at a table near the messenger and kept her eyes down discreetly.

The proprietor's voice broke the silence that had fallen at her arrival as he hastened toward her. "May I assist you in any way, my lady?"

Lynna ordered wine, and when the proprietor had returned to the kitchen, the messenger let his eyes slide with curiosity over the heavily hooded and disguised woman. Though her figure was obscured within the folds of her cloak, he could tell she was young and tempting; her eyes gleamed behind the half-mask, and beneath the lower edge, a pair of young, full lips curled in a self-satisfied smile.

He drummed his fingers on the table for a moment as he considered her. Rising, he sauntered to her table.

"Good evening, m'lady," he said, smiling broadly. His eyes caught hers through the mask and he noted the immediate quick sparkle in her glance.

The messenger was a young man of medium height, with one shoulder slightly higher than the other. Beneath a dark knit hat he had a thick crop of dusty brown hair. His brow was narrow and lined, his eyes set close on either side of a long nose with a sharp ridge. He wore a thick beard, matted with dirt, and his clothes were rugged and durable, fashioned from heavy brown linsey-woolsey that was creased and stained.

When he boldly seated himself across from her, Lynna folded her hands primly in her lap and expressed flustered innocence, though his approach to her was exactly what she had wanted. "Oh, sir, this is highly irregular—I'm afraid I don't quite know—"

"Let me introduce myself. Geoffrey Pike, at your service. And you are—?"

"Oh, nay." She shook her head very definitely. "I'm afraid I must not give you that information." She had every intention of eventually revealing an identity to him.

Surprise, then open curiosity crossed his features. "I understand." He grinned. "But whatever your secret, it would be safe with me, m'lady. I'm bound for parts far from here. No one need ever know we'd met."

He fell silent as a serving girl delivered a trencher of meat with two thick chunks of bread to the table. Behind her the innkeeper carried a can of ale and the lady's wine in a tall fluted glass. When they had moved away, Lynna sipped her wine and watched the man shove a large chunk of meat into his mouth.

He looked up speculatively. "Obviously your identity is very important. You force me to chance a guess."

"Sir, I detest your impudence."

Pike shrugged, the greater part of his attention on his supper. He downed a portion of his ale, wiped his sleeve across his wet lips, and observed, "M'lady, wherever your journey is taking you, I hope you have been provided a proper escort. These roads are extremely dangerous. Not only are there soldiers about, but highwaymen are thick, and a woman of quality such as yourself, poorly guarded, is easy prey. You should take great care.''

"Thank you for your concern, but I have sufficient guard for my purposes and needs.''

"Do you now? 'Sufficient for your purpose,' eh? Do you know what I think? I think you are no lady of quality, but some tempting bait. Lure your prey upstairs with some offer of perhaps an entertaining evening—''

"Sir! You dare—''

"—or even with the innocent excuse of seeing you safely to your chamber, and then lead him into a trap. For robbery, perhap?''

"This is unforgivable! Your manners are detestable. And for that matter you are most grievously wrong—''

"Am I?'' He pushed the tray aside and took up his can of ale. As Lynna watched him drink, a clot of grease sticking to his beard dropped off onto the table. She shuddered. It took all of her willpower to remain seated and keep him there for even a short span of time more.

The messenger set down his ale and studied her with his close-set eyes narrowing. "Perhaps then, you are seeking a little romp for your own pleasure. You find a stranger who attracts you, entice him to your table and from there to your bed? Refuse to share your identity, of course, so that after the fun, no one would be the wiser.''

Lynna seethed with revulsion. "You disgusting, over-stuffed—''

"Ho, now,'' he broke in. "Just because I see your game is no reason it can't still be played. Why, I'd be even more inclined to guard your secrets. What is it? An old and withered husband? Or one away at war?''

Lynna eyed him coldly, but refused to speak. As long as he continued talking, she could wait this out a little longer. She prayed fervently for Francis to hurry. From deep within her middle she felt the first stirrings of nausea. How she detested this man's ugly, smug face!

"Shall we take steps to remedy the situation?"

His suggestion took Lynna by surprise and she gaped at him.

"Let's go up to your room." His tongue darted out to wet his sagging lower lip as he grabbed for her hand.

"Sir!" Lynna cried in alarm, tugging at her hand. "Let go of me. You are greatly mistaken!"

"I think not."

She hissed through clenched teeth, all her ire spitting out with her words. "And what if I *would* lure you into a trap? You might find yourself with a split skull and no purse."

"I'll take my chances," he said, rising.

"I am no commoner to be trifled with to please your fancy!" Lynna cried in a desperate attempt to maintain an upper hand. "I am Lady Averil Maslin."

"Is that so?" He grinned, obviously giving no credence to her words. "I just might fancy nobility for a change, then. Where's your room?"

"I have no room!"

"Then we'll just have to find an empty one." His fingers tightened on her wrist and pulled her to her feet.

"Let go of me!" Lynna screamed. Frantically, she grabbed the edge of the table for a hold and the wine glass fell, shattering on the floor.

The proprietor was in the kitchen and, hearing raised voices and the breaking of glass, he burst into the common room. "You there! What is the meaning of this?" He advanced across the room and scowled at the messenger.

"Personal business between myself and the lady," the man said with a gruff surliness. "Don't interfere."

Frowning, the owner looked to Lynna. "Shall I hurry this one on his way, my lady?"

Pike leaned close to the proprietor and snarled, "I'm a soldier for the King, and if you do not wish to have your establishment set upon and burned to the ground, you'd best not stand in my way!''

"But, I have nothing to hide from the Crown," the owner protested in confusion.

"I'll invent something. But hear this—interfere with me now, and I'll personally see this entire place ruined!''

Fear brought a light sheen of sweat to the owner's face. He backed away hesitantly.

The messenger whirled to face the other two patrons gaping at them from the common table. He stared fixedly at first one then the other. "I'm in no mood for trouble, but could see each of you strung up." The two men looked away nervously.

"Come now." His voice was tight as he dragged Lynna from the table.

In a rush of naked fear, Lynna screamed out. She dug in her toes to keep from being pulled along with him, and her free hand flailed wildly for some object to grasp. Her fingers closed around a mug on the table in front of the two spectators, and she flung it at the messenger. Ale splashed over him as the mug glanced off his shoulder and fell, bouncing off the bottom step of the staircase leading to the upper rooms.

With a snarl, the man swung around. He grappled with her, tangling his hands in the bright cherry-red cloak, and managed to hoist her over his shoulder. For a moment, Lynna bounced on his thick shoulder, unable to catch her breath, but at last she screamed out, "Francis! Francis, *help*!''

Francis himself, with the messenger's fresh horse in tow, was on the way toward the inn. He heard Lynna's scream and threw the reins quickly around a pillar in front. When he burst into the inn, Lynna and the messenger were halfway up the stairs. With a cry of outraged anger, Francis flung himself after them. He grasped Pike, knocking the man down, and though he tried to catch Lynna, she slid past him head first and tumbled down the remaining stairs. Her legs struck the narrow walls of the staircase well, and she landed in a cloud of red satin.

The messenger regained his footing and swung around on the stairs, aiming a kick at Francis. It caught him in the belly, sending Francis backwards down the stairs. Pike descended close behind him and the two men stumbled over Lynna at the foot of the steps. She cried out loudly, dragging herself to one side to escape their heavy, bruising boots, and frantically righted her hood and mask.

Now that someone else had made the first move, the two patrons at the table darted up to join the fray. Francis was doubled up against a table as Pike advanced on him, but the two farmers jumped at the messenger from behind, trying to bring him down. With a wild swing of his arm, Pike sent the red-haired man scudding along the floor. The other man looked to his disabled companion, then with a scream of anger, managed to strike a fair-aimed blow to Pike's face.

Pike fell back, momentarily dazed as blood spurted from his nose. He put his fingers tentatively to the middle of his face and his hand came away dripping crimson. With a snarl, he leapt after the awkwardly rotund man who had struck him. But the menacing image of the proprietor with a heavy skillet in hand rose in front of him.

With so many ready to defend the woman, Geoffrey Pike decided against pursuing his original plan. He flung himself toward the outer door. Recognizing his saddle on the horse tethered in front of the inn, he swung onto the animal and rode hard away.

Francis dragged himself to his feet and crossed the room to where Lynna had taken refuge in a corner near the hearth. He pulled her to her feet gingerly.

"Are you all right?" he asked.

She nodded. "And you?"

"I think so." Francis was breathless and still hunched over slightly.

"The letter?" she whispered urgently.

"Here." He tapped his chest. "Do you feel strong enough to ride back now?"

"Aye! I can't stay here any longer!"

The other two men were being fussed over by an agitated serving girl and the proprietor was bringing a tray of ale from the kitchen when Lynna and Francis made their way from the inn to retrieve their horses.

Lynna limped slightly. Francis lifted her as best he could toward the saddle. They retraced their path from the inn and when they had rounded the bend that hid the inn from sight, Lynna reined her horse to a stop. Francis halted his steed and looked back in concern. On either side of the road, trees shifted uneasily in the night wind.

"Are you all right?" he asked. "What is it?"

"We did it, Francis! We really did it!" She ripped the half-mask from her face and flung it into the air as she gave a whoop of glee. Her eyes glowed strangely in the stark moonlight. Now that the deed was done and they were safely on their way home, she could barely contain her excitement. "We did it!"

When, on the following day, a messenger arrived in Oxford to see Prince Rupert and found himself without the letter he claimed he had been given, two of the King's soldiers were sent to backtrack on the trail the messenger had followed. They stopped at the inn to question the occupants. A young and thoroughly frightened ostler told them of the visit of Lady Averil Maslin and her manservant who had stitched the rip in the messenger's saddle. The innkeeper nervously recounted the events that had occurred there, and the soldiers relayed the information to Prince Rupert.

He listened to their report in a rising temper.

"Lady Averil Maslin!" he exclaimed, and his dark eyes grew even blacker in the ashen twilight, that last hour before the evening candles are lit. "So she's continuing where her father left off."

He dismissed the two soldiers with an angry wave of his hand. When they had let themselves out, Hammond, one of Rupert's officers, argued, "A woman? Surely you don't suspect last week's gunpowder theft was the work of a woman?"

"Not directly, nay, of course not. But perhaps one assisted."

Rupert stood by the window. The planes of his face, his heavy black hair, and his white shirt reflected the dimming light outside. He said with feeling, "But this one is a thorn in the side, to be sure. Remember the boy Mumbry brought to the room when we were in Abingdon? The one who was bringing us news of an attack on Maslin Manor?"

Hammond frowned and plucked thoughtfully at the blond, tapered beard on his chin. "I vaguely remember something like that. I must have had too much wine. But why? Who was he?"

"That was Lady Averil."

Hammond leaned slightly forward from the couch in surprise. "I'm beginning to see what you mean." He snickered with an evil little sound. "No wonder I thought the boy was another of Mumbry's kind."

"I think we all did."

"How did you discover it was Lady Averil?"

Rupert's dark concentration was building. He answered Hammond impatiently, "I had notices put up. One of the villagers, a servant for Sir John Walford, reported that a boy claiming to be Lady Averil had come to her door. The details of apparel and appearance matched."

Unyielding aristocratic arrogance burning in his dark eyes, Rupert added, "Her Majesty sells her own jewels and purchases arms for us, and then this kind of pestering theft occurs!" Abruptly, he strode across the room. "By God, if Lady Averil is capable of that," he said, "she's capable of more. I want her stopped."

At the door of his apartments, he turned and whistled sharply. "Come, Boy!" The white poodle that had been curled on its paws in a corner of the room scampered after him.

Rupert's booted footsteps reverberated in the dim hallway of the royal chambers as he went in search of the messenger, Pike. He had an urgent message to send to London.

News of Pike's mishap at the inn spread. Parliament sympathizers laughed into their ale as the story was told and retold with embellishments.

Averil herself heard nothing of this. She tried to speed the passage of time with thoughts of Camden and the approaching wedding, but her reveries of him invariably dissolved into images of his ship under fire in the Channel, masts toppling, the ship listing, and Camden's dark head disappearing into the sea.

Whenever she could, Averil went out in the coach, whether it was with Honor, or to accompany her aunt on visits to acquaintances, or just to ride aimlessly. But Lynna seemed to forever accompany her, and Averil grew increasingly disturbed by her cousin's predatory watchfulness.

Everywhere she went, she heard London citizens discussing the latest news items and rumors and agonizing over the dismal outlook. Prince Rupert was raiding in the Chiltern Hills and along the roads to London; for lack of funds and support for his men, the Earl of Essex, general of the Parliament forces, was threatening to resign. There were rumors of plots against Parliament; the prisons were overflowing with those accused of treason, and many were sent there without trial.

The unemployed swelled the number of beggars in the streets. The roads were choked with men, women, and children begging coins or lying ill and dying. It was thought by many that poverty was a sign of God's disfavor, but Averil could not resist the children who clung to the side of her coach as she passed, and she flung them what coins she had, hoping the money would be used for food and not ale to deaden a father's despair.

She wondered repeatedly why she had not heard from the Tottman. Surely he knew nothing of the threatening letter to Jacob—or did he? Was the Tottman even in London still? Had he learned of the letter and decided she was too great a risk to his safety? The last time she had seen him, he had been on his way to help the young couple who had been sent to the prison ship. Had something gone awry that night? Was the Tottman severely injured or even dead at this moment? Her imagination flogged her with gruesome possibilities.

In spite of her promise to Jacob not to see the Tottman again, Averil could not help scanning the roadways for any sign of him or the knife grinder. Just a glimpse of the Tottman or a word from Darby Kipp was all she craved, just to reassure herself that he was well and lived. She hoped desperately, violently, that he was safe.

On Wednesday, June twenty-eighth, the *Indomitable* docked again at Paul's Wharf and with the captain's return, the wedding date was officially set for the following Tuesday, July fourth.

CHAPTER
FIFTEEN

Camden and Averil were married at St. Sepulchre's Church in an early evening ceremony presided over by the aging and beatific Reverend Pritchard. Everything about that day—the church, the ceremony, the guests—had a blurred, dream-like quality to Averil. Dozens of candles, donated by Jacob and Mary Geneva, lit the interior of the church with a molten glow, while warm, dense shadows clung to the rafters overhead. The dark wood pews, the edges of which were dulled by years of being gripped by feverish, reverent hands, were almost filled with people. The Osgoods were present, as well as Eleanor Devenish and Edmond, the Woodbys, Sir John Walford, Morton, Honor, and more whom Averil recognized, and others she could not place at all.

The tip of Averil's head just reached to Camden's shoulder where he stood beside her. They touched not at all, but she was more potently aware of him than she had ever been before.

She wore her hair long and unbound in the sign of virginity.

It was draped with multi-colored ribbons, with more ribbons circling her wrists, her upper arms, her waist, and swirling from her gown, nearly obscuring the white satin skirt. Whenever she moved, she created an image of myriad shifting colors.

Reverend Pritchard's voice was nasal as he recited the words from his gilt-leather book. His nose was long and veined; his hands trembled with age. Or was it she, watching him, who trembled? A nervous, blissful energy surged through her.

When she repeated her vows, her voice was clear. Reverend Pritchard addressed Camden, who stood tall and erect, wearing flawless black velvet breeches and a silvery-grey doublet that matched the shine in his eyes. His voice was richly resonant as he spoke his promises to her. He reached out to take her hand, closing his warm fingers around her, and smiled with unmistakable love and pride as they were declared man and wife. With one hand at the back of her head, he kissed her with smiling lips.

After the ceremony, they returned to the Kirkland home. The guests trailed them in coaches and on horseback through the fog-shrouded streets.

Mary Geneva had created a superb wedding supper. There were meats in a wide array, larks and pullets, prawns and cheese, peas, asparagus, pastries, fruits. Many of the guests brought their own cutlery, so there was no lack in that respect, and Eleanor Devenish supplied extra plates. Jacob tapped the last few casks of wine he had in his personal stock in the cellar. An unmatched assortment of mugs and glasses were passed around as each guest received his share of wine.

Averil and Camden together occupied the head of the table in the dining room. Because there were too many people to be seated at the table, the remaining guests partook of the meal wherever they could—standing, sitting, in the large parlor, the dining room, the hall, on the terrace steps.

Averil felt Camden take her hand beneath the table. They had not had a single moment alone together this day, but

Averil felt as though a silken cocoon entwined them both, and the rest of the world passed by unheeded.

She sipped her wine and returned the squeeze of Camden's fingers as she listened to the sound of his voice in conversation with a guest to his left. Though she herself chatted superficially with a young man on her right, whose name escaped her repeated attempts to remember it, her senses were attuned to the presence and voice and touch of her husband beside her. Her supper remained virtually untouched on her plate. As though happiness were a palpable thing, it left no room inside her for anything else.

Camden turned from his conversation with the woman on his left. He bent his head toward Averil and his lips brushed the ribbons and strands of hair over her ear.

"The hours do drag, don't they," he murmured.

She looked up, smiling, and was not prepared for the exquisite promise she saw in his eyes. Her heartbeat quickened in response.

She dragged her eyes from his and looked down the length of the table, seeing, yet not seeing the varied guests. A pair of accusing tawny eyes caught her attention. Edmond Devenish's scowling gaze raked her, bringing out a flush of shame and guilt in her cheeks, though she could find no reason that she should feel that way.

Camden caught the look in Edmond's gaze and the corresponding embarrassment it caused Averil. With a pricking of discontent, he remembered Lynna's claim that Averil had promised to marry Edmond. When Edmond shifted his attention to Camden, he met a hard, steel-like stare that forced him to avert his eyes.

Shortly after supper Camden was drawn away by some of the men who were intent upon toasting him with a round of freshly refilled glasses. Averil, in turn, was surrounded by some of the women who chatted and laughed together about their own weddings and those of others. Beneath the gaiety, they watched her closely and nudged each other, grinning, whenever Averil's eyes strayed to the group of men.

Lynna stood with the women around Averil, but though she participated in the festivities with almost fierce gaiety, her look at the new bride was piercing with hatred. Several guests had brought musical instruments, and others gathered around them as a tune rose in the air. Honor's brother, a short, flat-faced young man, strummed the guitar he had brought and sang in a high, melodious voice.

Sir John strolled over to Averil. "A kiss for the new bride," he said lightly as he leaned down and kissed her cheek. "Congratulations, sweetheart."

"Oh, Sir John, I'm so happy!" She threw her arms around his neck and hugged him impulsively.

"I'm glad to hear that." His unlined, boyish face grinned back at her. "Frankly, when I received news of the wedding, I was not at all sure what to expect. It seemed so sudden. But you are your father's daughter through and through. Speaking of your father," he added, dropping his voice, "I sent a message to Prince Rupert enquiring about William."

Averil's smile faded. "What did he say? Have you received a reply?"

"Nay, it's been scarcely a month since I sent the letter." He shrugged. "We'll have to wait and see. If I hear anything at all, I'll let you know."

Sir John excused himself with a wink to Averil when he saw her new husband extricate himself from Percival's company and start toward her. Some of the guests were requesting a tune to dance to, and the amateur musicians complied. As the strains of a high-spirited melody filled the room, Camden took Averil's hand. They joined a line of people and stepped immediately into a fast-paced country dance.

The gaily colored ribbons in her hair lifted around her as Averil twirled to the music. She felt gloriously light. Camden led her through the patterns of the dance with a playful grin on his face. His teeth gleamed as white as the broad, square collar of his shirt.

The song continued through verse after verse, and couples dropped out, breathless, while new ones took their place on either side of the newly wedded pair. Averil never noticed. She danced the steps without thought or effort. All her attention was focused on Camden's smiling face hovering above hers, on the brilliant and compelling shine in his eyes. Flickering candlelight and dark shadows shifted behind his head as they crossed in time to the music. Faces passed by the outer line of her vision, but she paid them no heed.

When the last line of the song had been sung and the music ended, Averil collapsed against Camden's chest in breathless laughter. When she looked up again, the playfulness was gone from his face. The grey eyes were darkly serious, and Averil felt a sweet tension wind through her.

With a hand at her elbow, Camden led her to the side of the room where there were empty chairs. They sat side by side, and he put his arm behind her chair. With stroking fingers, he caressed the nape of her neck through the strands of hair and trailing ribbons. She grew suffused with warmth and a pleasurable weakness, and every inch of her longed for his touch.

Across the room, Esther Osgood jabbed her elbow into Mary Geneva's side and indicated the couple with a tilt of her head. "Isn't it time, Mary Geneva?" she suggested with a short laugh. The newly wedded pair had completed the first dance, and now the time had come for them to retire to the bridal chamber.

Averil's attention was drawn away from Camden when she saw Jacob and Mary Geneva winding their way through the crowd toward them. A beaming Jacob took her hands and drew her to her feet. He looked to Camden, grinning as he said, "We're going to part you two for just a few minutes, Captain."

She was handed to Mary Geneva who smiled nostalgically before drawing Averil into the center of the room. Mary Geneva had insisted on an old-fashioned ribbon ceremony

and as the guests gathered around, Eleanor Devenish helped
Mary Geneva carefully remove the decorative ribbons Averil
wore. Amid laughter and good-natured joking the ribbons
were passed around, one to each guest as a memento of the
occasion.

When that was done, Mary Geneva led Averil from the
room, inviting Eleanor to assist her. Lynna pushed through
the crowd and joined them. Averil looked back once as she
started up the stairs, and her eyes found Camden in the center
of a congratulatory group. Percival Osgood was pressing
another full glass of wine into his hand while Sir John clapped
him heartily on the back. Averil smiled to herself and ran
lightly up the stairs ahead of her aunt.

In Averil's chamber a fire burned with a cheerful, crackling
warmth. A candle was lit beside the turned-back bed. With
much excitement and laughter, Mary Geneva and Eleanor
helped Averil remove her white gown. Lynna hung back,
though no one noticed. Across the bed lay a gown Mary
Geneva had made for Averil. It was a deep blue satin gown
with a fitted bodice cut low and square. Flowing sleeves
reached to the wrists and were trimmed with lace. It was
a fine sleeping gown, and Averil had been touched when
Mary Geneva had presented it to her earlier in the day.

When Averil was attired in the smooth satin folds, Lynna
suddenly moved forward, reaching to take the hairbrush from
her mother's hand.

"I'll take care of that," she said. "And I'd like a few
minutes alone with Averil to talk. Please, mother." Lynna
smiled disarmingly and hugged the hairbrush against her chest
as she appealed to her mother. "You have the sack posset
to prepare now."

Mary Geneva nodded. "Not too long, though, Lynna."

When Mary Geneva and Eleanor had retired from the
room, Lynna turned to Averil, motioning her to sit on the
stool near the hearth. As Averil complied, Lynna began to
draw the brush slowly through the glossy strands.

The two women were silent for a time, each lost in distant and far different thoughts. Averil waited in trembling and terrified excitement, thinking of Camden. She was unaware that her cousin thought also of Camden.

Lynna's hands trembled slightly as she stroked the hairbrush through Averil's heavy waves, though it was not excitement but anger that ignited Lynna's thoughts. Soon Averil and the captain would be here in this room, sealing their marriage vows. Half mad with fury and jealousy, Lynna longed to revenge herself. She would make Averil regret ever meeting the captain! As she worked, Lynna concentrated on finding a means to achieve that goal, but her frustration and ire mounted as nothing of apparent use surfaced in her mind. At last she stalked away from Averil and slapped the hairbrush down on the dressing table. The unexpectedness of the action jerked Averil's attention back to the present.

Lynna planted her hands on her hips and glared at Averil. "Always the fortunate one, aren't you?" Lynna exclaimed, a half sneer in her voice. She had chosen to ignore the fact that her own home was still intact, her family safe—components of her life that were commonplace and therefore taken for granted. She pushed ahead, mindlessly, "My father could have offered the same dowry for me, but nay, he chose to spend it for you!"

Impatient with Lynna's outburst, Averil replied sharply, "But there was no dowry, Lynna. There was nothing your—" She stopped, suddenly realizing how her words sounded, how much more hurtful to Lynna this news might be. She sought some means of retracting her words, but Lynna laughed aloud. It was an ugly sound.

"No dowry?" Lynna repeated. "Do you mean you don't know?"

"What are you talking about?"

"The *dowry* contract." Lynna's triumphant smile deepened as a new idea skipped through her mind. She knew something Averil did not. Could she use this to her advantage?

Averil frowned as she said, "Both Jacob and Camden told me there was no dowry."

With a casual shrug, Lynna explained, "I saw the document myself. And read it. Every word. It was signed by both of them." At Averil's stunned expression, she shook her head in feigned sadness. "It seems they lied to you, cousin. Now why do you suppose they would want to do that?" She lifted her eyebrows in innocent wonder.

"I have no idea what you read, Lynna, but there was no dowry, and I was not lied to. Unless it was by *you*." Averil rose from the stool before the fire and turned her back on Lynna as if in dismissal.

Undisturbed by the accusation, Lynna said, "I suppose it would be something of a shock to hear. But I'm surprised you believed my father so completely. Heavens, I think we both know how manipulative he can be if it suits him." Turning away slightly, Lynna shot a sly glance from the tip of her eye to judge Averil's reaction. She caught the barely perceptible slump in Averil's shoulders, the slight downward tilt of her head. So! Lynna mused, this was indeed a weapon!

Averil turned around again until she faced Lynna, though her eyes darted elsewhere, never quite focusing on her cousin. Lynna grinned to herself as she added, "It was a handsome bargain, to my way of thinking. You should be mightily happy about it. But please, they've gone to the trouble of keeping it from you, so don't let on that I told you. Father tried to keep it secret from me, as well!"

Averil's troubled gaze finally settled on Lynna's face. "Why would they not tell me of it?"

"Heaven knows! There must be something to gain by the secrecy, why else would—"

"What did the contract say?"

Lynna studied her cousin almost sympathetically. "Honestly, Averil, I don't know that I should tell you—"

"*What did the contract say!*"

As if forced beyond her will, Lynna gave in with what

could have passed for a peevish sigh. "All right. When has a dowry ever been secret anyway?" So Lynna told her. She had spent a great deal of time in her father's study, perusing the contents, and now related every detail, relishing the increased depression she sensed in her listener. Lynna had no idea why this information should so adversely affect Averil, but she was half wild with a desire to destroy the relationship her cousin shared with Camden—a relationship that had been denied her—and so seized on whatever might crush Averil's happiness.

When Lynna had finished speaking, Averil eyed her cousin uncertainly. She opened her mouth to utter some protest, but realized it would be a futile protest. The contract as Lynna described it was too detailed, too plausible, and all too realistic when one knew the men involved, to not be true. Averil turned aside to stare into the flames leaping within the black, cavernous fireplace.

So Camden deliberately lied to her.

Tremors of hurt broke over her. Camden had said he would not be getting anything from Jacob, when in reality he was getting so very much!

She could not have explained why this news of the contract hurt her as it did—a worthy dowry should be a thing of pride. But she had been so desperately pleased to think Camden loved her and wanted her regardless of her lack of dowry. She had seized on the idea with all the youthful passion she possessed. She had wanted to be so loved by him. But in the wanting, she had been a fool—such a fool! she cried to herself. The pain rushed through her, great waves of pain that made her sway and tremble under their force.

Why did he lie? What purpose could he have had for lying? And the lie had come so easily to him!

Lynna, whose presence Averil had forgotten, uttered an excuse and started for the door. In that moment Averil heard the sounds of merrymaking and footsteps coming upward on the stairs. They were coming. *He* was coming. By tradition, the guests would see them put to bed. Panicking,

Averil cried out, "Nay, Lynna, don't leave now. Stay with me!"

Lynna shot her a part-triumphant, part-scornful look and left the room.

The laughter and accompanying footfalls echoed down the hall as the group approached. The door opened and Camden slipped inside, closing the door firmly behind him, barring entrance to all others. There was a moment of confused silence on the other side of the door, then a protest rose, and several hands banged on the panels. Camden swung out with one foot and snared a nearby chair. He dragged it to him and propped it under the doorhandle. The door was tested from the other side, and a loud voice cried, "What are you doing? Open the door!"

"Tradition stops right here!" Camden called back with a chuckle, arms folded, leaning one shoulder on the door.

"But what about the sack posset?" the voice protested.

"I never drink them!" Camden answered, grinning.

After a few more vigorous tries at the door and a spattering of ribald comments and jests, the disgruntled and disappointed group filed slowly away and returned downstairs. Like a sleepwalker awakening to her surroundings, Averil looked at her new husband with mingled apprehension and disbelief. He managed to turn every situation to fit his own desires, she thought. Her gaze fell on the waiting bed and her eyes widened in dismay. What have I done? she thought wildly. I don't know him!

Camden smiled apologetically. "I'm sorry if I upset your sense of propriety, Averil, but I was not about to let that group in here to see you in bed. Do you mind very much?"

She shook her head vaguely, aware not so much of the words he spoke as of the self-satisfaction and easy confidence which emanated from him.

Something of her wariness translated itself to him and Camden's eyes softened. He crossed the room toward her, but she backed away and he halted.

"Averil? Are you so frightened of me?"

When she remained silent, he reached for her and swept her to him. Averil stiffened in his arms. "Ah, Averil—I can be gentle," he murmured against her hair. He held her close, stroking her back. The satin fabric was still warm from the hearth. As she stood within his embrace, Averil felt again a measure of the happiness she had known earlier. She had been so happy, until Lynna had revealed the truth to her. At the thought, the hurt washed through her again.

Camden held her face in his hands, pressed little kisses over her face—such thrilling soft kisses. Maybe she could forget the lie for a while. His mouth moved to hers, covered it, slanted into a deep, hard kiss that almost wiped her mind clean of any other thought. Weak, she leaned into him, curiously ready to forget all else. Eager to forget all else. But she pushed against him, murmuring, "Tell me about the dowry contract."

Instead of answering, his mouth caught at hers once more, and the thrust of his tongue into her mouth was a streak of excitement. So potent were the effects that she struggled back up as if she were underwater. It seemed to take forever. With her hands trembling against his chest, she broke off the kiss. The grey eyes looked down at her, quizzical, faintly glazed with passion. "What . . . ?"

She felt his heartbeat beneath her hands, its rapid tempo so exciting. "You lied to me," she said, and her voice was no more than an ineffective whisper. "You said there was no dowry."

He lifted his head then and stared at the wall behind her as he stroked her arms. After a long puase, he glanced down into her eyes again and said, "Who told you?"

"So you admit to it now," Averil exclaimed, hurt washing over her anew. She tried to push herself away, but he held her against him.

"Averil! I didn't lie to you."

In anguish, she protested, "I know all about the contract! Lynna told me everything—and you lied, Camden. Why?"

"That evening in the coach, I told you the truth. I won't

be gaining anything—and certainly not in the way you're thinking.''

''Then why the contract!''

''That's entirely for Jacob's sake. To my mind it doesn't have anything to do with you, with us. It's meaningless for us to discuss this now, Averil.'' He closed his arms around her, holding her tightly. ''It has no bearing on—'' His mind on other things, he bent to kiss her. The wait had been long; this day alone had been far too long.

''But it *does*!'' She gave a half-sob and wrenched herself free of him. ''Uncle Jacob will be taking every cargo of yours for *four years*, and all depends on our marriage!''

Camden frowned slightly, eyes narrowing. ''I told you once that any business deals I might make with your uncle concern you not at all. And such is the case here.''

Averil stared up at him, aghast. She was part of an arrangement he had made with her uncle, yet here he was telling her in effect that she had no need of any knowledge of it—as if she were a hen or she-goat traded between them, not expected to understand or care who held her ownership. With almost a screech of fury, she demanded, ''How can the dowry contract *not* concern me when this whole arrangement hinges on our marriage!''

''Averil, if you know so much about this contract, then you must be aware of how much I've offered your uncle, but you don't know how little *I'll* be getting.'' Taking a deep breath and letting it out slowly, he went on, ''I don't have just the one ship, Averil—I have five, and all but one are engaged in trade. Not only that, but I have land both here and in the colonies. Can you honestly believe I'm in such desperate need of what your uncle can give me for just the one ship? I'd be able to find my markets with or without his help.''

Averil remained silent, unconvinced, and Camden explained, ''Your uncle was in need of help. You know what happened to his warehouse, don't you?''

Averil muttered savagely to herself, "So now I am just the solution to a problem."

In exasperation, he exclaimed, "Before you stand and pass judgment on me, perhaps you should consider the full truth, Averil! I paid your uncle for you. Monetarily I gain nothing, regardless of what you think you see in that contract. But I also gain *you*. And to me that means a wealth beyond anything Jacob could even dream of!"

He waited, watching her closely, but Averil said nothing. She was confused by his apparent wealth. Though she had expected he lived comfortably, she had never considered that he was so well off. And this concept, that he had paid Jacob . . . she was still too upset to sort it out in her mind.

Camden reached out to draw her to him, but she pulled away. "I don't know you," she said in a tight voice. "I'm realizing that now. Five ships! Land! What else don't I know? There's just too much . . ." She couldn't have explained it even to herself, but she sensed much more in him than had yet been revealed to her. He caught her arm again, determined, but she wrenched away. "You weren't going to tell me about the dowry contract, were you? That would have been a huge secret. For how long? Now I don't know whether to trust *anything* you say!"

"Averil, you don't mean that!" In exasperated surprise, he stared at her. "I love you. You trust that, surely?"

"Is it me you love?—or your profit?"

Catching her again, he pulled her to him and held her tight against her struggles as he said with grim fury, "I love you, and I married you, and I never lied to you! Why is that not answer enough for you?"

Averil struggled. His fingers bit hard into her arms to hold her. "You're hurting me, Camden," she protested.

His grip softened, but his eyes carried a hard glint of anger as he said, "I love you, and now that I've answered your questions—"

Alarmed by the hard light in his eyes, the grim voice, the

way his mouth compressed in determination, she tried to pull free of his grasp. But he trapped her in his arms, crushing her struggles against his chest.

"You're mine now, Averil. My wife," he said. "Don't fight me, I won't hurt you. I wouldn't do that."

He leaned to kiss her once more, but she felt too vulnerable, frightened of him and the hard, insistent way he was holding her. She tried to turn away. "Nay, don't, Camden," she protested.

Incited both by anger and long-repressed urgency, he scooped her up in an embrace that fairly lifted her off her feet. He felt the soft weight of her in his arms as he bent his head to capture that protesting but oh-so-provocative mouth. He hardly felt the rapid, frantic blows of her small fists on his shoulders as he kissed her. She struggled and twisted and beat at him. Her little cries were muffled against his mouth.

And then the blows softened. Faded. He felt her body slowly relax against his. Under the force of his kiss, her head fell back into the curve of his shoulder.

Abandoning her struggles, Averil melted under the onslaught of his kiss. Waves of sweet weakness broke over her. It was impossible to fight the pleasure he ignited in her. His mouth fairly devoured hers, his tongue hard and demanding, as he ripped apart her resistance. Desire flushed through her body, and she moaned under the fiery force of it. Instinctively, she curled her arms around his neck to hold him nearer and nearer.

He felt that sudden heat in the small, languid, lush form in his arms, and the excitement of her response almost made him lose control. He pressed his face to the curve of her throat, kissing her, breathing the sweet rose he'd smelled on her skin all day. Shifting her weight, he reached low behind her and felt the silken skin of one bare thigh. Her gown had slid up, trapped against his thigh. The touch ignited them; he let her slip back down to her feet as he slid his hands up the back of her legs and raised the hem of the blue satin gown.

Averil gasped at the soft velvet shock of his breeches against her bare thighs. His kiss had left her feeling half-drugged, but apprehension built in her mind again, scattering the languidness. In the firelight his shiny silver doubtlet was streaked with gold, his shoulders beneath the doublet appearing massive at this close range. Again, she was aware of his easy strength. Too strong, too strong. His eyes were too hot and hard, his arms too powerful as he tightened his embrace. How easily he had lifted her—she could have been no more than a doll! How insistent, how relentless he was this night! And when she felt his hands slide over her naked buttocks and touch the very center of her, she jerked involuntarily in astonishment, unprepared for the swift pang of pleasure she felt. His touch was exquisite, but even so she was abruptly alarmed. He was too strong, she too weak from his kisses, defenseless, completely vulnerable and at his mercy. At the realization, fear shot to her brain. She tried to wrench away, pushing and beating on him.

Ignoring her cries, Camden scooped her up in his arms and carried her to the bed. How beautiful were those white silken thighs! How he wanted to nestle there, feel the silk limbs part and close around him. He was on fire with need, passion grinding through him, relentless and undeniable. When he laid her down, she tried to roll away, but he held her still, pressing his weight down over hers. She pushed and beat at him, small fists raining inconsequential blows on his arms and shoulders.

"Averil, don't fight me." He was breathless at the way she twisted under him. "Let me love you—I won't hurt you. I'll be gentle. Oh God, Averil!" he exclaimed, "just be still for a minute, you don't know what you're doing to me!"

He tried to calm himself, to calm her. But the rapid panting of her breath kept pushing the soft breasts into his chest. He'd waited so long. And how exciting was the way she'd relaxed into his embrace minutes earlier, how tempting and responsive her mouth. Heedless of the blows, he lowered his head and kissed her, trapped her mouth with his, bruising and insistent.

But she pushed furiously at him and squirmed to escape. Her hair tangled across her face as she flung her head from side to side. He heard the gasps, the little cries. Carefully he pushed the strands aside and saw that exquisite face shining wet with tears. "Averil, oh Averil," he breathed. "It can't be like this, don't do this." He kissed her wet eyelids, her wet mouth, but she was too upset and beyond him. And his restraint was growing too thin.

"Trust me, Averil . . ."

But she was twisting all the harder, soft small hips jerking just under him, moving against him. That lush core of her was just under him. He wanted to yank the blue satin gown out of his way, touch and caress her, drive himself into that soft young body thrashing so wildly beneath him. He felt sweat breaking out all over as he tried to control himself.

It couldn't come to this, he thought. Not rape. She was crying, sobbing, angry and frightened, while all he could think of was getting that nightgown out of his way. . . .

And suddenly he was afraid of what he might do.

With a muttered curse, he released her and rolled away on the bed. He wiped his wet face with his hands. Averil leaped from the mattress and spun around to face him. Her hair tangled in shiny curls around her face and shoulders, the face between the strands glistened with tears. Camden swung his legs off the other side of the bed and stood up. He was breathing heavily, and for a long time he just looked at her.

"It doesn't have to be this way. Averil, I love you. I would never hurt you. Is it that I frightened you?"

But she remained silent, breathing hard herself. Her tears had stopped and she swept her hair back and wiped her cheeks with her palms. She wouldn't look at him, wouldn't meet his eyes.

His voice was almost toneless as he said, "I know you told me before I left for Amsterdam, but I want to hear it now. Do you love me?"

She drew in a ragged breath. "I don't know."

He started to walk around the bed toward her, but she backed away, watching him so warily that he knew a desperate, wretched fury. Scowling, he motioned to the bed. "Go to sleep then! I won't touch you."

After pinching out the candle, he walked to the hearth, and Averil, unable to decide what else she could do, climbed slowly onto the bed. She had never felt so confused. Nor so aroused, nor so frightened. She couldn't forget those exquisite moments when the hot insistence of his embrace and his mouth had taken her out of herself; she had answered him with an abandon unknown to her. She turned her head on the pillow to watch as he pulled the chair from the door and placed it before the hearth. He sat in the chair, his long legs stretched out in front of him, his attention on the small darting flames. He was deep in contemplation, fingers cradling his chin. Vibrant and rosy-yellow, the firelight glowed behind his stark black silhouette.

CHAPTER
SIXTEEN

When Averil awoke in the morning, she was alone. The pillow beside her bore the imprint of a head, and she knew Camden had lain there. In place of him there was a letter. She reached for it in trepidation, wondering if the message it contained would be a farewell. The thought that he may have left her already brought a desolate sorrow to her heart, and her hands were shaking as she slid from the bed. She went to the window and drew back the thick drapes to have light to read it by.

The sky that greeted her was leaden; fog hung heavily over the city and tangled in the distant church spires. It was still early, she noted. Had Camden slept at all? She unfolded the single sheet of paper and began to read.

"My dearest Averil," the letter said, "I leave you only for a short time as I must make the final arrangements for a home for us away from your aunt and uncle and Lynna. A close friend of mine, who is away at present, has graciously offered his home for our use for as long as we may desire it. It is in London and is adequately staffed, so it seems a perfect, if temporary, haven for us. I would reserve this evening for us alone. There is much I have to tell you. You say you do not know me, so I will share all with you and hold back nothing you desire to know about me. Perhaps then you can come to trust me, and we may begin anew, with no secrets between us, no regrets. I shall return sometime this afternoon for you. Till then, I remain yours in love and faith, Camden.''

A bright spark of hope burned in Averil's breast as she read and reread the letter. Then she folded it away in her drawer and took up a wrapper. Her feet were light on the stairs as she descended to the first floor. All was quiet. Jacob's study was empty, the large parlor put back in order with no evidence remaining of the previous night's celebration. Averil stood in the threshold, looking through the thick shadows. She could hear again a thread of music, hear the buzzing hum of voices, the clink of glassware, Camden's exuberant laughter. At the memory, a smile flitted across her lips. He had promised a new beginning, with no secrets between them, and she desired that with all her heart.

The quick swish of a broom broke into her thoughts, and Averil followed the sound to the dining room. She found Mary Geneva sweeping the boards while Jacob gingerly tested a mug of steaming ale at the table.

"Good morrow," Mary Geneva called briskly. "Your new husband was up and gone early this morning."

"Aye. Is Honor about? Do you think you could spare her for a time to help me pack? Camden has found a place for us to live, so I'll be leaving today."

Jacob winced as the hot liquid in the mug burned his mouth. "I suppose that is all for the best," he mumbled. He looked up with reddened, bleary eyes and moaned. "Oh, my head hurts."

" 'Tis no wonder," Mary Geneva observed in disgust. "You were most definitely celebrating last night." She put aside her broom against the wall. "Averil, would you have time this morning to come with me and pay a call on Reverend Pritchard's wife? He told me last night that she's been indisposed and sorely missed not being able to attend your wedding. Honor can pack your things in our absence.''

Averil nodded, remembering Mrs. Pritchard from the years of visiting London with her mother, though her memory of the woman was still filtered through the eyes of the child she had been.

Impulsively she embraced Mary Geneva. ''Thank you for the wedding, aunt. It was lovely. And thank you also for the shelter and aid you have given me these last months.''

Mary Geneva smiled expansively, and Averil turned to Jacob, who grunted in embarrassment as she kissed his cheek. ''And thank you, Uncle Jacob. I know it was not easy for you to open your home to another and provide for me as you did.''

Jacob reached for her hand and patted it as he replied gruffly, ''I'm glad all has turned out well for you now. The captain is a fine man.''

Honor was summoned from the kitchen garden where she was gathering asparagus shoots, and she accompanied Averil to her chamber. Mary Geneva had Jacob pull out several small trunks for Averil's use. As Averil dressed, she gave instructions to Honor concerning the packing of her gowns and belongings. Morton readied the coach for them, and within the hour, Averil and Mary Geneva were sitting in the front parlor of the Pritchard home being entertained by the frail but still vivacious Mrs. Pritchard.

Though Averil enjoyed the interlude for what small time she could concentrate on the conversation, her thoughts slipped away repeatedly to images of shining silver eyes above a shining silver doublet.

The two visitors declined the offer of dinner, and after kissing Mrs. Pritchard, Mary Geneva and Averil departed in the coach to return home.

They had gone no more than a short distance when they turned a corner and Averil caught sight of Camden at the door of one of the houses. He had his back to the street, and Averil wondered if this was the house he had referred to in his letter. Curious, she craned her head to see it. The structure was small and narrow, two stories high, and set flush with the road. It was a dreary home in a cramped, dismal street. She would never have chosen it of her own accord and knew a moment's disappointment.

As they drew near, she started to call out to Camden, but the door of the house swung open and she recognized Francis Bowers at the threshold. Averil froze at the coach window as Francis grinned at Camden and invited him in. As the door closed behind him again, Averil sagged back against the seat.

Francis Bowers had been involved in the trap set for the Tottman that night on London Bridge. She believed him responsible for the incidents for which her father had been accused and arrested, responsible for the threatening letter sent to Jacob and the subsequent damage to his warehouse stock. The Tottman had warned her of him. Averil felt cold inside, her fingers icy.

What manner of business could Camden have with Francis Bowers?

She could not bring herself to speculate on what she had seen. But once she and Mary Geneva arrived home, and Averil had gone up to her room to check on the progress Honor had made with her things, her mind burned. Honor had already completed the packing, so there was nothing for Averil to do but wait. In that blank time she could not wipe from her mind the image of Camden and Francis Bowers together at the doorstep. She sat gingerly on the edge of her bed and closed her eyes.

How much did Camden know about her through Francis? What was he doing there today? As she had passed the doorstep, it had been obvious to her that the two men knew each other—that they were more than just passing acquaintances.

What could it mean?

Francis wanted the Tottman. Was Camden also involved

in that? Regardless of how he felt about her, he could still
be intent on capturing the Tottman. There was too much she
didn't know about him!

Then another thought burst through her mind. Camden
intended to speak with her tonight, intended to tell her about
himself. Would he reveal this association with Francis?

Neither Camden nor Francis Bowers noticed the coach that
passed in the street as they stood at the door, nor the white
face that stared at them from the window. Francis grinned
at the deadly gleam in his visitor's eyes and stepped aside
for the other to enter.

When the door closed behind him, Camden thrust a paper
under Francis' nose and demanded, ''What the devil are you
up to!''

Francis was triumphant, but said nothing as he led the way
into the small front room. Decorated in drab blues and
browns, it was almost bare of furnishings—a low chest stood
against one wall and two ladder-back chairs with a small table
between them flanked a cold, odor-ridden hearth.

''Have you seen this?'' Camden questioned.

Francis paused in the center of the room and turned to face
Camden. He eyed the sheet of paper crumpled in Camden's
fist. ''Aye. An interesting piece,'' he said.

With a harsh exclamation, Camden flung the paper down
on the low table. It was a copy of *Mercurius Britanicus*, a
Parliamentarian newsheet. Published weekly, the paper
contained satirical stories and rhymes ridiculing the Royalists.
It was a fairly new venture, distributed hand to hand, the
Parliament answer to the Royalist newsheet, *Mercurius
Aulicus*.

Featured prominently in this issue was the tale of a Royalist
messenger stripped of his papers and pride by a Lady Averil
Maslin and her manservant Francis. It was complete with
a cartoon depicting the messenger as a pop-eyed rat being
chased by a hooded noblewoman wielding a skillet.

"I don't care what in hell you were doing," Camden said. "You can throw yourself into the river for all I care! But how did Averil get linked with this?"

Francis rubbed his hands over his mussed hair as he considered his visitor. It was high time the conceited, overbearing dog got taken down a peg, he thought. So he said simply, "She participated in the little adventure, that's how."

"She wouldn't do anything of the kind!"

Francis remained calm. "Oh, you think you know her, do you? You're bloody sure of yourself! Well, my friend, for once you are terribly, wonderfully, wrong. Now, why don't you remove yourself from my house!" He started to cross to the door, but Camden grabbed his shoulder and yanked him around.

"I wouldn't mind cracking your neck." Camden's eyes were unnaturally bright; his muscles swelled ominously. "Who was with you and what happened?"

Angrily Francis jerked himself free of Camden's grasp. "Damn you! Filthy son-of-a-whore! Averil was with me, just as the account says in that sheet!"

"Why would she do something like this, eh? Answer me that!"

"You really don't know, do you?" Francis laughed his anger and derision. "Don't you know how much she has against that Prince Rupert? And *why*? It seems to me you don't know very much about her. But I'll tell you this much, old *friend*—Averil's eating out of my hand now and you can't do a thing about it!"

"I don't believe you!"

"Oh? Have you been around here lately?"

White-lipped with fury, Camden stared at him. Before he had sailed that day, Averil had been like one lost. Had something happened while he was in Amsterdam? Had Francis, someone from her past life, gained her trust? Had she turned to him in her desperation? A pain in his head pounded unmercifully. He tried to marshal his thoughts, but the lines of anger, doubt, and confusion only tangled him deeper.

That scene last night. He thought it was because he had frightened her. But was it just her way of rejecting him? And what about the things Lynna had told him? They were ugly, unbelievable things. But then there was that sharp accusing stare Edmond Devenish had leveled at her at their wedding supper the evening before. Had Lynna spoken truthfully when she said Averil had agreed to marry him, had used him? How much of what Lynna had said about her was true? Was he really so sure of Averil? Or had he only projected onto her what he wanted to see, ignoring all else?

He recalled his meeting with Jacob the day he proposed the marriage arrangement. Jacob had protested Camden's accusation that he had struck Averil by saying—what was it? 'You don't know her as I do . . . you don't know her character.' Something to that effect.

He didn't want to believe any of them—Jacob, Lynna, or Francis—but could he so blindly discount three separate testimonials against her? He left Francis' house, the sense of caution that was so natural to him reasserting itself with uncommon power.

Shortly before two in the afternoon, a coach drew up to the door and Averil watched from the front room window as Camden alighted. She had ceased her tears long ago and her eyes betrayed no redness. But a nervous tremor seized her as she watched him approach the door and heard the heavy knocker strike through the silence.

Honor admitted him, and when he appeared in the doorway, Averil looked at him warily, measuring him, wondering, and was dismayed by the distance in his gaze.

Averil's spirit felt frozen inside her as she made her farewells to the family. Camden's smile was forced as he accepted the good wishes. Jacob, Mary Geneva, Honor, and

Morton saw them off, and Averil watched the figures recede as the coach bore her away down the street with her new husband. A terrible emptiness engulfed her.

Camden occupied the seat across from her and Averil finally dragged her eyes to his. From beneath slightly lowered eyelids, he watched her. They sat in silence. Neither moved except for a gentle, involuntary sway whenever the coach rocked. She wondered where they were going but asked nothing, and he volunteered nothing.

They turned into the crescent-shaped drive of a home near the beginning of the Strand where it met Drury Lane. Two wrought-iron gates guarding the entrance and exit to the circular drive were swung back and latched open. A recently erected brick wall enclosed the front courtyard. The expensive, four-storied structure they halted before was built of pink stone, two matching staircases extended like wings from a main entrance on the second floor. Rows of sparkling, lead-patterned windows gazed back at her blankly as Averil alighted from the coach on Camden's arm. Along the brick wall to the right of the home, a gardener was clipping hedges, and the fragrance of sweetbriar hung in the still air.

"Why are we stopping here?" Averil asked in bewilderment.

Camden looked around at the well-tended shrubs and studied the row of yew trees lining the property's left boundary. They had grown half again as high as the house. "This is your new home."

"This is your friend's home?" Averil questioned, her voice sliding to a whisper of surprise. "I never expected this much."

Camden's face was blank. He took her arm and turned her around to the coach. "And this is Hosiah," he said, extending his hand to indicate the driver. "He is the son of the couple who oversee the running and maintenance of the house and grounds. This coach is at your disposal, and Hosiah will be glad to take you wherever you desire. Hosiah, this is my wife.''

Hosiah, a young man with crinkly blond hair curling over his eyes, ears and collar, grinned shyly and nodded to her. Averil looked at him in surprise; she had thought this to be a hired coach and driver.

At Camden's nod, the young man clicked his tongue to the two horses and the coach was led to the left side of the house and disappeared behind it on a pebbled path.

Feeling a hand at the small of her back, Averil looked back again to Camden. They approached the right wing of the staircase that ascended to the heavy main door.

''Who is your friend—the one who owns this home?'' she asked.

''Denningham's his name,'' Camden said absently, his eyes traveling to the top of the steps.

Waiting to greet them at the upper landing was an older woman dressed all in black, with a white linen cap on her head. Before Averil and Camden reached her, a girl of perhaps thirteen, dressed similarly to the older woman but with a long, linen apron tied around her waist, ran eagerly out of the door. She had pink flushed cheeks and light blue eyes, a pretty girl, and her chest heaved as if she had come running from a distance.

''Averil, I'd like you to meet Mrs. Quint and her daughter, Ruth,'' Camden said, smiling to the older woman when they reached the landing. ''And this is my wife, Mrs. Warrender.''

Averil's attention caught on her new name, so effortlessly spoken, as if they had been man and wife for years. Little goosebumps—whether from apprehension or pleasure, she could not determine—flitted along her skin. She managed a smile for both women. Ruth tucked one foot behind the other and bobbed a quick curtsy, but said nothing. Her bright eyes returned to Camden almost immediately.

Mrs. Quint was perhaps forty years old, short, rounding—a good-humored woman. She took Averil's hands. ''Ah, madam, how very good it is to meet you and have you here.'' She smiled happily and proudly. Her full-cheeked face bore a healthy pink-and-cream glow, and her eyes were light blue with straight, sandy-colored lashes. "And that be Mr. Quint pruning the bushes there. But he doesn't speak much, so you mustn't take it amiss if he doesn't greet you."

The residence Averil was ushered into a minute later was spacious and clean. Every inch—from parquet floor and dark wood balustrade to the floral motifs finely carved in the mantels—was polished and gleaming. The intricately detailed ceilings in each room were swept free of cobwebs, and their plaster whiteness reflected a soft brilliance down into the rooms. But each room Averil peered into, though tastefully decorated, seemed arid and lifeless. It occurred to Averil that the rooms bore no stamp of use, no comfortable feeling of personalities impressed upon the surroundings. She felt a mirroring aridness in her heart.

Camden had remained outside talking to Ruth as Averil followed Mrs. Quint into the house, but now he entered behind Hosiah and Mr. Quint, shouldering trunks which they carried up to the second floor. Mrs. Quint, Averil, and Ruth hastened after them.

"These will be your chambers, madam," Mrs. Quint announced.

Averil was shown into a suite of rooms, four in all, opening one into another. There was a sitting room, a spacious and airy bedchamber, a dressing room which opened into both the bedroom and sitting room, and a smaller room, completely barren of furniture, off the far side of the bedchamber.

After showing her through the suite, Mrs. Quint left Averil in the sitting room and returned to the dressing chamber where the men had taken the trunks. Alone now, Averil sat on the edge of a holly-green satin couch. She had not realized she was so tired.

She sat facing the hearth in which a brazier of sea coal glowed warmly. The mantel above it was artfully carved with cherubs, and paintings in gilt-edged frames filled the walls. Everywhere Averil looked, her eyes met the luster of oiled wood and the shimmer of rich colors.

After Mrs. Quint and her and son and daughter had departed, Camden strolled toward Averil, removing his silver doublet, the one he had worn the day before for their wedding, and tossing it over the back of the couch. He crossed to a tall, gleaming, dark-wood cupboard beside the hearth.

"Would you like something to drink? You look tired," he said.

Averil started to shake her head, then changed her mind. "Aye, please." His back was to her and she looked at the tall, strong frame, the thick shoulders narrowing to a lean waist and hips. Why was the sight of him still so pleasing to her? she wondered dismally.

After pouring two cups of a light amber wine, Camden brought hers to her and settled himself on the couch beside her.

"Soon you'll be free to do as you wish, but I want to have a little talk first," he said as he raised the cup to his lips.

"I thought that was to take place this evening," Averil commented.

"I won't be here this evening."

Camden sighed imperceptibly as he looked at her lowered profile. How was he supposed to begin? he wondered. Excuse me, my dear, but are you deceiving me? Have you been waylaying messengers in the dead of night? A muscle clenched in his jaw, and he stroked his face absently, watching her.

Ah, but she really was a lovely thing. He glanced over the swelling breasts, the curve of waist into hips. He thought of her response to him in the coach that evening. The depth of her passion had frankly surprised him; he had not expected such in a woman so young and inexperienced. But what had surprised him more was the intense pleasure he had known. . . .

He ground his teeth together, angered that there might be truth in his doubts about her, angered that doubts even existed. Not realizing there was an edge in his voice, he said,

"I hope you were able to keep yourself entertained while I was in Amsterdam."

Averil darted a small, confused glance at him. "Oh—aye."

"Did you get out often?"

"Occasionally," she answered, uneasily.

"Incidentally, Francis Bowers sends his best regards."

Though he had expected some response to this mention of Francis, Camden was unprepared for the immediate and ghastly draining of color from her face. He stared at her in frank astonishment, then struck again, before she could rally herself.

"He says you're greatly to be thanked for the success of his recent mission."

Averil swayed, her green eyes glazing over with horror. Instinctively, Camden reached to catch her, but she pushed weakly at him. "Nay," she gasped out. She fought for breath and shivered like a half-drowned kitten. "Don't touch me."

He sat back, hating himself, furious with her. "Did you think I wouldn't find out?" he asked. "Did you think you could keep all this hidden from me?"

Averil's hands fluttered to her face, covered her mouth, trembled over her eyes. Even with the reflected crimson-pink glow from the hearth on her, her skin looked bloodless. "I'm not feeling well," she moaned. "I—" She started to push herself up from the couch, but Camden held her down with a hand on her shoulder.

"I'm not finished yet," he said without inflection. He reached out with one foot and kicked over a wooden coal bucket from beside the hearth. It clattered and rolled to a stop near Averil's feet. "Use that if you have to."

Dropping her face wearily into her palms, Averil felt the grief welling up inside her. They had caught the Tottman. That was what the reference to Francis' successful mission meant. And that was why she had heard nothing from him these last weeks! When had this taken place? Had she been in any way responsible? Sobs of anguish broke hotly in her throat.

"At least you're capable of remorse," Camden said in angry disgust. "Now that we've got that much out, why don't you tell me the rest?"

"Why," she managed to say, "do you need to know anything more? You already have what you want!"

"I don't have *half* what I want from you—what I'm going to get from you!"

"The reward," she said dully.

In one fluid movement, a tightly wound spring was released and he leaped to his feet. "The reward money for the Tottman? Is that what you mean?" he exclaimed.

"Isn't that what you want from me? From Francis?" she said looking hard at him through her tears. "Do you want your *share*?" Sarcasm broke through in her voice. "Or are you more interested in having it all for yourself!"

Fury and disbelief were etched starkly in his face. "Oh, Jesus," he muttered hoarsely, turning away and rubbing his hand over his face. Everything they had said about her was true!

Averil, watching him pace, was abruptly struck with a new and stunning thought. If they didn't have what they wanted, could that possibly mean they didn't have the Tottman yet? Heat from excitement and hope flushed upward into her face. They'd never learn anything from her! Never! Loyalty to the Tottman flamed higher than ever before in her heart.

But what had been Francis' successful mission? Her brow drew sharply into a frown, she bit thoughtfully at her lower lip.

"Such worry, Lady Averil," Camden said with heavy sarcasm. "What is it—you don't like sharing the money?"

Averil started at his voice. He was staring at her with such icy contempt that the pain of it was a blade in her heart. *He knew.* She should have expected he would know her true identity if he knew Francis Bowers, but the shock of hearing him call her this, the tone of his voice, the contempt in his eyes, all set her trembling with hurt and uncertainty.

She took a deep, shaky breath and asked, "How do you know Francis?"

"Oh, he and I were schoolmates at Westminster and then Oxford—many a year ago," he replied with tight-lipped unconcern. "Nothing to what your history is with him, is it? Tell me, just how close *are* you?"

In quick anger Averil almost choked out a retort, but she halted herself. She wouldn't let him goad her into revealing anything. She had to guard the Tottman. "Excuse me, please," she said and stood up to leave the room.

"You aren't even going to grace my question with a lie of denial, are you," he said, stepping in front of her and barring her way. "And you're not excused. I have more questions for you."

The lines of his face were hard, his eyes ice. His cold fury was an almost palpable force. Averil stared at him. Her legs and stomach felt watery with fright.

"I never should have married you!" she cried suddenly. "I never should have believed your lies!"

"You accuse *me* of lies?" he shouted.

She darted toward the doorway. He caught her forearm and yanked her back with such force that her skirts snapped.

"Don't touch me!" she screamed.

"Don't worry," he said through gritted teeth. "I have no intention of *ever* touching you again!"

CHAPTER
SEVENTEEN

Averil lay in the oversized bed. In misery she wondered what her future held. If it was anything like the emptiness she felt now, she did not think she could bear it. She suddenly missed Mary Geneva and Jacob terribly; she missed her room at their house, Honor's chattiness, even Jacob's loud roar as he complained of the expenses the household incurred.

On a table beside the bed lay a tray with her supper on it. Mrs. Quint had delivered it earlier with soothing concern for Averil's health. Apparently Camden had told them she was ill. She could not bring herself to touch any food now.

Much later, as she lay in bed sleepless, Camden returned. She heard him moving about in the sitting room and dressing room. Apprehensively, she waited, but he did not open the door into the bedchamber. Though she tried to prevent it, the bright contempt she had seen earlier in his eyes returned to her mind and brought on a rush of fresh, raw pain.

In the morning, he was gone again and though she found his clothing in evidence in the dressing chamber, she saw no sign of how or where he had passed the night.

Mrs. Quint was pleased to see Averil up and about. "Aye, there's a bit more of a spark in you this mornin', madam," she said, smiling approvingly, as if she had been responsible.

Averil sat at the worktable where Mrs. Quint cracked almonds for a marchpane. She reached for a handful of the nuts to begin cracking them herself, not so much from a desire to help as to divert her mind.

"Have you known Captain Warrender very long?" Averil asked.

"Nigh on eight years it be—as long as we've been employed here. Here now, madam, there's no call for yourself to be workin'. Just rest and I'll fetch you a hot ale." Mrs. Quint swept the almonds from their pile in front of Averil and ladled a mugful of a steaming brew from the pot set to keep warm on the stones in front of the fire.

Averil did not protest, but curled her fingers around the mug and let her palms absorb the heat. Returning to her work, the older woman continued.

"Aye, the captain there—and such a fine man he is too, madam, though I don't doubt you know that well enough yourself. He shows up at the door whenever he's in port. Which is not often enough for Ruth here." The ruffle of her day cap quivered as she chuckled. Her mild blue eyes, almost colorless against the pale lashes, glanced significantly to Averil. "He'll make a first-rate father, but you'll have to be watching that he don't spoil the babes." Tickled, Mrs. Quint laughed again.

Averil tried to smile in return, but the sadness in her heart was only increased. Though she was in part enthralled to hear this woman speak so of Camden, another, deeper part of her struggled against it.

"Tell me something about the owner—Mr. Denningham," she suggested, eager to change the subject.

"Mr. Denningham?" Mrs. Quint cleared her throat and fingered the white cotton ties of her day cap. "Well now, there's another fine man!" She lifted her eyebrows in a facial shrug and her fingers paused, cradling a fat woody almond.

"I'll tell you something, madam," she said earnestly. "It's about our employment here, and I trust'll not go beyond the two of us, eh?"

When Averil nodded, Mrs. Quint said, "Them two men, they've got a good heart, if you know what I mean, madam. It's a rare wonder in these days." She shook her head with emphasis. "But as I was saying—before we came to work here, we were employed in another household for a good many years. You'd think with a sterling record of service they'd have been a bit more understanding, but not them! The lady's diamond-pearl earbobs and bracelet disappeared and they looked to me as the guilty one. Personally, I think it was the husband—gambling and running up the bills like he did all the time. He pawned 'em for sure, I'll stake my life on it." With vehemence she cracked the almond in her hand.

"So your family was dismissed?" Averil suggested.

"Aye, and a hard time it were too. No good word for us, not from them. For want of funds, we couldn't pay our bills—it don't take long nowadays to find oneself a debtor. But we were innocent, madam, I swear it."

Averil sipped at her drink and nodded.

"Mr. Denningham found Mr. Quint in—well, it was in Newgate, I have to admit it. He paid the debt for us—two pound ten—and hired us on. A kinder man you'll not find."

Before Averil could make a reply, Ruth leaned into the doorway. She wore a tall-crowned black hat over her day cap and a basket swung lightly and emptily from one arm. "Hello, Mum," she called cheerily. "I'm off now, so what d'you lack?" In the contrast from sunlight to the dimmer interior of the kitchen, she did not at first detect Averil's presence. "The captain's leaving for the wharf and he's offered to drive me in his coach."

"Mind yourself and fetch me a bit—"

"The captain's still here?" Averil exclaimed. "I didn't see him."

Ruth flushed deeply and mumbling, "Ma'am," dropped a quick curtsy. "Aye, he's been a'working in his—in the study, ma'am. If you want to see him, he's around front with Hosiah."

Averil made a small, negative motion of her hand.

"Oh, and Mum, he wants me to tell you he's leaving for Stepney. Won't be back for a day or two."

Averil looked away to cover her poignant disappointment. He was leaving. And he had not mentioned it. The shift from his caring to his indifference was so complete, Averil could well believe he had never loved her.

Mrs. Quint said, "A bit of sugar, a neat's tongue, and a mess of turnips for me, Ruth—there's a girl."

Restless and feeling very much alone now, Averil left the kitchen and walked out through the rear courtyard garden. Mr. Quint, a short man with stocky legs, was at work weeding the massive flower beds. He watched her with squinted, opaque eyes, but did not nod or speak or otherwise acknowledge her presence. She kept her distance.

She dined alone that evening. The long dining room with its rows of portraits on the walls was lit by only one candle set near her end of the table. Beyond the bright flame, the opposite end of the room faded into shadows. In the deep silence, Averil could hear herself breathe, chew, swallow. She pushed the solid lumps of meat and vegetables around on her plate for a time, then set down her fork and fled the room.

"Thank you, Hosiah. Here will be fine." Averil squinted up at the young man sitting on the driver's bench of the coach. The sun lay heavy in the sky—a dry, airless noon—and the stench was high from the running sewers that scored so many of the roads. "In about three hours," she added.

Hosiah nodded to her. "Aye, ma'am, I'll be here," he said, and whistled to the horses to start them off.

Using the excuse of browsing the shops for an afternoon, Averil had asked Hosiah to drive her to a corner at Paul's

Churchyard. But once the coach was out of sight, she headed down the road to Fleet Street.

Though she was attired as conservatively as she could manage from her wardrobe, Averil still caused any number of curious glances once she arrived in Fleet Street. Her clothing was of obviously better quality than the typical housewife out for her shopping, and she was unescorted.

She paid no heed to the onlookers as she wound her way amongst the porters and animals in the road; her every attention was on locating the one-eyed knife grinder. She had to hear of the Tottman—was he well and safe? Had he been successful in freeing the people from the prison ship? Had he any more news of her father? And she had to warn him of Camden's relationship with Francis Bowers and her suspicions that her husband likewise was working to apprehend him.

Just to learn that the Tottman was still free would satisfy her immensely.

Beneath the light cloak she wore, her gown was beginning to cling to her damp skin. And though she had worn her most comfortable and serviceable pair of shoes, they were not meant for extended walking. A blister grew painfully on her right heel. Anxiously she watched the length of her shadow in the dirt of the street, gauging the passage of time.

She avoided the squalid area near the Fleet Ditch, one of the worst sectors in the city. Then, far ahead of her in the street, a tavern door swung open and Darby Kipp emerged. Averil's heartbeat hit an erratic, excited rhythm and she put up her hand to catch his attention. But though she thought he had seen her, he started away up the street, shuffling awkwardly, his whetstone careening from side to side.

Averil hurried her steps, breathlessly pushing past the people in her way. But despite her efforts, the distance widened perceptibly. Because of the cluster of people around a dancing monkey, she lost sight of him, and when she passed the crowd, the knife grinder was nowhere to be found.

For as long as she dared, Averil hunted along the street. In an agony of searching, she peered into evil-smelling side alleys, pulled open shop doors to scan the interiors, and braved long looks and laughing invitations when she entered taverns. But Darby Kipp was not to be found.

And she realized he had not wanted to be found.

Had the Tottman abandoned her because of the letter to Jacob and her marriage to Camden? Somehow, he must have discovered a potential threat in her. And he had instructed Darby Kipp to avoid her.

The following day she again went out, but this time to see Sir John. She could wait no longer to know if he had received any reply to his letter to Prince Rupert. Sir John was not in when she called on him, and she turned her steps back to the coach in disappointment. She had genuinely wished to see him, even if there had been no message from Rupert.

Despite Mrs. Quint's cheerfulness, frustration and loneliness pressed in on her. Camden was gone from her, the Tottman was not to be found, and Sir John was absent whenever she tried to see him. And so she took on the increasing and inescapably feminine burden of waiting.

Early morning sunlight slanted into the bedroom through a window in the dressing chamber and fell across Averil. She felt its welcome heat pressing into her arm, her hip, the side of her face as she leaned closer to the looking glass. Was it a trick of the light or did she really look this pale and lifeless? Her eyes were washed-out and tired, her cheeks thinner, lips colorless and unsmiling.

She wore only a smock; her feet were bare, and her hair hung loose and tangled down her back. Sighing sleepily at her pale reflection, she dipped a corner of a towel in the water basin and scrubbed her face. She still could not accustom herself to the feel of the almost constant layering of London grit on her skin or in her mouth.

A shadow fell over her and blotted out the sun, causing

goosebumps from the sudden coolness to start out on her arms. She looked up. Camden stood in the open doorway between the dressing and sleeping chambers.

He was fully dressed, wearing a vivid burgundy doublet and breeches, the doublet trimmed in silver thread and buttoned only over his upper chest. From his right hand hung the swordbelt he had returned to the dressing chamber to find. He had seen Averil approach the mirror and study her reflection. The sight of her, the simple white smock and just-visible bare feet, the sleep-tangled strands of hair curling over her back and about her waist, had awakened in him a tender yet urgent need for her. Knowing he would not have her now, but unable to turn away from the sight of her simplest, unaware actions, he watched her in bitter fascination.

His involuntary step forward suddenly struck the sun from her and now she was aware of him. He regretted the loss of that natural unawareness in her; now she stood stiffer, her face severe in his shadow. The hand that reached for the towel to hold in front of the smock was moved in the complete awareness of being observed.

"You've returned," she said without inflection, in the bluntness of unease.

"I'll be seeing your uncle this morning," he said. "I plan to invite them to sup here soon." The idea had only just occurred to him.

She never changed her expression. "I'd like that," she said.

Wishing she would express something, anything, but the unchanging stiffness, he scowled as he asked, "Is everything to your liking? There is nothing else you need?"

She shook her head.

He turned to leave again through the dressing chamber, but Averil cried out, "Camden!" and he looked back.

She hesitated, the towel clutched at her breast. There was such a look of pleading in her face that he became angry again. He had no room in him for forgiveness.

Tightly, he asked, "Did you wish to say something?"
Her face worked, but she said nothing, so he departed.

During the following days, Averil saw virtually nothing of Camden. He was absent from the house most of the time and retired to the study in the evenings. Most of his meals were taken there, Averil discovered. He continued to sleep in the sitting room of the master suite, but he did not seek out his make-shift bed until long after Averil had retired for the night.

Sometimes Averil awakened in the morning to hear him moving about, hear the splash of water as he shaved in the dressing room. But the door between the two chambers now remained closed. He never opened it to look in on her, and though she wished to see him again, her stomach always leaped fearfully whenever she thought of going to the door herself.

As the day of Jacob and Mary Geneva's visit arrived, Averil could not deny the excitement she felt. Her loneliness had increased so that the prospect of guests for supper began to take on the dimensions of a royal visit. She bathed and prepared her hair leisurely so as to help fill the hours till they arrived.

As she toyed with the curls over her forehead, Averil wondered if she could hold up the pose of happy new wife in front of her aunt and uncle. Mrs. Quint and Ruth, though they never made verbal reference to it, were aware of the discord. Would Camden say anything about their estrangement? Would the evening become a charade of wooden gestures and polite, forced conversation? She sighed at the thought, laying her head across her arms, already weary of the tension that would fill the evening.

It was not until many minutes later, when Mrs. Quint entered, that she roused herself. Mrs. Quint gathered clothing for Camden, then departed hastily, full of the importance of seeing to a supper for guests.

Averil dressed in the same red satin gown she had worn the night of the party Jacob and Mary Geneva had given. The sides of the skirt were drawn up to the waist and she wore beneath it a petticoat trimmed with yards of silver lace. At her ears swung pearl earrings, and a simple pearl necklace circled her throat.

When she finally descended the stairs to the main floor, Averil heard voices coming from the formal drawing room and she realized their guests had already arrived. Eagerly, she crossed the parquet floor of the hall and entered the drawing room. It was a deep, broad room decorated with gold and blue fabric at the walls and windows. Though it was daylight still outside, a multitude of candles were lit throughout the room and flickered brightly. A fire burned low in the great hearth. Its heat was unnecessary, for the day had been warm. Two tall windows on the right side of the room stood open, admitting a faint fragrance of honeysuckle and roses with the twilight breeze.

Averil's eyes found Camden first. He was seated in a chair with his back to her, and as she momentarily cast a pleased eye over the brushed, faintly waving dark hair with its bronzed streaks, her heart leaped and she almost lost her courage.

On two matching couches flanking the hearth sat Mary Geneva, Jacob, and Lynna. Jacob chuckled when he saw her approach and rose to kiss her. Now that Averil had been removed from their responsibility, Jacob and Mary Geneva were delighted to see her, and their voices were vigorous and excited as they exclaimed over her. Even Lynna was friendly, kissing Averil in greeting.

Camden rose and took her hand lightly. When Averil glanced to him in surprise and uncertainty, a faint smile touched his lips and eyes. With his gaze warm on her, the feel of his fingers firm around hers, Averil's pulse quickened in happiness. It seemed to her that time and eternity fluttered to a halt, held that one moment apart and inviolate for them, then resumed, fluidly.

Mary Geneva tucked her arm through Averil's. "I vow, I've never seen such a lovely home! Would you show me some of the other rooms, dear? I would love to see more." She rolled her round eyes expressively. "Wait till Eleanor hears about this! She'll be paying you a call just to see that I'm not exaggerating in my description!"

Lynna joined them, but the two men chose to remain in the drawing room to talk. The women crossed the hall to look into the dining room first. Ruth was putting the last touches on the table in preparation for serving supper, and Lynna strolled over to the young girl. She spoke quietly to Ruth, and in a moment the two were deep in conversation. There was something about Ruth's attention to what Lynna was saying that surprised Averil. She wished she could hear the conversation, but her aunt was drawing her toward several paintings on the opposite side of the room.

"My dear, dear Averil, but these are exquisite," Mary Geneva exclaimed. She reached out a hand to a portrait reverently, not quite touching it. "However did the captain find such a home?"

Averil dragged her eyes from Lynna and Ruth as she answered. "It belongs to a friend of his, a Mr. Denningham."

"What a fine family these Denninghams must be. Wealthy, as well, no doubt." She turned to Averil. "You must tell me about this Mr. Denningham. All about him."

She tucked her arm through Averil's as they sauntered to the door. At the doorway she turned and called to her daughter, "Lynna? Shall we see the other rooms now?"

"In a moment, Mother. Why don't you and Averil go along. I'll catch up to you."

At supper they were seated intimately at one end of the long table—Averil and Jacob on one side, Mary Geneva and Lynna across from them, and Camden at the head. Averil sipped the claret in her cup and listened to the easy-flowing conversation, the brief spurts of laughter. The amiable mood of the group transmitted itself to her, and she was able to put aside much of her uneasiness at being near Camden again.

He gave no indication that anything was amiss in their relationship; whenever a more personal question was directed at either of them, he deflected it adroitly. Averil was grateful for the tact he displayed.

Averil found her eyes lingering on Camden more and more often. She watched the shifting expressions of enthusiasm, seriousness, and amusement on his face as he talked; admired the way his fashionably tailored, blue velvet doublet fit snugly over his shoulders; examined the long, dark fingers of one hand resting on the table.

She thought suddenly, unexpectedly, of that hand and those fingers touching her, and a swift rush of pleasure flooded her. Searching his hair, she discovered the faint strand of silver, and she thought of those moments in the coach when she had first noticed it. A small smile touched her face, as if she and Camden shared some special secret. She listened to the comments he made, enjoyed the sound of his laughter, tried to still the butterfly-flutterings in her middle whenever he spoke to her.

She noticed also that his gaze became faintly brooding when he looked at her. Frequently he shifted his attention to Lynna and studied her face and listened to her with thoughtful interest.

They were halfway through Mrs. Quint's well-turned mutton roast when Jacob made mention of the gardener he had encountered on his arrival.

"He's a sour one, to be sure," Jacob vowed. "Wouldn't so much as look in my direction when I asked about the care he used on those musk roses."

Camden explained, "He cannot speak."

"Cannot speak?" Jacob snorted derisively. "Seems more likely he's mean of spirit and refuses to speak."

"Nay. 'Tis a sorry tale, but one that should not be forgotten. One night some six years ago he was set upon by a band of young drunken men intent on doing mischief. When he refused to speak to them or even acknowledge their presence, they decided to pay him equally—and cut out his tongue."

Averil caught her breath, aghast at the tale. Camden's eyes sought her out and there was sadness in his look. She met his eyes wonderingly. Could such compassion be evident in a man who practiced deceit?

After supper, when Mrs. Quint brought earthenware pitchers of warm, spiced wine to the table, Camden rose. "If you women will excuse me, there is some business Jacob and I must attend to."

As the men departed the dining room, Mrs. Quint passed spiced wine to the women and beamed broadly at Mary Geneva's profuse compliments on the meal. Recognizing a kindred spirit, Mrs. Quint fell into energetic conversation with Mary Geneva, and Averil and Lynna carried their wine with them as they returned to the drawing room.

"Averil, you'll never guess!" Lynna exclaimed as they entered the room and were out of earshot of the dining room. "I met Francis Bowers in London just recently. Do you know, he's known the captain for years!"

"Oh?" Averil's face felt stiff, resisting, as she took a seat on one of the couches. Lynna chose the opposite couch.

"Aye! I wonder if he ever visited Francis at Maslin Manor. I certainly would have remembered him if I'd seen him. Now, I don't mean to be disloyal to you, but Francis says it was the captain who wrote the letter to Father about you. He's determined to catch the Tottman and even wagered one hundred pounds to Francis that he could do it! Of course, I haven't—Oh! Averil, are you ill?"

Averil stared at her cousin, her eyes widening as Lynna's face seemed to grow smaller and fade into a dusky shadow.

So it was all true then. All true.

Somewhere inside her, she had refused to believe the worst of Camden. Her heart had held out against the evidence. But now . . . Now there was nothing to hold on to anymore.

After the others joined them, she felt stiff and unfeeling. In desperate panic, she watched Camden.

Though he tried to join in the conversation, Camden was aware of Averil's looks in his direction and the shadowed wretchedness in her face. Tonight, for her sake, for the sake of the Kirklands, he was playing the role of the loving husband. But the initial pleasure of being near Averil again had gradually melded with and then given way to anger. His fury with her was now a solid presence in his chest, and he hated her for her deceit, hated her for this enthrallment with her which he still could not rid himself of, hated her for this painful pressure in his chest.

Camden and Averil stood side by side in the front hall as their guests departed. When he had closed the door behind them, Camden leaned against it as he looked at Averil. Her emerald eyes stared back blankly, lost.

His gaze slid down the slender column of her neck to the neckline of her gown. It was low—low enough to hint at the curves of her breasts that were now rising and falling with her breathing. Past the poisonous dip at her waist, his gaze lingered on the gently rounded hips, and he had visions of a soft, smooth stomach and a small cluster of curls above exquisitely tapered legs.

Averil saw the pupils of his eyes dilate until his gaze was almost black. Her chest tightened in fear and she started to turn away, but he caught her by the waist. In alarm she twisted and pushed hard against him. But he was holding her too tightly and his face above hers was unrelenting, the darkened eyes glittering.

"Nay, Camden," she pleaded, unable to raise her voice above a whisper, "don't. You said you wouldn't touch me!"

Rage pounded through Camden, and his back and chest were wet with the sweat of it. "*Someone* touches you." He was breathing harshly, holding her against her struggles. "Francis? When I was away? Or was it earlier than that? When you two started plotting together?" Fleetingly, in the distant corners of his mind, he rebelled at the rage, but another part flared with unthinking ruthlessness. "There's nothing of the virgin in your passion!" He closed his hand in her hair and pulled her head back as his mouth came down on hers, violently. He ground her hips against him, forcing her body in an angry caress on him.

Abruptly, he released her and Averil stumbled away from him. Ruth hesitated by the post at the foot of the staircase.

Camden's voice was harsh with restrained fury as he said to Ruth, "You can put out the candles now."

Averil fled blindly up the stairs.

Behind her, his steps echoed as he followed, taking two and three stairs at a time. In the hallway she tried to run, but he caught up to her and pulled her with him into the sitting room of their chambers, flinging the door closed behind them.

Tears splashed down Averil's cheeks and she struck back at the hand that held her. Then, wanting to hurt him for everything she had learned now about him and all the pain she felt because of it, she struck at him in a frenzy. But he grasped her wrists and held her fists out of reach of his chest.

"Averil?" he said, and again, urgently, "Averil!"

But she was beyond hearing or caring; her anger brought the sobs out in hoarse, choking sounds. She wrenched her arms, trying to strike him, wild with anger and grief, until she was spent and could only push ineffectively at him. But still he held her away.

Averil tried to calm her ragged breathing, not looking at him, feeling wilted and defeated.

"Why?" she said, her voice low and hoarse from her sobs.

"I'm sorry, Averil," he said. He paused and dropped his hands from her wrists. "I don't have an explanation to give you."

When Averil looked up, his face was drawn and still, the grey eyes watchful but tired, as if he felt as exhausted as she did.

His mouth opened, twisted, moved as if he wanted to speak but could not. At last he said, heavily, "If there is another man . . . If something happened while I was in Amsterdam . . . I was angry earlier, I know, and you had every right to be angry with me." He paused and looked at her steadily.

But his mouth twisted in unconcealable misery as he asked, "*Is* there another man you love?"

Hardly thinking to consider or decide, moved only by the ache in her heart, Averil reached up on her toes and drew that miserably twisting mouth to hers. She kissed him tentatively, exploring, holding his face between her palms.

As she kissed him, his hands came up slowly, ever so slowly, slid through her hair, and cupped the back of her head. Several strands of hair, loosened previously, slid in loops and tangles over his fingers and down her back. He returned her kiss, his mouth expressively gentle over hers.

Groaning softly against her mouth, he muttered, "Love me, Averil. Let me love you."

He kissed her again. His mouth moved over hers and described every curve and facet of her lips and face. He was so careful, so exquisitely tender, that Averil almost wept with the delight. And she knew in those moments that this was where she longed to be. At peace with him. Loving him. She understood now that he loved her, and she him. She curved her arms around him and he dropped his mouth to her neck, her shoulder.

With his thumbs he brushed the sides of her breasts where they were pressed to his chest, and when he kissed her again, his mouth hard with passion, she felt her own need of him plunge into the center of her. Against her abdomen he was thick, solid, insistent.

Even as he tried to be slowly gentle, his breathing grew heavy, and his hands more purposeful. He released the laces at the back of her gown, then those of her stays, until all were free and he swept the garments down away from her. They caught at her waist, held by the sash of her gown. Averil felt the cool air on her bare skin and every nerve ending in her body quivered with exquisitely raw waiting.

His warm palms covered her breasts. His fingers stroked the swollen, curving sides of her breasts. When his mouth found hers again, she closed her eyes, trembling under the

impact of the sensation. Her hands moved up his chest, over
his shoulders, over his arms, exploring the hardness of him,
the strength and solidity.

His hands were ardent and caressing, touching her breasts
until they were taut and aching. She had never felt a man's
touch in this way, and she was flushed with pleasure so
intense, so extraordinary, that it swept through every inch
of her, leaving her burning. And she needed his hands on
her all the more.

She wanted to melt into him, to fit herself to the shape
of his chest and loins and thighs. Sliding her arms around
his neck, she pressed into him, straining toward a closeness
with him.

Camden held Averil hard to him, and through his shirt
he felt the heat of her skin. His breathing was ragged, and
his desire was almost a scorching pain throughout his body.

But he knew another pain that needed release as well, and
was as acute. As he plucked impatiently at the knotted sash
that held the gown at her waist, he muttered, "About . . . the
Tottman, Averil . . . and Francis . . ."

Averil went rigid. As if he had struck her, a small,
involuntary cry broke free. She did feel as if she had been
struck. Now, at this most pure of moments, when she was
so open to him and defenseless against him, he would ask
about the Tottman. Love each other they might, but his goal
was the destruction of the man for whom she felt so much
loyalty.

Her reaction, her cry of muffled shock and fury and pain,
stopped him, and apprehension broke over him like a wave
of icy water. He had made himself vulnerable to her and
then, when she had pulled away, the proof of where her
loyalties lay had come screeching into his brain. Francis
Bowers. He felt shredded, annihilated. What had come over
him to almost trust her as he had? He watched her scoop the
gown up to cover herself. She had lied to him, deceived him.
Her kind of love was meaningless! He held himself rigid,

afraid that if he spoke or touched her, he would do something ugly.

Camden's eyes were hot with fury as they faced each other barely an arm's length apart. But before Averil felt the first stirrings of alarm, he had wrenched open the door and was gone.

Averil tossed about restlessly in the bed. She touched herself tentatively where his hands had been, but experienced such anguished longing for him that despair overwhelmed her.

Wide-eyed, she stared into the heavy shadows above her. She thought of the Tottman, thought with confusion of the decision he had made. A deliberate decision, he had said, and she began to understand something of the depths of a despair that would have forced him to make such a decision—a decision that put his very life in danger. With a new horror, she thought of the trap on London Bridge.

She had to protect the Tottman—had to! But at the expense of her marriage? At the expense of what she so longed for? Why—*why* of all the men seeking to destroy the Tottman—did it have to be Camden? Where should her loyalties be? With Camden or the Tottman? She owed both. She wanted to owe both. To whom did she owe the greater duty? Never before had the conflicts of loyalty and love been so acute. Curling herself into a tight, desolate ball, she wept bitterly and found no rest until after the sky had begun to glow in a dark crimson dawn.

That afternoon, wrapped in her cloak and hood, she paced the neatly laid-out walks in the rear garden. The sky was heavy and dark. A strong wind whipped her. It carried the London dust with it, and behind that the scent of far-away rain.

By mid-afternoon, the first heavy drops began pelting the ground. Dismally Averil pulled her hood closer about her face and started back toward the house. She met Camden walking toward her in the center of the main path.

"Averil, I'd like to talk to you." His face was bland, expressionless. Fat raindrops pelted him, spotting the white shirt with faint circles. She hurried past and up the rear stairs to the open door where welcoming light spilled out into the storm-darkened day.

Camden followed her. Averil was ascending the stairs briskly when he reached the front hall.

"Averil!" he called up to her.

She stopped and looked back, one hand on the gleaming balustrade, the other untying and removing her hood. He stood in the center of the parquet floor in the lower hall, his arms relaxed at his sides, his manner secure.

"There are some questions between us that should be—"

"Nay," she interrupted. "Nay, sir, I will not be subjected to an inquisition." Her anger was like a vibration just beneath the surface, and she continued up the stairs.

"*Averil*!" This time her name was an explosion that echoed around her and bounced off the ceiling. She gritted her teeth but did not stop until she reached the master chambers, where she tried to close the door on him. But he was there behind her, forcing it open with his forearm.

Averil faced him in a quiet fury. She saw anger and tension in his face, in the clenched muscles along his jaw, in the brightness of his eyes. "So you think to use force," she cried, "but I refuse to tell you anything!"

"We have much to discuss."

"We have nothing to discuss!"

He snapped impatiently, "Then why don't you *listen*!"

"There is nothing I care to hear from you." Averil started to remove her rain-sprinkled cloak.

"Not even that I'm leaving?"

Her fingers paused at the ties under her chin, then she went on calmly and drew the cloak from her shoulders. All the anger had deserted her. She dropped the cloak and muff onto the couch.

"Are you saying you're never returning?"

"That's exactly what I'm saying. If the winds are right, I leave in the morning. You're free to remain here. I'll leave you some money before I go and periodically send additional sums for your living expenses. I'll stay in contact with the Quints, so if there is anything else you need, inform Mrs. Quint and I'll make what arrangements are necessary. Do you have any questions?"

Averil stood very still, defeated. "But where will you go, Camden?"

He muttered in disgust, "Does it make a difference?"

CHAPTER
EIGHTEEN

Camden watched from the quarterdeck as his ship was kedged out into the middle currents of the Thames. Below deck, eight men labored to turn the capstan. The ship rolled sluggishly in the water.

It was mid-morning and the sun was bright and distant in a sky laced with high, scudding clouds. A crisp wind snapped at his face and arms as he looked across the deck, watching the progress of the ship. It was customary for the captain to relay all orders through his first mate and to address his men only on formal occasions, but Camden knew each of his crew members personally. He depended on their loyalty and fostered that through a closer contact with them.

"Lay your sails to the yards!" his voice boomed across the deck. "Make ready to set sail!"

"Yea! Yea!"

"Hoist your sails half mast high! Loose the topsails!"

"Yea! Yea!" Sailors scrambled up the ratlines, their steps easy and sure as spiders on a web.

"Haul the cat!" he directed, and the anchor was drawn in.

There was a rhythm to his voice as he gave the orders, a rhythm to the chanted response. It was a rhythm that was soothing to him—a rhythm of order, of purpose, of movement toward a common goal.

"Heave out your foretopsail! Cross your yards!"

"Yea! Yea!"

"Heave out your foresail!"

"Yea! Yea!"

Turning, dark hair blowing about his face, Camden called down the shaft to the helmsman in the steerage room below the quarterdeck, "Ho there! Turn her steady, we're into the wind!" The joints of the whipstaff and rudder creaked in response.

"Out with the main-topsail! Haul the sheets!"

"Yea! Yea!"

"Let fall your mainsail!"

With a great creaking in the timber of masts and yards, all the square, white sails were sheeted home. They spread, snapping, catching the wind, and curved taut and full. The bowsprit dipped to the currents, rocked back slightly, and the ship surged powerfully through the waters.

The *Indomitable* was a beautiful ship. Fashioned of fine English oak, she was trimmed with bright gilded carvings on bow and stern, and there were those on shore who squinted into the sunlight to watch her slide proudly past.

Ahead on the river, the drawbridge section of London Bridge was being raised for the ship, and as they passed, Camden waved to the man above him. The man returned the greeting and the bridge section was lowered back into place over their wake. They glided by Tower Wharf and the imposing, formidable stone outer walls of the Tower of London.

Instead of turning the ship over to his first mate and retiring to the great cabin now, Camden remained on the quarterdeck. The wind felt pleasant on him, washing out his tiredness, relieving him of his anger. He allowed himself to rest there in the surcease of emotion and effort, in the exquisite peace of effortless movement and rhythm.

His gaze lifted to the white sails, beautifully full-bellied with sun and wind, a sight that never failed to move him. He felt with joy the powerful push of the water beneath him. And he felt no longer apart from, but a part of it, this greater rhythm—the rhythm of the currents of the river; the rhythm of the sun beyond the sails; the rhythm of time, of elements and seasons, of life itself.

The sensation filled him, filled his thoughts and all his senses with a heady exultation that flooded deep in him. It was an exquisite sensation—of beauty and cleanness and completion.

Turning, he walked to the rail and peered back toward the dwindling, haze-snared spires of the city. He thought of his life before he knew Averil, of what he would now return to, and the old weariness of all his efforts overwhelmed him. At that moment he knew he would never leave her as fully as he had planned. Forever there would be that spark of her carried with him. There was no logic to this knowledge; it was simply a knowing, and as such was irrefutable.

Camden leaned both hands on the rail and his brow furrowed in thought. If he should return to her, would she accept him? He had to know the truth about her! But it was alarming to contemplate testing her—what if she betrayed him? Could he face the results? He straightened and cast one last look behind the ship as he turned from the rail.

Two men approached Camden as he descended the steps from the quarterdeck. Turning into the narrow hall that led to the great cabin, he motioned for them to follow him. One was Richard Cheyney, the ship's first mate, and the other, a nineteen-year-old man named Giles Nessel.

Both Cheyney and Nessel were aware of an unusual current of tension in their captain's manner. In the cabin, they took seats across the table from Camden as he unrolled several maps and spread them on the table surface. A square of white sunlight from the row of tall windows behind him fell on

Camden's back and cast his shadow onto the maps.

"After I leave this evening, Cheyney, take the ship down to here," Camden pointed with his index finger to a place on the map just north of the Thames estuary. "Instead of two days, wait three for me."

Cheyney nodded his acceptance, though he commented uneasily, "A two-day delay there is dangerous enough, but"—he shrugged—"if you see no other course."

"Why the extra day?" Nessel asked.

After a hesitation, Camden outlined a simple idea he had in mind concerning Averil.

When he had finished, Cheyney and Nessel remained silent in thought. They exchanged brief glances, Nessel's brown eyes wide in a deceptively angelic face—a face that frequently caused older women to smile at him with impulsive maternal warmth.

Cheyney's collar-length blond ringlets hung damp and windblown, and he shoved his fingers, like a comb, into the tangle behind his right ear. "You can't do this alone," he said.

"I can't risk so many lives."

Nessel protested, "But you are the Tottman, my lord, and your cause is the cause of each man on this ship!"

Though Giles Nessel had a fierce if reckless bravery and a quick mind, he was also quick-tempered and inclined to rashness—characteristics Camden sometimes found uncomfortably resminiscent of himself at that age. But he took a special pride in the young man. Camden studied him with a frown.

"I wonder if you realize how very final this might be."

Cheyney said, "But think on it. I agree with what Nessel is trying to say—for you to take unnecessary risks now is unfair to all who have worked with you."

Long ago having come to respect his first mate's opinion, Camden at last conceded. "So be it," he said with a sigh. Looking to Nessel with a small, humorless half-smile, he commented, "But you'll have to guard your own flank."

The young man gave a short chuckle, remembering the night recently in Stepney when Camden had saved him from a surprise assailant.

"We'll need six or seven others, Cheyney, so you'll have to make do with a reduced crew for a time."

Camden pulled out his pipe and tobacco. After filling the white clay bowl, he asked, "How fares our guest, by the way?"

John Ernestus, costumed in old breeches and tunic belted at the hip, waited below in the 'tween decks. A week earlier, in protest of the handbills John Pym was having circulated and posted all over London, he had spoken out vehemently in Parliament. The handbills in question proclaimed that Catholics had killed thousands of Protestants in Ireland and that, at the invitation from His Majesty, Charles Stuart, they would soon be invading England. Not caring about its untruth, Pym had circulated these handbills in an attempt to further turn the people against their King. The resulting panic and isolated riots that had erupted in London as a result had angered Ernestus to the point of jeopardizing himself by speaking out against this action.

Through Percival Osgood, clerk for the House of Commons, Camden had learned enough to make him suspect a secret arrest of Ernestus had been ordered. It had been relatively easy to spirit Ernestus away, and it was now generally believed he had run away into hiding. But news had reached Camden that Ernestus' wife and two-month-old daughter were being watched. The man could not return to see them and, in a panic lest Pym cause their arrest, he had pleaded for their deliverance as well.

Cheyney answered Camden, "Well, he's under severe strain—"

"Aye! I can well believe it."

"—but he won't cause any problem for us. He's learned enough to hold his tongue and wait this out. Have you any thoughts yet on the business of his family?"

"Nay, I've been preoccupied," Camden admitted.

Cheyney and Nessel drew their chairs closer as Camden lifted a sketch of the streets of London from the stack of maps on the table and placed it on top. They considered their choices and discussed possibilities. As they talked, pipe smoke circled above them and clouded the shaft of sunlight.

Nessel used broad gestures when he spoke; Cheyney frequently tapped the deep indentation in his chin. Camden's concentration was evident and focused in his eyes which were bright, intent, lit with animation.

Cheyney was leaning forward in his seat as he said, "And we can use Pottle again for a forgery."

"Nay, not this time." Camden shook his head briskly. "Let's go back to—"

"A shawl!" Nessel sketched a circular shape over his abdomen. "It would work with a shawl!"

Camden chuckled. "Can you imagine if it slips?"

"Or the babe seeks a teat?" At Cheyney's remark, all three men were abruptly laughing.

It was mid-afternoon when the town of Gravesend slid into view. The ship anchored there for customs. All outgoing vessels passed through customs at Gravesend, while London-bound ships stopped at Dover. Camden carried a cargo of cloth, soap, and saltfish.

When the formalities were concluded and the customs officials had departed, the three men met again in Camden's cabin. It was not until some hours later, when the ship slid past the estuary that led to the naval yards in Chatham, that they concluded their plans.

When night had fallen, Camden buckled on his swordbelt and shoved two pistols into the waistband of his breeches. From his chest in the cupboard beneath the bunk, he pulled out a black cloak, a broad-brimmed hat, gloves, and a satin mask. He donned all but the face mask which he tucked inside his black doublet. Taking up a large pouch from the bottom of the chest, he left the cabin.

The deck glowed with a thin yellow light from the ship's

lantern. Most of the men were scattered, eating their supper, and the few of the dogwatch nodded briefly to him. Camden crossed to the rail and peered toward the dark southern shore. All was quiet save for an intermittent creak from the loose whipstaff and the soft whisper of water against the hull of the anchored ship.

Richard Cheyney approached, bringing a shuttered lantern. "Any sign yet of Nicodemus?" he asked.

"Nay, but it's early." Camden glanced past Cheyney to Nessel who joined them at the rail. "The boat's lowered?"

Nessel nodded.

Three pair of eyes returned to search the shore and after some minutes, Cheyney exclaimed, "There." He pointed to a spot farther east on the river where a light gleamed briefly in signal.

Cheyney unshuttered the lantern and signaled in kind. He looked over the rail to his captain, who was already climbing down to the small boat that rocked against the side of the ship. "May all go well," he called down.

Nessel rowed Camden to shore, and when the boat slid into the weeds, Camden climbed out onto the muddy bank and gave the boat a shove to help Nessel return to the *Indomitable*. Then he climbed the short steep bank to where Nicodemus waited. The bearded man held the reins of two horses.

Using a thin slit of light from the lantern, they picked their way carefully over the hills toward the road that led to London.

After Camden's morning departure, Averil wandered forlornly into the dressing room to search out what she would wear that day. She was surprised to find much of Camden's clothing still there, and for a moment she was hopeful that he might return. But her optimism was dashed as she realized it could change nothing in their relationship.

She picked idly through his clothes, wondering if she might

find something she could use in her charade as the lad. Averil knew she should resume her search for her father, but she felt no enthusiasm for the task. She felt only defeat and a violent loneliness.

This will pass, she thought, trying to comfort herself. But the image of her future bereft of Camden stretched out before her like arid wasteland. Not even the thought of returning to Maslin Manor with her father could lift her grief, for she knew there would always be an empty place left in her life.

Averil found nothing in Camden's wardrobe that might be usable. His clothing was far too large for her. At last she decided she could risk his wrath if she took a shirt and breeches and cut them down to fit her. He might not even notice they were missing. She spent the day in her chambers, cutting and stitching. Her progress was slow, revealing the heaviness in her spirit.

The following morning, Mrs. Quint came to her chamber. ''Madam, there's a peddler back of the house. Says he has business with you.''

''A peddler!'' Averil repeated, rising from her seat before the cold hearth. At Mrs. Quint's initial knock on the door, she had shoved her basket of sewing out of sight behind a chair. In confusion, she followed Mrs. Quint down to the rear door.

Darby Kipp waited on the flagstones of the courtyard. With his whetstone beside him he stood patiently, ignoring Mr. Quint, who sauntered past and set himself to work near the edge of the garden. Dazed with elation, Averil fairly skimmed the steps as she descended to him. But she was unhappily aware that Mr. Quint was near enough to hear most of what might be said.

Darby Kipp spoke first. ''I be 'ere on the matter of a debt ye owe me, ma'am. I sharpened yer shears fer ye, if ye remember, and ye were unable to pay then.'' His clear eye gleamed intelligently in his parched face. ''I've come now to collect.''

Averil's spirits fell. She well remembered the day he mentioned. It had been the day of the abortive attempt to rescue the couple from the inn on London Bridge. Darby Kipp had refused payment for sharpening her shears by saying the Tottman paid him for his services. What had happened now? Was Kipp no longer in the Tottman's employ? Where then was the Tottman?

Averil mumbled in a scarcely audible voice, "Aye, I'll fetch the money for you."

As she started to return to the house, the knife grinder called cheerfully, "Should ye 'ave any knives that need a touch at the stone 'ere, I could do it now fer ye."

Desiring to prolong the knife grinder's stay and learn more from him, Averil returned with a tray of what paring knives and cleavers she could find in the kitchen. Darby hummed to himself as he worked. From a window in the house, Ruth watched. Averil balanced the tray in her hands as the old man took up the first knife. But then, as he removed his hand, she caught sight of a folded square of paper under the blades. It had to be a message from the Tottman, and with effort she kept her hands from shaking. Her eyes fixed on the visible edge of paper as if she could read it there.

After paying Darby Kipp, Averil slipped the message into her palm, returned the knives to the kitchen, and hurried to her chambers, where she unfolded the paper and read eagerly.

The Tottman instructed her to meet Nicodemus that night in front of the White Hart Inn in Southwark at nine of the clock. She should be prepared to be absent for several days. There would be no need for her disguise as the lad, the note said. A coach would be sent for her, and she was to inform the necessary servants that she would be staying with her aunt and uncle for the time.

Averil reread the scant message several times before laying it in the hearth and striking a spark to it. When nothing but cinders remained, she broke those up with the poker.

The Tottman had not abandoned her after all! He lived

and was well—and free!

Several days, she repeated to herself in wonder. Would he be taking her to her father? Overcome by the thought, Averil sat down abruptly on the couch.

When she could think clearly again, Averil realized that she had preparations to make if her departure was to be believable. She retrieved her cloak and muff from the dressing chamber and hurried down the stairs. Locating Hosiah, she asked him to take her to visit her aunt.

Mary Geneva and Lynna were home when she reached the house in Aldersgate Street. Averil chatted with them for a little less than an hour, trying not to appear nervous or preoccupied, then took her leave and Hosiah drove her home again.

When she swept through the front door, she found Ruth in the hall. The young servant was tying the strings of her black hat as she prepared to leave for her morning errands.

"Where might I find your mother, Ruth? Is she in the kitchen?"

"In the drawing room there, madam," Ruth answered, without meeting Averil's eyes.

Passing the girl, Averil opened the drawing room door and looked in. Mrs. Quint knelt before the hearth, sweeping out the ashes.

"Mrs. Quint," Averil called, "I've just been visiting my aunt and she's invited me to stay with them for a few days. They will send a coach for me this evening."

Mrs. Quint's face was flushed red from bending forward, but she smiled at Averil. "Aye, and that'll be a good tonic for you, madam, I don't doubt, what with the captain away now."

Behind Averil, Ruth departed quietly.

The serving girl passed through the gates and sauntered toward the meatseller's shop several blocks away. It was her first stop. In the past she had always enjoyed these outings, but in the last few weeks, since the captain and his bride had arrived, she felt uneasy on her errands. As she neared the shop, she craned her head to see if Mrs. Warrender's cousin, Lynna Kirkland, had arrived yet. The two met regularly. She was not sure she liked Lynna, but for the sake of the captain's happiness, she knew she must do what she could.

As usual, Lynna was outside the meatseller's shop, waiting impatiently. Her blonde hair was tucked demurely into a starched day cap, her face bland and expressionless above a plain gown. Around her shoulders she hugged a black scarf.

When Ruth approached, Lynna met her with a concerned frown. "And how is my cousin faring, Ruth? Has there been any change?"

Ruth sighed as they moved to the side of the shop, out of the stream of pedestrians. Her light blue eyes were shadowed and she looked sadly at her companion.

"Nay—at least not for the good. Since the captain sailed, she's been even more down in her temper. She hides herself away. Mayhap y'should talk to the captain again."

Lynna frowned and glanced at the people passing. "We'll have to wait."

"When he returns?" Ruth asked hopefully.

"But I've explained—he won't listen to me, he won't see how ill Averil is."

"I'll speak with him," the girl said in sudden determination.

"Nay! Let me do it," Lynna said sharply. "I promise you I'll bring the matter up with him as soon as he returns. In the meantime, continue to watch her." Lynna started to leave, but Ruth looked perplexed and put her hand on Lynna's arm to stop her.

"Have you forgotten then? Mrs. Warrender will be with you."

"With me?" Lynna repeated, leaning toward Ruth and lifting her eyebrows in surprise.

"Aye. She told us after she returned from visiting today.

Mrs. Kirkland invited her for a few days' visit.''

Lynna laughed lightly to cover her amazement. "Aye, my mother did mention she had asked Averil to come. She never said when, though.'' Her voice rose as if in question, and Ruth answered readily.

"This very evening.''

Lynna nodded a brisk farewell to Ruth and hastened away, her mouth twisting into an ugly grin of excitement. This was it! she thought. Averil had never been invited to stay with them; it was a fabrication on her cousin's part. Averil was obviously up to something she wanted no one to know about. It had to be the Tottman! There was no other explanation. At last, she had been successful!

How easy it had been to convince Ruth Quint to watch and report to her on Averil's activities. And Averil herself had given credence to the story that she was sick in her brain and needed watchful care. Ruth had reported to Lynna that the young bride had been unfriendly, nervous, and given to odd behaviors and humors.

Lynna chuckled over her victory as she hailed a passing hackney. She gave the driver directions to Francis Bowers' home.

A hackney coach arrived at half past eight. Averil bid goodbye to Mrs. Quint and climbed inside. She had packed a small case with some necessary items, including one fresh gown and chemise, a pair of stockings, and a nightdress.

The driver took her to Southwark and drew to a stop in front of the White Hart Inn. Though Averil scanned the street through the coach window, she found no sign of Nicodemus. She described the bearded man to the coachman, and he searched the inner courtyard of the inn, but returned with a shake of his head. Alarmed, Averil asked the driver to wait. When he expressed some discontent, she thrust a silver coin through the window to him to ease his mind.

As the minutes dragged by, Averil's tension wound tighter. Surely the letter had said tonight, surely it had specified the

White Hart Inn, surely Nicodemus was to meet her. Had she arrived late? Had she missed him? Had there been—? Then she saw him walking along the street toward her.

Averil flung open the door and stepped from the coach. The relieved driver sprang down from his perch and, at Averil's nod, pulled her case from the floor of the coach and deposited it on the street. Nicodemus looked ill at ease and almost angry as he retrieved the case, hefting it to his shoulder. He said nothing to her as he walked quickly through the stone archway into the inn's courtyard. As the hackney coach rolled away, Averil lifted her skirts from the mud and hurried after Nicodemus.

They went directly to the stables where two horses stood saddled and ready. There was no sign of an ostler. Nicodemus strapped her case behind a sidesaddle on one horse, then lifted her onto the horse's back as easily as if she had been a kitten.

He swung his bulk into the saddle of the other horse. "Stay with me," he ordered.

Averil had no intention of doing otherwise and guided her horse after him. They traveled the streets at a steady pace, neither leisurely nor urgently. Nicodemus held his back rigid and glanced from side to side nervously. He kept to the busier streets until they passed through the gate in the old Roman wall surrounding the inner city. Then they made their way in darkness to the torch-lit sentry gate at the defense line that circled London. After showing their passes, Nicodemus lit a lantern he had carried on his saddle. He held it out on a long pole to light their way as they advanced into the night.

Averil had not been outside the city since the previous April when she had traveled there from Abingdon, and the rumors she had heard of Prince Rupert and his men raiding along the roads frightened her. She tried to still her rapid heart-beats by reassuring herself that the Tottman knew what he was doing, and she trusted him completely.

They had not gone far when Nicodemus led them off the main road and they passed through a heavy grove of trees

where huge, fat branches wove a canopy over their heads.
The outline of a white-washed cottage with a steeply pitched,
thatched roof appeared through the trees. Nicodemus guided
them through the open door at one end of the structure, and
Averil found herself in a stable of sorts. Many such cottagers
occupied the same building as the stables, the family living
in one end, the animals at the other.

No sooner had they cleared the threshold than the portals
behind them were thrown shut. Averil looked around in
alarm. Behind her stood a slim young man she had never
seen before and the Tottman. He was attired severely in a
long black cloak, black hat, and black mask.

Unafraid now and weak with relief, Averil leaned against
the Tottman as he lifted her down from her saddle. She looked
up into the black mask and he touched her cheek lightly with
the back of one gloved finger.

The Tottman looked over her to Nicodemus, who was dismounting. "Anything?" he questioned in the harsh rasp.

"Nay," was the answer.

The farmer led them into the family's living quarters. The
Tottman had to duck through the low doorway and kept one
hand on Averil's arm as they entered. The room they emerged
into was a main room of sorts, lit by two burning rushlights.
There was no one else in evidence, though a cradle stood
by the hearth.

Nicodemus took a pewter mug from a nail on the wall
where pots and pans and bunches of dried herbs hung and
helped himself to ale from a small barrel in the corner. The
farmer did the same, filling two mugs and handing one to
Averil.

As they all seated themselves around the table, Averil could
contain herself no longer and asked the Tottman, "Is it my
father? Have you found him?"

"Nay, this has nothing to do with your father."

Averil regarded the black face with dismay. "What is it,
then? Why am I here?" But the Tottman merely shook his
head.

The other two men said nothing, though Averil looked at each in turn. The young farmer's small brown eyes fixed on her curiously, but he glanced away when Averil's eyes met his. Nicodemus stared back at her, his black eyes narrowed in a malevolent gaze. The tension at the table was thick. Averil dropped her gaze to her mug as fear crowded in on her. She did not touch her ale, but instead tucked her hands inside the muff in her lap. On the table in front of her, a tiny insect swooped and darted about the thin flame of a rushlight.

The Tottman sat across the table, watching her. Averil lifted her head and regarded him silently. Her gaze slipped over the contours of the mask and along the strong line of his shoulders beneath the long cloak. She had feared for his safety more than she had realized. Beneath the confusion in her mind lurked a strange and violent joy.

"How long must we wait?" Nicodemus asked with a growl.

The Tottman answered, "Till morning if need be."

"I don't like it," the bearded man retorted. "I don't like sitting here, able to do nothing—"

The young farmer snapped impatiently, "Get yourself more ale if it'll help."

Nicodemus glared at him wrathfully, but rose and refilled his mug.

"Please," Averil begged the Tottman. "What is it? Why can't you tell me?"

The silence was broken by the creak of the stool as Nicodemus took his seat. "Tell her," he said. "Why not?"

The Tottman ignored him. "In time," he answered Averil.

She looked around the table and all eyes stared back watchfully.

The soft whinny of a horse outside broke the night's stillness. All heads came up and froze. The Tottman cocked his head to listen, though the black eyeslits bored into Averil. From somewhere near the cottage, a man shouted. Almost immediately the sound of a musket shot split the night. Nicodemus jumped from the table, dropping his mug as the

Tottman extinguished the rushlights. The room was plunged into darkness.

"Hold her, keep her quiet," she heard the Tottman say. Immediately she was grasped and held against the farmer, his hand over her mouth. Averil's shock was so great, she could have made no sound had she wanted to.

Outside, the noise increased as more guns were fired and voices shouted in surprise. Averil heard a long scream of pain and was reminded of the attack on Maslin Manor. She thought she would faint.

The Tottman was at the window drawing back one of the shutters to peer out. In the bursts of flames and sparks from the guns he could see the shapes of men, perhaps ten or fifteen, scattered among the tree trunks, and others of his own men dropping onto them from the thick, overhanging branches. Instantly, Nicodemus was beside him, leveling a pistol through the glassless window.

"Don't be a fool!" the Tottman rasped at him, flinging the pistol aside. "You can't see well enough to know who to aim at! Get the horses ready. Jamie will have to come with us."

As Nicodemus spun around to comply, the Tottman drew his two pistols from the waist of his breeches, prepared them quickly, and climbed out the window. Crouching, he ran the length of the cottage and continued around to the back. His eyes stabbed into the shadows of the trees behind and to the side of the cottage, searching for any telltale movements or the gleam of light off a polished musket barrel or sword.

With the sounds of a fight taking place in front, any who had circled to the back would have rushed the cottage by then. Satisfied that Nessel and his men had jumped the attackers before any could separate to surround the cottage, the Tottman crossed into the trees and slipped around toward the front.

The struggle continued only briefly, for the attackers had not expected to find themselves victims of a trap, and they retreated swiftly. The Tottman found Nessel, who limped slightly in the aftermath of the fight.

"I don't know if they're all gone. The rear—" Nessel began breathlessly.

"Nay, I searched there. It's clear. How are the men?"

"Some are wounded, though I can't say how seriously. We lost no one, but neither did they."

"They'll return soon. Can you ride?"

"Aye."

"Take the men back to the ship as quickly as you can. Nicodemus and I will handle it from here."

When the Tottman returned to the cottage, Averil still sat in the grip of the farmer. Her shoulders shook and tears streamed from her eyes. Nicodemus had readied the three horses in the stables and relit one of the rushlights in the main room.

Averil watched the Tottman as he entered the room and laid his pistols on the table. She heard his harsh, sharp breathing and sensed the contained violence in his every move.

Something was strangely, terribly wrong.

CHAPTER
NINETEEN

The Tottman gestured abruptly. The farmer released her and stepped back. For a frozen eternity, the Tottman's black stare held hers, and the silence thundered in Averil's ears.

"I loved you." His whispered rasp was more terrifying to her for its quiet than had he shouted. "Dear God, how I loved you. Yet you could betray me!"

Averil's heart struck violently against her ribs. The blood pounded through her head, and the back of her neck clenched up in tight pain. She was panting and tried to speak, but could make no sound.

The Tottman turned away. "I need something for a gag," he directed. "I can't have her scream or call out if they return."

At his words, the significance of all that had transpired flared through Averil's mind. The Tottman blamed her for the attack. She burst out, "Nay! You don't understand! I was not part of that—"

Nicodemus said in disgust, "Jesus, just kill her now."

From the Tottman's mask the eyeslits burned blackly. She shrank against the table. "It's not what you think!" she cried urgently. "I haven't betrayed you!"

When the Tottman answered Nicodemus, his voice had a toneless, brittle quality. "There is information I want yet from her."

The farmer handed him a clean rag and the Tottman thrust it across Averil's mouth, muffling her protests. He ignored the pleading in her eyes as he tied the ends behind her head and drew her hood up over her hair.

The light was extinguished and they departed the room. She was carried on the Tottman's horse, so that he could keep one arm around her to still her movements and prevent her from pulling off the gag. The farmer and Nicodemus rode the other two horses. As they departed the stable, the Tottman called an order to Nicodemus, who hung back momentarily. He sliced a small branch from one of the trees and dragged it behind his horse to wipe out the signs of their passing. They could not risk a light now, and the speed of their flight was hampered by the thick black night with its hidden trees and slippery bogs.

With the iron band of the Tottman's arm around her, Averil sat motionless, but her thoughts crashed chaotically. Someone had set a trap for the Tottman, had followed her to the meeting place in the cottage. Though every ounce of her cried out against it, she knew the someone had been Camden. She had not traveled to the wharf to see his departure; he had obviously not sailed. Instead, he had tricked her and followed her to this cottage. Nicodemus had been nervous and watchful as they traveled through London earlier, the tension of waiting had been evident while they were at the cottage. The Tottman had suspected her!

Did he believe her guilty of treachery because of her marriage to Camden? The logic of that assumption seemed inevitable. She wanted to protest to him, to explain what she now knew, but the gag in her mouth prevented any coherent sound from emerging. So she waited in stark misery.

After an hour of traveling slowly and silently through the
dense forest, they came at last to another cottage, larger than
the first. It was two-storied, its brick walls laced with vines.
Four chimneys in a row thrust upwards from the roof against
the star-speckled sky. As the muffled thump of horses' hooves
in the dirt quieted, the cottage door opened and a young
woman stood framed in the doorway.

The group dismounted and the farmer, Jamie, led all the
horses toward an adjacent structure. The Tottman held
Averil's arms at her sides as they entered the cottage. As
they passed the woman, she gazed hard at Averil and murmured, "So it went awry."

In the small parlor an elderly man stood waiting for them.
His hair was pure white, his stance straight and proud. He
cocked his head slightly at the sound of the footsteps, and
Averil saw that he was blind. His eyes were colorless, the
irises sliding about at random.

"I bid you welcome, though I know what your coming
here signifies," the man said.

Averil wrenched one hand from the Tottman's softened
grip and pulled down her gag. She turned in his arms,
pleading. "You must listen to me! I told no one about
tonight!"

The Tottman leaned down, his voice carrying a cruel and
ruthless bite. "Words mean nothing to me now." He lifted
his head and motioned to the young woman. "Take her
upstairs, Mary."

Averil did not look at any of them as the woman, Mary,
lifted a rushlight and led her out of the room and up a narrow
stairwell in the center of the house. She took Averil across
an open room to a smaller chamber. After Averil had stepped
inside, Mary closed the door, and she was left alone in the
darkness. She heard a bolt being set in place against the other
side of the door, then the woman's footsteps melted away.
Averil stood still, numb. When it became apparent to her
that neither Mary nor anyone else would be coming to the

room, she felt her way toward the cot she had seen there and lay down on it, curling her body into a tight ball in desolation.

Dawn came swiftly. Steady rain fell outside. Averil stirred from the cot, drawing the folds of her cloak tightly about her against the damp morning chill in the air. She tested the latch on the door and found it opened easily. Blowing on her cold, numb fingers, Averil descended the stairs slowly. The wood steps creaked under her weight. As she emerged from the stairwell, the young farmer was waiting for her. In the blue-grey morning light, his features looked more angular, his nose was thin, his nostrils pinched. Soundlessly, he motioned her toward the rear of the cottage. Averil followed the hall he indicated, and stepping outside under a long roof, found herself facing the open doorway of a warm kitchen. Jamie was behind her. She entered.

The blind man sat at the table, his back to the cheerfully burning hearth. His long white hair was combed back from his face, and his cheeks were smooth and pink. He wore a chamois jerkin and had a walking stick propped against the table beside him. There was no one else about. The farmer brushed past her to return to his seat at the table.

"Come in, lass," the blind man said. "Fetch yourself a mug. The ale is hot and hearty, and there is cheese here."

Silently, Averil took a mug from the cupboard the man indicated and dipped herself some of the ale kept warm in a pot beside the hearth. Rosemary twigs floated in the brew, adding a pungent fragrance and taste.

The blind man held up his mug. "Fetch me another as well, lass."

Averil sat next to him, across the table from Jamie. She broke off a small chunk of the cheese and looked to the farmer. He scowled blackly, and she lowered her eyes.

"Where are the others?" Averil asked hesitantly.

The farmer demanded, "Ye mean, where is the Tottman? I'll not be telling ye—ye'll not be interfering again with any o' his plans.''

''Nay, I didn't mean that! I wouldn't do anything of the kind,'' Averil insisted, her voice pleading as it rose on a high note.

''Stop it!'' the young man cried. ''Because of you, I've lost me farm! Yer friends'll be watching it, won't they?''

The blind man broke in firmly, ''Jamie, you knew the risks. And the Tottman will do as he promised and provide a new home for you and your family.''

''Meanwhile me wife and child are in hiding!'' Jamie cried in frustration. ''I can't abide being here now—with *her*!'' He thrust himself up from the bench. ''Call out to me if you need help,'' he said, and left the kitchen.

Averil pushed aside her cheese and ale and buried her face in her hands. ''What can I say?'' she cried. ''How can I convince anyone?''

''Come now, lass,'' the old man said impatiently. ''Use your energies for repentance, for God's wrath will be far greater than the Tottman's.''

''What will the Tottman do now, do you think?'' Averil asked warily.

''That I cannot say, for I do not know his mind on the matter. But he has given Jamie orders to keep you here, and I agree with him.''

''For how long?''

''Three, perhaps four days.''

Averil stared into the thick brown liquid in her mug. The Tottman had said words meant nothing; how could she prove herself to him? There *had* to be a way!

A horse-drawn cart wound slowly up High Holborn in the hazy grey hour of sunset. Because of the stench from its load of excrement and muck and disintegrating food, most of the traffic in the road backed off from it, and so its progress was fair. The driver hunched over the reins. A greasy, tan wool cap perched jauntily to one side of his head; his dark, equally greasy hair stood out in rigid clumps under the cap's edge. His heavy coat and tan jerkin, belted under a broad sagging belly, were stained with the excrement and rotting food that was his business. He seemed oblivious to the stink and whistled to himself, swaying easily with the cart as it bucked and sank over the ruts and broken cobbles in the road.

Beside him sat a smaller figure, also hunched, his hat tucked down to his collar, a black patch over one eye. Had the light been any stronger and clearer, his advanced age would have been more noticeable, but the fading light robbed the two figures of details.

Had any of the nearby pedestrians, who detoured to avoid the cart with its load of muckish slop, been told it was the Tottman who passed thus amongst them, they would not have believed it. Because of this, and because no one would be inclined to come near the cart could they avoid it, Camden had decided on this means of removing Mrs. Ernestus and her baby from the city.

Camden had found the cart unattended at the rubbish dumps in Moorfields, just north of the old Roman wall that surrounded the inner sectors of the city. Filling it had been easy enough; roads were slimy with animal droppings and slops tossed out from kitchens and bedrooms.

From High Holborn, he turned left into Chancery Lane where it skirted Lincoln's Inn Fields. The Ernestus' rented London home faced the Fields. Four-storied, it was made of timber and white stone that had long ago gone blackish.

Whistling unconcernedly, Camden eyed the street and was momentarily dismayed to find there were sentries now posted at the house. Two leaned negligently by the front door, and Camden knew more would be set to watch the rear.

"Eh, Darby, we're going to be earning our place with this one."

"I just want t' live through the stink o' the muck," the old man answered, scowling in ill humor.

"Aye! If I ever come up with this trick again, convince

me otherwise!''

They lapsed into silence long before Camden guided the
cart near the door and pulled back on the reins to halt the
horse.

'' 'Ere now, move off! Don't stop that thing 'ere!'' The
nearest sentry screwed up his face and exclaimed, ''Aah!
I said move off, swine!''

But Camden was scowling angrily. ''Y'bloody beggars like
it well enough when I've cleaned yer privy cellars! Where's
th' door, I've a mind t' be done and home to m'supper.''

''There's been no call fer a raker—''

''It's not from 'ere, but from th' owner, Lord Washburn!''
Behind the sentry a curtain moved in a downstairs window
and two women, then three, were peering out at him. ''Wi'
th' weather bein' as warm's it is, 'at cellar'll raise a fine
stink! D'ye think ye'll like it better, then?''

''By God, ye'd best be quick with it! G' on. Round behind
there.''

Camden guided the horse through a narrow, bush-lined
alley skirting the house and maneuvered the animal till the
back of the cart drew up within a half-man's length of the
cellar entrance. One of the sentries from the front had come
around the far side of the house and was explaining the
presence of the raker to the two who waited indolently in
the alley by the back wall. One of them pushed himself away
from the house and sauntered nearer to watch. Climbing down
from the driver's ledge, Camden was relieved to see that
the man stopped while still a good fifteen feet away.

Camden's steps were slow as he approached the cellar and
leaned down to pull up the single, wood door. Everything
he did now—every step, every movement—felt leaden and
dragged at him. As if the very spirit of life had gone out
of him, he felt himself as empty as a husk.

He dropped down into the cellar, hearing behind him the
scratch of Darby's voice cursing under his breath as the old
man climbed from the cart and followed him to the cellar.

Darby knew to be slow about drawing out the shovels and wooden buckets, giving Camden a chance to enter the upper, first floor of the house.

Camden climbed the stairs and hesitantly pushed open the door, finding himself in a finely polished hall. The three women he had earlier seen peeking out the window stood in a huddle at the end of the hall, horrified at the sight of him intruding. The young woman attired more generously than the others would be Mrs. Ernestus, he guessed, and Camden addressed her, hastily, before any might cry out or scream in alarm.

"I come from Mr. Ernestus. I'm a friend. He gave me this for you." He held out a ring, but the light was growing increasingly dim and he knew she could not see it. "I've come to help deliver you to him."

She approached. "John?" Though at first wavering, her manner grew bolder and she reached for the ring. "Aye! You come from John!" Behind her the serving maids crept nearer.

Mrs. Ernestus looked radiantly at him as she clutched the ring to her breast, and in that moment Camden saw something of Averil in her. The image, the remembrance, was a scorching pain in his body. He was sweating with the hurt of it as he loosened the belt under his swollen mid-section and withdrew from under his shirt a carefully wrapped bundle of clothes. In it were wool cap, dusty breeches, a patched shirt and coat, and a pair of shoes stiff with age.

"Listen to me now, for we have to be quick," he said as he thrust the bundle into her hands. "Dress yourself in these and tie the maids. You have some ties or sash—"

At her surprised gasp and the sudden look of alarm she shared with the two other women, he explained sharply, " 'Twill appear they had no part in this. You don't want them punished or imprisoned?"

"Oh ma'am!" one of the servants cried, still cringing along the wall.

Mrs. Ernestus nodded her acceptance of Camden's words, and he said, "When all is ready, bring your child and come down to the cellar. Do you understand?"

Again she nodded, and he let himself back down to the stairs, seeing behind him in the hall as he closed the door the two servants rushing toward Mrs. Ernestus and one of them hugging her.

Darby was stomping around on the dirt of the cellar floor and thumping a bucket irregularly as he waited. "Took too long," he said as Camden reappeared. "Can't breathe proper any more."

Both men set to work shoveling out the steaming mass of garbage, kitchen scraps, and contents from chamber pots that filled part of the cellar. Under the watchful eye of the distant sentry they moved back and forth from the cellar to the cart, dumping their buckets.

Anxiously, Camden watched the twilight descending. In the cellar they were already working in near darkness, and the sentries would soon be questioning why they lit no light there. But the stark brightness from even one candle would reveal the youthful and lovely features of Mrs. Ernestus.

As he once more returned to the dark pit of the cellar he brushed against a human form. "Madam?"

"Aye," she whispered back. "I'm ready."

"And the babe?"

"Here."

Flinging off his coat and shirt, Camden explained, "I'll wrap the child to my stomach with a shawl here. It's the best we can do." Using the shawl as a pocket to carry the baby in, they settled the small form against Camden's midsection, but the baby squirmed and gave a tiny wail of protest.

Mrs. Ernestus said, "Wait, I can put her to sleep."

But Camden whispered urgently, "There's no time. Tie the ends of the shawl around my back."

The baby fretted and made small sounds of whimpering, as if she were working up toward a full, vocal wailing. Willfully calming himself, Camden held the tiny tucked-up body to the warm curve where his chest descended to his stomach. With firm and unmoving hands, he held her still. He had soothed his own infant daughters in this way, and he now mourned them silently. Gradually, beneath that warm firmness, the baby calmed. Camden felt a tiny, shuddering exhalation tickle his skin.

"Help me on with my shirt," he directed softly. "I don't want to let go of her yet."

Carefully, one hand on the baby at all times, Camden drew the shirt over his head and worked his arms into the sleeves. He moved his hand from her slowly and slipped the belt around himself, buckling it under the little bulge of the child. Because of the open neck of his shirt, he knew she would have air enough. The coat he had worn was large and he was able to draw the edges close around his stomach to conceal the odd bulge and any movement she might make.

Darby still labored with the buckets and shovel. But now, just as they were ready to leave, a sharp strong light pierced the gloom of the cellar. The sentries had lit a lantern.

"Damn!" Camden muttered.

Darby handed him the last bucket and the shovel. "Ye'd best be off now, eh," he said. He gave his eye patch to Mrs. Ernestus to wear.

According to their plan, Darby would have slipped away on foot after they departed, but now with the lanterns lit he would have to wait there in the cellar until such time as the sentries put out their light. Though they had not originally known of the presence of the sentries, Camden was not overly worried about leaving Darby; the knife grinder had been fairly able to melt away, even before his own eyes, twice before.

Taking the woman to the foot of the outer steps, Camden made her wait. He ascended the few stairs, with a slow and steady rhythm in his steps to soothe the baby, and set the bucket and shovel onto the loaded cart. The sentry who had earlier watched them had now joined his companion on the stairs leading into the rear of the house, a distance of barely twenty feet from the cart. By the light of their lantern they

were casting dice to amuse themselves. Camden retrieved
a rag from the seat of the cart and carried it back to the cellar.

"Mop your face with this to keep it covered and hunch
up, like an old man. You'll only have a few feet of ground
to cross to the cart," he explained, reassuring the woman.

Mrs. Ernestus appeared calm enough to him while they
were still in the cellar, but once into the light, she faltered
and began to shake. Camden had seen the effects of panic
before and he moved as quickly as he dared without jolting
the infant who now slept.

He sidled against her and grasped her elbow, holding it
hard to his side so she could not bolt and run. Reaching for
the rag, he grasped the edge of it just as her fingers released
it. She struggled momentarily, but seemed disoriented enough
to allow him to direct her. Shooting a quick glance at the
sentries, he saw they were concentrating on their game and
had not noticed.

They reached the head of the cart and Camden said tersely,
under his breath, "If you want to see your husband, climb
up there." She stumbled against the cart, fumbling like one
blind, her hands grasping ineffectively at air.

He could not help contrasting Averil's quick-minded
performance with this, but the unexpected thought of her
plunged him into sudden, mournful rage. Silently excusing
himself, Camden put his hand under Mrs. Ernestus' buttocks
and hoisted her to the narrow ledge of a seat. He climbed
up beside her and thrust her head down to her knees as he
reached for the reins. The baby squirmed and rubbed her
face on his stomach. Tiny fists clutched.

The cart lurched forward. Mrs. Ernestus seemed to come
to herself and grasped the rag Camden had thrust beside her
face. Though she put the cloth to her face, she remained
partially hunched over as they passed the sentries.

"Unspeakable swine! Ye'll 'ave me blood, won't ye?"
one of the men exclaimed to his partner. At the sound of
the cart, they glanced up.

Jeers of "Good riddance!" and "Take the stink with ye, ye filthy rakers!" followed the cart.

The rain had started up again. It ran in tiny streams down all the windows and kept up a monotonous drone as it pelted the roof and surrounding trees. The woman, Mary, had gone to take word to Jamie's wife, and so Averil was alone with Jamie and the blind man. Despair dragged at her, but Averil refused to allow it to govern her. She worked tirelessly through the hours, throwing herself into the oblivion of activity to keep the desperation at bay, but still there was a lifelessness in her.

On the evening of the third day the rain finally let up and the only sound outside was an occasional drip from the sodden roof or the splatter of wind-swept moisture striking the windows. Averil had cleaned the pewter dishes, scrubbed the table, swept the floor one last time for the day, and was seated at the table mending a rushlight.

The blind man, whom she had come to learn was named Simon, shuffled into the kitchen. Averil knew it was he; Jamie kept away from her as much as he could. Simon, though, had been friendlier. He sat often at the kitchen table, talking with her and warming himself with the hearth fire at his back. Averil had come to like and respect Simon. He asked now for a mug of ale and, as he seated himself and laid his worn walking stick beside him, she fetched it for him.

"Thank you, lass," he murmured appreciatively as he heard the soft thump of the mug being placed before him. He sipped at the ale and asked, "What is it you're doing now?"

When she told him, Simon puckered his lips thoughtfully. "I wouldn't have expected such a talent in you."

Averil smiled ruefully. "I watched Jamie do it last night," she said. "And I wouldn't call my efforts talent." She pushed aside the crudely affixed stalk. "The Tottman should return soon," she murmured.

"Ah, so he will." Behind him the fire hissed as it licked at a wet stick of wood and the amber-tinged light undulated over the walls. "And have you decided how you will go about proving yourself to him?"

"Nay. I can think of nothing." Averil flattened her palms on the table and studied her fingers. "I wish I knew why he has come to doubt me at all." She shook her head wonderingly. "He said he loved me."

Simon smiled into the air between them. "Aye, I know he does. And what he feels, he feels deeply—it strikes to the very core of him and he has no defenses. But you tell me now, if he loves you, and you love him—why is there this distrust?"

Averil stuttered in surprise, "I? Love him? But nay, that cannot—"

"Lass," he scolded gently, "I may be unable to use my eyes, but I have my ears, I have my mind—and you, were you truly of a mind to, could have run from here easily so many times. But you stayed to prove yourself true to him. You not only respect our Tottman, but you feel much for him. I hear it in your voice. I hear the groanings of your very soul, I do."

Averil's voice faltered. "Oh nay, I can't love him. It isn't—"

"But you do," Simon persisted.

"Aye," she whispered, stunned by the truth she had never admitted to herself. An overwhelming wonder held her. "But how can I love him when I have never even seen his face?" she protested.

Simon laughed. "You're asking that of *me*?"

A deep blush crept over Averil's face. "I wasn't thinking," she mumbled in apology.

"But nay—you *were* thinking. The love sprang from all you knew of the Tottman without the use of your eyes. The eyes can deceive, lass."

Averil thought of Camden and agreed reluctantly with Simon. "This talk of love is useless," she said at last, heavily.

"It doesn't alter the situation. And I am married to another," she added, half to herself.

Simon shrugged. A smile sat at the corners of his lips, his pale eyes wandered blankly. "Pardon an old man's attempts to help." He felt for his stick beside him and pushed himself up from the bench. "For whatever comfort this is to you, I know you could not have betrayed the Tottman."

Averil caught his hand. "You believe me? Oh, tell him, please! He would listen to you!"

"Mere words again, lass. But I will do what I can." He shuffled from the room and Averil heard his steps ascend the stairs to his room.

Jamie appeared in the doorway, his brown eyes sharp and accusing. He waited as usual to escort her to her room before taking his rest. Averil rose and retired to her small chamber under the eaves, pondering all the while this disturbing revelation.

That night the Tottman returned. He was alone. After seeing to his horse, he entered the cottage. Jamie met him, blinking sleep from his eyes as he asked, "Did all go well? Where is Nicodemus?"

The Tottman swept the moisture-laden cloak from his shoulders and hung it on a peg near the door. He kept on his hat and mask; Jamie did not know his identity. "Aye, it went as we planned. Nicodemus continued on last night to take them to the ship."

"Simon has kept a room prepared for your return," Jamie said, trailing the Tottman across the parlor to the hearth. "The usual one."

The Tottman lit a candle from the dying fire and asked as he straightened, "How have you fared? How is Averil?"

"There were no problems here, but Mary has not returned yet. I have had no word from my wife—"

"I stopped there briefly. Your wife is well and eager to be with you again. Tomorrow Mary will return and you may go."

"But where are we to live? Our own cottage is now

known—surely it is not safe to return there!''

The Tottman had started to leave the room but paused at
Jamie's protest. He reached inside his black broadcloth
doublet and pulled out a flat pouch. Tossing this to Jamie,
he said, ''While in London I made arrangements for you.
To the west of the farm where your wife is staying is a tract
of land that now belongs to you. There is the deed.''

Jamie looked at the pouch in his hands in awe. ''I own
it?'' he asked, amazed.

''Aye. You deserve it, Jamie. I had intended to do such
for you regardless of what happened.''

Leaving Jamie in the front parlor, the Tottman turned his
steps toward the stairs. He held the candle ahead of him to
light the way. But as he neared Averil's door, his steps began
to slow. Weariness invaded him and he almost turned away.
He halted outside her door, reluctant to face her, reluctant
to condemn her.

CHAPTER
TWENTY

The feel of a hand on her shoulder awakened Averil and she bolted upright in bed, eyes staring in alarm. Beside the cot stood the Tottman, a wavering candle in his hand. He wore black breeches, a doublet crossed diagonally with a swordbelt, a black, wide-brimmed hat, and the mask over his face. His shadow lay flattened on the side wall and reached up into the cobwebs of the corner of the ceiling.

Averil blinked against the light as he set it on the table beside her. Turning, he walked away to the farthest shadows, and Averil drew the blanket around her. Though she wore a linen smock that covered her from neck to wrists to toes, she felt vulnerable and naked to the empty black stare in his mask. She pressed her fist to her breast where her heart hammered dully.

For several long minutes they watched each other. At last, Averil could bear the strain no longer and looked aside, murmuring, "What do you plan to do now?"

"That depends upon you," the Tottman answered, his voice rasping loudly in the room.

"How little you know of me," she said through a tightly restricted throat, "to ever imagine I could betray you. What have I done to make you believe such? Didn't I help you that night at the inn on the bridge? Why would I wish you ill when you're my one hope of saving my father?"

"Aye, we'll speak of that night at the inn." His harsh rasp was heavy, the words forced, as he continued, "The case against you is this: you were present when Peter Oxton was murdered at the Nag's Head Inn. You were present when Francis Bowers set the trap on London Bridge. You waylaid Rupert's messenger with Francis, and you led him to the cottage."

Averil blanched with surprise and fear. "I knew nothing about those! *You* asked for my help that night on the bridge!"

"And very convenient it was for you and Francis. When did you begin plotting with him? Was it before you first came to me?"

Averil shoved her fingers into her hair and gripped the roots in frustration. "I have no regard for Francis Bowers, *none*! I would never willingly align myself with him in any way." She dropped her hands to her lap as she looked past the light to the tall, black figure. "Why would you ever think I would?"

"So you also deny waylaying the messenger to Rupert?"

Averil frowned against the light, realizing he had set it there to fully illuminate her while he himself watched from the shadows. She could smell the mingled scents of rain and night air in his clothing and the sweet pungency of the leather of his swordbelt. She wished she could touch him.

"I don't know how to answer you," she pleaded. "Will you believe my denials?" Unable to look on him for the ache in her heart, she gazed past him. In his shadow, a cobweb floated, fairy-like. "You no longer believe in me . . . and my husband has betrayed me. . . ." Should she tell him now what she knew of Camden's intentions?

"Your husband?"

"Aye," Averil murmured, frowning. "I married Captain Warrender."

Thoughtfully, the Tottman stroked the side of his mask with one gloved hand. "Tell me, are you in truth an honorable wife to this husband?"

Averil glanced swiftly to him in concern. "Aye," she said and wondered if he might misunderstand her loyalties.

"And what of love?"

She hesitated. "Aye, I love him." Did he know of Camden's alliance with Francis Bowers? Would her declaration of love be construed by the Tottman as an admission of similar guilt on her part?

"What of me, Averil? What are your feelings toward me?"

Averil looked down at her lap. As she did so, her hair fell forward, veiling her face. "I would rather not discuss this. There is no point."

"But there *is* a point. Answer me please, Averil."

"Why?" she protested, flinging her hair back and looking at him bitterly. "What good would saying I love you do? Where is the sense in that when I am already torn apart by my feelings for both you and my husband? The secrets I have from him, the secrets I hide from you . . . they've trapped me."

The Tottman's voice knifed through the air, halting her. Each word was distinct and hard. "What secrets do you keep from me!"

"It is my husband," she confessed.

"What does he have to do with this?"

Averil hugged herself tightly. Now that the moment had arrived, she found herself reluctant to accuse Camden. What would the Tottman do? Kill him? A keen sense of loss gripped her. But she had already lost Camden, hadn't she? And she could not stand aside mutely and see the Tottman caught in some trap her husband and Francis Bowers might set.

The Tottman exclaimed in mild exasperation, "I have no patience for playing games this night. Tell me what troubles you about your husband, Averil.''

Averil pushed herself up from the cot and lifted the blanket higher around her shoulders, hugging it across her chest, as though it could conceal and protect her. ''My husband desires to trap you,'' she said in a dead tone.

''My God,'' he exclaimed softly. ''What would make you believe this of your husband?''

Drawing in a quavering breath, she plunged ahead. ''He has admitted to knowing Francis well, and has questioned me about you on several occasions. And then my cousin told me Camden wrote a letter to my uncle in which he condemned me for my involvement with you and that he'd wagered a hundred pounds that he can capture you. Oh, please! Believe me when I say I would not have married him had I known all this!''

The Tottman shook his head slowly, mutely. Then she heard him sigh. ''Yet you say you still love him?'' he questioned.

Dismayed, Averil looked away. ''Aye, but I love the man I thought him to be, not what I know of him. Oh! This is so difficult!'' She drew in a deep, unsteady breath. ''It is as if he is two men. I love him, yet I also hate and fear him.''

Pressing her fingers to her temples to ease the newly blooming ache there, she said, ''I knew nothing about the attack on Jamie's cottage. I had no knowledge of that, though I am sure now that it was led by Camden or Francis.''

The Tottman turned away from her and she heard a short, mirthless laugh as he rubbed one hand over the mask. ''All right,'' he said, looking back to her again. ''I believe you, for what you have said explains much that has puzzled me about your behavior.''

Averil's relief was short-lived. Her worry started afresh when the Tottman strolled across the room slowly, then returned, head bent, fingers cradling his chin in a pose of concentration.

''What will you do now?'' Averil asked fearfully. ''What will you do to Camden?''

"Do to him?" The Tottman seemed surprised out of some deep thought. "Nothing. He's not guilty of those things you attribute to him, Averil."

She looked at him in wonder. "Not guilty? But I saw him, I heard—"

"Nay, I should have explained this to you long ago. Your husband did none of those things, nor is he trying to trap me." Averil started to protest, but he shook his head. "The reason is simple," he said, peeling off his gloves and hat and tossing them to the cot. As Averil watched in fearful amazement, the Tottman reached behind his head to untie the mask. When it was removed, she looked into grave yet startlingly vivid grey eyes.

In fright, she cried, "Camden!" She thought she might scream. "You tricked me! Oh, dear God in heaven, what are you doing here?"

"You doubt me even now? I am the Tottman, Averil. Do you want me to prove it?"

Averil shook her head wildly, hysteria clouding her eyes. "What have I done?" she mumbled, distractedly.

Camden cupped her chin and lifted her face until she was looking back at him. Her eyes were desperate. He smiled, tiny creases appearing at the outer corners of his eyes. "I remember a certain young boy named Jeremy Halmes, a dirty urchin with a fighting determination . . . and, truly, a very lovely face. He sought me out at the Red Gate Tavern, but though I refused him at first, he finally convinced me to help him save his father. Do you remember that day, Averil? You were so angry with me—and I was sure I had never met a more incredible woman."

Averil squeezed her eyes closed. She pulled her face from his touch and hung her head.

"I had just arrived in London with a full cargo of wine, and when I learned at the wharf office that your uncle was a wine merchant, I made good use of that cargo." Camden grinned at her. "And what a profit it brought!"

Averil listened numbly as his voice washed over her.

Camden continued, reminding her of the night Nicodemus
had led her to the lodging house on the bridge where he had
been waiting. While Nicodemus led her through a twisted,
lengthy route, he had paid a short visit to the Kirklands on
his way to the inn. He recalled for her small details of their
meeting there and many more incidents from that night which
Averil knew and remembered all too vividly. She was aware
of a hard lump in her chest. Her throat felt dry, her eyes
stung. It had been Camden all along.

Camden!

"You asked me that night when I returned you home if
you could see my face," Camden continued, "but how could
I show you the face of a man you claimed to detest? Just
that same morning you had been so furiously insistent that
you wanted to have nothing to do with me. And I had lived
too long with caution and distrust—I couldn't risk putting
the knowledge of who I was in your hands." He watched
her with quiet speculation.

Averil shook her head slowly, in confusion. "Why didn't
you tell me after we were married?"

"I intended to. Remember that letter I left for you the
morning after our wedding? I would have told you in that,
but against my will I found reason to doubt you." His voice
dropped away. "Believe me when I say these weeks have
been a torture for me."

"Why would you doubt me?" Averil watched Camden's
face closely in bewilderment, but deep within her heart a
sweetly painful joy was blooming.

As he told her of Lynna's visit to his ship and the
accusations she had made, he rubbed the back of his neck
as if he felt an ache. He tried to describe for her the sequence
of events that had led him to confusion, then doubt, and finally
to belief in her duplicity with Francis.

"I knew the determination and strength you had, Averil.
I knew what you were capable of when it came to something you felt strongly about. You sought me out, didn't

you—and look what you went through to find me." His eyes narrowed. "Lynna! How many of our troubles stem from her!" Camden swore softly. "And to think I almost left you."

Averil reached up to touch his face. She wanted to weep with the joy. "I'm so happy it's you," she murmured. "I was so torn with loving you, yet fearing you. Never did I guess you were the Tottman. Oh! It's still so hard to believe!"

"You can believe," he assured her, smiling. He put his hand to her face, stroking back the tangled tendrils of silvery hair that curled forward over her shoulder. Then his breathing quickened and he cupped her cheek with one hand. It was an intent gesture, poignant with meaning and longing.

Averil's heart leaped in response. Her voice was a bright whisper as she exclaimed in wonder, "How I love you!"

He tilted her face to him to kiss her, and when her mouth opened under his kiss his heart pounded and a thick rush of pleasure surged in him. Finally, he tore himself away, and after pulling the thin blanket from her shoulders, he gathered her up in his arms.

"Where are we going?" she whispered as he carried her into the narrow, dim hall. She pressed kisses to his cheek. His skin was still cool from the night and she smelled the rain in his hair.

"To a bigger bed!" he exclaimed. "It's high time, Mrs. Warrender."

A fire burned low in the small, cheerful room they entered. After kicking the door closed, Camden carried her to the draped bed and laid her down, dropping a light kiss to one breast through her smock before straightening up again. She looked back at him with such open trust that he knew an ache in him that was at once both terrible and tender.

Averil watched him lift the swordbelt over his head and shrug out of his doublet. When he crossed to the hearth at the foot of the bed and dropped to his heels to add more wood against the night, she marveled at his litheness. He moved with an easy masculine grace, light, full of repressed energy.

And she wondered how she had ever failed to connect the two men, Camden and the Tottman, in her mind. But then she realized that perhaps, somewhere deep in her heart, she had never confused them—the man of sunlight, wind, water, and the elements of life was only the other half of the man of night and blackness and death. Her feelings for each facet of the man had fed and built on the other.

She slipped from the bed to go to him, unable to bear even this brief separation. When she touched the back of his head and stroked her hand downward over his shoulder, he straightened. His eyes were intense, yet smiling as he gazed down at her. She lifted her arms, sliding them around his neck, and he caught her to him in a fierce embrace.

Thick waves of joy exploded through her and her mouth clung to his, her body molded to his. He lifted one hand to hold the back of her head against the force of his kiss, and his lips and tongue met hers with fierce urgency. When he broke away, his movements were quick, and he lifted the smock over her head to discard it. Averil felt the heat of the hearth fire pressing intimately on her skin. When he stepped away, she opened her eyes slowly, wondering, lost in the shadows of her passion for him. She caught the glitter of hunger in his eyes as he gazed at her.

"Ah, Averil," he muttered, and there was something softly fierce in his voice that was like a caress. "You're more beautiful than I remember."

She knew without words that he was thinking of the night he had pulled her from the river. The Tottman. *Her* Tottman.

He rid himself of his boots and thick woolen socks, peeled off his shirt and breeches, and she began to tremble in the waiting as she watched the firelight etch the hard contours of his chest and loins. The sight of him sent a thrill of longing through her. She now wanted to know fully every secret of him, every secret of this shadowed man. When he returned to her, she leaned on tiptoe, pressing herself to him.

She was stunned by the feel of his naked body, of

the hard, warm skin, the crisp hair on his chest, the heat and heaviness of him against her abdomen. He stroked the hair that cascaded down her back, and he reached lower, softly, slowly, as if in wonder, curving his hands around her buttocks. His touch was so exquisite, so near the center of her, that she quivered with sharp, expectant pleasure. As if her mind ceased to function, the world around her receded, spinning away to a tiny reality, and was gone. There was only this moment, shadowed and soft and warm, with Camden's body and hers. When his mouth found her throat, she arched her head back in delight. His tongue traced the pulsing vein in her throat, and he bit softly into the tender flesh of her shoulder.

He held her breasts together between his hands as he drew one taut nipple and then the other into his mouth. The taste and texture of her skin filled his head and his senses, and at her small, trembling cry of delight his passion sharpened.

Such pleasure, that mouth on her nipple, the faint scratch of his beard on her breast. She was breathless with it, and suddenly, exquisitely weak. Averil leaned into him, bending her head to his shoulder, her hair cascading down his chest. He was so strong, so strong. Had it not been for the warm, sure arms curving around her, she was sure she would have been unable to stand. She spread her fingers over the warm, rigid muscles of his shoulders and chest. So wondrously made was he! She reached to touch the hard, heavy member pressing so insistently between them. When her fingers curved around him, she heard the sudden catch in his breathing, and her own excitement quickened with his. Experimentally she touched him, cradling the weight, moving her fingers along the length of him. A tremor went through him and an instant later he pulled her hand away.

"This is too good," he whispered. "I won't be able to last."

The discovery of her power to cause him such excitement

burst through her mind and an entirely new vista, fertile and ripe with potential enjoyment, opened before her. In a haze, as if drugged by the deep shudders of pleasure, she clung to him, his hands and mouth ardent on her, caressing, leaving her breathless. And then, as his hand slid up her thigh and slipped between her legs, she arched involuntarily in wondering surprise. The pleasure was extraordinary. Never had she known such pleasure, and when she uttered aloud an involuntary gasp of excitement, the sound had the shape of his name.

Camden heard the sound of his name wrapped round with her pleasure and thought he had never heard anything that so thrilled him, so moved him. Between her thighs she was almost unbearably warm, and he wanted to be there, thrusting deep, to heaven. Quickly, impatient, he lifted her and carried her to the bed. He laid her down across the quilt, and the firelight tossed liquid coral light over her taut breasts and smooth stomach and the shadowed juncture of her thighs. He swept aside the silken strands of hair curling over her breasts and hips. His, this beauty. And he was burning up, almost painfully hard with arousal. A drop of perspiration skidded down his cheek.

As he lay over her, Averil clutched her fingers in his hair. That scent of night rain emanating from his face and hair would forever in her mind be linked with these moments. Forever it would remind her of moments made rapturous by the first experience of a woman's passion. Clinging to him, dazed with passion, she had hardly been aware that he'd brought her to the bed. Shuddering with the thick waves of desire engulfing her, she reached for him, wanting to hold him close. So close. She was only dimly aware of the radiant eyes so bright in the shadows as he loomed over her.

Unable to wait another moment to be where he so wanted to be, Camden forced her thighs open with his hand and one knee. He found the wet warmth he sought and slid himself into her. Such pure, intense pleasure shot through him that his arms trembled under his weight. Something deep and savage in him exulted in that moment.

"Oh, woman of my heart!" he breathed.

Below him, she twisted restlessly, crying out. He reached one hand beneath her hips to hold them both still together. He tried to wait, tried . . .

Averil clung to him though the ache of his presence burned between her legs. Her world was abruptly shadowed and hurting. But even as he moved himself in her and she cried out again, the burning pain was quenched by pleasure, intense and piercing. Losing herself in the passion, she moved her hips, sharpening that excitement he ignited in her.

Camden thrust into her again, past control. He felt her response matching his, climbing with his in an elemental and savage rhythm of movement. His breathing grew labored; he heard the rising tempo of her gasps. The heat of their joined excitement coiled tighter, tighter, until it could no longer be contained, and it exploded inside them, flinging them both into waves of excruciating fulfillment.

Averil lay in Camden's arms, eyes closed, experiencing a languid contentment so pervasive she thought she could not move a single muscle even had she wanted to, which she did not. Camden laughed softly, rolling onto his back, and wiped his wet face in the crook of his arm. "All those nights!" he groaned. "And you were so near!"

Averil opened her eyes slowly and smiled. She rolled to him, within the curve of his arm, and propped herself on her elbow, her head braced on her hand as she carefully traced the outline of his mouth with one finger. Light and shadow from the hearth fire flickered over his dark face. "I wanted to love you. Oh, Camden! How I wanted to be close to you!"

"I could tell. But I couldn't understand why you refused me so vehemently." He flung out his arm, grasped a pillow, and tucked it behind his head.

"All that time I was trying to protect the Tottman." Averil

peered at him closely as he turned his head to look at her.

"Protect me?" he murmured. "Why?"

She lowered her eyes and studied the hard line of his jaw. "I couldn't forget what you told me—about your decision, about why you did what you did as the Tottman." Venturing to meet his eyes again, she caught a strange, dark dullness that worried her.

He said vaguely and distantly, "I thought I had thoroughly disgusted you when I told you that."

"I was fearful," she admitted, "but that was just at first."

Camden continued as if she had said nothing. "I wanted you to know, but I'm not sure why. I think I was warning you, or testing you—I don't know." He rubbed his face, closing his eyes, and rested the back of his hand on his forehead.

"What a night that was," he said. "I remember your scream. I heard you screaming as you fell, and I was so afraid—for both of us." He looked up at her, his eyes distant with remembering. "But I couldn't let myself think about it. I just jumped after you." He sighed. "But tell me something. How could refusing me, refusing to make love, help the Tottman? What were you thinking of?"

Averil frowned slightly, musing. "I just felt so much loyalty to the Tottman—I loved you so desperately, but I thought of you as an enemy of the Tottman, and therefore my enemy."

He laughed softly in amazement and faint disbelief. "Let me get this straight then, it's a bit confusing. You were fighting me to save me?" He stroked her back as he commented absently, "You and your loyalty."

"Camden?" she began hesitantly, tracing his face with the tip of one finger. "Can you tell me about the Tottman—about that decision you said you made?"

"Oh, Averil," he murmured, reluctance dragging at his voice. He reached for her fingers where they rested against his cheek. "That's not something you want to know." He pressed her fingers to his lips as he lapsed into a brooding silence.

"I want you, Camden. Everything about you."

Watching the strong, dark face, the grimace that twisted his features, Averil waited. At last he began speaking, but his voice was slow, almost without inflection, as if by not voicing them, he could keep his emotions from touching him.

"When my wife and daughters were killed—Averil, I should have been there! The thought has forever haunted me that, had I been there, I could have prevented it. But I was here in England." Uttering a heavy sound of disgust, he pulled his arms from around her. He sat up on the edge of the bed. "I just can't forgive myself for it. I could have saved them! So many times I've been there with them in my mind, I've saved them over and over. Oh dear God, that I had been there!"

"But it wasn't your fault!" Averil protested, stroking his back. "You couldn't have known."

He gave a short laugh without humor. "Fine sentiment, but it doesn't change anything. It doesn't change what happened."

Averil held her tongue, unsure of this bitter self-damning element in him.

"I wanted revenge, Averil, wanted to—" His voice fell off abruptly. "I wanted to *kill*! I wanted to *die*! You can't understand this, I know, and maybe I shouldn't even talk about it. But . . . you see, a knife became like another hand to me. I searched out fights in every port I put into, looked for anyone and everyone who'd take up a weapon. And in the ports I saw, there were plenty. Some of those places— oh God, Averil, it makes my skin crawl just to think of it."

In horror he wiped his hand over his face, as if he could erase from his mind what he knew. And there fled through his mind images of blank, humanless faces—faces he had wanted so much from, faces of men who could have given him deliverance, but who had given him in the end only the death mask.

When he turned his head to look at her, Averil saw the heaviness in his face, the cindered dullness of his eyes.

"I hated the man I had become."

"And then there was the decision," she said quietly.

"Aye." He sighed, rubbing his palms together absently. "I agreed to help my father's friend. Simon, in fact. And in doing so I began to see, as if for the first time, the injustices and pain around me. I couldn't close my eyes to it, Averil. I couldn't ignore it. It was there all around me—everywhere. And I could feel it as if it were my own pain. All those people needed help, and I needed a way to escape myself." He fell silent, pensive, leaning his elbows on his thighs. "To redeem myself."

"But you've done so much that's good, Camden," she protested.

Looking at her absently, he reached out and stroked her hair. "You were protecting me?" he repeated. His teeth gleamed whitely in a slow smile. "Do you know—I think I like that."

He bent his head to the curve of her shoulder. She felt him sigh against her skin as he kissed her, and she lay back on the bed, arms around his shoulders, drawing him with her.

CHAPTER
TWENTY-ONE

When Camden awoke, the room was bathed in the buttery golden light of full morning. Averil slept curled against him. As he eased himself from the bed, carefully so as not to wake her, he smiled to himself. Her hair lay under his shoulder and back, fragrant, downy curls that were like silk on his skin. After adding wood to the hearth, he donned his clothes and left the room briefly.

Averil woke to the feel of a warm mouth gently brushing hers. She blinked her eyes open. Camden's face hovered over hers, yellow sunlight slanting across his hair. "I just can't resist you," he whispered, smiling. She laughed softly, happily, as she slid her arms around his back. He peeled back the quilt and dropped a light caress of a kiss on the quickly rising peak of one breast.

Later, spent yet very aware of each other, they sat in bed and sipped the mugs of ale Camden had brought back to the room. He had left them by the hearth to stay hot, and the bread he had also brought on the tray was fragrantly warm.

Averil gazed admiringly at the man beside her. He was more handsome to her now than ever before, and at his nearness her entire being felt vibrantly alive.

"You don't have to return to London today, do you?" she asked, cradling the mug of ale between her hands.

Camden smiled as he broke a chunk of bread from the loaf. "Nay, today is ours, to spend as we want—and I know how that'll be! All too soon we'll have to return and be separated again." At her questioning look, he explained, "I can't be seen in London—I'm thought to be on board ship."

Averil accepted a chunk of bread and turned it in her hand as worry dragged at her heart. "You've never truly left when your ship has sailed then, is that it? You have your other work—the Tottman's work—to see to?"

"I've gone on some trips. I still have a very real business."

"Camden?" Averil said, her voice high in a plaintive appeal. "What about my father?"

He looked at her sadly, reluctant to speak, and stroked her forearm as he said, "I haven't located him yet, Averil. After talking to Mrs. Brimby at the inn in Abingdon where you met Prince Rupert, I followed Rupert's trail to Birmingham. There was more than a month's delay between us, and there were few in Birmingham who could remember anything about Rupert's prisoners. Most of the prisoners were taken to Oxford, and though I searched there next, I couldn't find a trace of him. I don't know whether that isn't a blessing— the prisoners at Oxford are crowded into stinking buildings, treated like beasts, starved—"

Camden broke off as he raised his mug to his lips and drank. Averil watched him in silence, her heart twisting with love, though she experienced a brooding heaviness at his words.

"There are people in different places around who know me," he continued, placing the mug on the tray across his lap. "I contacted them with the request to alert me should they learn anything concerning your father. I followed up as best I could on any reports of his whereabouts, but in each case I was too late.'' Camden rasped his thumb over his chin and his eyes narrowed in frustration. "Rupert is playing an odd game here.''

''But aren't you an ally of Prince Rupert's?'' Averil asked. "Couldn't you have gone to him directly?''

''Hardly.'' Camden grunted. "I'm as much a mystery to him as I am to Parliament. And I've helped many a Parliamentarian as well as Royalist.''

Averil put her bread on the tray, untouched. She sipped at her cooled ale but had no interest in finishing the drink and set it aside too. Camden pushed the tray onto a low coffer near the bed and continued speaking.

''In every place where I searched for your father, he had been removed to another place before I could reach him. Then a little more than three weeks ago, I lost track of him altogether.''

''What will you do now?''

''People are watching for him, Averil. There will be some news.''

She sighed, hugging her knees to her chest under the quilt. She propped her chin on her knees and squeezed her eyes closed against the first fat tear that threatened to fall. Camden reached over and turned her face to him. His eyes were soft as he leaned toward her and gently kissed her lips.

When they drew apart, he stroked the hair falling over her shoulder, lifting strands to sift between his fingers. A frown spread slowly on his brow, and his grey eyes stared past her to some indefinable point. She moved close beside him, resting her knees against his hip.

''Camden? You're leagues away—what are you thinking?''

His glance dipped and flickered back to her face. "I can't help wondering who followed you to Jamie's cottage. Someone knew you would be meeting me, someone engineered that trap.''

''Francis Bowers,'' she said in disgust. "But how would he have known?''

''There's something else that plagues me,'' he said, absent

in thought. "Obviously Lynna and Francis are working together, and though they're clever, there is someone else who controls them."

Averil caught her breath in fear. "Who? Do you have any idea?"

"None," he admitted.

Would she lose him? He was a wanted man, a five-hundred-pound reward on his head. If he were caught, his would be one of the prize heads staring into the wind on a spike above London Bridge. Averil's fear climbed.

The quilt slipped away from her as she rose on her knees beside him. She laid her hands on his shoulders and his head lifted as he peered at her questioningly, warmly. She leaned her head to his, her hair sliding around him, veiling them both in intimate, protecting shadows.

"Love me, Camden," she whispered. "Love me now."

The following morning, Camden again rose early and went to the coffer in which he had stored his leather pouch the previous morning. Averil, aware that the warmth of her husband's body had been removed, stirred and roused herself slowly. They'd had little sleep during the night. She sat up with the quilt draped around her waist as Camden set out the contents of the bag on a low table and propped the looking glass before him.

He caught sight of her in the mirror and paused, smiling, before returning his attention to his work. "Today we have to return to London," he said.

Averil asked hopefully, "Can we not remain here longer? The Quints won't miss me, and you're thought to be on board ship."

Camden paused and glanced over his shoulder at her. "It's a tempting idea, but I must return. We'll be apart only for the daylight hours, Averil." His eyebrows lifted slightly as he grinned. "I can still return to you every night."

Averil realized that she must be content with that, for the time being, and she propped her arms on drawn-up knees as she watched him curiously. He uncorked a small flask and spread some of its contents, a brownish liquid, over his face and neck.

"What are you doing?" she asked.

"It's an infusion of walnut leaves," he explained as he worked. "I can hardly return you to London today and risk being recognized." Camden turned to her with a grin on his face, his skin now a heavy swarthy tinge beneath the stubble of dark beard he had left on his face.

Averil laughed aloud and climbed from the bed to draw closer as she watched. He covered his head with a wig of thin, stringy black hair that brushed his shoulders, added a straggly, ill-kempt moustache, and donned a pair of spectacles. He squinted at Averil's reflection in the looking glass, his lips thinning and twisting down at one corner. Averil gasped with laughter.

"What!" he bellowed. "Are ye bein' disrespectful then, m'girl? Ye'd best keep a civil tongue in yer 'ead or I'll flay y' good!" Chuckling at her laughter, he leaped from the stool to catch her, but once she was in his arms, he groaned. "I can't even kiss you or I'll get this damned stuff on you."

As he turned and walked back to pick up his clothing, Averil's smile faded. "You have several such disguises, have you not?" she said, remembering Percival Osgood's account of the Tottman as a blond man with a scar along his face. Her fear for his safety pressed in on her again.

"Aye, several," he said, tying his breeches and reaching for his shirt.

"Camden? When I first met you, you had black hair—almost coal black. How did—?"

He was laughing as he tugged the shirt over his head. "You've just said it exactly," he exclaimed. "Coal." Tucking the white shirt into his breeches, he said, "These streaks where the sun has bleached my hair are too recognizable—I always have to cover them somehow."

He finished dressing, donning the black doublet and wide-brimmed hat, though when he faced her once more his right

shoulder hunched in, and his hands shook. His clothes hung
on him oddly. The change in Camden was dramatic, and
Averil looked him over wonderingly. He appeared as a nondescript man, a merchant perhaps, or a surveyor; he could
even have been taken for a porter dressing finely in some
employer's cast-off clothing.

He straightened his shoulders and said with a grin, "Do
you know, I love seeing you like that." He gestured at her
nakedness, at the bright strands of hair tangling over her
breasts and brushing her hips. "In all seriousness, you'd
better get dressed or I'll be smearing walnut stain all over
that beautiful skin."

Simon beamed when they made their farewells to him. He
opened his arms to Averil, and she hugged him gladly and
kissed his smooth cheek. In the stable, Camden saddled his
horse, the black beast Averil had seen him on in the forest,
and another for Averil. He leaned over from his saddle and
kissed her lightly before they rode out into the brilliant
sunshine.

The journey back to London took slightly more than two
hours. There were soldiers on the road, and Averil's heart
jolted painfully when she saw them, realizing now how
precious Camden was to her, and how precarious his position
was as the Tottman.

After the clear sunlight and fragrant breezes they had
enjoyed earlier, the London streets were dismally grey with
smoke and dark from the many tiers of overhanging buildings.
The smells from the open sewers running along the sides
of the road burned Averil's nose. She wished they could have
stayed with Simon, wished they could have gone anywhere
but back to London. Her heart was heavy.

Camden hailed an empty hackney coach passing them.
When the driver stopped, he handed Averil into the interior.
"I'll see you tonight," he murmured. He gave several small
coins and directions to the driver and the hackney rolled
away. Averil leaned out the window to look back. She
watched Camden swing himself into the saddle and turn the

horses down one of the side roads. She wondered where he would go today, what he would do.

Mrs. Quint hurried down the long flight of steps as Averil alighted from the coach. "Madam, it's a picture you look!" she exclaimed. "That visit was just the right thing for ye, now wasn't it!"

Averil laughed, realizing that the deeply rooted contentment she felt must be evident. "Aye, I could stand a hundred of them!"

They chatted together as they ascended to the front door. Averil looked around the entrance hall with its parquet floor and bright plaster ceiling and thought of the day when Camden's ship would return and he could move freely about the rooms, sup with her in the dining room, share the master suite with her. Her heart jumped a beat as she thought of him joining her in the bed later that night.

Ruth ran in from the back of the house and cried, "Hullo, ma'am," with such relief and delight that Averil felt very much as if she had come home. As the girl lifted her case and they climbed the stairs together to Averil's rooms, she remembered Camden telling her he had nine brothers and sisters. What richness there must be in having so many people to love and to be loved by in return! she thought.

When the serving girl had departed the room, Averil crossed to the window and peered out. Camden had promised to come to her tonight, but how would he reach her? He could not enter by the front door and risk meeting any of the Quints; he had told her they did not know his identity as the Tottman, and so they would expect him to be on board ship. There were no trees here in front of the house, no vines, nothing but a sheer wall. Yesterday she had wanted to stop time; now she wished to hurry it toward nightfall.

She returned to the window as evening drew on and a few linkmen with their torchlights were visible in the Strand. Bathed and rested, she wore the blue satin gown Mary Geneva had made for her wedding night. She swung open the window to peer out, her gaze moving restlessly over the flowers and bushes lining the drive. Beyond the outer gates, a man rode by slowly on horseback, and a torch he carried splayed his shadow on the cobbles around him. A small dog with two boys close on its heels darted through the circle of light. Averil sighed into the evening wind that brushed through her window as she waited.

The minutes trailed past slowly, lengthening into an hour, and still there was no sign of him. Restlessly she paced by the window. Another hour stretched past, and yet another. It was past midnight and a dread alarm spread through her. Still she waited. When a bellman called out the hour of one, she backed away into the room.

She knelt before the hearth, staring into the low crimson embers, and tried desperately to stem the panic that threatened to engulf her. Resolutely, she placed more wood on the grate. With a small bellows she blew the embers to flame and when the new wood had caught fire, she rose to her feet. But when she turned, she faced a tall, black-cloaked man.

"Camden!" she cried joyfully and threw herself into his arms. "How did you get in? I heard nothing."

"There are trees behind the house, and I came over the roof. As for your not hearing me—" He closed her tightly in his arms as she curved her body to fit his. "I suppose I've been forced to move in silence too often."

Averil was reminded of his stealth and easy grace as he had maneuvered across the rooftops that night on the bridge. "I was so worried when you didn't appear earlier. I envisioned something terrible happening to you."

Camden said heavily, "Today I saw an execution—on Tower Hill. And I couldn't help picturing you there."

"Oh, Camden! Don't think that way!" In spite of herself, a shiver ran through her. She was thinking not of herself on Tower Hill, but of Camden facing his execution.

"I've been so damned selfish in wanting you with me," he said. "But now I've made arrangements for you to leave— that's what delayed me. I have friends in Devon and it would be safer for you there."

She clung to him desperately. "Nay, I can't leave you!"

"But you must! I couldn't bear it if anything were to happen to you."

"Don't ask me to do this!"

Camden dragged her hands from around his neck and gripped her upper arms. A dark stain was still visible on his face and his eyes were starkly bright in contrast. "Listen to me, Averil. There will be no leniency for the wife of the Tottman, no matter who she is."

"But what if I never see you again?"

"Have you ever seen an execution?" he snapped impatiently. "Perhaps you should!"

She leaned her forehead to his chest. "Please, Camden. Don't be like this."

"Averil, trust me," he said. "You don't know what you're up against here!"

She said earnestly, "I'd return, Camden. I'd find a way to be with you."

He turned away, agitated, angry, wanting to shake her until she could see reason. "Averil, don't even talk like that—you'd never make it from Devon!"

"But I'd try," she said. "I can't lose you now, and I'd return if there was any way at all."

"By God, you would try, wouldn't you." His voice sharpened in anger. "Averil, how can I—"

"Let this be my decision, Camden!" she exclaimed. "I've seen what happened to my home, I've seen what happened to Peter Oxton, I was with you on the bridge the night Francis sprang that trap. I'm frightened, aye! I can't deny that! But let this be *my* decision."

He stared at her in silence for a moment, then muttered, "Damn! If I could, I'd leave too, Averil. We'd leave together. But I couldn't live with myself."

"I know what you mean," she answered quietly.

He looked at her in exasperation.

"I'm more frightened for what might happen to you than to me," she said. "And if I left now, I couldn't live with myself.''

Frowning, he glanced away and exclaimed, "This isn't easy, you know!" At last he pulled her into his arms. He let his breath out in a long sigh. "All right. But, Averil, if the time ever comes again when I ask you to leave, you must go. You'll have to do that for me.''

Camden departed during the last black hour before dawn. He returned again the following evening, and every evening after.

They kept the fire in the hearth blazing up brightly through the nights, and its light warmed the green and gold hangings of the room and drove out the formless black night pressing in at the windows. Sometimes they laughed together and he teased her by speaking in the hoarse, rasping tones of the Tottman. Other times they were solemn, pensive, talking quietly as they held each other. She could talk of her father and Mrs. Fairchild and her mother now for the first time since that fateful morning, and she talked freely, gratefully.

She asked once, "What do you do during the day?''

"Usually I sleep." He grinned at her, his head propped on his elbow, and stroked her thigh. "We don't seem to do much of that at night!''

"But where?''

"Different places. Sometimes I wander by the gates out there, but I've never seen you.''

"Maybe I should wander out that way more often.''

"Nay," he said. "Stay where you're safest.''

"Couldn't we meet somewhere? Like we did at the Red Gate Tavern?''

"Averil, you don't realize the risks. We have this much, here, at night. We can't ask for more.''

She sighed. Idly brushing her hand through the dark mat of hair on his chest, she asked him about the thing that worried her the most. "Do you do much as the Tottman?''

"Aye.''

Quietly she said, "Today Mrs. Quint told me the latest

rumor—that the Tottman had managed to free two Adamites from Ludgate prison." She looked at him questioningly.

His eyes were soft and grave. "Don't ask me about it, Averil. You're better off not knowing."

Some nights their passion was a fury, and they explored each other with a sensuality that burned them both to their very souls. And some nights they joined together with a tender care for each other so joyful and exquisite that Averil almost wept in his arms.

"Such peace I know with you," Camden murmured in wonder. He stroked her skin lightly, moving his hand down to cup the warm smoothness between her thighs. "You receive me and hold me in you . . . and when I'm inside you, Averil, I feel such peace."

Averil savored every moment they shared, so it was with great trepidation that she heard him say he must leave for a time.

It had been almost three weeks since they had returned to London. He had made love to her with a special lingering tenderness this night, and now he was leaving the bed to find his clothes. Averil pulled on a pink satin dressing robe and sat on the edge of the high bed.

By the flickering firelight, she watched him move about the room. For all of his height and breadth, he had an animal grace that she never ceased to admire. A sense of foreboding shadowed her world.

"Why, Camden? Why must you go?"

He smiled reassuringly at her distress. "I have to meet my ship," he explained, tying his breeches. "Cheyney will be returning soon and I have to be on board—we're bringing a cargo of arms through, Averil. But then, my heart," he reminded her, "I can return to London—and to you—by light of day." He smiled wistfully. "I miss not seeing you in sunlight."

"When do you leave London?" she asked.

"Now." He pulled on his shirt and tucked the tails into

his breeches.

"So soon!"

"Actually, I should have left several days ago. I'll have to make haste now."

"How long will you be away?"

The mattress dipped as he sat beside her to pull on his boots. "A fortnight at most."

"A fortnight?" she repeated, and it seemed to her half a lifetime. "Let me go with you."

Camden looked at her with an amused smile and leaned over to kiss her lightly on the forehead. "I'm traveling to the coast, Averil. It's not a safe journey at any time."

When he stood up to put on his black doublet, she sighed but remained silent, biting back the pleas and fears that pushed up so strongly inside her. She heard him readjust the buckle of his swordbelt; then he returned to the bed.

"Promise me something, Averil," he said, catching hold of her arms and leaning down to meet her eyes. "Don't leave these grounds. I know that may be hard to do, but it would be safer. Do you remember those two men who followed you one day? They're still in London. I've spotted them several times. As yet, I haven't been able to determine their purpose, but I want to be very careful."

Averil shuddered involuntarily and he pulled her to her feet. "*Promise* me, Averil. don't go out until I return—not even with the whole damned Quint family with you!" When she nodded, he kissed her quickly, fiercely, then was gone.

After Camden departed, Averil smoothed the rumpled bedclothes to remove any trace of his presence. It was something she did each time he left. But though she tried to sleep, she only tossed fitfully in the empty bed and rose at the dawn, feeling morose and listless. Before this, the days had been long enough, but now the nights would be equally long and lonely. She fussed over a piece of lacework that morning, but it seemed incredibly boring.

When she heard a coach rumble up the drive and stop before the outer staircase, she put the needlework aside gratefully. She emerged from the drawing room just as Ruth was admitting the newcomer.

It was Sir John Walford. He wore a charcoal grey doublet and breeches, and a wide ruff collar circling his throat. His unlined, youthful-looking face split into a smile when he caught sight of her.

"By gad, sweetheart!" he exclaimed, beaming. "You look exceedingly well. Marriage appears to agree with you."

Averil greeted him excitedly. She had almost forgotten that Sir John had sent a letter to Prince Rupert inquiring after her father and had promised to let her know the results. Eager for any news now, she took his arm and led him into the drawing room. As Walford settled himself comfortably on one of the couches before the hearth, Averil asked Ruth to bring wine for them.

"Is Captain Warrender here?" Walford asked. At the negative shake of her head, he seemed satisfied and smiled, the expression giving his face an even younger appearance. "I have some news for you—but wait." He launched into idle talk, but after Ruth brought wine and cups and retired from the room once again, he leaned toward Averil. There was urgency in every line of his long frame.

"I think I may have found your father, Averil," he said with tense excitement.

Averil was pouring wine for Sir John, but at his announcement her hand shook and the wine splashed onto the table. "My father?" she repeated, her voice squeezing to a whisper. "Where is he?"

"In Oxford."

"He's alive!" Averil's mind felt near to bursting. She ignored the spilled wine. "Where did you learn this? Was it from Prince Rupert?"

"Nay, I met a man who had traveled from Oxford recently. He saw your father there and recognized him."

Walford accepted the cup Averil handed him, his attention fixing on her flushed face and the glassy, preoccupied stare in her eyes. He sipped the heavy burgundy, then lowered his cup and cradled it between his hands.

"Averil . . ." He hesitated. "I'm not certain I should have told you this. There's really nothing we can do."

Averil came out of her chair and crossed to one of the tall windows. She looked out on the long, shaded drive ending at the black gates. Camden had only just left. He would be gone up to a fortnight, he had said. Too long!

"But we must do something," she protested, turning back to Walford.

"Averil! What do you imagine the two of us could do against the King's army at Oxford? By gad! There must be hundreds of prisoners alone!"

"If I could just see him again," Averil said, hugging her arms around herself. "One look—"

"Have you forgotten Rupert's intention to find you? Even leaving the city is gravely dangerous for you now."

"Come with me," Averil pleaded. "No one need know who I am."

"Think about this, Averil!" He waved one arm in a broad arc through the air. "Supposing you did, by some miracle, actually catch a glimpse of your father—what then? Would you be content to return here? Knowing you, I'd say you would then work on some means to get a message to him. You were always a stubborn child, impulsive and spoiled."

Averil walked slowly back to the chair and sat as she poured herself a portion of wine. She was angry now with Sir John and unhappily aware that Camden was somewhere on his way to the coast and there was no way she could reach him. Unless . . .

Averil remained silent, thinking, staring hard at the center of the table in front of her.

"Think of your father!" Sir John exclaimed. "If you were arrested in Oxford, do you know what it would do to him? It would destroy him! For once in your life, think of the other people involved!"

Averil let her shoulders droop and murmured, "You're right. It's just so difficult to accept."

Walford was instantly contrite and regretful. "I understand your feelings, but I'm glad you can see reason now. Give me your word you'll do nothing rash."

When Averil had given her promise, Sir John excused himself and took his leave. At the outer door, he kissed her perfunctorily on the forehead, then descended the steps to his coach.

Averil closed the front doors and waited in the hall till the sounds of his departing coach faded. Then she snatched up her skirts and raced up the stairs. She detested having to deceive Sir John, but knew he would have stayed and argued with her till she agreed with his point of view. Every moment counted now, and she could not tolerate even the briefest of delays if she were to locate Darby Kipp or Nicodemus. Surely one of them would know a way to get a message to Camden!

But she had promised Camden she would remain on this property. Averil decided the circumstances were imperative enough to override that promise, and especially if she managed this with special care so as to ensure her safety.

She hurried down the hall and into her chambers. In the dressing room she burrowed into a chest and pulled forth the shirt and breeches of Camden's that she had begun altering to fit her. She had almost finished the task the morning Darby Kipp had appeared at the door. Only one leg of the breeches remained to be altered. There was no time now to do a complete job of it, so she took up her shears and whacked off the extra length. With quick fingers she plucked at the cut edge and pulled and frayed the threads.

Among Camden's belongings she found a knit cap that would suit her purpose and a short cloak. On Camden's tall frame the cloak extended only to the top of his thighs, but on Averil it hung well below the knees. She removed a sheet from the bed to cut into strips to bind up her hair. There remained only the question of shoes, but Camden's were far too large, and her own too obviously feminine. After several frantic moments, Averil finally chose a sturdier pair of her own shoes, without tall heels, and decided she could wrap her feet and shoes with strips of linen discolored with ashes from the hearth.

When her costume had finally been assembled and donned, Averil surveyed herself in the looking glass. Aside from the brown knit hat that bulged strangely over her hair, the effect was passable. The wrapped shoes reminded her shockingly of the many beggars she had seen with tattered wrappings around their feet. Though the cloak was far too fine, she hoped it would not draw undue attention. There were those in London who sported odd assortments of clothing pieced together from hand-offs from the parishes' charity.

After lightly greasing her face and hands with soot from the back of the hearth, Averil crept uneasily from her room. To her relief, she saw none of the Quints as she slipped down the staircase and departed the house. Gaining the shadows of the high brick wall at the property's boundary, Averil waited, catching her breath. Then, with a long, boyish stride, she emerged through the wrought-iron gates and turned east toward the center of the city.

CHAPTER
TWENTY-TWO

Sir John Walford peered through the coach window in amazement as the young boy strode through the gates. Had Averil not told him of her escape to London in the guise of a boy, he would never have recognized her now. He had been right in suspecting she might attempt some drastic step in the wake of the news of her father. Briefly leaning from his coach, he pointed her out to his driver and ordered the man to keep her in view.

This feat proved impossible. Averil moved with a spritely step through the crowds, but the lumbering coach soon became tangled in the congested traffic and Walford lost sight of the brown, bobbing head. He swore to himself after the coach had tried several side streets with no sign of her. She just might get away with this little undertaking, he thought admiringly, but wished heartily that he knew where she was headed. He tapped his fingers on one bony knee as he considered what he should do next. At last he instructed his driver to return to Southwark.

Averil had seen the large coach, and recognizing it as Sir John's, had ducked into a narrow alley between a tavern and a gunsmith shop. She had no intention of being returned home unceremoniously and with an accompanying lecture from Sir John on the dangers of such foolish behavior. When the coach passed by, Averil returned to the street.

The air was hot and close, blanketed by a heavy layer of smoke from the soap-makers' fires. Keeping alert should Sir John return along Fleet Street, Averil maneuvered through the pedestrians, but could find neither Nicodemus nor Darby Kipp. She questioned several peddlers, but they shook their heads, none having seen the aging knife grinder that day. And though she wound through alley after dismal alley in what she believed to be the right location, she was unable to locate Nicodemus' cottage. In the streets, scruffy children watched her warily; dogs sniffed at her heels; a gaunt, sharp-faced woman protested shrilly when Averil questioned her about Nicodemus.

Averil grew distracted with worry but steadfastly continued her search until the afternoon light had waned to a pale grey. Feeling a dark frustration that bordered on fury, she at last gave up her search and retraced her steps toward the Strand. She strode up the long drive and into the house, no longer caring if any of the Quints saw her attired as she was. What did it matter now anyway? she thought bitterly.

Averil wandered into the study without encountering any of the servants. After closing the door behind her, she crossed the dim room and sat in the hard but serviceable chair behind the desk. Whether it was sitting at the desk where Camden had spent many an hour, or catching some faint essence of him that lingered in the dark wood of the desktop or in the leather bindings of the few volumes neatly stacked to one side, Averil felt unexpectedly close to him in that moment. A soft moan tore from her as she longed for him.

With a paralyzing ache in her heart, Averil lay her head

on the smooth desktop and mourned for both men—Camden and her father.

She imagined her father being beaten with fists and cudgels. She saw blood oozing from his nose and mouth and trickling through the thick black hair of his head. At the image, a blue-white blade of pain pierced Averil's chest and she jerked upright, breathless with panic. She could not let that happen to him!

"Camden, *Camden*!" she cried aloud. She remembered what he had said about Prince Rupert playing a game of some sort. Every time Camden got close to her father, he was moved again—until sometime in late July when Camden had lost all trace of him. Now she had learned her father was in Oxford—but would he still be there in two weeks when Camden returned? Or would Prince Rupert have secreted him away to another location? Camden might arrive too late, and her father would be lost again.

An unexpected idea occurred to Averil then—a frightening, stunning idea that set her heart racing. What if she traveled to Oxford to watch and to follow should her father be taken elsewhere? If she left a message here for Camden, he would come to her swiftly. And if her father were moved, she could contrive some means of contacting Camden to let him know their whereabouts.

Averil remembered her own journey from Abingdon, thought of the dangers from soldiers or highwaymen along the roads, and almost discarded the idea entirely. Just half a year ago such an undertaking would have been entirely unthinkable to her. Since then she had braved much and accomplished much. The thought gave her courage. She also had her disguise, a horse to use, and money—all three factors lending her a certain degree of confidence. And Oxford could not be more than a day or a day and a half away, she estimated. If she left now, she could be in Oxford by tomorrow evening. Suddenly she did not know whether to laugh or cry, and one long tear rolled down her cheek. She wiped it away, chiding herself for such weakness when she had a journey to plan.

Averil reached for quill and paper and wrote out a brief message to Camden. After folding the paper and sealing it with a fat red blob of wax, Averil left the study to search for Mrs. Quint. She found the woman in the kitchen house bending over a steaming kettle in the hearth. The air in the room was moist and smelled pungently of onions.

"Mrs. Quint—it's Averil, Mrs. Warrender," she explained quickly when the woman's eyes grew large with surprise at finding a bold and grimy lad in her kitchen. "I must leave London now. I realize this must appear strange," Averil indicated her garments, grimacing slightly, "but I think 'twould be safer this way."

"Madam!" the woman exclaimed. She was momentarily speechless and her ladle dripped soup onto the flagstones. Her faded blue eyes darted over the soot-streaked face, the strange clothing. "I don't ken your purpose," she said in confusion.

"Mrs. Quint, I have to leave London. It's an extreme situation—an emergency. You can't believe I'd do this if it were for anything less?"

The older woman's face flushed. "Is it the Watch, madam? Are you in trouble of some sort? Why, I'll keep out the whole King's Army, I will. You'll have nought to fear here!"

"Nay, it's not like that, but I can't explain it to you. Please just trust me, Mrs. Quint, and tell no one. You can tell your family I've gone to see my aunt again. Give this to Captain Warrender immediately upon his return."

She thrust the sealed letter into the woman's hand. Mrs. Quint said severely, "Now if you're running away from 'im, madam, that's a serious mistake you're makin', it is."

"Oh nay, nothing like that!" Averil's patience was growing thin. "Ask Hosiah to saddle a horse and leave it tethered at the front. Then he should return to his duties. Please make

certain he is occupied elsewhere and doesn't see me leave
on the horse."

The tone of Averil's voice halted Mrs. Quint's next
intended outburst of shocked incredulity. Never before had
the young woman been so firm or issued directives in such
a way. "It goes against me good sense, madam," she
muttered darkly. She licked her lips in her confusion. "Aye,
then, it'll be as you say, though I don't doubt it'll be the
shame of you to think back on't."

Muttering to herself, Mrs. Quint left the kitchen to find
Hosiah, and Averil wrapped a section of cheese and some
meat in a napkin for herself before slipping back to the house.
She went upstairs to her room and took the coin pouch
Camden had left for her.

She waited uneasily in the front drawing room by the
window until Hosiah appeared, leading a horse which he
tethered to one of the stone balusters of the staircase. When
Hosiah disappeared again, Averil left the house quietly.
Though every instinct warned her to run back to her room,
she mounted the animal and turned its head toward the outer
gates. Riding astride was a new experience for her, and Averil
grimaced with the unaccustomed position.

She panicked some time later when she neared the guard
stationed at the road leading out of London. In her haste to
be off, she had thought of neither the required pass, nor the
quickly descending darkness of night. Briefly she debated
returning to wait until the morning before setting out again,
but having already made good her departure from the Quints,
she was loathe to try to repeat it on the morrow.

She studied the guard as she approached. He was bearded
and slovenly in his manner, and Averil suspected he might
be open to a bribe. Anything was worth a try now, she
thought wildly.

She was right. The guard eyed her suspiciously for a
moment, but took the three shillings she offered him and
pushed them into a pocket dangling from his waist. Deciding
to brazen a little further, Averil succeeded in purchasing one

of his lanterns. He grinned at her as she gave him an additional three shillings for the light, and she saw that his teeth were coated with a greenish slime. With a shudder, Averil hurriedly thumped her horse into motion. She distrusted the guard and decided to put some distance between them before he grew curious as to just how much money she carried.

The ground was soggy from the summer rains, and her horse slid often in the mud of the road. When she was several miles from London, the winds picked up and grew sharp. Averil hugged the cloak closer around herself and began to wish she had waited till morning before embarking on this journey. Goosebumps stood out on her arms, and she cast many apprehensive glances around her. The lantern she held shed a wide circle of yellowish light around her. Beyond that the blackness deepened as night closed in. As she passed them by, her light gleamed and faded on the muddied leaves of bushes and trees banking the road.

Some time later the moon eased from behind a thick crop of clouds. Its light bathed the rolling hills ahead with a silvery cast and shed an eerie, unnatural brightness down on her. The road was clearly illuminated, and Averil urged her horse to a gallop, hoping to swallow the distance to the first inn as quickly as she could.

Fifteen miles from London, and much to her relief, she entered the town of Uxbridge. Averil slowed her horse to a walk as the streets narrowed. No one was out at this time of the night and Averil heard clearly and in unnatural loudness the slopping of her horse's hooves in the mud. She held the lantern high and looked anxiously for an inn.

Her light illuminated the rows of cottages crowding the road, then slanted off a creaking, swinging sign that hung from a wrought-iron arm farther down. In the weak light, she saw that the building was an inn and hurried toward it, tethering her horse in front before entering. Only one patron occupied the common room. He slumped on a wooden bench near the fireplace, his chin sunk on a thick, barrel-like chest.

The owner, a thin, hunched older man with a white beard, brushed off the tables with a soiled dark cloth. He saw Averil enter but went on with his work, ignoring her presence.

Drawing up her courage, Averil said briskly, "I'd like a room for the night."

He straightened and looked her over. Scratching at his beard, he said, "Six shillin's fer the lodging, an' ye pay now."

"I want a private room. And I have a horse out front."

" 'At'll be extra—three shillin's more fer the room and four fer the animal."

Averil gave him the required amount, not knowing if he cheated her or not, and not really caring, and he took her up the stairs. The heavy rumbling sound of someone snoring in his sleep issued from behind one of the doors. The room she was shown to was next to it.

After the owner departed, Averil removed the brown hat and linen bindings from her head and rubbed her scalp with her fingers as she glanced around. The room looked comfortable and clean. Fresh white curtains hung at the window, the rush mat on the floor was new, the chamber pot gleamed from a recent scrubbing. She was tired, and her body ached not only from the unaccustomed strain of riding astride the horse, but with the tension that had gripped her through the last half a day as well.

The flock bed draped with linen hangings beckoned her, and Averil lost no time in pulling off her cloak and shoes. Her breasts ached when she removed the linen bindings. She washed her face with water from a pitcher on the dressing table, then brushed the dust from her breeches and shirt as best she could before extinguishing the rush candle the proprietor had left and stretching out with a luxurious sigh on the bed.

But she jumped up almost immediately and ran to the door, her fingers sliding along the panel in the dark as she searched for a lock. There was none. She had not expected to find one—the use of locks on inner doors was not a widespread practice. But she had hoped it might be different here. There were no articles of furniture she could move to bar the door with. Feeling vulnerable and alarmed, she returned to the bed.

But who was to know the boy was really a woman? she protested to herself. Or who that woman was?

The snoring continued loudly from the next room, but Averil was too weary to care. She thought fleetingly of Camden's warm body beside hers, and her heart was heavy. But before another minute passed, she was lost in sleep.

A creak of the floorboards woke her. She opened her eyes wide, staring into the soft blackness of the room. The moonlight had disappeared completely; the snoring had ceased. She lay still in concentration. Had she truly heard the sound? Or was it her imagination?

Then she smelled the dense fetidness of someone near and a hand gripped her mouth.

With a muffled shriek, Averil jumped in fright, but she was held down immediately. In blind, mind-burning terror, she thrashed against her unseen attackers, her screams held back behind a bruising and sweaty hand. She bit the fleshy pad of the palm over her mouth and drew blood.

'' 'S God's my life! She's a bitch!''

One of her assailants shifted away from the bed, then a rush candle was puffed to flame from an ember in the hearth and the light was brought close to illuminate her. Averil ceased her struggles in momentary horror as she stared at the faces of the two men hovering over her. Both were attired in dusty chamois breeches and leather coats with swords swaying from thick belts around their waists. One sported a soft beaver hat, the crown ringed with a gold-link band. He had medium brown hair, a thin moustache over wide, dry lips, and a sharp point of a chin.

The man who held her scowled harshly. His hat had been knocked to the floor, and he had straight black hair falling around a narrow face with glittering amber-yellow eyes. He wore a black T-beard and moustache.

They were the two men who had followed her from her uncle's home one afternoon, the ones Camden had seen in London and warned her about. An oily, sickening panic rushed through her.

With a sudden burst of energy, Averil broke from the loosened grip the one man had on her, but she was flung down again immediately. The man who held her down grunted in exasperation. "She's going to be too much trouble to tie up," he said. He removed one hand briefly as he lifted a small cudgel from his belt.

The other exclaimed in alarm, "Careful with that thing!"

Averil's eyes burned in terror as the cudgel came down on the side of her head. An excruciating splash of pain filled her, and she slipped away into a soft brown oblivion.

She was dimly aware of movement, of horses, of cool winds, of sun, but could neither move nor utter a sound, though she tried. Her head ached. Voices surrounded her, but she could make no sense of the words. She thought she was falling. Then a shout pounded through her skull. Sensations came and went, with no sense of order or reason.

Averil felt the hot pressure of sunlight. She stirred, realizing that she lay face down on the ground, lush, damp grass crushed under her cheek. Someone grasped her shoulder and rolled her to her back. She groaned aloud as the movement brought fresh pain spearing through her head.

When she managed to get her eyes open to a squint, she saw a man looking down at her, his eyes dulling and yellowed. He was one of her abductors, the man who had struck her. Dropping to one knee beside her, he reached for the waist of her breeches.

In sick desperation, Averil tried to cry out, to move, to cover and protect herself. But his hands seemed to be everywhere on her at once. She screamed but heard no sound; nausea rose in her, and she knew the horror of feeling as if she did not exist.

Suddenly another voice burst out, "What in hell d'you

think you're doing!'' The man above her was dragged away
by his companion. ''We weren't to lay a finger on her! Those
were his orders, by God!''

The yellow-eyed man struck out, knocking loose the other's
grip on his arm. His voice growling with restrained anger,
he answered, ''How is he going to know?''

The two faced each other, sunlight burning between them
and blinding Averil where she lay huddled on the ground.
She wanted to climb to her feet and run while they were
distracted, but she could not make her muscles move as she
wanted them to.

''*She'll* tell him! Remember what he did to that other
fellow? Had him sliced up into bits! Eh? Remember *that*?''
He was furious. He shook his fist under his companion's
nose. ''I don't want to be dancing on the end of the gibbet
because of *you*!''

The first man waved aside his friend as if he were a
persistent insect and looked down again at Averil. ''She won't
tell him.''

But the other whipped out a knife from his belt and put
it to his companion's midsection. Anger added an evil edge
to his voice. ''You want it so bad, I'll get you a whore. One
that won't get us strung up or cut to ribbons.''

For a long time they stared at each other in silence. The
yellow eyes of her assailant narrowed. He leaned down,
gathered up his hat from the ground and knocked the dust
from it, then stalked away until he had disappeared into a
thicket of trees.

Averil tried to sit up. She touched her burning head. Her
temple was swollen and crusted with something stiff that
extended down the side of her face. When she realized it
was her own blood, she had to stifle a rising scream.

An uncorked, half-empty bottle of wine was shoved into
her hands. She looked up at the man who had pulled the knife.
He stared down at her with unfriendly eyes as he wiped the
sweat from the back of his neck.

"Yonder is a stream. Clean your face. Don't think you can get away—I'll be watching. Hurry back. We've a long way to go yet." With steps made sharp by impatience, he turned away and walked back to the nearby tree where three horses were tethered in the shade.

Averil crawled carefully to her feet. Gripping the bottle, she half walked, half slid down the small slope to a narrow, swiftly rushing stream. The water was deep and icy and the shock of it on her skin cleared her head. Sitting back on her heels, she looked around.

Rolling, verdant hills stretched away in each direction, the soft greenness broken by scattered clumps of pink and yellow field flowers and thin copses of trees. She could not tell where she was. The horror of her situation broke over her and suddenly she was crying, her breathing ragged. She had tempted fate, tested her luck once too often. Camden had told her she did not know what she was up against, and he had been right. Camden! she cried silently.

The horse she rode was led by a rope secured to the saddle of the man who had tried to rape her. The two men spoke little enough to each other and not at all to Averil. Though she asked them where they were taking her, she never received an answer. They traveled all that day and the next. Late in the night on the second day they halted.

Averil was led into a darkened, empty building and left there. A guard, a different man than either of her abductors, took up a post just outside the door. Averil stood alone and frightened in darkness that was solid and oppressive. She wondered where she was, what would happen now. The black air smelled of dust and faintly of moldering hay—it was a stable, she realized.

A skittering of tiny claws on the wood floor startled her. Shivering with fright and revulsion, Averil retreated to hug the door where she had entered. Though she tried to remain alert, weariness settled over her and she eventually fell asleep, sitting up with her back against the door.

She woke slowly, her mind dull. Birds twittered; someone outside laughed. Averil dragged open her eyes. Split timbers reinforced warped wood plank walls and a sloping roof. A cracked and dried leather harness hung from a nail on the wall to her left. Everywhere splinters of sunlight shone through the planks and pierced the dim interior of the structure. There were no animals in the stable. It was bare of hay, feed, or any of the trappings of a working stable. She became aware of more voices outside and before she could move away, the door against which she had slept was pulled back.

Framed in the rectangle of brilliant light was the silhouette of a man. Averil recognized the man with the T-beard and yellowing eyes. She huddled beside the door, staring up at him.

He bent and lifted her to her feet. Averil was unable to tolerate even his smallest touch and pulled her arm from his grasp. "Where am I?" Her voice sounded fuzzy in her ears.

He took her arm again, squeezing it in his hand as he led her from the stable. Outside, the sunlight was too bright for her and Averil ducked her head. Her hair was a mass of tangles, bits of straw and dirt clinging to the strands. She was barefoot, dressed only in the breeches and linen shirt of Camden's that she had worn to leave London. The shirt had come out of the waist of the breeches and hung in wide folds that flapped loosely around her in the breeze.

They crossed a dirt yard bordered by groves of ash and hawthorn trees. Several groups of men, wearing dusty doublets and breeches and shoulder belts hung with powder flasks, turned to look at her with curious resentment. She avoided their eyes.

The man led her to a large, three-storied, stone house, the walls of which were laced with green vines. Sun-warmed roses blooming against the back wall lifted a sweetly thick fragrance into the air. She was taken inside the house, through a dining room where more men stood about drinking from mugs, down a dark corridor and into the front parlor. It had been taken over for an office, and a large table serving as a desk dominated the room. Behind the table sat a man with dark eyes and long, curling black hair.

Prince Rupert.

At the sight of him, fear climbed inside her like a living being. She doubled over, one hand to her mouth, afraid she would be violently sick. Perspiration broke out across her brow. An arm around her prevented her from falling.

"For God's sake—someone get her a bucket," she heard Rupert say in disgust.

Averil pulled in a deep breath. She pushed away the pot thrust at her. The man holding her straightened her on her feet, and her eyes locked with the dark gaze Rupert fixed on her. She was pushed toward a chair set in front of Rupert's desk. Her knees quivered and buckled, and she sat.

"All right, leave us now," she heard Rupert say. Shuffling footsteps departed, the door was closed with a creak of hinges. Averil stared at Rupert, unable to breathe.

He leaned across the table, his palms flat on the surface as he said quietly, "So . . . Jeremy Halmes, Lady Averil, Mrs. Warrender." He pushed himself to his feet, the black curly hair sliding around his face and shoulders.

Averil saw him walk around the table and bend to stroke the fur of a small white dog that lay in a square of sunshine. It was the same dog he had had with him at the inn in Abingdon. Her heart struck painfully against her ribs. Though she felt frozen in time, unable to move, her thoughts crashed with mounting hysteria. What would he do? What did he want? What could she do? Could she move to the door—get away? A silent scream filled her head.

Rupert straightened, his back rigid. "Where is his lordship, your father?" he asked. His black eyes pierced her.

Averil stared back at him. What was he saying? Every muscle of her body clenched in panic.

Rupert continued, "The two of you have played me for a fool, haven't you!" With one hand braced on the back of her chair, the other on the table, he leaned down. His dark mane of hair swung forward.

"I have enough trouble now with Cromwell and his damned Ironsides. Your interference is wearing on me. Where is the Earl?"

Averil saw only the glitter of one gold pendant on his green doublet. It filled her vision in monstrous proportion. She tried to speak.

A low sound of anger rumbled from him. "Are you listening to me!" he demanded. Suddenly he yanked a handful of her hair, half lifting her from the chair. Averil squealed in painful surprise.

"Where do you get your information? Who tells you about the movement of the munitions? The messages?"

Averil gripped his fist against the pain in her scalp. His skin was hot. "I . . . don't . . . know!" she managed to say, though it was barely a whisper. "I don't know anything about—"

"Do you think I'll believe that? You're not like any other woman—I've found out quite a lot about you." His voice tightened to a harsh whisper. "By God, I'll have your neck stretched. Tell me, where is his lordship? Who gives you information?"

"I don't know what you're talking about! My father has never done anything like that—and I don't know where he is. *I've been trying to find him*!"

Abruptly, he released her and Averil dropped into the chair, pressing her hand to her head where the scalp burned. Rupert tugged his green satin doublet back into place. His dark eyes, smudged with arrogance and anger, stared down at her.

"You hang tomorrow," he said.

"This is a mistake!" Averil cried. She fought for breath again in the horror of the moment. "You've got the wrong person—I've had nothing to do with this! Nor has my father! I *swear* it!"

Rupert ignored her. His voice rose as he called out for someone beyond the door. When the man entered, Rupert said, "Take her back."

"Nay, nay! Believe me, I've—"

But with an impatient yank, the man lifted Averil to her feet. She stumbled as she was led out to the hall. The walls of the corridor seemed to close in on her; the hard stares of the men in the dining room separated and twisted away at odd angles in her vision. She stumbled against a chair and never felt the floor when she hit it.

When she became aware of herself again, she was lying on the floor of the empty stable. Outside she heard loud voices, murmuring voices, laughter, shouts. A trencher holding bread and meat sat on the floor beside the door.

Gingerly, but driven by panic, she stood up and walked around the stable. She tested the walls, pushing against the warped planks with the flat of her hand. They were thick, too thick to break even if she'd had a tool of some sort. Through the tiny spaces between the boards, she peered out. The yard beyond was filled with men. They were busily inspecting weapons, cleaning out musket barrels, weighing swords in their hands. A cart stood to one side, loaded with wooden crates. Some of the crates were open and sitting in the dirt of the yard. Other men were removing gun parts from the opened crates. Some filled the flasks attached to their belts with black powder from a barrel on the back of the cart.

Averil circled the interior of the stable, peering through any crack that was large enough to admit light. The front and right side of the stable looked out on the yard where the men were occupied with their weapons. The rear abutted a thick stand of trees. Between the trunks Averil could see a green meadow stretching out to a distant hill. There were almost no shadows, which meant the sun was high overhead. Through the wall on the left of the stable she saw a road. It was empty, though a layer of dust hung in the air as if there had been recent movement on it. In a field across the road she caught sight of more men. Curious, she walked down the wall till she found another large crack.

Now she could clearly see rows and rows of men, hundreds of them, drilling. They did not fire their weapons, but knelt, aimed, went through the motions of falling back, reloading. Some had muskets that required stands to brace the barrels on.

She saw Prince Rupert astride a horse, moving through the ranks. He shouted instructions, but she could not hear the words clearly. Sometimes he pointed, harangued a slower subordinate, then whipped his horse to another side of the field, his black hair flying like a banner behind him. Always he watched and forced his men through round after round of drill.

Averil wished she knew where she was.

She went to the door and listened. She could never get out while all the soldiers were just beyond in the yard. She peered through the planks of the door and looked directly into the broad back of a soldier standing guard. He was so close she could have touched him with a piece of straw thrust through the crack. Her keeper sighed suddenly, shifted his position and called out a laughing comment to a friend Averil could not see. She backed away from the door. After another inspection, she was forced to admit to herself that the only way out was through the door. Though old, the stable was solidly built.

The collar of the forgotten harness might prove a weapon to strike someone with—if she got the opportunity. Averil hefted it. Her strength was such that she could hope only to momentarily stun someone with it and thereby gain a chance to run. It was definitely risky—but it was her only chance. She would have to wait, she knew, until the soldiers had retired for the night.

Averil held the collar, testing it, and then crouched by the door to wait out the hours. At length the light in the stable waned, grew shadowy, then faded out completely. When the light was gone, the soldiers' voices scattered and finally there was silence.

Averil went quietly to the crack in the door to peer out. She could see nothing, but she heard the guard shift position and knew he still waited at his post. Averil listened intently, her ears pounding in the empty silence. There were no footsteps approaching.

She hefted the collar and called to the guard.

"What d'ye want?" he grunted.

"I want to see Rupert," she said, trying to keep the trembling out of her voice. Her heart pounded violently.

"Ye'll 'ave to wait till morning—can't disturb 'im now."

"This is important!"

"It'll 'ave to keep," the guard cut in.

Averil waited a moment. "I need more water," she tried.

Her keeper uttered a sound like disgust. "Ye've plenty, so close yer mouth."

"I . . . I spilled it."

" 'At's too bad."

Averil realized she was crying. Angrily she wiped her cheeks and said, "I'm hungry."

The guard responded sharply, "Well now, y' don't seem t' be able t' make up yer mind *what* ye want. Will it be me next time, sweetheart?" His voice slid into a greasy tone. "Ye want me t' keep ye company?"

In a burst of panic, she fled from the door. She sank to her knees, shaking. Rupert had promised she would hang come morning, but even so she could not bring herself to call the invitation that would make this man open the door. The terror of what might happen should she not be able to get away from the guard held her paralyzed and unable to call him in. She sobbed, pressing her face to her knees.

There must be a way! she thought frantically. Something would happen, surely!

Time slipped past. Averil's hopes slipped away as silently and stealthily as the passing of the hours.

Eventually she slept—a light, restless sleep. Every gentle rustle of wind or animal stirred her awake. Then a rustling seemed too close, too pronounced. Her ears strained. Someone was moving outside the side wall of the stable.

Averil came to her feet, lifting the harness collar. She

crossed to the door and listened intently. After a long minute, she heard a quick scraping sound. With a strange gurgling noise, a heavy bulk slid down against the planks. Averil took one panicked, unconscious step back, realizing the guard was being murdered. The stealthy scrape was repeated. The sound of it rasped against her nerves and unsettled her stomach.

The latch on the door was tested, something slid away, and then the door swung back slowly. She caught her breath, not knowing what to expect.

Then framed against the starlit sky she saw a tall, cloaked, masked form. Every ounce of her cried out with joy.

"Camden!" she breathed, her relief rushing tears to her eyes. As she dropped the harness, she missed the briefest of hesitations in the black-garbed form. She threw herself into his arms. "Camden, oh Camden!"

Averil knew the difference the moment she touched him. The shoulders were thin, the form not so tall as Camden's, the cloak he wore was musty and rank-smelling. She flung herself away in painful surprise.

The man caught her arm. "Averil, it's Sir John. We must hurry!" He pulled her toward the door, and they stepped over the prostrate form slumped across their path.

"Sir John?" Averil mumbled, not able to make sense of the moment. She followed him numbly, instinctively. They turned and ran along the side wall of the stable and into the grove of trees behind it. The night air was crisp, and she welcomed its chill on her face. They slipped wordlessly through the trees and ran on through the meadow. The tall grass swished against her legs and bare feet.

Sir John led her on to the bordering forest. Within the denser shadows two horses were tethered to a sapling. He helped her into the saddle of one of the animals, then mounted the other.

"I hope you're able to ride a goodly distance tonight," he said over his shoulder. He pulled off his mask and tucked it inside his shirt. "We have to make haste and put miles between you and Rupert. By gad! What a fool you were!"

Averil looked at him in anguish. "I should never have left London, but oh, Sir John! I'm so glad you came! Prince Rupert intended to have me hung tomorrow!"

"Probably just a bluff."

"He doesn't have my father—he wanted me to tell him where he was."

Walford hesitated a moment. "We have to get back to London."

"Where are we?"

"Near Gloucester."

By the light of the myriad twinkling stars overhead, they picked their way with care along the narrow road. Averil wore no cloak and she huddled in the saddle, shivering not only with the night air on her lightly clad body but also with the after-shock of her brush with death. Before long she drooped with exhaustion.

Dawn came swiftly; they had been on the road for only two hours. Sir John increased their pace as the light grew stronger and illuminated the road. Somewhere behind them, Averil heard the distant rumbling of a cannon. The sound rolled toward them like the far-off thunder of a summer storm. When they had traveled another hour, Sir John led the horses off the road and into a thicket of young oak trees.

"We'll pass the day here," he explained. "Gloucester has been under seige by the Royalists, and London is sending its militia. Better not to press our luck on the road."

He gave Averil his cloak and she curled under its warm folds, her head pillowed on a bulging tree root, and slept. They traveled through the following night, again sought shelter and waited out the daylight hours. Early in the morning of the third day, London came into view.

The streets were beginning to come alive with the multitude of early tradespeople, tinkers, and peddlers. On all sides, as Averil and Sir John made their way through the city, they heard the peddlers' cries.

"White-hearted cabbages!"

"What d'ye lack?"

"Fresh sweet milk, sweet milk. Any milk here?"

Averil smiled through her weariness, glad with every ounce of energy she possessed to have returned. Sir John reached across from his horse to squeeze her hand reassuringly.

"Come back with me to my home first, Averil," he suggested. "We have still to discuss the matter of William's whereabouts. I suspect he may have escaped and returned to Maslin Manor."

Averil looked to him quickly, her eyes brightening despite her tiredness.

"And aye, sweetheart, I will go with you this time."

Before another hour had passed, Averil was slipping into a steaming tub of water in a bedchamber Sir John had graciously provided for her temporary use. She slid low in the water, relishing the feel of the heat on her aching muscles, the soapy bubbles sliding over her skin. For a long while she lay with her head against the back rim of the tub, her hair floating around her.

The tub sat before a brightly flickering hearth in a spartanly, though elegantly, decorated chamber. Red and gold hangings surrounded the narrow bed and were pushed back in thick folds at the two small square windows. The floor was bare of mats or rugs, but there were several plush stools and a dressing table with a gilt framed mirror; beside her a tapestry-backed chair held several clean linen towels. After she had lathered herself briskly and scrubbed her hair, the water had cooled, and Averil was forced to climb from the tub. Sir John had left a dressing gown of his for her. She put this on and was sitting at the dressing table, pulling a comb through her wet hair, when Sir John knocked at the door and asked for entry.

He was freshly shaven and had changed into a clean suit of clothes. His smile was as bright as Averil's when he entered. Averil thought he looked younger than ever. If it were not for the tell-tale grey heavily shot through his dark hair, he could have passed for a man half his age. His body was still lean, and the fresh black doublet and breeches fitted him well.

"Did you enjoy your bath?" he asked, coming around to sit on a stool near her. "Actually, it was appalling the way Prince Rupert treated you. Someone of your station deserves better handling, no matter the circumstances."

Averil lowered the comb. "How did you find me?"

"I followed you, of course. You avoided me in Fleet Street that afternoon, but I took a chance on your trying to reach Oxford and so waited on the road."

"You should have stopped me then," Averil said in a small, regretful voice, "before all this happened."

Sir John wagged his finger at her. "You were already being followed, little innocent. I could do nought but follow your followers." He laughed at that, shaking his head. "But, as you said, 'tis all over with now. We'll not talk of it again."

He rose and walked across the room to the door. "I'll see if I cannot find you something a bit more suitable to wear. Then we can talk over the matter of your father. In the meantime, feel free to rest. Actually, sweetheart, you look deathly tired."

Sir John left the room. As Averil lifted the comb again to her hair, she heard the clear and unmistakable sound of a bolt being shoved home on the door.

CHAPTER
TWENTY-THREE

Averil lowered her arm and turned to look at the door. A small frown of confusion puckered her brow. She walked to the door and tested the latch carefully, but it refused to budge. Rattling it loudly, Averil called out for Sir John. There was no answer, though she called and thumped her fist on the portal for several minutes. Somewhere below her in the house, a dog set up a savage barking.

At last, Averil left the door and returned to the dressing table. Had it been an accident—the bolted door? Or had Sir John some reason to protect her in this house?

She waited restlessly for his return. From the window, she stared out at the dense, overgrown forest behind Sir John's home. A ruined garden lay between the house and the trees, a rotting pale fence tipped and swayed at the property's boundary. In the garden, untrimmed vines and shrubs spread straggly limbs over the ground; everywhere sturdy weeds sprouted through the brown, soggy covering of dead leaves. The sky had grown dark with clouds, leaden and low, and a fine mist thickened the air.

When Sir John returned, he brought two servants with him. One was the kindly, aging man Averil had met twice before, the other a youthful giant attired in a black broadcloth suit of clothes embroidered with silver thread. He wore swinging gold hoops at both ears. Ignoring Averil, they moved back and forth in the room, emptying and removing the bathing tub. Sir John held a gown out to Averil and smiled as she accepted it.

" 'Tis a bit wrinkled, I know, and may not fit you all that well, but it is a gown at least and not like those hideous garments you arrived here in. I'm sorry, I don't have any of the—um, other things you women wear underneath."

Averil held the gown up to study it, and a musty smell wafted from its folds. Made of faded green velvet, it had puffed, flowing sleeves trimmed with stiff, ivory lace at the wrists, a low square neckline, and tiny clusters of seed pearls sewn in shapes of flowers over the bodice.

He handed her also a small pair of slippers, green, with scattered seed pearls sewn on the instep. As Averil looked from the gown and the slippers to Sir John, she recalled the Tottman telling her that Sir John had been married once, briefly. These garments had belonged to his wife, she realized, and the thought of Sir John's loss melted her heart. But it was strange that she had never known about it, or about this house.

"Sir John, when you left earlier the door was locked and I don't know if—"

"Aye, it was locked," he replied in a reluctant tone. "And 'twill remain locked, but only for a few days at most."

Averil cast a confused look at him and glanced aside to the two servants shouldering the tub out of the room. "But why? I don't understand."

"Now that you've given me the information I needed from you, I cannot allow you to leave just yet. But look"—he gestured around the room with a wave of his hand—"I know how to treat a lady of quality. Not like Prince Rupert at all. He's a damned beast, if you ask me. Too hot-headed, too closely governed by fire and passion and all that. Nay, it is logic and a clear, controlled mind that one needs. He's losing this war, but I'm not.'' Sir John smiled at Averil's flushed, awe-struck expression.

''But—'' Averil faltered. ''But, Sir John, what are you saying?''

He shrugged. ''I needed to discover the Tottman's identity, and you supplied that for me.''

Averil drew in a sharp breath, remembering the moment he had entered the stable, attired as the Tottman, and she had cried Camden's name in her relief. Bewildered, Averil shook her head. Instinctively aware that she should shield Camden, she stammered, ''The Tottman? But nay, that is not right—why, I merely mistook the form in the night. It was so dark and I—''

''By gad! I'm not a simpleton, Averil! I've suspected his identity. You merely confirmed my suspicions.'' He shook his finger at her. ''So don't think to alter the facts with cheap protests. I intend to see the man arrested, and nothing will stop that now.''

Averil stared at him in stunned horror, unable to piece together his words, his intentions. Her mind was snagged with the memories of Sir John as her friend, her ally, her father's long-time companion. Then, as he walked over to give a directive to the older servant, the truth burst through her mind.

Camden had spoken of a man who controlled Francis Bowers. It was Sir John! He had known Francis at Maslin Manor.

Averil felt as if she had been struck in the stomach. She stumbled, crumpling the gown against her middle, and groaned aloud. ''Oh, nay! Oh dear God! It can't be you!'' Averil gasped air into her lungs and pleaded, ''Why? Why! He was helping find my father for us.''

Sir John swung around. ''But your father is beyond help, sweetheart. He's in the Tower.'' He looked pityingly at Averil's stricken face. ''During the confusion of the battle at Bristol, the Earl was released from the Royalists in error. His reappearance in Abingdon certainly stunned me, but with a few words to the nearest Parliament commander, to the effect that your father had been an associate of the Tottman, he was arrested and transported to the Tower. Let me see,''—Walford pinched his lips together—''your father's execution is scheduled for Saturday, September ninth—just three more days! So you see,'' he said with a shrug, ''there's no help for him.''

''You betrayed my father?'' Averil breathed painfully, unable to believe this added treachery.

Walford spoke patiently. ''I certainly enjoyed your father's company, Averil. But we're engaged in a war at the moment, and because of that, certain things become not only expedient but necessary.''

''But I thought you were—didn't you send a letter to Prince Rupert about my father?''

''Aye, but I also sent Francis and your cousin, Lynna, after the messenger. Lynna was so decidedly eager to join Francis, I engineered a little experiment to see if she was up to the test of working for me.''

The full magnitude of what she had done flooded Averil's mind and she panted sharply with the horror of it. She had given the Tottman's identity to this man; Camden was no longer safe and he did not know it! In a few days his ship would dock, and he was entirely unaware of the danger!

Averil looked about wildly, clutching the velvet gown to her still in a death grip. She had to get away! With a savage cry, she flung the gown and shoes at him, the shoes striking his forehead with a thump, and then she was flying toward the door. She cleared the threshold and was swept up into the air by the young giant of a servant who had been standing just beside the door in the hall.

Averil shrieked and clawed at him, but he merely laughed with a deep, reverberating sound and carried her back into the room. Sir John was stroking his bruised temple with his fingers. His mouth thinned as he gestured the servant back.

Averil was set down and the man retreated, closing the door
behind him. She flew at Sir John in a frenzy of outrage and
fear. With a muttered curse, he slipped quickly to the side,
grasping one of her outstretched hands and twisting it around
behind her back. She cried out with the pain.

"I'd rather not have to hurt you, Averil," he said, his voice
whispering between his teeth as he held her arm tightly. "You
were always a very clever, entertaining child, and I have
no quarrel with you."

When Sir John released her, Averil threw herself across
the room. "Why are you doing this?" she begged in a ragged
voice. "What have you to gain from my father's death?"

He looked at her in surprise. "Land, of course. Maslin
Manor and all your father owns."

"Maslin Manor? You'll never—why, it's been taken by
the Crown!"

"You are a woman after all, my dear, so let me explain.
With the aid of Cromwell's new cavalry troops, the Ironsides
I believe they're called, the tide of the war has changed, as
I suspected it would. The King will never again have the
complete and absolute power he enjoyed previously. Parliament will have power. And when this necessary struggle has
reached its end, I intend to emerge with all your father's
holdings."

Averil listened, aghast. "You were the one," she exclaimed
in stupefied amazement. "Prince Rupert accused my father
of—of stealing guns, but that was *you*!"

Sir John laughed delightedly. "Oh, you do have a quick
mind."

Averil sat wearily on a stool near the window. She hugged
the dressing robe close around her as she said dully, "*You*
wrote the letter to my uncle and destroyed his wine."

Sir John cleared his throat and looked suddenly disgruntled.
"An unpardonable fit of anger on my part, Averil. That was
when I learned from Francis that you were indeed working
with the Tottman—he had recognized you in that little fiasco

on London Bridge—and you had *lied* to me, told me Darby Kipp knew nothing!''

Averil looked up, her eyes dark with loathing. "You'll not get Maslin Manor. Even should Parliament win, lands are awarded to the *worthy*. I don't see that you merit any such reward."

"Sweetheart!" Sir John laughed loudly in disbelief. "And I thought you were so clever! Think about it! I will have handed over the Tottman. Isn't that merit enough?"

"I won't let you do it!" she cried savagely.

"You're going to stop me?" Sir John looked her over in derisive amusement. "When your captain docks, he'll be arrested as soon as he steps foot on land, and the next time you see either your father or your husband 'twill be their pickled heads staring down at you from the spikes on the bridge."

After Sir John departed, Averil remained sitting beside the window. She lowered her head till it touched her knees. What have I done? she thought in overwhelming despair.

Later, when the light from the window had darkened and the rain had begun to splatter down over the house and trees, Averil lifted her throbbing head. She tried to summon even a small spark of hope, but felt nothing. Soundlessly she crawled to the bed and lay across it. Hugging her arms around herself, she rocked on the soft mattress, groaning with the knowledge that, in the end, it really was she who had betrayed the Tottman.

Averil opened her eyes slowly. She could see nothing in the darkness, but knew something horrible was there—it seemed to surround her and press in on her like a deadly, vaporous cloud. And then she remembered where she was and what Sir John had said. The image of the grisly, brine-soaked heads impaled in the wind above London Bridge sprang afresh to her mind. With a shudder, she pulled herself up to a sitting position, one leg curled under the other.

Her body felt stiff and aching and she winced as she slid from the bed. How long had she slept? Moving on unsteady limbs, she felt her way to one of the windows and pushed it open.

The incoming gust of wet night air chilled her, but she leaned out, breathing deeply. She could not determine the hour; all was a soft black.

With the window wide, Averil moved back through the dark room. Camden was unaware of what was happening here. She was the only one who could make a difference now. She had to get away to warn him!

How? How! her mind cried. Camden had lowered her down the side of the inn—perhaps she could rig a rope of some sort here. With what?

She groped her way to the bed and ripped back the blanket. When she had removed the sheets, she knotted these together, but they were not long enough. Averil groaned and leaned her face into the curtains of the bed. With a gasp of surprise, she felt the fabric, then ripped down the panel from its rings. She tied this to the sheets, praying all the while that the knots would hold. With one end tied to the bedpost as anchor, she dragged the rest to the window and dumped out its length.

Knowing she could never slip through London wearing a man's dressing robe, she dressed herself in the gown and slippers Sir John had given her. Then, shaking with fright and excitement, Averil climbed through the window.

But this was far different than being lowered on a rope tied around one's waist. She could get no solid hold on the fabric and though she tried to wrap her legs and arms around it, her weight dragged her uncontrollably down the makeshift rope. Wildly Averil gripped the material to stop her flight and keep herself from dropping off entirely, but the friction burned into her palms and scraped her legs. At last she came to a stop halfway down and hung there trembling, her heart jumping crazily in her chest, icy rain running down her arms and face.

As she was pondering how to maneuver herself the rest of the way down, a slopping, shuffling sound caught her attention and she looked over one aching arm to see a man with a lantern come around the side of the house. Fear shot through her. She had no time to move either up or down, so remained still, hardly daring to breathe, hoping that somehow, with the darkness and rain, her presence would go unnoticed.

The light grew brighter as the man approached. When he was directly below her, he stopped, and Averil dared one small look down. He was smiling up at her, squinting his eyes against the rain. She had never seen him before.

"Good morrow, my lady," the man began pleasantly. "If you'll just climb back up there now."

"Please, you don't understand!" Averil begged. "Sir John intends to kill my father—"

"Aye, my lady."

"—and my husband!"

"Aye, my lady. Back up you go."

Recognizing that she had no choice and could fall too easily if she delayed there, she attempted to climb up the fabric. After watching her slip and struggle, the man told her how to use the stones of the side of the house as stepholds for her feet, and in that manner Averil continued the rest of the way to her window and climbed through.

"Now toss down the other end of the sheets, my lady."

When Averil had done so, the man departed, calling back, "If you try such a thing again, we'll have to tie you in that room."

Angrily Averil banged the window closed. Tears of pain and frustration coursed down her cheeks. Her arms and shoulders felt on fire and the palms of her hands were scraped raw.

In the morning Sir John barged into her room and with angry swipes ripped down the remaining bed curtains. He tossed these into the hall outside her room and went on to bring down each of the drapes at the windows. Averil cowered as he marched through the room gathering candle-holders, the pitcher, vases, every small object that could be used as a weapon, and flung these into the mound of curtains in the hall. Without a word, he left the room, and the wooden bolt was again thrust home, this time with an angry vehemence.

Averil moved to the door. She flattened her palms on the panels and bit at her lower lip in angry frustration. Through the door she heard distant voices, and she pressed her ear to the seam above one hinge, trying to listen.

The words were indistinguishable, but she recognized the high, clear tones of Francis Bowers' voice. Her panic deepened as she realized that time was moving forward, drawing ever closer to the moment when Camden would reach London, ever closer to the date of her father's execution. She squeezed her hands into fists and struck the door. She beat her fists against the wood over and over in a fit of despair.

Late in the morning, the elderly manservant brought her a tray of dinner. Averil presented a stiff back to him. Without saying a word to her, the man set the tray on the dressing table and departed. Momentarily Averil debated flinging the tray against the door, but experience cautioned her that she needed the nourishment if she was to be of any use to herself and to Camden. So she ate slowly, tasting nothing, swal-lowing hard over the lump of bitter anguish that welled up in her throat.

Through the afternoon she paced the dimensions of the room. Worry and fear and a lonely desolation chased her. There had to be something—something!—she could do.

When the day drew on to the supper hour, Averil dragged a stool to the door. She lifted its bulk and practiced a swing. It was such a clumsy maneuver, Averil almost cried with the exasperation she felt with herself. But if the same manservant—the older, weaker man who had brought her dinner earlier—also came to bring her supper, perhaps she could manage to knock him down. Anything to give her a moment's start out the door. She was sure she could outrun him and flee the house before anyone else could be alerted and come after her.

She soon heard the footsteps approach her door, and she waited poised beside the threshold, the stool held high though her muscles shook with the effort. The bolt was slid out, the panels swung open, and she brought the stool down sharply toward the unsuspecting elderly man.

But he was surprisingly swift in his movements. Before Averil could change tactics, he had managed to knock the stool aside with a swing of his forearm. It was struck from her grasp and crashed loudly to the floor. The man had not even dropped the tray of supper he balanced in one hand. He stared hard at her, and Averil's eyes widened fearfully.

The noise of the stool falling to the floor alerted Sir John. Averil heard him leaping the stairs, and then he strode into the room behind the manservant, his face flushed with fury. Averil backed from the door.

"Take that thing out!" he ordered the servant, indicating the supper tray. "She doesn't deserve it."

The man left the room, and Sir John scowled at Averil, exclaiming, "I'm beginning to think Rupert had the right idea! You don't deserve deferential treatment." As he advanced toward her, Averil skittered from his path, but he lunged for her and snatched her back to face him. He bent her over his arm, his thumb digging into her throat. Averil gagged and choked, twisting to escape the hand that squeezed her neck. Her pulse thundered in her ears and she thought her face would explode.

Slowly he released his fingers. Sobbing, clutching her bruised throat in one hand, Averil sagged weakly. She tried to push herself away from him, but his arm still held her.

His face was tight as he warned, "I said before I have no quarrel with you, Averil, but don't try my patience any further.''

Sir John released her and Averil darted to the far side of
the room. She cowered there, watching, as he opened the
door and dragged out the stool. Then he returned, staring
sharply at her, and pulled the other matching stool from the
room, the tapestry-backed chair, and a small table that had
stood beside the bed. The chamber was bare now but for
the bed, dressing table and a wardrobe—all items too large
for Averil to move.

Twilight filtered through the chamber and created dusky
shadows that crept toward her from the corners of the room.
Without a candle now, she waited on the bed, pensive and
preoccupied, as night stole the last of the faint light from
around her.

Early in the morning, a harsh, impatient clamoring on a
door somewhere within the depths of the house woke Averil.
She lay on her side, fully clothed, on the mattress. As the
sharp rapping continued, she lifted her head, then slid off
the bed and crossed quietly to the door. With her ear pressed
to the seam, she strained to hear. The main door in the hall
below was rattled and pounded on continuously until finally
someone opened it.

A furious voice exploded in the lower hall and Averil
recognized it as Francis Bowers'. ''Where in hell *were* you?
The Royalists could have taken all London in the time it took
you to get to the door! Where is Sir John? I want to see him!''

Averil's brow puckered in concentration as she listened,
wondering what had caused such agitation in Francis.
Whether it was from excitement or consternation, she could
not determine. Then she heard the heavier tones of Walford's
voice, but he was calmer and the words were muted, running
together into an indecipherable rumble.

Francis interrupted Sir John. ''His ship was sighted last
evening coming up the Medway. He should reach London
and dock sometime this morning!''

Averil knew immediately that he referred to Camden's
ship. A small sound of agony broke from her. Her ears

struggled to differentiate the sounds, but try though she might, she could not determine what Walford was saying in response. Whether Francis Bowers had calmed down and departed, or the two men had moved out of the hall and into another chamber downstairs, their voices dwindled off to nothing in her ears.

The uncanny silence crowded Averil. It throbbed and reverberated through her head. Finally, she backed from the door and turned, facing the thin morning light in her chamber.

Camden was returning!

Oh nay! *Nay!* She thought her heart would explode. In a few hours, he would be arrested. All of London would turn out for his execution—jeering, cheering. Every crew member from the *Indomitable* would be methodically led to Tyburn Hill and hung till dead.

All because of her!

She had to do something! But what could she do? What? What!

In agitation she paced the small area of the room, her movements quick and tight. Her brain burned feverishly, wildly. And then the first faint inklings of a desperate idea flared across her mind.

The surrounding brilliance of the clear morning mirrored Camden's mood as the *Indomitable* nosed its way through the sun-splintered surface of the Thames on its approach to London. After the anchor splashed home in the middle currents across from Paul's Wharf, Richard Cheyney was dispatched to arrange docking space.

Camden stood high on the poop deck, his legs braced wide against the slow rolling of the ship beneath him. Impatiently, he narrowed his eyes in the white sunlight, tiny etched lines radiating outward from the corners of his eyes as he did so. He had much to do after they docked and would be unable to get away for several hours yet. But just being in London again brought out in him an unbearable eagerness to see Averil again.

He looked toward the wharf for Cheyney's return. Several ships were docked there, and sailors swarmed across the decks and crowded the wharf around them as cargoes were either loaded or unloaded. Carts and wagons waited. There was the usual number of merchants milling about, some engaged in heated conversations, some watching his ship speculatively.

The sailors not occupied with the handling of cargo from any of the other ships lingered around the port office or wandered the wharf in a desultory way. Some watched his ship from tavern doorways; others milled about in small groups; still more lounged in the sun, their pipes sending tiny smoke puffs drifting away in the breeze.

Frowning, Camden glanced across his ship. His men were busily furling sails, coiling the lines, clearing the deck in preparation for docking and beginning the unloading—experienced seamen who knew their jobs.

As he shot his attention to the wharf once more and studied the crowd, an uneasiness slid over him.

Richard Cheyney was returning now to the ship. Docking space had been granted them, and Camden's attention was momentarily diverted as they began the procedures to kedge the ship into dock.

As they halted briefly while the small boat ahead of them lifted the anchor once more and carried it closer to the dock, Camden returned his gaze to the wharf. He leaned his hands on the rail, all of his instincts alerted. His attention moved amongst the figures in the throng, picking up details, watching movements, studying activities.

Abruptly, Camden straightened. He spun away from the rail and leaped down to the quarterdeck. With rapid strides he crossed the quarterdeck and descended the steps to the main deck. Richard Cheyney was below the mainmast, watching the furling of the main course as Camden approached him.

"As soon as we're docked, get Nessel and meet me in my cabin."

Cheyney looked around, surprised, but nodded.

Camden entered the narrow passage leading to his cabin. He stripped off his shirt and tossed it across the bunk.

When, some ten minutes later, Nessel and Cheyney entered the cabin, Camden sat at the table. Scattered in front of him were a yellowing white wig, a towel, a jar of white powder, and dish of water. A reflecting glass leaned on a black knit hat. Camden had already affixed a matted and greyish beard to his face.

"What is it?" Cheyney asked as Nessel pulled the door closed behind them.

Camden mixed some of the powder and water together in his palm as he said, "Something's amiss, but I'm not sure yet just what it is." He touched the paste he had mixed to his left eyebrow. "Have you noticed the crowd at the wharf? There are too many sailors, and the majority are not occupied with any of the ships currently docked."

Nessel frowned. "I don't understand."

Camden looked up, his fingertips smoothing a pad of short, blond hairs. "When have you known that many seamen to linger at the wharf when they've no work to do there?"

Cheyney uttered a small exclamation and asked, "What do you suspect?"

"I don't know," Camden admitted. "But there are too many men out there engaged in nothing more than waiting. And I'm not sure for what." He looked down into the reflecting glass as he created a bushy blond eyebrow above his left eye from the pad of hair. "I have to find out."

"Do you think they're on to you?" Nessel asked.

"It's possible." Camden pulled the yellowing, oily-haired wig over his own hair, slid a black eye patch down to cover his right eye, and said, "I'll need your help, Nessel. Gather some of the men—five, I'd say. We'll depart the ship in a group, but then I want each man to wander the dock at his leisure, keep his eyes skinned, his ears sharp. Have them report anything that seems out of the ordinary."

Nessel nodded, and Camden threw back the lid of his trunk,

·ummaged through the clothing, and pulled out a dingy shirt and faded, colorless coat. Cheyney rose to help his captain dress. Camden pulled off his boots and changed into a baggy, shapeless pair of brown breeches as he continued speaking.

"I don't know what will happen, but I want everyone prepared for any possibility. Cheyney, should anyone come aboard asking for me, tell them I'm in my cabin meeting with someone and cannot be disturbed. I trust you to judge the situation and defend the ship. If need be, leave port altogether."

Cheyney murmured, "Aye, Captain," as he reached out to assist Camden into the coat.

After shoving the black knit hat down low over the yellow hair, Camden took a slim-bladed dagger from the chest. Pensively, staring at the winking blade, he turned it in his hand for a moment, then thrust the weapon into a pocket beneath the coat.

When Camden next appeared on deck, he looked much like an aging and scummy, though fit, sailor. Even his own men searched dubiously for any signs of their captain beneath the thin whiskers, the eye patch, the loose-fitting breeches, and the folds of the long, shapeless coat. His shoulders bowed in, and he rolled on his feet like a man who had braced himself on the deck of a ship since first he could stand upright.

He was among the first group of men allowed off the ship and as he maneuvered through the merchants converging at the foot of the gangway, he licked his lips as though he thought of nothing but a long mug of ale. He shuffled across the wharf in a pair of cracked and salt-stained shoes. The one visible grey eye squinted and roved over the crowd with a piercing scrutiny.

Camden approached two sailors who were lounging indolently against an empty cart. One sucked at a pipe, the other, a younger sailor, eyed a particularly comely woman who strolled by on the arm of one of the better-dressed merchants.

"Eh there, 'earties!" Camden addressed them. "Where's

the best place fer a man to quench 'is thirst? A strong drink, now mind ye, none o' this watered spittle.''

The younger man pulled his attention away from the woman and indicated two taverns farther down the way on the road leading north from the dock. "Either o' them 'ud do. No finer English ale in the whole of the city.''

The other sailor looked annoyed at the interruption. Camden nodded to the young man's suggestion and inquired conversationally, "And what ship might ye be with?''

The one sailor's annoyance seemed to grow and he glared ill-humoredly at Camden while the younger piped quickly, "The *Pride of Dorset.*''

Camden knew the ship; it was in the service of Parliament, currently patrolling the North Sea with the Earl of Warwick's fleet. The young sailor had obviously blurted the name of the first ship that came to mind. They were from no particular ship, Camden knew, and his upper lip tightened imperceptibly.

His companion, wiser, plucked the pipe from his mouth and growled sharply, "We *were* with the *Pride of Dorset.* But ye're from the *Indomitable* there, are ye not?'' he questioned, eyeing Camden shrewdly as he replaced his pipe in his mouth. "What's yer captain like?''

"Eh, 'e's a mean master, that 'un,'' Camden answered, scowling. "But what—ye're not thinkin' o' signin' on, are ye?''

"Mebbe. Where's the captain now?''

" 'Spect he's in 'is cabin. Lazy whoresons 'er always—''

But before he could finish, the man with the pipe took his companion's arm and hustled him away without another glance. Camden watched, and then his attention leaped ahead of them and he saw a face he recognized. Francis Bowers wore a scruffy set of breeches and a torn jerkin, and he lounged in the sunlight against the outer wall of the port office. His face was grim, with a pinched look about the eyes and mouth, and he whittled nervously at a small piece of wood.

The presence of Francis Bowers in this situation confirmed
Camden's fears, and the last of his hopes died quietly. His
identity as the Tottman was known.

And Averil? Had she been arrested?

At the thought, rage split through him. His eyes were
momentarily blinded by the force of the blood in his veins,
and his muscles turned to fire. He wanted to feel Francis
Bowers' face and bones splinter and crush beneath his hands,
rip the last whimpering bit of life and blood from his throat.

As if he heard the siren-like song of death calling him,
Francis Bowers looked up from the piece of wood he held,
and his eyes met Camden's. That glance was all Camden
needed to remind him of what needed yet to be done, and
he slowly hunched his shoulders again and turned away.
Forcing himself with all the control he possessed, Camden
moved toward the nearest tavern, measuring his steps so they
were slow and ambling. He stepped off the end of the wooden
wharf and eased himself down to a sitting position in the
dirt alongside the wall of the tavern.

From here he had a clear view of the wharf, including
Francis Bowers and the *Indomitable*. Drawing one leg up,
he rested his forearm on his knee and tried to calm himself.
He wondered where Averil was, if she had been arrested
or not. This time he would have the truth out of Francis
Bowers. And he longed for that moment to come swiftly.

He surveyed the area carefully. Discounting the numbers
of true sailors who would have reason to be at the wharf,
he estimated Bowers had between twenty and thirty men.
They must be intending to take the entire ship, he decided.
But, if that was true, why had they ignored Nessel, himself,
and the other handful of men who had accompanied him off
the vessel?

Camden let his eyelids droop and watched Francis Bowers
surreptitiously. How long would Bowers just watch the ship
before making any kind of move? He looked agitated.
Camden doubted the man had the patience to wait for long.

He was correct. Francis Bowers was thinking about making

a move toward the ship. He had seen the first group of sailors
descend the gangplank to disperse through the crowd, and
though he had studied each in turn, none had resembled
Camden Warrender. After that, no one had departed and those
remaining aboard were going about their duties leisurely.
When the ship had first approached the dock, Warrender had
been visible at the rail, but after retiring out of sight in the
general direction of his cabin, he had not reemerged.

Francis was impatient. Ever since Walford had told him
the identity of the Tottman, he had been livid about the joke
Camden had played on him. He wanted revenge now, and
his goal was too near. His nerves were fraying with the
prolonged wait. They were supposed to take Warrender first,
alone and quietly. Then the ship would be boarded and the
crew disarmed before any were alerted. Though several
sailors had departed the ship, Bowers' first goal was the
captain, so he had let the men go rather than create a scene
on the wharf that would tip those remaining on the ship to
their danger.

The fact that he was equipped with a goodly number of
men—Walford had wanted every edge—made him bold, and
Francis reasoned it would be just as easy to take the whole
ship now, with Warrender on it, as it would be to pluck him
from the dock should he appear. As he thought about it now,
he decided the odds were in his favor. With those sailors
gone from the ship, his men outnumbered those remaining.

Buoyed, he threw aside his stick, pushed himself away from
the wall, and strode purposely toward the moored vessel.
He paused once beside a small group of men, and after he
spoke to them briefly, three of the brawnier of the men
detached themselves from the group and followed him.

Camden watched, every sense alert, muscles flicking.

From where he stood beside the port office, Nessel also
watched. All across the wharf there seemed to fall a sudden
hush, and the shrill laugh of a whore in teasing conversation
with one of the sailors from another of the docked ships lifted
loudly in the air. Almost imperceptibly the aimless shifting

movements of the crowd changed, and more and more men drifted toward the *Indomitable*.

Bowers slowed his approach and after climbing the gangplank and dropping onto the ship's deck, he was met by Cheyney. They exchanged words that seemed to grow heated quickly, and then Bowers pushed Cheyney aside as he and the three men disappeared toward the stern. Obviously they were headed for the captain's cabin.

"There's trouble, eh?"

At the sound of the deep rattling voice just beside him, Camden whipped around, every muscle tensed for a spring. It was Nicodemus. The bearded man dropped to his haunches beside Camden and looked ruefully toward the *Indomitable*. "They must suspect ye of something. D'ye think they know?"

"I'm sure of it."

On board the ship, Camden's men were gathering behind Cheyney, who was watching some activity out of sight in the stern. Nicodemus pulled gently at the tip of his beard as he watched. "How did they find out?"

Camden shook his head. "When Bowers leaves here, I'm going to follow him. Nessel has some men who can cover me. Try to get to Cheyney. Tell him to take the ship down to our usual spot below the naval yards. Tell him to hold there as long as he can safely do so."

At that moment a shout drew his attention and he jerked swiftly to his feet as a struggle broke out on the deck of his ship. Bowers and his three men were being forced off the ship. All across the wharf there was a surging movement as men thrust themselves toward the *Indomitable*.

Instinctively, Camden shot into the throng. Nicodemus followed.

Camden let his voice slide into an old man's cackle of glee, crowing, "A fight! 'Tis a fight!" as he slammed his elbow into the midsection of an unknown sailor beside him. The man doubled up with a grunt and toppled back against another who lost his balance and landed, skidding, on his buttocks.

Elsewhere in the crowd nearer the gangplank, Nicodemus followed Camden's example, cracking one man's jaw with a powerful jab from his fist, mashing another's nose.

Nessel and the other sailors from his ship had taken the cue and also turned on the men around them. Several merchants hastily scrambled toward their coaches or hurried away on foot. But fighting was a sport, an entertainment in a savage world, and a lure too hard for some men to resist. The sailors who had been working on the other nearby ships dropped their crates and barrels and swarmed eagerly into what was now becoming a widespread fray.

Camden swiftly ducked aside from an unknown assailant. Warding off stray blows, he dashed through the crowd to the outer fringes and watched the proceedings from there. Francis Bowers was caught in a struggle halfway down the gangplank. Cheyney and the men on the ship had swords up and were squeezing Bowers and his three companions down the narrow gangplank. One of Bowers' men was clipped in the shoulder by a blade and plunged down into the narrow strip of water between the dock and the hull of the ship.

More of Camden's men ranged themselves along the length of the main deck, forcing back those who tried to scale the side of the ship. At the foot of the gangplank, Nicodemus, who had wrested a sword from an attacker, was holding off any attempt by the men on the dock to board the ship by that means.

Camden saw Bowers throw a look around the dock at the wild melee taking place. Utter dismay showed in his features as he realized that his attempt to capture the Tottman was failing. He flung himself from the gangplank and jumped onto the edge of the dock. His two companions did likewise, and with the removal of that obstacle, Cheyney and the men behind him swarmed down the gangplank and onto the wharf to further fight off their attackers.

With several of his men following, Bowers disengaged himself from the throng and strode angrily past Camden without so much as a glance at the hunched figure.

Camden gestured quickly to Nessel who was attempting to defend himself and keep an eye on his captain at the same time. The fight was continuing full force as Camden slipped stealthily from the wharf with Nessel and four other men trailing him at a distance.

CHAPTER
TWENTY-FOUR

Averil sat back on her heels in front of the hearth. Her hands
were black with soot, more soot smeared the front of her
gown, and a grey-black smudge marked her cheek where
she had reached up gingerly to push back her hair. Once,
at a time of such innocence it seemed to have occurred years
ago, she had told Sir John how she escaped the soldiers who
attacked Maslin Manor. Would he remember? To make certain he did, she was leaving broad clues to help remind him.

She surveyed her work as she wiped her hands clean on
a dirty linen towel she found in a drawer of the dressing table.
Ashes from the hearth had been scattered, some swept out
slightly onto the floor; sooty handprints ranged across the
face of the hearth; scrape marks were clearly visible in the
blackened back hearth plate.

Was it too obvious? she wondered with some concern. Or
would he take it, as she wanted him to, as signs of a clumsy
attempt to hide herself in the flue? His chimney was far too
narrow and slanted, not like the ancient straight flues at

Maslin Manor. But would that immediately occur to him? She needed to deceive him only momentarily, and perhaps this would work. The whole idea was a tremendous risk, easily thwarted, and fraught with improbabilities, but she was desperate now. This might be her last chance to get away to warn Camden.

After cleaning her hands, Averil replaced the towel in the drawer, then squeezed behind the dresser. This entire scheme depended on Sir John coming to her room alone, and to do that she had to summon him somehow. Levering herself against the wall, she forced the heavy piece of furniture forward until it tottered unsteadily and fell crashing and splintering to the floor.

She waited. Then she heard footsteps—faint, light, hurried. Quickly she retreated to the wardrobe, stepping into the dark, musty, empty interior and closing the door till only the faintest of cracks remained. The wardrobe stood between the fireplace and the door, one of the reasons the scheme had seemed so plausible to her earlier. Now she had serious doubts. Foolish! she cried to herself.

The wooden bolt was slid back, the door pushed open, and she heard a single pair of footsteps entering the room. Averil's eyes were wide, peering through the tiny line of light at the edge of the wardrobe door. It overlooked the hearth, nothing more. Her body trembled violently, her heart pounded.

The footsteps stopped. Averil held her breath. Then a low laugh reached her ears. It was Sir John! And he was alone. He crossed to the hearth, and as he passed the wardrobe his shadow fell across the crack. Averil watched him, waiting.

He stood facing the hearth, his hands clasped behind his back, and he looked supremely amused as he studied the black handprints on the face of the hearth. With one shiny black shoe he brushed the ashes on the floor.

"Come out, Averil," he said conversationally. "I know where you are, so you'd best hurry along now." He waited.

"Come now, Averil, I know you're in the chimney. At the moment I'm merely amused, but if you delay, I'm liable to grow quite vexed with you."

His gaze roamed over the face of the hearth, his head tilted as if he listened for something. "Averil? Soldiers are already at the wharf. There's nothing you can do now."

Averil's heart plunged; she squeezed her eyes closed.

When she heard Sir John move, she blinked open her eyes again and peered anxiously through the crack. He squatted down in front of the ash-strewn hearth and felt upward into the flue with one hand. He found nothing. Cursing her soundly, he planted one foot directly in the ashes and gingerly shifted his position until he was squatting half-in, half-out of the fireplace. He ducked his head under the broad stone face of the hearth and peered up into the chimney.

This was just the moment Averil had been counting on; Sir John was in an awkward position and would be temporarily—but oh, so briefly!—unable to make a grab for her. Without pausing to think about it, Averil clutched her skirts high in one hand and hurled herself from the wardrobe. Her pulse was frantic; her legs seemed unable to propel her toward the outer door. It gaped wide, but appeared so far away, receding.

Behind her Sir John was moving. She cleared the door, turned, and plunged down the hall. She heard Sir John shouting. She never distinguished what he shouted, for her pulse was clamoring too loudly in her ears. Around the top newel post, she rushed at the stairs blindly, her feet barely skimming the steps. She flung herself across the lower hall and wrenched open the broad front door.

The sight that greeted her in the blinding morning sunlight halted her so swiftly that her hair flew in a wild arc around her and she almost fell. Some dozen men dressed in ragged clothing were just clearing a thick grove of trees at the edge of the road. They were coming up to the house, Francis Bowers at the head. As yet, they had not spotted her.

Behind her Sir John was running down the stairs. She could not return into the house. Panicking, Averil snatched up her skirts again and flew to the right, toward the dense overgrowth of trees and shrubs that encroached on the property. Just as she plunged into the heavily wooded area, Sir John burst from the front door.

Averil ran on. Within seconds she heard them coming behind her. They crashed through the bushes and the dead leaves and twigs. Terror sliced through her stomach and jolted upward into her brain. Her breathing was ragged. It dragged out harshly between dry lips as she ran, zigzagging through tree trunks and holding up one hand to push aside thin, tangled branches. She never felt the twigs and brush that cut her arms and yanked at her hair and gown.

Then she heard the dog, and the snarling, vicious sound of it grew louder behind her. Averil's nostrils flared. A thin whine of fear and exhaustion broke through her lips. She would never be able to outrun it! Her breathing was painful now, the air scorching her lungs; her leg muscles stiffened.

Through the savage barking of the dog she heard the spritely cheerful music of a flute. Her brain refused to comprehend it at first. Was this some trick life played upon the damned? To somehow lighten the horror of impending death?

But nay, it was the fair! Today was September eighth, and the Bartholomew Fair had begun in the grassy, sloping meadow where she and Camden had picnicked once with Mary Geneva, Lynna, and Edmond. There were people just ahead! Crowds of sane people to protect her.

With a desperate burst of energy, Averil raced toward the sound. The trees were thinning ahead. Little blotches of red and yellow tents showed through the woods. She could reach it!

When she was several yards from the edge of the woods the dog caught up to her and sprang. Its fangs closed on the flowing skirt of her gown, and Averil was wrenched backward by the dog's weight. As she was flung to the ground, she emitted a scream of unholy terror that shattered the stillness of the forest.

For one numbed instant, Averil's mind recorded the dip of a bird in the burning blue of the sky overhead. Then she threw herself into a tight ball, covering her head with her arms. But the dog never attacked.

Tensing, Averil peered tentatively around her. The dog was a massive, long-haired beast with yellowed eyes and a wet, bitten, bleeding tongue lolling from slack jaws. It lay still at her feet. From its thick neck a dagger protruded, blood coursing across its heavy shoulder.

She dragged herself away from the dog and tried to sit up. Her brain was just forming the question—who?—when a tall figure bent over her. The man had a matted grey beard, greasy hair, and an oppressively frightening black patch over one eye. She was sure he was one of the men who had arrived in the group with Francis Bowers. With a wild cry of denial, Averil twisted away, striking out at him as she struggled to get to her feet and flee once more.

But he held her tightly. "Averil, it's me! It's Camden, be *still*!"

Averil caught her breath. In wonder she searched the face above her own. His one visible eye was a vivid grey, blazing with love and anxiety. "Camden?" she breathed. "Oh, Camden!" She flung her arms around his neck.

"Are you all right?" he asked urgently.

She nodded, unable to speak. Camden lifted her to her feet, and Averil leaned against him as a curious fuzzy darkness seemed to grow around the edges of her vision. "Sir John," she breathed. "It was Sir John all along. He tricked me. He knows who you are."

"So I've discovered." Bracing Averil with his arm, he leaned down and pulled at his dagger. It squeaked against bone as it came free of the dog's carcass. He wiped the blade across his thigh and shoved it back into the inner pocket under his coat.

"And my father—he's in the Tower." The darkness was

receding. "He's to be executed in the morning!"

"Hurry now, I hear them coming," Camden exclaimed, grabbing for Averil's hand.

Camden pulled her along with him as they emerged into the brilliant, colorful, noisy confusion of the fair. Around them were bright red tents and stalls trimmed with ribbons fluttering in the breeze; a trained bear wearing a jewel-studded collar walked on his hind legs behind a roped-off barrier as they ran past. There were fire-eaters; jugglers spinning red, green, yellow balls in the air; morris dancers weaving through the crowds and piping a light tune on their flutes.

And everywhere, from one end of the long grassy meadow to the other, were the citizens of London. Not only did the sunshine provide a respite from the wet summer weather, but the fair was a respite from the harshness of life in a world torn asunder by civil war. Ale, small beer, and wine flowed freely. Small cooking booths fried fragrant delicacies for the general consumption, barbers cut hair and shaved customers. Everything was for sale—horses, pots, jewelry.

Camden had to slow his pace as they became caught up in the crowds of fair-goers. Averil clung to his hand. She was bumped and jostled on all sides and feared being separated from Camden. The feel of his strong fingers, the warmth of his palm, were reassuring, and Averil felt a surging joy. He was still free!

Somewhere to her left, she heard a sudden shouting commotion, and angry voices grew in volume. When Camden halted abruptly, Averil stumbled into him. She flung her hair back and looked around quickly, alarmed. "What is it?" she asked breathlessly.

Camden did not answer her immediately. He tore off the eye patch that partially obscured his vision and swept his gaze around. "Bowers and his men are trying to surround us." He looked down at Averil, his mouth hardening as he said, "We'll have to run again. Can you make it?" When Averil nodded, he looked past her and jerked his head.

Seeing the motion, Averil spun around and caught sight

of a small group of men fanning out behind them and disappearing into the crowd. "Camden!" she started to cry in warning, but he had taken her hand and was pulling her with him.

"Those are my men," he flung back over his shoulder.

They emerged behind a sun-faded turquoise tent. Here the numbers of people had thinned, and Camden increased their pace, dodging and leaping the lines that secured the tents. They were running downhill. Averil's feet slid over the soft, moist weeds and moss, the wind tossed her hair and skirt.

Ahead of them, at the foot of the slope, was a grove of trees where horses and empty coaches waited. They had almost reached it when three men, each bearing a long, ugly wooden staff, broke from the side and cut off their path.

Camden flung Averil behind him. His hand fumbled into his coat to reach the dagger. At that moment, to Averil's alarmed eyes, a fourth man, a lanky, long-legged sailor carrying a staff, rushed up. The newcomer did not attack Camden, but turned to engage the three armed men who had blocked their path. As still another sailor ran toward them, the first man motioned wildly to Camden to go on.

For the space of a heartbeat, Camden hesitated, and Averil saw some bright, indefinable spark of emotion in his eyes. Then he had grasped her hand once again and they were darting to the side toward the edging of trees. Behind her as they ran, Averil heard the reverberating cracks of staffs meeting. Camden pulled her on and they circled back through the branches and tree trunks toward the animals and coaches.

After lifting Averil onto the back of the closest horse, Camden swung himself up, throwing one leg over the horse's head as he settled himself in front of her. Averil hugged his waist as Camden kicked the horse into motion, and they shot out into the clearing and onto the road toward London.

A cry went up behind them as the horse's owner caught sight of his animal being ridden away. There was a surge of movement toward the other horses and shortly a party of riders appeared on the road, giving chase.

Soon they were on the bridge and pedestrians scattered before the onrushing hooves. They plunged into the shadowed archway of one of the buildings built over the roadway, and when they emerged into blinding sunlight again, Camden saw Nicodemus at the side of the road. After they had entered the tangled, traffic-filled streets of the city, Camden abandoned the horse for the pursuers to catch, and he and Averil set off on foot. He led her through alleys and branching side streets till they came at last to Nicodemus' cramped cottage. It was empty and murky inside.

After closing and bolting the door, Camden pulled Averil into the circle of his arms, and they stood locked tightly together. She pressed her cheek against his chest, her arms around his back. Beneath her ear his heart thundered, echoing the wild throbbing of her own. A long shudder passed through him.

"Oh, Jesus! Averil—" he muttered. "I was afraid I'd never see you again." His mouth moved across the shining tangle of curls above her ear. "I was afraid I'd never hold you again."

Averil groaned and pressed her face into his shoulder. Inwardly she writhed with shame and fear of what might have happened to him, for what might still happen to him. She whispered, "It's my fault. It's all my fault!"

Camden cradled her face between his hands and peered intently at her. His voice rumbled up from his chest and broke as he demanded, "Were you harmed in any way?"

She shook her head.

"Tell me what happened!" he said.

Averil squeezed her eyes closed, ashamed and humiliated by what she had to tell him—that it was she who had given away his identity.

"Averil," he pressed urgently. "It's important for me to know *all* that's happened."

He was right, she told herself. He had to have the knowledge of Sir John's treachery to arm himself. So for his sake and his safety, she told him everything that had occurred since his departure that night. His face drew taut in shock and fury.

"My God!" he breathed.

She felt a violent tension vibrating in him. His breathing grew labored. The muscles in his arms hardened and he stood rigidly in an effort at control. His fury emanated from him like a solid, palpable force that frightened her. His nostrils flared as he said again, his voice a hushed explosion, "My God!"

"I'm sorry, Camden! It's my fault that they know you now!"

He stared past her, his eyes glittering slits. "Those men— You might have been killed!" He flung himself away with a savage twist of his body. "I could kill them! I *should* have!"

"It's all right, Camden," she begged.

"It's all right," he repeated without inflection. He seemed to struggle with himself. With a visible effort, he brought his attention around to her again. Drawing her into his embrace, he asked softly, "They didn't harm you?"

"Nay," she said, holding him to her, stroking his back. He cradled her head against his chest, and his arms tightened.

"I don't know what I would have done if I'd lost you!" he whispered.

"Or I you!" she said. "But what will you do now? They know who you are!"

"There is yet the matter of your father's safety, isn't there?"

Averil's heart leaped in fear. "Nay," she protested. "I never thought I'd say this, but though I'd do anything to save my father, I can't risk losing you. You are more important to me! Please, Camden, save yourself!"

"How can I do that?" He drew away to meet her eyes. "In the years to come, you wouldn't be able to look at me without regret, knowing I abandoned your father, forfeited his life to save my own. I can't do it. I don't want something like that between us."

He started to release her, but she quickly grasped at him.

"Averil, I have to make some arrangements for you! Stay here. You'll be safe, and I'll return as quickly as I can." His lips caught at hers. "Bolt the door after me. And don't open it for anyone but me!"

A brief streak of light penetrated the room as he let himself out. Averil crossed the short space, debated calling him back, warring with herself, then pulled the heavy bolt firmly across the door to lock it.

It was almost two of the clock and the traffic was light as Camden turned down Thames Street, the stink of oil, tallow and hemp strong in his nostrils. Approaching Paul's Wharf cautiously, Camden wondered if his ship and crew had managed to get out of port safely. The sight that greeted him froze him with cold dread.

The *Indomitable* was still docked as he had left her that morning, and there was no sign of any of his crew. Instead, it was under guard and a crowd of soldiers was unloading his cargo.

Camden ducked back out of sight behind the rear wall of a building. What had happened! When he left the wharf earlier, the victory had seemed so surely his! He paused there a moment, thinking hard, then pushed away from the wall and strode back along Thames Street. After turning north, he reached Carter Lane. His pace slowing, he entered the Rose and Holly Tavern and stopped just inside the door as he sought out the comely form of the owner's daughter, Kat.

Business was slow today. Three men lingered over their dinner at one end of the main table as they discussed a business arrangement; a young man and woman nestled close to each other on a bench at a side table near one of the windows; five soldiers, standing around a table where they tossed dice, swigged bottles of wine and alternately cursed or exclaimed over their luck at the game.

Through the far door into the semi-attached kitchen, Kat was visible. She sat on a high stool, plucking white feathers from a chicken held on a towel between her knees. From around the edges of her day cap, dark wisps of hair had escaped and hung in front of her ears. Camden walked into the kitchen and closed the door behind him. He pulled off the facial whiskers and plucked at the bits of white paste on his skin. Kat glanced up from her work, a grimace pulling at her features until she recognized the customer who had sought her out.

"I swear, you find the nastiest clothes—you look enough to scare a poor girl to death!" She wrapped the chicken in the towel and thrust it into a basket at her feet.

"Has Darby been by?"

Kat rose, wiping her hands on her long, grease-stained apron. "Not yet."

"I'll wait for him." He stripped off his baggy coat and shirt and poured water from a bucket into a bowl he took from a shelf. "Get me some ale or wine, would you, please? I'm parched as the devil."

"I heard some talk today that there was trouble at Paul's Wharf," she said.

"Aye," Camden answered simply, and Kat nodded in understanding.

She pulled the cork from one of the bottles of wine standing out on the table. After taking a quick sip, she brought the bottle to Camden. He was scrubbing at the paste on his face but paused to take the bottle and tilt it for a long drink. Then he handed it back and bent down to splash water over his sweat-glistened chest.

Kat watched, her black eyes troubled. "I thought it might be your ship. There's been another fifty pound added to the reward for you, and I was so frightened—"

"Darby and I will need a room," he interrupted. "Can you join us?"

Kat nodded. "My father'll be back soon. Will it be for long?"

"Nay, I've left my wife alone at Nicodemus' cottage and

have to get back."

At the sharp intake of her breath, Camden straightened and met her eyes as he reached for a towel.

"You're married now?" Kat questioned, her piercing black eyes going liquid with sorrow. "Oh, aye, I should have guessed— When you didn't—" Her lips twisted.

"Kat," Camden began gently.

"Nay!" she cried. "Don't try to explain anything! I know what you're going to say—there were no promises between us. And you always said you'd leave, too. Oh Lord! The number of times you said *that*!" She turned away and planted her hands on the worktable, leaning her weight into her arms.

Camden flung aside the towel and reached for his shirt. He said nothing.

Kat straightened from the table and used the hem of her apron to wipe her cheeks. "Don't mind me," she said bitterly, drawing in a ragged breath. "You were always honest, weren't you."

"I can only say I'm sorry, Kat."

"Aye, so am I! When did this happen? Nay, I know—it was before you went to Amsterdam, time before this."

"Something like that," he said, adjusting the shapeless coat on his shoulders.

From a hook beside the door, Kat grasped a large iron key and tossed it to him. "Use the back stairs," she said. "The last room on this side is empty. I'll bring Darby up when he comes."

He started to turn but paused, hefting the key. "I've been found out, Kat," he said quietly. "I'll be leaving London tonight."

"Oh Lord," she breathed, her face slack with shock.

He looked long at her. "I want you to know I'm grateful for the help you've given me."

She nodded vaguely and he let himself out the rear door. He sidestepped slimy green puddles in the alley, climbed the steps alongside the back of the inn, and fitted the key into the heavy padlock on the door leading into the second floor.

Within minutes Darby Kipp and Kat joined him in the room. Camden had pulled closed the shutters at the windows and lit a fat candle on the table beside the bed. Darby and Camden sat on the edge of the narrow bed, Kat leaned against the wall facing them. Camden quickly related the incidents that had occurred that day, including the final bit of information he had just gained concerning the fate of his ship.

Darby shook his head, his gnarled fingers clasped together in his lap. "And yer crew?"

"It's my guess they're being held on board. Kat, could you find out?"

"Aye. Do you want me to go now?" She twisted the edge of her apron in her fingers. Her eyes were swollen.

"Not yet. There's more to discuss first. I need to find some men who'd be willing to fight without knowing the reason for it."

Darby Kipp chuckled. "There's plenty o' men 'ereabouts who'd give their right arm fer a chance in a good fight, the reason be damned."

"And I've got some regular customers who fit the bill. They'd tear this place to pieces for their fun if we're not careful to water their drink a mite."

"Ye're thinkin' of fightin' fer yer ship?"

"Aye. Can you two arrange to have twenty or more men here tonight for me?"

"What time?" Kat asked.

Camden propped his elbows on his knees and rubbed his forehead. "I can't say with any certainty. My wife's father is being held in the Tower. I have to get him out first."

Darby's breath whistled around his one front tooth. "In the Tower! Eh, now ye've gone mad! Ye'd be wiser to take that ship o' yers and leave as quick as ye can. What wi' the men o' Parliament on t'ye now, ye'll be lucky to get y'self away!"

"I'll need that luck, won't I? I also need you to get the

drawbridge up when the *Indomitable* is heading out. Can you get to it?''

The old man agreed. ''Not a bit o' trouble.''

Frowning thoughtfully at the candle flame, Camden said, ''And just in the event I don't make it back here tonight, would one of you send word to my brother Nathan? Tell him about Averil. She'll be alone then.''

''Your wife?'' Kat asked.

Camden nodded. ''Would you let her wait here for me? She's in considerable danger herself.''

''I'd like to meet her.''

Though Camden grinned, his eyes held Kat's in a silent warning. He stood up, and the candle flame swayed wildly in the draft. ''Nicodemus should be returning soon. Darby, come with me now and bring Averil back. I'll see you tonight, Kat.''

Camden and Darby left and returned through the streets, the light from the afternoon sun casting their shadows like watery ghosts across the dirt and uneven cobbles behind them. Averil admitted them when Camden knocked at the door and called quietly to her. She looked wonderingly at Darby Kipp as the knife grinder bobbed his head and grinned at her. The two men entered the cottage and Camden closed the door.

'' 'Tis a pleasure t' see ye again, ma'am,'' Darby said. Gallantly, he took her hand and kissed it.

''Thank you,'' Averil murmured. She looked in confusion to Camden.

Absently, Camden lifted one of the wayward strands of her hair as he said, ''She'll need a cloak, Darby, and some clothing for the journey.''

''Where are we going?'' Averil asked.

''Home,'' he replied, smiling, and Averil's heart lifted in soft excitement at the thought. He said, ''I want you to go with Darby. He'll take you to a safer—''

Averil broke in. ''Nay, Camden, please don't go to the Tower!''

"Do this for me, my heart. Go with Darby."

Averil saw the veiled sadness in his eyes as he drew her into his arms. He kissed her tenderly, his lips lingering on hers. To Averil, his kiss had the taste of good-bye. When he released her, she turned away swiftly to cover the tears in her eyes.

CHAPTER
TWENTY-FIVE

After Averil departed with Darby Kipp, Camden rummaged through the contents of the various shelves and drawers till he found a pipe and tobacco. He lit the pipe and settled himself at the table in the gloom, his eyes narrowing in concentration. He had not wanted to admit it even to himself, but the task before him was almost impossible—almost. Due to the war, however, the Tower was filled to overcrowding and the number of known escapes had increased; chaos was inherent in a situation where there were too many prisoners and not enough trained guards. It was the one point in his favor. Still, he had no idea where, in which of the many towers, William Maslin was being held.

The arrival of Nicodemus interrupted his thoughts, and he watched the large man step into the room, fling a bundle onto the sagging cot, and close the door behind him. Nicodemus' eyes were shining and black beneath the thick brows as he grinned at Camden.

"All's well, Cap'n. I talked to Cheyney like ye wanted,

and yer ship's safely out of London. She'll be waitin' fer ye near the Channel, as usual.'' Nicodemus shifted his dusty black hat from his head to the table and sought out his mug and ale from a barrel on the floor.

Camden did not move. Nicodemus had lied to him.

The bearded man straightened from the ale barrel and tipped his mug to his lips. ''Ahh. Now there's a drink to quench a man's thirst. Where's yer lady? I would 'ave expected to see 'er 'ere.''

Camden's watchful gaze grew piercing. How did Nicodemus know he had succeeded in finding Averil? At once he remembered seeing the man on London Bridge earlier that day. Nicodemus had seen him—and Averil—clearly. The man's presence on the bridge and heading south, the direction he and Averil had just come from, had bothered him at the time, but too many other things had claimed his attention since then. What had he been doing there?

Camden drew hard on his pipe in grim concentration. Then with a sudden flash of insight, the unexplained puzzles of that day fell into a logical order. And he suspected Nicodemus had thrown in his lot with Walford.

Never very remarkable on his own, the big man had been slavishly devoted ever since Camden had bested him in a fight. Now that Camden appeared bested, had he switched his devotions? Did he give his loyalty only to the strongest, regardless of cause or purpose? Camden glanced at him assessingly.

And if Nicodemus had turned on the crew of the *Indomitable*, that would explain the fact that his ship was under guard now, and also why Nicodemus had lied about it. Any of the remaining men Francis had brought with him to the wharf could have told Nicodemus about Bowers and Sir John Walford. That was why he was heading south on the bridge at that time—to find Walford.

Sick with disgust, Camden watched Nicodemus drain a second mug of ale. He hoped he was wrong.

He hoped Nicodemus hadn't brought a detachment of

soldiers with him. The possibility sent a rush of raw fire through his muscles.

He stirred from his chair and knocked the plug of tobacco from his pipe into the hearth. "Averil's with the Quints," he answered Nicodemus' last question. "There was no need for her to remain here."

Nicodemus settled himself on the other cane-bottomed stool across the table from Camden and said, "So what's in yer mind now?"

Camden frowned slightly. "Averil's father is being held in the Tower. I have to reach him." Nicodemus had probably learned this already from Walford. He felt his scalp crawl as he wondered what else was coming, if Nicodemus had truly sold out. "This will take some careful planning," he added.

Nicodemus took the proferred cue. "I think I've got a way we can get t' the Earl. Just today I found us some interesting bits of clothing."

Camden lifted his eyebrows in invitation, and Nicodemus began laying a plan out for him. As the man spoke on in his gravelly voice, Camden considered the situation thoughtfully.

The fact that Nicodemus had arrived equipped with a plan for taking the Earl meant there were no soldiers lurking in the street. Walford wouldn't count on Camden being there at Nicodemus' home that afternoon. But they counted on his continued trust in Nicodemus. A trust that would lead him into a trap in the Tower of London.

Walford, he decided, would be prepared to arrest him whether he went first to his ship or to the Tower. Francis Bowers must be on board the *Indomitable* now, making himself comfortable in his cabin, waiting out the time till Camden made a move to take his ship.

Camden rose and paced the small dimensions of Nicodemus' room. It was difficult for him to keep a serious expression on his face as he heard out Nicodemus' scheme for him. Never would Camden have considered such a blatant-

ly obvious plan like entering the Tower as a clergyman come
to pray with the condemned man on the eve of his execution.

But that was just what he would do tonight, he knew. It
was his means of entering the Tower grounds. The guards,
surely alert to the plan, would be most willing to have him
enter the Tower. Leaving again was the problem that now
occupied Camden's mind, for it was obvious he was not
intended ever to set foot outside those stone walls again.

The room's murky darkness grew thicker as the light faded
outside, and Nicodemus lit a sputtering candle. As they talked
together, Nicodemus set out bread and meat for them for
supper. When Camden attempted to discuss a possible way
of getting back out of the Tower with the Earl, Nicodemus
seemed less interested and muttered vaguely, "We'll 'ave
t' kill a few guards. I 'ave my knife—you don't 'ave anything, though, do ye?"

He could see that Camden was not wearing his swordbelt.
Camden shook his head in the negative, though beneath his
coat, the dagger rested securely in a pocket.

After finishing the meal, they donned the heavy black
clerical robes Nicodemus had brought in his bundle. "Didn't
get any o' them hats," the bearded man said with a grunt
of dismissal. Disguising his face was not worth the trouble
now to Camden, but he thought it odd—and another slip on
his companion's part—that the other man had not thought
to mention it. When the two were dressed, they departed
into the narrow street.

The night's cool winds ruffled Camden's hair; he wore
no hat and had the distinctly unpleasant impression of being
escorted bare-headed to an execution. Nicodemus wore his
unadorned black hat. His face was almost obscured between
the low crown of the hat and the thick curly black beard that
started high on his cheekbones. Camden studied him as they
walked.

He would have to kill Nicodemus, he realized with a sudden
piercing ache of loss. Though never a particularly imaginative
partner, he had been nonetheless a staunch and relentlessly

loyal man. Until now. But Nicodemus knew the other people who had aided the Tottman, knew things that were far too dangerous for too many people.

At the next street Camden turned south. There were passenger boats aplenty they could hire for the trip down-river to the Tower, and he wondered if Nicodemus would try to avoid the wharf to keep him from seeing the *Indomitable*. He wanted to give the man one more chance, but he knew it was a hopeless gesture.

As he expected, Nicodemus halted him. "Nay," the bearded man protested. "We can take a boat from the Swan Stairs."

"That's almost to the bridge," Camden exclaimed. "Why there?"

"I have a friend who'll take us to the Tower. Very trust-worthy."

After looking hard at his companion, Camden nodded as if he accepted this. Nicodemus would make certain they were well past Paul's Wharf before venturing onto the river. With the thick cloak of night enveloping the *Indomitable*, it would not be visible to them from the Swan Stairs. He fell into step beside the other man once again. They were silent as they continued through the dark streets lit sporadically from the windows of alehouses and the torches of passing linkboys.

Behind the Old Swan Inn, several boats were tied and waiting to transport customers from the inn. Nicodemus hailed one of the boatmen, who called back a stinging obscenity of a greeting. When the boatman had rowed the boat around, Camden and Nicodemus descended the stone steps and climbed into the small, rocking craft. Though the boatman tried to joke with Nicodemus as they swept down the black river, Nicodemus was too tense to offer more than a half-hearted reply now and then.

Camden watched Nicodemus, alert. There were too many unknowns, too many variables operating this night, and he knew he would have to rely on instinct alone if he were to be successful.

Ahead, the turreted outer walls of the Tower rose high above the roofline of the city with a powerful, sullen menace. The small boat angled toward the bridge and plunged through the foaming waters beneath it. Cold water sprayed the three men. The small boat wove a path through the high-sterned, black-hulled frigates moored off Tower Wharf and made an approach to the Tower Stairs. Nicodemus alighted first and strode ahead of Camden across the wharf to the guard waiting at the gate house. In the bright light of the two lanterns on either side of the doorway, the guard peered closely at Camden. Camden noted a flicker of excitement deep in the man's eyes—it was brief. Camden felt naked to inspection. The guard would remember his face.

Nicodemus assumed a suitably solemn mien as they followed the guard across the drawbridge that spanned the moat. Water from the Thames circled the Tower and sighed against the stone walls. At the entrance to the Tower at the Gate, three guards awaited them.

The first said with unnecessary enthusiasm, "They're to pray with the Earl of Armondale."

Three pairs of eyes searched Camden's face and he met them openly. There was morbid eagerness, derision, barely concealed contempt in their faces. As he looked to Nicodemus, Camden tried to control the scorn in his own gaze. Did the man honestly believe he would not have been alerted by this so very obvious charade? Camden thought about how little he had known of Nicodemus. But he knew enough to be leery of the man's brutish strength. It was one of the characteristics in Nicodemus he had used often enough in the past not to be cautious and wary of it now.

As they passed through the arched gateway in the inner wall of the Bloody Tower, Camden glanced upward, past the raised portcullis, and noted the guards barely visible on the turreted roof above them.

To their left after they emerged into the inner grounds, by the light of sparsely placed torches, he saw the lushness of a garden near the lieutenant's lodgings. It seemed strangely incongruous after the somberness of the outer walls. With the overflow of people being sent to the Tower by Parliament, nearly a thousand now, the lieutenant of the Tower had been forced to give over his quarters to house more of the prisoners.

Not only were guards and prisoners housed in the Tower, but grooms, servants, people who worked in the Royal Mint and armory, and all manner of other employees from cooks to clerks lived within its walls as well. None of the many people going about their business across the gardens and walkways paid the guard and two cloaked men any attention, and Camden knew that only the guards needed for the deed were aware of the scheme to trap him here.

Camden and Nicodemus were led to Coldharbor Tower, one of two twin circular towers guarding the innermost enclosure of the Tower grounds. A sentry stood at the door of the tower, his halberd braced beside him.

The guard who had accompanied them unlocked the small wood and iron-reinforced door. They had no light with them and the interior was palpably black. Just as he ducked inside, Camden glanced to Nicodemus, his attention catching on the tension in the bearded man's face, the too-bright glitter in the hard eyes. The time was drawing close, Camden knew, and the sudden sharp beating of his heart sent a rush of naked excitement through him.

His right hand snaked into the folds of his cloak and reached toward the dagger lying in the pocket beneath the coat. Carefully he withdrew the silver-handled blade. He knew the moment was near at hand, and he would have to strike first.

With the guard in the lead, Camden behind him, and Nicodemus in the rear, they ascended spiraling stone steps. Camden's shoulders brushed along the narrow walls on either side of him in the black twisting tunnel of the staircase. He felt the damp chill from the walls, and his nostrils flared with the musty stench of centuries of despair and death that enveloped him.

He caressed the warm handle of his dagger. It had been

like another hand to him once. Blinking against the blackness that seemed to have swallowed him, swallowed all of them, he contemplated killing the guard.

He imagined sinking his dagger into the hard-fleshed body, but it was not the body of the guard he pictured; it was the sinewy, dark-skinned body of a savage. At the image, his heart pounded, the excitement swelled in him and sharpened. *He would kill again.* Oh, the sweet and piercing ecstasy of it! Kill and kill!—for all his losses. Long repressed, revenge and black joyful rage burst through his mind, and he wanted to feel again the hot splash of blood over his hands, smell again the hot sweetness of it, know the dark excitement that could surge in him and engorge him and obliterate all else.

But deep in the corners of his mind, a scream of denial welled up.

He saw again an icy, drizzling January night when he had watched, by torchlight, steam rise from the blood. It had been utterly meaningless to him. He had watched without thought, as mindlessly as the lowest of the animals. And he had drawn nearer only to seek the warmth.

At the memory, sweat erupted from his every pore. He felt himself tottering on the brink of that supreme blackness of self-hate. It yawned before him, that black chasm, unbridgeable. He would lose himself again in that despair, that rage.

The cry of denial swelled in him and filled him and burst from him. And he heard, aghast, the echo of his anguish reverberating off the stone walls.

The movement of the three men on the steps halted.

Camden brought the handle of his knife down sharply on the back of the guard's head and spun to meet Nicodemus, but he was too late. Nicodemus' knife bit into his lower back, and his own turning momentum dragged the blade along his rib until it sliced free at his side. Pain and fury exploded in him, and he kicked hard into the darkness.

Nicodemus grunted as the blow caught him in the groin and tossed him backward down the black hole of the stairwell.

Camden followed Nicodemus, his hands on the walls at each side to help him negotiate the steps. Sweat seeped down his face. There was no sound save his own drumming pulse in his ears.

He knew Nicodemus had arrested his fall, he had heard the scraping of his body on the stone come to a stop, but where the man was at the moment he could not tell. Was he waiting? Coming slowly back up the steps?

Blinking hard against the eerie blackness that surrounded him, Camden eased himself down slowly. His ears strained to hear any sound, a soft breath, a whisper of cloth against cloth, the slither of a fingertip on the stone. The activity in the outer yard of the Tower grounds was completely shut out behind walls that were more than a foot thick. He heard nothing.

Bracing himself against the fire in his side, Camden waited. Then he caught the smell of Nicodemus—a rank, yeasty odor that came to him over the smells of the musty damp walls and his own blood.

Nicodemus was a large man, bear-like. With his bulk confined in this small space, there would be no way for the man to maneuver. Camden held his dagger close to his chest, blade out, and crossed his left arm in front of him. There was a change in the air; he sensed the heat emanating from somewhere just below. Nicodemus was coming up toward him. He waited, counted slowly to himself, felt the sweating, moist heat grow stronger, caught the smell of the man more pungently.

With a sudden lunge, Camden thrust his dagger downward into the darkness. Its blade rang against something metallic, and knowing it was Nicodemus' blade, he struck out with his left forearm to knock it aside just as his own dagger met and plunged into hard flesh. His fingers sank against cloth; he had caught Nicodemus in the upper chest, and he twisted the blade sharply. His other arm ground the man's wrist against the cold stone wall. Nicodemus' weapon fell and clattered onto the steps. A gasping grunt came from deep

in the man's throat, but he uttered no other sound as he
staggered back. Camden's blade came free of Nicodemus'
chest. He heard the crack of a skull on stone, the slithering
sound of the body sliding down, the repeated bumping of
a head on steps. Then all was quiet.

Panting and shaking, Camden sagged against the wall and
pressed his wet face to the cold, damp stone. He dragged
himself around and retraced the few steps to the unconscious
guard. Dropping to his knees, he tugged up the man's buff
coat and wiped the blood from his hand on the other's shirt.
Then he sliced a piece of the shirt free with his knife, folded
it, and gingerly pushed it inside his own shirt to press against
the pain and blood from his wound.

For a long time he sat with his back against the wall,
motionless. He had not fallen; the black chasm of his nightmares existed no longer. He was aware of the spark inside
him, the spark of peace he had gained loving Averil, that
little spark of her he carried now. He calmed the shaking
in his body.

Finally he pushed himself to his feet, took the guard's
sword and the key the man had held in his hand. Somewhere
in this tower, he knew, he would find Walford and then
William Maslin.

Camden climbed the stairs, carefully feeling along the stone
wall until he encountered a small wooden door. Beneath his
fingers he felt the opening of the lock and he fit the key into
it. At his side, his warm blood soaked into his clothing; he
set his teeth against the hot pain. When the door was
unlocked, he pocketed the key, hefted the sword in one hand,
his dagger in the other, and thrust the thick door open.

The room was small, square, lit by a lantern set on the
floor at the feet of Sir John Walford. That one sat easily on
the end of a narrow, wood-frame cot against the opposite
wall. Beside him sat another man, a finely dressed gentleman.
Two guards, one at each side of the room, stood watching
the door.

In all there were four cots along the stone walls, but only

one prisoner was in evidence—a man slumped on the cot beside the one on which Sir John sat. This man had thin black hair hanging around his face; his eyes were sunken. Thick hemp rope bound his hands together. Despite the hopeless expression in the thin, parchment-like face, the resemblance to Averil was startling.

Camden registered the scene in the space of an instant as he flung the door open. The gentleman with Sir John looked stricken at the sight of the tall, armed man with the starkly glittering eyes who stood in the threshold. Sir John had barely begun to snarl an order to the guards, but they were already reaching for their weapons.

One slid a sword from its sheath at his hip. The other had only just aimed a pistol at him when Camden's dagger swept toward him and buried itself to the hilt in the man's chest. The pistol, clenched in the guard's hand, barked deafeningly in that small room and a puff of black smoke erupted from the barrel along with a ball. The stray ball chipped sprays of pulverized stone off two walls as the guard fell.

The other guard lunged toward Camden with his sword swinging in a wide arc designed to fling Camden's sword from his hand, but Camden met the swing with his blade and took a chip out of the other's weapon when the two blades crashed against each other.

Camden easily parried the other man's advances, pressing in with ripostes that forced his opponent back a step. With the space as small as it was, the swords of both men nicked the walls time and again. They fought directly before the doorway and were thus blocking the only means of escape for any of the other occupants. The gentleman tried to back away, his face and arms flinching at each ringing blow of the swords. Sir John scowled.

He slipped to the body of the guard on the floor and, putting one foot against the man's ribs, jerked free the dagger. With the weapon in hand, he tried to find a way to maneuver close enough to Camden to kill him, but with the glittering deadly blades cutting the air around them, he could not find an opening. With a snarl of rage, Sir John threw down the dagger and knelt beside the guard on the floor as he searched for a powder flask and another ball with which to reload the pistol.

Camden knew what the man intended, and realizing he had no defense against a pistol now, he felt a surge of new strength in his arms and shoulders. At the first opening, his long blade winked in the lanternlight as he thrust it past the other's blade and into his chest. The guard fell but did not cry out, and his sword clanked on the stone floor when he dropped it.

Sir John tried one desperate lunge to retrieve the sword, but he halted abruptly, half bent with one arm outstretched, as the tip of Camden's hot, crimson blade touched him warningly under his chin.

Camden jerked his head to indicate the other side of the room. "Sit down," he rasped, breathless.

Sir John backed slowly toward the cot where the other gentleman had seated himself abruptly. His eyes were thin slits.

"Where do you think you can go now?" he said furiously. "You're known! Your deeds are known! And there is a witness here!" He indicated the gentleman beside him, who shook visibly. "Or do you intend to kill us all?"

As Camden turned his attention to the other man, Sir John's glance skated across the stone floor and he saw the forgotten dagger barely four feet from him.

"And who are you?" Camden inquired brusquely.

The gentleman glanced around uneasily before answering, then summoning some reserve of dignity, he replied, "Sir John Conyers, Lieutenant of the Tower."

"Untie that man and use the ropes to bind this one." His sword swept out indicating first the Earl, then Sir John.

Camden stepped back to allow the lieutenant to pass in front of him to the other cot. As he did so, Averil's father started to cry out a warning and pushed himself off the cot.

At that instant, Walford seized what seemed to him his last opportunity. As Conyers stepped in front of him, he suddenly leaped up, shoving Conyers at the Tottman, and lunged for the dagger. The Earl tried to reach it first.

The force of the lieutenant's weight as a projectile threw Camden backwards. The two men crashed down together on the edge of one of the empty cots, and Conyers was knocked senseless when his head struck the frame. As they thudded to the floor, the lieutenant's heavy body anchored Camden's arm and shoulder. Before he could free himself, he caught sight of Sir John. The man held a dagger and was at that moment starting to thrust it down for a fatal stab into Camden's chest. Camden tried to lift his sword.

Before Sir John's weapon could find its mark, two hands appeared around the man's head. A bit of hemp stretched between those hands cut into his forehead, and he was momentarily pulled back before the hemp slipped free again.

But the delay, though it was by a mere hairsbreadth, gave Camden the time to swing his sword into position. The tip of his blade struck Sir John's chest as that one, unable to check his momentum, plunged forward, impaling himself. The dagger twisted sideways in Sir John's fingers and its tip sliced the cloak and swept only a shallow cut on Camden's chest before it clattered away. Sir John's weight dropped over him. With an immediate roll, Camden repulsed the man's heavy body and flung him aside over the lieutenant.

Breathing heavily, Camden pulled his sword free and dragged himself to his feet. Averil's father, weakened by his terrified lunge at Sir John, sagged down on the cot. His hands and body shook, his face was a deathly white.

"I saw him. . . ." the older man breathed. "I saw him look at the knife and then . . . I was afraid I'd be too late."

Camden picked up the dagger and sliced the hemp that bound the Earl's wrists together. He looked deeply into the man's face. Though the Earl was a tall man and had once been robust, the past months had taken their toll on him. His frame had thinned, his black hair was lank and laced with silver strands. His deep brown eyes were filled with a yearning despair; over his long patrician nose and high cheekbones the skin was stretched into an almost translucent white. A long neglected beard grew on his face.

"How do you feel?" Camden asked. "Are you all right? Will you be able to walk?"

"Oh, aye," the Earl said, catching his breath and attempting a slight smile. "I was treated well. It made little difference to me, though—I sometimes wished I had died long ago." His voice dwindled away.

Guessing at the reason for the man's deeply rooted unhappiness, Camden said, "Your daughter is waiting for you."

The sunken brown eyes stabbed sharply up at Camden. "What? Averil? She's alive?"

"Aye, not only alive, but well and safe. We'll have to hurry now."

"But—" The Earl faltered and gestured to the body of Sir John. "He told me she was dead, killed by Prince Rupert's men the day they seized Maslin Manor."

Camden smiled faintly. "She escaped them. Now wait here, I'll return in a moment."

Camden left the dazed Earl, and taking up the lantern, stepped out of the chamber. The yellow light illuminated the tunneling staircase and the moaning form of the guard slumped on the steps leading down from the door. Grasping one of the man's arms, Camden dragged him into the room.

"Take his breeches and doublet off him and tie him," he said.

Then he went back out and descended the stairs to where the body of Nicodemus lay wedged sideways between the narrow walls. Sadly, and with an effort, he dragged Nicodemus up to the small room.

Closing the solid chamber door again behind him, Camden

pulled off his cloak then carefully removed the shapeless coat beneath it. The linen shirt he wore was wet with dark blood that covered his side and extended down his leg. In the aftermath of his exertion, Camden's wound throbbed with a renewed flaming onslaught, and the sweat from his body had soaked the shirt, lending the material a damp, cold feeling.

The Earl paused in his attempt to tie the first guard. His stare locked on the scarlet stain. ''I didn't realize you had been wounded,'' he muttered. ''Tell me what must be done, let me do it.''

Camden grunted in pain as he moved to the inert mass that was Nicodemus. ''Here, help me get this cloak off him.''

Together the two men wrestled the long black cloak from the body, and straightening, Camden handed the garment to the Earl. ''Put this on,'' he instructed. ''You've the beard for it, you'll have to be Nicodemus.'' He studied the Earl assessingly. ''But you'll have to wear more beneath the cloak. Nicodemus is notably bigger.'' The Earl nodded and together they stripped all of the doublets from the men on the floor.

Briefly Camden left the room again, lifting the lantern high as he descended the steps until he found Nicodemus' hat and the knife the man had earlier wielded and dropped. When he returned with the items, William Maslin had donned the various doublets and coats and finally the cloak. With the extra padding, his form was extraordinarily close to that of Nicodemus himself.

''I knew they were planning to trap the Tottman here,'' the older man muttered, shaking his head. ''I listened to them talking, and knew there was nothing I could do to warn you or save you. They also had plans for your wife—you're married?'' the Earl questioned, the surprise and puzzlement frankly revealed in his face.

''Aye.'' Camden gingerly pushed his arms into the first guard's undamaged coat and buttoned it over his linen shirt. ''I wed your daughter, Averil, two months ago.''

The Earl was stunned. He slumped down on the cot. "Dear God!" he murmured. Camden said nothing as he searched out a pair of breeches and boots that might fit him.

The Earl murmured again, "My daughter? And the Tottman?" He looked up at Camden, his face wreathing with a pleased smile. "I—I'm overwhelmed. I don't know what to say."

"We have your approval then?" Camden said.

"Of course! Dear God, I'd never hoped for such a match, but I approve most heartily. You're a worthy man. I could ask for none braver, or more honorable." The Earl stood up again and the two men grinned at each other. "Do you love her?" the Earl asked.

Camden gazed at the other man seriously. "Aye," he replied. "Aye, I do love her."

William Maslin's smile remained fixed on his face. He nodded his head, a sudden glitter of wetness in his eyes. Abruptly he looked away. "Tell me now," he said firmly. "What are we to do?"

"It all depends on your strength, your lordship," Camden said. He slipped on a swordbelt, adjusting the strap over his shoulder until it reached the length he needed. "Unfortunately you'll have to do most of the work, since you'll be Nicodemus."

The Earl frowned. "If Averil is waiting, my strength will be sufficient. But quickly now, tell me what I should do. I am most impatient to be gone."

Camden quickly sketched the rudiments of an idea and handed him the black hat to wear. One of the guards had been wearing a triple-barred helmet and Camden pulled it on to help conceal his own features for he had been clearly seen earlier.

William Maslin folded his hands, palms together, as he watched and listened to Camden. "Aye, I can give it a fair try," he said at last. "Nicodemus was here earlier. I saw him and heard his voice."

Nodding, Camden handed him the knife Nicodemus had used. He took for himself one of the swords which he cleaned before sliding it into the scabbard at his hip. They left the lantern in the room and when they had stepped onto the stairs, Camden locked the door again behind them. He slipped the key into a pocket beneath his coat.

At the foot of the spiral steps, Camden knocked loudly on the outer door to alert the guard. When the door was opened for them they emerged into night air that was noticeably warmer and drier than the air inside the Tower. The guard halted them with his halberd braced between two hands. Cautiously his gaze slid over the two figures. The night's shadows were thick, and Camden hoped they would conceal his features.

The Earl, his black hat low over his brow, his unkempt beard concealing his lower face, grunted low in satisfaction. It was an eerily like imitation of the real Nicodemus, and Camden peered at the man sharply. Reassured that the Earl could handle himself, Camden edged into the shadows behind him. Unobtrusively, he reached to grasp the hilt of his sword.

'' 'Tis done,'' the Earl exclaimed. "They've subdued the Tottman.''

The guard frowned at the Earl. "So where are you going? You're not supposed to leave until the lieutenant has given me the permission for it.''

"It's his wife," the Earl growled. " 'Ave ye forgotten then? Conyers wants her arrested now, before any word of this leaks out and she disappears. D'ye want t' go against 'im?''

Behind the Earl, Camden chuckled inwardly. So this was where Averil got her talent for mimicry.

The guard shifted his feet, confused and unsure. He was well aware, as had been the Earl, that there were plans to arrest the Tottman's wife. But he hadn't known it was intended for tonight. "But the lieutenant—''

Accustomed to issuing orders and having his way, the Earl

pushed the halberd aside. "We'll be back before they're even done up there," he said with a disgusted grunt.

The guard lowered his halberd and stepped from their path. Before moving past him, the Earl added, "Yer man, Conyers, doesn't want anyone allowed in 'til we return." As the guard nodded, the Earl and Camden walked quickly away.

Camden cast an admiring glance to the Earl and was dismayed to see the man's lips trembling with weakness, his steps faltering slightly. He knew he could not touch the man now or support him. To do so would risk revealing that the figure was not the robust Nicodemus. He whispered urgently, " 'Tis not much farther."

The Earl said nothing. Camden slowed their pace slightly to make it easier on the man, all the while praying the Earl would not pass out before they were safely away. Averil's father had handled the guard with remarkable skill, but Camden knew it had severely depleted his reserve of strength.

They passed under the portcullis in the archway of the Bloody Tower and turned to the right along the space between the two sets of walls. At the Gate, when they faced the two guards, Camden hung back. He turned his head away from their torch so the shadows were deep on his face. The Earl drew himself taut with a formidable display of control. He was at first laughingly boisterous about the successful capture of the Tottman, then smug as he told them he would return with the Tottman's wife.

The guards responded as Camden had suspected they might. They cast sly looks at one another and shared a ribald joke concerning the woman in question. For them it was a red-letter day, and they were in the mood to be festive. That murdering, traitorous legend of a man, the Tottman, had been captured at last.

The Earl brushed past them as they laughed, and Camden followed, keeping his face averted. They proceeded along the causeway to the Middle Tower. Earlier, as Camden had laid out his plan to the Earl, he had suggested they take this

exit from the Tower rather than out to the wharf where
Nicodemus' boatman friend might be lingering.

At the Middle Tower the charade was repeated. Though
these guards had not set eyes on the man Nicodemus before
now, Sir John Walford, escorted by the lieutenant, had
spoken to each earlier and described the large bearded man
to them. They knew the plot was afoot and now greeted the
news of its success with exuberant cheers.

With growing respect, Camden regarded his father-in-law.
Camden and the Earl walked on, past the Lion's Tower where
the Royal Zoo was housed; the ominous roar of a hungry
beast echoed across the causeway. The Earl stumbled once
as they approached the Lion's Gate, but Camden moved
beside him and tried to use his own body as an unobtrusive
brace for the older man.

When they reached Tower Street, the Earl made a sudden
grab for Camden's shoulder. He had overtaxed his strength.
His breath wheezed out between dry lips as he shuddered
uncontrollably.

CHAPTER
TWENTY-SIX

A commotion from the common room below—hearty voices, laughter, curses, the clanking of tankards—rose into Averil's room. She sat on the edge of the bed, staring at the thin shafts of light that pierced the gloom, clawlike, from between the planks of the floorboards. Dust motes and tiny winged insects danced in the yellow light. Beside her rested the small traveling case Darby Kipp had brought to her earlier. Somewhere he had also obtained a deep red wool skirt, a snowy linen blouse, two petticoats, and a black shawl.

Averil had changed as soon as she could, abhoring the sight and feel of the green velvet gown Sir John had given her. Because she knew she would need it, though, she had reluctantly packed the gown in the case. Attired in the fresh blouse and skirt, she waited. Kat had brought her a light supper, but had then quickly returned to the common room.

Averil rose from the bed and paced through the smoky shafts of light from the room below. Torment festered inside her. What was happening? Where was Camden? What was he doing? Would she ever touch him again? Hold him? Love him?

Miserably afraid, she threw herself across the bed and lay on her back, staring at the low cross-beams above her. She became aware of a change in the sounds creeping up from the common room. There was a low-pitched intensity in the air, a tone of expectancy and eagerness in the voices. She heard the heavy tread of footsteps climbing the stairs and then crossing the hall. Who would it be?

The door was pushed open and Kat entered, carrying a candle and a gleaming helmet. Behind her Camden stood framed in the threshold, one arm supporting a heavy-set man in a long cloak. Camden's face was strained and white above a buff coat, but his eyes fastened on her in relief. With a muffled cry of joy, Averil threw herself to him, circling his neck with her arms.

"Oh! I was so frightened for you!" Averil groaned, lifting herself on her toes to kiss him.

With his free hand, Camden held her against him as he returned her kiss. Then his lips smiled against hers.

"Averil," he murmured. "Averil, I have your father."

Averil drew back in surprise and confusion, her eyes darting to the heavy-set man beside Camden. As tired but warm brown eyes found hers, she gasped with recognition.

"Father! Oh, dear heaven!" Instantly they were clasped in each other's arms, both crying, exclaiming over the other.

Camden stood back, a broad smile on his face. He glanced across to Kat, who dabbed at her eyes with the edge of her apron.

With tears coursing down her face, Averil looked at her father in wonder. "I never believed—I didn't think I'd ever see you again!"

"And I thought you were dead!" The Earl blinked back his own tears as he stroked her hair. "Averil . . . my Averil."

They clung together in their happiness, seemingly oblivious to anything or anyone else, but when Camden started to leave the room to give them more time alone, Averil reached out to halt him.

Tucking her arm through his, she smiled tenderly at Camden. She turned to look at her father, beaming with her happiness as she said, "Captain Warrender and I are married."

The Earl matched her smile. "Aye, so I've learned! And I'm—" His eyes darted to Camden as he repeated, "*Captain* Warrender?" He looked at Camden with surprise, then inquisitive amusement. "You haven't told her?" he said with a smile of disbelief.

"What is this?" Averil asked, her perplexed gaze darting between the two men, who seemed to share some joke. "Do you two know each other? What haven't you told me?"

Camden smiled at her. "It was never something I found I could tell you, but there's no time now to explain," he said.

As he disengaged his arm from Averil's, his lips clenched. The fabric of his shirt, stiff with blood and adhering to his skin, was pulling painfully at his wound. At his movement the lower edges of his coat lifted and parted slightly, giving Averil a startling view of the scarlet stain on white linen.

Averil's face blanched with shock and fear. "Camden!" she breathed. "You're hurt! We have to do something!"

Kat moved involuntarily toward Camden, but he held up his hands to halt both women. "Nay," he said. " 'Tis not bleeding now."

"But Camden!" Averil protested.

He cut her short, firmly, catching her hands in his own. "The shirt will have to be soaked away first and I have no time." He turned his attention Kat. "Were you able to find out if the crew of the *Indomitable* is still on board?"

"Aye," she said. "They're there—in the hold."

He had half-feared the men would have been removed elsewhere, which would have seriously delayed the departure. But Nessel and the men who had followed him from the wharf? Had they returned to the ship and been arrested? "Are there any extra customers here, those who know nothing of what we'll do tonight?''

Kat shook her head. "Nay, I hurried all the others on their way."

"Good. Bar the door when you get downstairs, for we can't let anyone else in now. "Sir," he said, addressing Averil's father, "unfortunately, my ship is under guard. If I succeed in freeing it, Averil and I will be leaving London tonight for my home in the new colony. Will you come with us?"

The Earl looked from Camden to Averil's imploring face and back to Camden again. "I am grateful you extend this invitation," he said sincerely. "My home and lands here are not available to me now, and as I have been tried and declared a traitor, I do not have anywhere else to turn. Besides," he added, nodding and smiling at his daughter, "I would hate to find and lose Averil again in so short a time. Thank you, I would be pleased to go with you."

"Bring Averil to the wharf. When I've gained control of the ship, I'll want to leave immediately."

Kat and Camden departed the room and descended the stairs, Kat going at once to secure the main door. Camden entered the main room, and by the light of the few candles in their wall sconces, stood looking over the groups of men. They were a common, indistinguishable lot, representing all manner of trades, including beggary. Some were scarred from previous fights, others partially maimed. They exclaimed over the upcoming fray.

" 'Tis the Puritans, I can smell it!"

"Stuff John Pym with his own two-shilling passes!"

Camden's eyes came to rest on a group of five men at a table near the kitchen. It was Nessel and the others from the *Indomitable*. Relief washed over Camden and he strode toward them. He laid his hand on Nessel's shoulder.

"Have you talked to Kat?"

"Aye, she told us of your plan."

"I'm going ahead to the wharf. Give me fifteen minutes

or so, then bring this crew along.'' He gestured with his head to the room. ''Keep them eager.''

At Nessel's nod, Camden went into the kitchen, finding there the helmet he had worn from the Tower, and left by the rear door into the alley.

Camden paused at the corner of Jacob Kirkland's warehouse and peered toward the *Indomitable*. It was past two in the morning now. Had the alarm been given at the Tower? Did the soldiers on board the ship know of his escape? The gangplank had been removed, and there were no soldiers on the wharf. On deck he spotted three men on watch, though he could not be sure who or how many they were with the moonlight slanting across the deck and the shadows of men and masts melding. A high musical sound of wind in the rigging reached his ears and he was satisfied. They would need every breath of wind to fill the sails this night.

Ducking back behind the wall of the warehouse, Camden pulled on the helmet. With a casual step, he sauntered into view and crossed the wood planks of the wharf toward the ship. Two of the guards came to the railing and peered down at him as he paused on the wharf in front of them.

''What's yer business?'' one of them requested sharply. He had a long pike in his hand, its evil, moon-gilded point aimed skyward.

Camden settled his weight on wide-spread legs and gestured the length of the ship with one finger. ''Is it true what I hear about this ship?'' he asked, grinning through the bars of the helmet.

''What?'' came the response.

''That it's the Tottman's ship?'' Camden pressed.

The two guards exchanged glances. A third joined them at the rail. ''Where did you hear that?'' demanded the first man.

''Why, down at one of the taverns. Have you got the

Tottman there?''

''Nay,'' another voice said. ''Get away with ye. Are ye drunk or daft or what?''

''How do you know you don't have him? I was at Newgate once—same day the Tottman slipped someone out. I got a good look at him then. Didn't know it was him at the time, but I remember him well. He's clever with disguises, that one. How can you be sure he's not here and pretending to be one of his own crewmen? Eh? Let me on. I'll take a look over the prisoners.''

There was a confused whispering conference on deck. Camden glanced behind him, wondering how far back the men from the tavern were and hoping they would not appear just yet.

''Listen to me,'' Camden demanded. ''Who's going to get that five hundred and fifty pound reward money, eh? It's ours if we identify the Tottman. Tonight! Split it four ways and it's still a fair pretty sum, don't you agree?''

The three men obviously agreed; the plank was sent out for Camden. He climbed quickly onto the deck. ''Where are they?'' he asked as he stood before the three guards.

Though he knew the way well, Camden hung back and allowed them to show him to the hatch near the forecastle. One of the soldiers fetched a lantern and held it aloft, its bright light illuminating the ladder that descended to the 'tween decks area and from there into the deep hold. The other guards stayed on deck while Camden and the man with the lantern started down.

Camden moved softly, hearing the slumbering noises of the soldiers asleep along the length of the deck. He followed the faint, shuttered light from the lantern the man ahead of him carried, and they proceeded quietly down the next ladder into the main hold.

Camden had arrived that morning with a partial cargo of munitions that Cheyney had loaded on in Amsterdam. There had been crates of muskets and swords, barrels of black powder, two cannons, and cases and cases of musket balls. As soon as he had descended to the hold, Camden could see that most of the munitions had been removed. But there were still several crates they had not had time to unload today.

The guard led him to the stern and there Camden found his crewmen, bound and gagged. Some were sitting up, others lying down; most were awake, their eyes glittering apprehensively in the lanternlight as the figures of two soldiers picked their way toward them.

Averil and her father arrived at the dock shortly ahead of the group from the tavern and waited in the opening of the alley beside the port office. Passing them, the men's torches cast a stark, undulating light across the wharf, the fat trails of smoke drifting over the deck of the ship, and their voices were loud and coarse and eager.

A shouting alarm erupted on the ship, and in the resulting explosion of noise and confusion, Averil saw Camden emerge on the deck. His sword flashed in the stark illumination of torches and moonlight as he fought a slow, erratic path across the deck. Soldiers were lined along the rail, holding back the tavern men who attempted to scale the hull, but Camden worked his way through the melee and managed to hoist the plank for them to reach. The men on the wharf uttered shouts of encouragement and cheers as they swarmed onto the main deck. For the most part they wielded whatever manner of weapon they had been able to find—small cudgels, sticks of furniture, knives, staffs.

Averil kept her eyes trained on the tall, dark-haired man who was her husband, her breath catching as he engaged first one soldier, then another. Whenever he ducked from her sight, her heart jolted in pain, and she thought he had been cut down. Her father tried to turn her away from the sight of the battle, but Averil refused to be distracted, pushing aside his arm. The Earl looked at her oddly, but turned his attention to the ship once more.

His more experienced eye discerned the slow, gradual changes occurring on board—the soldiers were being surely and methodically pressed back. First one, then another leaped from the deck of the *Indomitable*—some onto the wharf to disappear into the night, others plunging into the river.

As the battle dwindled, Averil spotted Francis Bowers. He limped painfully across the wharf, one hand pressed to his side where a blackish stain seeped over his shirt and fingers. His face was twisting harshly in a grimace of pain and defeat. When he passed the opening in the alley where Averil and her father waited, the Earl made as if to call out to him, but Averil halted her father with an urgent hand on his arm.

The men from the tavern group were exclaiming in their victory as they marched off the gangplank. Some limped or held themselves protectively. On the ship, Camden stood watching as the decks were cleared. Still grasping his sword, he slowly lowered the point till it touched the deck. Across the ship, men were hoisting still forms and carrying them down the gangplank to dump on the dock. Averil heard a shouted, "All's clear below."

"It's time, Averil," the Earl said, taking her by the hand. "He's got to get away before word of this brings more soldiers here to stop him."

Following her father's lead, Averil ran toward the ship. Camden met her at the head of the gangplank. She fell into his arms and buried her face against his chest. Lines were cast off, voices shouted. Beneath their feet the deck lifted and rolled slowly as the ship slipped from the dock.

Averil drew away from Camden's embrace, her eyes wide. "Your wound," she gasped. Instantly she was plucking at the buttons of his coat. In the waning moonlight she could see the blackish stain of blood soaking through it, and he was bleeding profusely.

"You're bleeding again!"

"Aye," he answered, his voice dim and hoarse with tiredness. "We won't need to soak the shirt away now."

Leaving Cheyney to oversee the setting of the sails, Camden and Averil entered his cabin. The Earl followed. After lighting a brass lantern over the table, Camden lowered himself gingerly to sit on the edge of the bunk. Averil's mind flew.

"I'll need soap, water, some towels," she muttered aloud to herself.

"There." Camden pointed to the lower cupboards in the wall beside the bunk. "Thread and a needle as well," he added. "Any one of the men can fetch you the water."

As Averil dashed to the cupboard, the Earl's eyes fixed on her in disbelief. "Why, my dear! Are you going to do this yourself? Shouldn't you let one of the others see to it? Surely they've had more experience—"

Averil cut him short with an impatient glance as she deposited a basin, a chunk of soap, and a stack of clean towels on the table. She did not bother to answer her father, but left the cabin to search out a man to fetch water.

The Earl was perplexed. Camden wanted to laugh, but said, "Has she changed so much?" He reached for a full, uncorked bottle of wine Francis Bowers had left behind in the litter of food and empty bottles on the table.

William Maslin snorted, but smiled somewhat ruefully. "Aye, that she has. When last we were together, she"—the Earl shrugged—"she was a child."

"She's been through too much since then," Camden exclaimed as he tilted the bottle to his mouth.

When Averil returned, Nessel trailing her with a full bucket of water from one of the barrels in the hold, Camden had removed his shirt and was holding a towel to his side. His darkly tanned chest and back glistened with a heavy sheen of sweat.

After Nessel departed, she sat beside Camden and took the towel from his hand, catching her breath at sight of the swollen, ugly gash in his side. With her lips pressed into a thin line, she set to work cleaning it. At her first touch, Camden grunted involuntarily.

There was silence for a while as both men watched her.

Growing distracted by their attention to her work, and not wanting them to see how her hands were beginning to shake with strain, Averil reminded them of the conversation earlier at the tavern. "We have time now. What was it you haven't told me yet?" Her curious, probing gaze darted from one to the other.

William Maslin laughed softly, but Camden held himself rigidly still for Averil's ministrations, only a flicker of a smile touching his mouth and eyes.

"Shall I do the honors?" the Earl suggested. At Camden's tight nod, he addressed Averil with an air of formality, ceremoniously sweeping out his hand to Camden. "My dear, may I present your husband—his Lordship, the Earl of Denningham."

Averil's fingers froze as she was tying off a stitch. Her glance snapped to Camden and she stared at him incredulously. "His Lordsh—*Denningham*!"

Her look of stunned bewilderment stabbed at Camden's heart, and his gaze softened. "I should have told you sooner," he said, "but I never used the name. Before now, I never quite believed myself worthy of my father's title."

"Denningham!" she repeated. "I should have known! That was *your* home!"

"Aye," he said.

She looked to her father, who smiled happily. "And how did you know this?" she asked, accusingly.

Camden uttered a short laugh. "So all the dark secrets will be out this night, eh?" he said. "Shall I do the honors this time?"

"It is your turn, I believe," William Maslin deferred. "She'll not rest until her curiosity is satisfied."

"Very well." Camden looked down at her, a smile in his eyes. "Your father helped me in my work as the Tottman. He and my father had been good friends before my family left England, and when I sought out your father, he agreed to help in any capacity. Maslin Manor was a shelter for quite a number of people leaving London or leaving England entirely." He smiled broadly. "And that's how I knew your name that day you came to me at the Red Gate Tavern, though I'd never actually seen you before."

Averil's astonished gaze sought out her father for confirmation of this incredible news. "But how was it that I never knew any of this?" she begged.

"We never used the main house itself, Averil," her father explained. "And you were so young, so innocent. I had no intention of involving you in such dangerous activities as those of the Tottman here."

At this last statement, Averil stifled a laugh of her own.

When she had finished tying a strip of clean linen towel around his waist, Camden rose and donned a fresh shirt he had pulled from a trunk in a lower section of the cupboard.

After showing the Earl to a cabin he could use for the journey, Camden leaned close to Averil and whispered, "Come with me, I want to share something with you." He led her out onto the main deck, and they turned and climbed the steps to the quarterdeck. The wind was strong, sleek, and chilled. Averil shivered, but Camden put his arm around her to keep her warm.

Cheyney halted Camden as they passed. When the blond man smiled and nodded to Averil, she gave a gasp of surprise, recognizing the face of the man she had encountered with the Tottman at the Red Gate Tavern.

Cheyney said to Camden, "Sorry to disturb you, but we'll be coming up to Gravesend before too long. Should we stop for the customs procedures so as not to arouse suspicions, or do you think a messenger would have reached there by now to alert them?"

"Keep all the sails out, we're not stopping," Camden answered. Moving past Cheyney, Camden took Averil up to the highest deck, the poop deck. He put his arms around her and she leaned into his chest as they looked out over the black glimmer of the river, the soft, dusky grey sky ahead of them on the eastern horizon. Beneath them, the waters surged past, splashing and foaming against the wooden hull. He said softly, "Someday we'll return, Averil. I promise you that."

She smiled and turned to look up into his face. "I have no regrets. You're my home now."

Camden caught and smoothed her wind-tossed hair. His eyes were soft, grave, warm. "You, with all your love and that incredible loyalty I never quite believed in before— Averil, you've given me back myself. Do you know what I'm saying?" He smiled slowly. "I've found peace with you. I've found worthiness with you. Forgiveness for so much—"

Averil felt the tears of love welling up behind her eyes and she pressed her fingers to his mouth. He felt the catch in his heart, heard the catch in his voice, as he said, "You've set the Tottman free."